The American Journalists

A COLLECTION OF THE POLITICAL WRITINGS OF WILLIAM LEGGETT

William Leggett

ARNO
&
The New York Times

Collection Created and Selected
by Charles Gregg of Gregg Press

Reprint edition 1970 by Arno Press Inc.

LC# 76-125702
ISBN 0-405-01681-6

The American Journalists
ISBN for complete set: 0-405-01650-6

Reprinted from a copy in
The State Historical Society of Wisconsin Library

Manufactured in the United States of America

A COLLECTION OF THE POLITICAL WRITINGS OF WILLIAM LEGGETT

Wm Leggett

A COLLECTION

OF THE

POLITICAL WRITINGS

OF

WILLIAM LEGGETT,

SELECTED AND ARRANGED,

WITH A PREFACE,

BY

THEODORE SEDGWICK, Jr.

IN TWO VOLUMES.

VOL. I.

NEW-YORK:
TAYLOR & DODD.

1840.

H. LUDWIG, PRINTER,
72, Vesey-street, N. Y.

PREFACE

In preparing for the press a selection of the writings of William Leggett it is proper to state the precise object which has been had in view. The wish of his friends is to re-publish such of his writings as will give a true picture of the mind and character of the man whom they so much lament; and in discharging the duty confided to me I have endeavoured faithfully to carry out this idea. To do this, however, it has not been thought necessary or desirable to revive and perpetuate the temporary controversies, in which the editor of a newspaper becomes almost inevitably entangled; and therefore, although many of the pieces of this class were, at the time they appeared, among those which attracted the most attention, they have, with few exceptions, been excluded from these volumes.

But beyond this I have omitted nothing on account of its peculiar character, and have re-published all those articles from the Plaindealer, and Evening Post while under the management of Mr. Leggett, which will give the most vivid idea of the vigour of his style, the originality of his mind, and the force and independence of his character.

I have excluded nothing merely for the reason of its being contrary to the prevailing or popular opinion, and on the subject of Slavery I have inserted many articles which go far beyond the tone of either of the great political parties of this day.

It will not be supposed, however, that the Editor of this publication, or the friends who have sanctioned it, adhere to the views expressed upon all the controverted topics which these pages contain. Many of those most attached to Mr. Leggett, and most devoted to the leading doctrines of his political faith, were at the same time the most opposed to the course pursued by him on particular subjects. But I have not thought myself at liberty to omit any articles for this reason. The effect of suppression would be to give a very imperfect idea of the mind and character of Mr. Leggett; and to suppress them from any apprehension of injuring the sale or circulation of the work, would be a subserviency to popular prejudice, which the author, of all men, would have been the last to permit.

In this collection, therefore, I have endeavoured to embody such of his writings as will serve to convey a just idea of the ability and virtues of the author, and perhaps I may be permitted, in a few words, to point out those attributes of peculiar merit to which they may justly lay claim.

The intellect of Mr. Leggett was of a very high order. His education was originally, in matters of mere accomplishment, defective; but perhaps, in other respects, it could not have been better calculated to form the able and intrepid man, whose memory these pages are intended to perpetuate.

Nurtured in moderate circumstances, unspoiled and unpampered by the seductions of affluence, his life was one of widely diversified experience—first a woodsman in the wilds of the west—next wearing the uniform of the navy and breasting the waves under the constellation banner—soon the victim of a harsh if not tyrannical commander, he threw up his commission, because his complaints were denied a hearing—then exposed to grievous hardships and to all the temptations of a great commercial metropolis—last a leading partisan editor—all these chances and changes were well fitted to make a hardy, self-relying man—an intellectual athlete.

But it is not to this education that Mr. Leggett owed his vigorous eloquence—his copious style—his close logic—his eminent powers of generalization. These attributes incontestably distinguished him. His articles are often prolix, often perhaps defective in other respects of style; but it must be reflected that there are no circumstances so unfavourable to composition as those under which an editor writes. The unavoidable haste—the eternal interruptions and distractions—the impossibility of concentrating the mind on the subject—the necessity of repetition—the want of time to condense;—all these are sufficient reasons why the Press has in this country no higher literary character. But all these difficulties were, in a great degree, surmounted by him; and when it is remembered that the greater part of his articles were composed in the back room of a printing-office, amid the din of the press and the conversation of political loungers, it will be, I am persuaded, thought remarkable that he overcame them to so great an extent. I do not mean to overrate the merit of his writings. I am aware that very great deduction is to be made for the excitement under which they were first read, when they were animated and quickened by a deep interest in the events with which they were connected—that great deduction is also to be made for the strong bias which a similarity of political sentiments creates; but I am convinced that the admiration these writings excited is no delusion, no mere temporary feeling; and that the reputation which Mr. Leggett attained, during his short career as an editor, could not have been acquired unless his writings had possessed merits of an abiding character. What, then, was that character? What are the claims which these productions present to a permanent place in our literature?

The foundation of his political system was an intense love of freedom. This, indeed, was the corner-stone of his intellect and his feelings. He absolutely adored the abstract idea of liberty, and he would tolerate no shackles on her limbs. Liberty in faith—liberty in government—liberty in trade—liberty of action every way,—these were his fundamental tenets—these the source alike of his excellencies and his defects.

His love of freedom made him the warm and constant advocate of universal suffrage. He ever looked coldly if not with positive disinclination upon the different laws proposed for registering voters; he could not endure the idea of any impediment upon the liberty of the citizen, and he preferred the evils which resulted from a want of registry to those which he feared might follow from a system that should impose any restraint or qualification upon the right of suffrage.

In the same light he looked upon every effort to exclude foreigners from the polls. His love of liberty was far too catholic and comprehensive to be bounded by any line of language or birth, and he could never tolerate the hostility often expressed to the adoption of foreigners into our political family. As to freedom of trade, he was equally consistent. He from the first warred against the tariff, and a federal bank. He was the leader of those who raised the standard against the monopoly system of incorporated banks; and one of the first to insist upon the total disconnection of government from its fiscal agents. In like manner, he reprobated all the state inspection laws, and one of his last productions in the Plaindealer is that in which he advocates the idea of a free trade post office, or a system by which letters should be carried, as goods and passengers are now, by private establishments. In this respect the merits of his writings cannot be overrated; he must ever be remembered as one of the most able and consistent disciples of that school of commercial freedom which is destined ultimately to bind the whole civilized world in bonds of peace and amity—of that school of political science whose end and aim are to simplify and cheapen the operations of government.

His reading was extremely copious, and his style of the most vigorous and manly order. On the topics which excited him he poured forth a flood of reasoning or it might be of denunciation and invective which forced the mind irresistibly along and aroused the most sluggish intellect. His language often rises to a commanding eloquence, and is always earnest, impressive and powerful.

I have no desire or intention to pronounce a mere eulogy, an inconsiderate and sweeping panegyric. It would be I am convinced, the thing most repulsive to his own feelings. Mr. Leggett had unquestionably defects in his intellectual organization—he generalised too much—he pushed out his theories without a proper reference to the time and means necessary to perfect them, and to persuade their adoption—and what was a greater defect for one who desired to lead the public mind on matters of daily and hourly importance, he was not sufficiently practical, nor did he listen with sufficient attention to the suggestions of practical men. His views when most correct, were frequently urged with a vehemence and impetuosity which prevented their adoption, and he often in this way displeased and alienated moderate men of all parties.

To this, which might perhaps be termed an impracticability of conduct, are to be ascribed some singular inconsistencies of his views on various topics. He was an author and a consistent advocate of the right of property and of free trade. But he at all times opposed the introduction of an international copyright law. No one was a more zealous and unflinching enemy of mobs, but he with almost equal ardor opposed the passage of any law granting indemnity to their victims. He detested slavery in every shape, but he was totally hostile to any action of Congress on the question in the District of Columbia. This diminished his influence as a party leader, for which station indeed he was not fitted, except in periods of great excitement and violence.

He was certainly at times deficient in forbearance towards his opponents, and indulged in a violence of language wholly unjustifiable. But in extenuation it is to be recollected that no writer connected with the press, was so unfairly and indeed indecently attacked as he was during the time when he had charge of the Evening Post. It must not be forgotten, that he was abused and calumniated in a manner almost unprecedented, even in the annals of the American press, and that his errors in this matter, were, to a great extent, errors of retaliation.

Nothing could form a greater contrast with the vehemence of his writings, than the mildness and courtesy of his social life. I have repeatedly witnessed the surprise of those who knew him only through the columns of his paper, when accident brought them personally in contact with him. No one more enjoyed the pleasures of society—no one allowed less of the bitterness of political controversy to infuse itself into his social relations. His naval education, and "the grave and wrinkled purposes of his life," gave dignity to his manners, and he had a softness and delicacy in his character which the acrimony of political strife had no effect to diminish.

His style is often diffuse, and it may occasionally be charged with rhetorical extravagance, but to this a sufficient answer is perhaps to be found in the fact that these writings are newspaper articles; written under the spur and excitement of the hour, and often with the intention and under the necessity of appealing quite as much to the passions as the judgment. It is an unhappy obligation, but one apparently imposed upon the conductors of the press, that they are compelled to arouse the public mind and stimulate it to action; and this is often to be done solely by infusing into the system, not the wholesome mental food of truth, but the powerful and dangerous excitants of invective and declamation.

Another and one of the highest attributes of the author of these works, was boldness—courage. He had no conception of what fear was; physically, morally and intellectually, he had no idea of the meaning of the term. No personal danger could appal him; no theory did he ever hesitate to adopt because it was scouted by the prevailing opinion, and no cause did he ever fail to espouse because it was destitute of friends. When the mobs first attacked the abolitionists in the city of New-York, he had not made the subject of slavery one of very particular consideration, but he was the earliest to denounce the popular violence, and to call upon the municipal government to suppress it by the most vigorous and effective weapons. The same course he pursued in regard to the Bank. The vehemence of his attacks upon that institution brought him into direct and frequent collision with members of the mercantile classes, but never was he deterred from this path by any apprehension of injury to his interests. The course pursued by the paper (the Evening Post,) during the crisis of 1833 and 1834, was extremely injurious to the pecuniary affairs of that journal which had previously, by its opposition to the tariff, made itself to some extent a favourite of the commercial community.

This same courage taking what is perhaps the higher shape of fortitude, showed itself in a manner equally remarkable in his private life. Amid the reverses of fortune, when harrassed by pecuniary embarrassments—during the tortures of a disease which tore away his life piece-meal, he ever maintained the same manly and unaltered front—the same cheerfulness of disposition—the same dignity of conduct. No humiliating solicitation—no weak complaint for a moment escaped him.

But the intellectual character of Mr. Leggett, marked as it was, was far inferior in excellence to his moral attributes. It is to these he owes the respect and affection in which his memory is held—it is to these that the influence his pen acquired during his life is chiefly attributable.

At the same time it should be said that it is difficult to distinguish between his intellect and his character. They both derived force and support from each other, and it is not easy to draw any dividing line. There is nothing of that incongruity which history exhibits in some of the greatest men upon her page, where extraordinary mental power has been unsupported by moral energy.

His great desire on all the questions which agitated the country appeared to be the attainment and establishment of *truth*. The vehemence of his temperament and the force of his original impressions often had an obscuring tendency upon his mind. But against these he was forever striving. No one familiar with him but must have perceived the progress his mind was continually making, and the manly independence with which, when once convinced of an error, he denounced and cast it off.

Truth was his first love and his last—the affection of his life. His most favourite work was, I think, Milton's Areopagitica, and the magnificent description of Truth which it contains was constantly on his lips.

Equally remarkable with this, was his superiority to all selfish considerations. He was doubtless sometimes misled by his passions and his prejudices—never by his interest. No personal considerations could weigh with him a moment, when set in opposition to what his deliberate judgment convinced him was the cause of truth. Nothing can more satisfactorily prove this than his conduct on the abolition question. The first time that this matter distinctly presented itself, was in the summer of the year 1835. The administration was then in its palmiest days. The contested elections of 1834 had terminated successfully. The attack of the President upon the Bank, had been sustained by the state of New-York, and to appearance the government had established itself in an impregnable position. At this time Mr. Leggett was the sole conductor of the Evening Post, the leading, if not the only administration organ in the city of New-York. He had edited that journal during the warmest part of the conflict, and on every ground he had a right to demand and expect the support of the party in power.

At that moment Mr. Kendall, one of the most prominent members of the government, issued his well-known letters to the postmasters at Charleston and New-York, in which he justified, to a certain extent, the conduct of those officers who had stopped the mails containing what he termed, the "incendiary, inflammatory and insurrectionary" manifestoes of the abolitionists.

That party at this time, was a small and unpopular sect. It is always painful to utter a syllable detracting from the merit of persons unquestionably animated by the impulse of a high moral principle — more especially of men combating with the baleful institution of slavery. But the truth should at all times have precedence. Wisdom of conduct is as necessary as integrity of purpose. The unpopularity of the abolitionists was not wholly without cause. They had done injury to the progressive cause of freedom, by a violence of denunciation which the good sense of the country pronounced unjust and dangerous. Their proposed measures were not sufficiently distinct to be intelligible to the people; and their leading organs had not manifested a proper cient deference either for the great charter of the union or for that spirit of concession and harmony upon which our political existence depends, and which forms the corner-stone of the Constitution itself. It is however with the fact that we are here principally concerned. But a few months before, they had been the victims of mob-law in New-York, and they were preeminently unpopular with the commercial classes of the north, whose interests had taken the alarm, and who had enrolled under the dark banner of the detestable institution. Thus disliked by their immediate neighbours, they were absolutely abhorrent to the people of the South. They in fact stood alone, a small and uninfluential sect, professing ultra and impracticable doctrines, without power or support. In this matter of the post-office law, they stood unsustained, except by justice and freedom.

But this was enough for Mr. Leggett—that an unjust and unconstitutional power was attempted to be exerted against them was enough for him. Contrary to the urgent solicitations of many of his personal friends—against the vehement representations of most of his political supporters, and particularly in contempt of all consideration of interest, he declared war against the doctrines of the administration. He grappled, without fear or hesitation, with the Posmaster General himself, and in terms ef eloquent reprobation denounced and derided this new censorship of the press.

This conduct can be ascribed to no cause whatever but his love of truth and his utter superiority to sordid motives, and from the moment he adopted his line of proceeding, he steadfastly persevered in it. No considerations moved him. The administration organ of the state denounced him. The mouth-piece of the government excluded him from the party pale, but these things he heeded no more than the blasts of the winds: or if they produced any effect at all, it was to arouse him to a more vehement and more unsparing opposition of the measures of the government. So far as individuals and motives were concerned, he may have been carried too far by the violence of his temperament; but we can scarce pay sufficient honour to the boldness, the independence and the integrity of his conduct.

This same line of action he pursued until he was prostrated by illness in the fall of 1835, and obliged to abandon the Evening Post.

He established the Plaindealer in the fall of 1836. The first number was published in December of that year, and the last in September, 1837.

It is in this periodical that his best pieces are to be found; and it is from this that I have comparatively made the largest selections.

The paper was established originally as a democratic paper; but the boldest attacks upon the course pursued by the government towards the abolitionists are to be found in its columns. While at the same time, there is no more vigorous support of the Sub-Treasury scheme than its pages contain.

His mind was too sagacious not to perceive that the adoption of this measure must inevitably lead to the great desideratum of American legislation—an ad valorem tariff, and a revenue reduced to the actual expenses of the government.

In connection with the subject of Abolition, I have reprinted his article upon Mr. Van Buren's Message of 1836; not that I think it just, but because it is oneof the most conclusive proofs of Mr. Leggett's independence. Abolition of slavery, in the District of Columbia, is environed by difficulty, and the President should not have been charged with a want of courage or honesty, without more conclusive proof than the Message itself afforded. I have also republished this article for another reason, to which, in giving increased publicity and permanence to so severe an invective against the President, it is right to call the attention of the reader. There is no better evidence of the superiority of Mr. Van Buren to personal resentment, and it furnishes indeed the strongest argument in favour of the chief magistrate on the subject of the paper in question. He could scarcely within two years have appointed Mr. Leggett to the Guatemala mission, at a time, too, when that gentleman, broken down by illness, was without influence or power, unless he had been conscious that the attack was unfounded. It is impossible that newspaper articles can be always correct. The merit of Mr. Leggett's writings is that they were always *honest.*

The Plaindealer also contains some articles on a subject which must ultimately engage the attention of the American people—that of direct taxation. Mr. Leggett has ably put forth the leading arguments in favour of this, the only fair, uniform, and democratic mode of raising funds for the support of the government. It is not one of the least proofs, of his far-sighted views, and the enlarged and philosophical tone of his legislative theories.

Such is a very brief sketch of the character of the author of the writings contained in these volumes. It is necessarily imperfect. The reader has the opportunity of completing or correcting it from his own observation. No man's personal qualities were ever more deeply impressed upon his works.

The death of Mr. Leggett is deplored with a regret that arises as well from public as private considerations. We grieve for the loss of an accomplished man of warm attachments, ardently devoted to his friends, and ready to make any sacrifice for them. But if possible we still more deeply lament the death of an eloquent and independent politician, thoroughly imbued with the cardinal principles of Liberty—of one with no superior, and scarcely a rival in his vocation, who, whatever his faults, had merits that a thousandfold redeemed them; his richly stored intellect—his vigorous eloquence—his earnest devotion to truth—his incapability of fear—his superiority to all selfish views, are forever embalmed in our memory.

Most especially do his friends deplore the time and circumstances of his death. Life appeared to be opening brightly, and the clouds which had hung around him seemed on the point of dispersing.

Every year was softening his prejudices and calming his passions. Every year was enlarging his charities and widening the bounds of his liberality. Had a more genial clime invigorated his constitution, and enabled him to return to his labours, a brilliant and honourable future might have certainly been predicted of him. He would not have left a name only as the conductor of a periodical press—he would not merely have left these transient and fleeting memorials of his ability and rectitude. It is not the suggestion of a too fond affection, but the voice of a calm judgment which declares that whatever public career he had pursued he must have raised to his memory an imperishable monument, and that as no name is now dearer to his friends, so few could then have been more honourably associated with the history of his country than that of WILLIAM LEGGETT.

A COLLECTION

OF THE

POLITICAL WRITINGS

OF

WILLIAM LEGGETT.

BANK OF UNITED STATES.

[*From the Evening Post, March*, 1834.]

In answer to the many objections which are urged with great force of argument against the United States Bank, and against any great national institution of a similar character, there is little put forth in its defence, beyond mere naked allegation. One of the assertions, however, which seems to be most relied upon by the advocates of the Bank, is that it has exercised a most beneficial power in *regulating the currency of the country.* Indeed, the power which it was supposed it would possess to regulate the currency, furnished one of the chief grounds of the support yielded to the original proposition to establish a United States Bank, and the same topic has occupied a prominent place in every subsequent discussion of the Bank question in Congress. It is maintained, in favour of the present institution, that it not merely possesses that power, but that it has exerted in it the most prudent and salutary manner. This is made the theme of many high-wrought panegyrics. It is triumphantly put forth by the journals in the interest of the Bank; it drops from the lips of every Bank declaimer at political meetings, and is asserted and re-asserted by all the orators and editors of the Bank party, with a confidence which should belong only to truth. Many persons, indeed, who are strongly opposed to the United States Bank on moral grounds; who view with dismay its prodigious means of corruption; and shudder with abhorrence at the free and audacious use it has made of those means; yet accede to it the praise of having at least answered one great purpose of its creation—namely, the regulation of the currency of the United States.

It is to be feared that men in general have not very precise notions of what constitutes a regulation of the currency. If the meaning of this phrase is to be limited to the mere sustaining of the credit of the Bank at such a point, that its notes shall always stand at the par value of silver, then indeed must it be admitted that the United States Bank has, for the greater part of the time performed its functions in that respect. Yet no praise is to be acceded to it on that score; since such an effect must naturally and almost inevitably flow from the self-imposed obligation on the government to receive its notes at their nominal amount, at all places, in payment of debts due to the United States. There is not a bank in the country, accredited and endorsed by the Government to an equal extent, that would not as certainly maintain its paper on a par with the precious metals. Indeed, most of the well-conducted institutions in the Atlantic cities, without the advantage of such countenance from the Government, have preserved their paper in equal credit; or, in other words, have been equally successful in *regulating the currency*, so far as the term implies the affording of a convertible paper substitute for money, which shall pass from hand to hand as the full equivalent of silver coin. The doing of this certainly constitutes an important branch of the regulation of the currency; but there is another and more important branch, and in this the United States Bank has totally and most signally failed.

What is regulating the currency? It is the furnishing of a medium of circulation, either metalic or convertible at par, equal in amount to the real business of the country, as measured by the amount of its exports and the amount of actual capital employed in commercial business. It is the furnishing of that amount of circulation, which is actually absorbed by the commercial transactions of the country—by those transactions which rest on the basis of the exchange continually going on of the commodities of one country for those of another. When bank issues are limited within this circle, the notes of the bank in circulation are founded on the security of the notes of merchants in possession of the bank, and the notes of the merchants rest on the basis of goods actually purchased, which are finally to be paid for with the products of the soil or other articles of export. The maintaining of the circulation at this point would, in the strict and proper sense of the word, be regulating the currency. It would be supplying the channels of business to the degree requisite to facilitate the operations of commerce, without causing those operations to be unduly extended at one time, and unduly contracted at another. It would be causing the stream of credit to glide in an equal and uniform current, never stagnating, and never overflowing its boundaries.

When bank circulation exceeds this measure, an inevitable derangement of the currency takes place. The par of value between the paper representatives of money and money itself may still be maintained; but prices are raised, and raised unequally, and the dollar no longer accurately performs its office as a measure of value. The effects of the expansion of the currency are first seen in the rise of the prices of foreign fabrics. This leads to excessive importation on the part of the competitors anxious to avail themselves of the advance. Goods are purchased from abroad to a much larger amount than the exports of the country will liquidate, and a balance of debt is thus created. The payment of this balance drains the country of specie. The bank, finding its paper return upon it in demand for coin, is obliged suddenly, in self-defence, to curtail its issues. The consequence of this curtailment is a fall of prices. Those who had ordered goods in expectation of deriving the advantage of the high prices, are obliged to sell at a sacrifice, and are fortunate if they can dispose of their commodities at all. Those who had been deluded, by the fatal facility of getting bank favours, into extending themselves beyond the limits of that fair and prudent credit to which their actual capital entitled them, must necessarily be unable to meet the shock of a sudden withdrawal of the quicksand basis on which their business rested, and are thus compelled to become bankrupts. A state of general calamity succeeds—most severe in the commercial cities, and measured in all places by a rule of inverse ratio to the excess of the preceding apparent prosperity. These sudden expansions and contractions of the currency have happened too frequently in this country, and have been followed by effects of too disastrous a nature, for any reader to be ignorant of them.

Has the United States Bank never caused distress of this kind? Has it never caused the amount of circulating medium to fluctuate? Has it never stimulated business into unhealthy activity at one time, and withheld its proper aliment at another? Has it never poured out a sudden flood of paper money, causing the wheels of commerce to revolve with harmful rapidity, and then as suddenly withdrawn the supply, till the channels were empty, and every branch of business languished throughout the land? There are few of our readers who cannot, of their own knowledge, answer these questions in the affirmative.

For the two or three years preceding the extensive and heavy calamities of 1819, the United States Bank, instead of regulating the currency, poured out its issues at such a lavish rate that trade and speculation were excited in a preternatural manner. But the inevitable consequences of over issues did not fail to happen in that case. A large balance of debt was created in Europe, and to pay that debt our metalic medium was sent away from the country. The land was soon nearly exhausted of specie, and still the debt remained unliquidated. The bank, in order to bring business to an equipoise again, exchanged a part of its funded debt for specie in Europe, and purchased a large amount of coin in the West Indies and other places. But it still continued to make loans to a larger degree than the actual business of the country, as measured by the amount of its exports, required, and its purchase was therefore a most ineffectual and childish scheme. It was but dragging a supply of water with much toil and expense, from the lake of the valley to the summit of an eminence, in the vain hope that, discharged there, it would continue on the height and not rush down the declivity, to mix again with the waters of the lake. The specie, purchased at high rates in foreign countries, was no sooner brought to our own, and lodged in the vaults of the bank, than it was immediately drawn thence again, by the necessity of redeeming the notes which poured in upon it in a constant stream in demand for silver. In one year, 1818, upwards of fifteen millions of dollars were exported from the country, and still the debts incurred by the mad spirit of overtrading were not liquidated. The bank itself was now on the very verge of bankruptcy. At the close of its business on the 12th of April, 1819, the whole amount of money in its vaults was only 71,522 dollars, and it at the same time owed to the city banks a clear balance of 196,418 dollars, or an excess over its means of payment of nearly 125,000 dollars. A depreciation of its credit was one of the consequences which had flowed from this state of things, and the notes of the United States Bank—the boasted institution which claims to have regulated the currency of this country—*fell ten per cent. below the par value of silver.*

But the greatest evil was yet behind. The Bank was at length compelled, by the situation in which the rashness of its managers had involved it, to commence a rapid curtailment of discounts. An immediate reduction took place of two millions in Philadelphia, two millions in Baltimore, nearly a million in Richmond, and half a million in Norfolk. This sudden withdrawal of the means of business was, of itself, a heavy calamity to those cities; but the system of curtailment was persevered in, until the foundation of a great part of the commercial transactions of the United States, and of the speculations in land, in internal improvement, and other adventures, which the facility of getting money had induced men to hazard, was withdrawn, and the whole fabric fell to the ground, burying beneath vast numbers of unfortunate persons, and scattering ruin and dismay throughout the Union.

The same scenes, only to a greater extent, and with more deplorable circumstances, were acted over in 1825. There are few inhabitants of this city who can have forgotten the extensive failures, both of individuals and corporate institutions, which marked that period. There are many yet pining in comfortless poverty whose distress was brought upon them by the revulsions of that disastrous year—many who were suddenly cast down from affluence to want—many who saw their all slip from their grasp and melt away, who had thought that they held it by securities as firm as the eternal hills.

But not to dwell upon events the recollection of which time may have begun to efface from many minds, let us but cast a glance at the manner in which the United States Bank *regulated the currency* in 1830, when, in the short period of a twelvemonth it extended its *accommodations* from forty to seventy millions of dollars. This enormous expansion, entirely uncalled for by any peculiar circumstance in the business condition of the country, was followed by the invariable consequences of an inflation of the currency. Goods and stocks rose, speculation was excited, a great number of extensive enterprises were undertaken, canals were laid out, rail-roads projected, and the whole business of the country was stimulated into unnatural and unsalutary activity. The necessary result of the spirit of speculation thus awakened was the purchase of more goods abroad than the commodities of the country would pay for. Hence vast sums of specie soon began to leave the United States ; scarcely a packet ship sailed from our wharves that did not carry out to England and France a large sum of money in gold and silver ; and it is estimated that in 1831–32 the specie drawn from the country did not fall short of twenty millions of dollars. The Bank of the United States, failing to accomplish the bad design for which it had thus flooded the country with its paper, now began to try the effects of a contrary system, and resorted to coercion.

A reduction of its issues must inevitably have taken place in the nature of things, nor could all the means and all the credit of the Bank have removed the evil day to a very distant period. But it had it completely within its power to effect its curtailment by easy degrees, and to bring back business into its proper channels by operations that would have been attended with little general distress. But this was no part of its plan. Its object was to wring from the sufferings of the people their assent to the perpetuation of its existence. Its curtailments were therefore rapid and sudden, and so managed as to throw the greater part of the burden on those commercial places where there was the greatest need of lenity and forbearance. The distress and dismay thus occasioned, were aggravated by the rumours and inventions of hired presses, instructed to increase the panic by all the means in their power. Of the deplorable effects produced by this course, the traces are yet too recent to require that we should enter into any particulars.

The Bank has not yet exhausted its full power of mischief. Since its creation to the present hour, instead of regulating the currency, it has caused a continual fluctuation; but it is capable of doing greater injury than it has yet effected. It is perfectly within its power to cause a variation of prices to the extent of twenty-five per cent. every ninety days, by alternate expansions and contractions of its issues. It is in its power, in the short period that is yet to elapse before its charter expires, so to embarrass the currency, so to limit the amount of circulating medium, so to impair commercial confidence, and shake the entire basis of mercantile credit, as to produce throughout the whole land a scene of the most poignant pecuniary distress—a scene compared with which the dark days of 1819 and 1825, and those through which we have just passed, shall seem bright and prosperous. And there are indications that the Bank will do this. There are signs and portents in the heavens which tell of a coming tempest. There are omens which foreshow that this mighty and wicked corporation means to use to the uttermost its whole machinery of coercion, to wring from the groaning land a hard contest to the renewal of its existence. We trust the People will bear stiffly up under the infliction. We trust they will breast the storm with determined spirits. We trust they will endure the torture, without yielding to a measure which would destroy the best interests of their country, and make them and their children slaves forever.

Regulation of the currency! What a claim to set up for the United States Bank! It has done the very reverse: it has destroyed the equal flow and steady worth of the currency: it has broken up the measure of value: it has kept the circulating medium in a state of continual fluctuation, making the dollar to-day worth a dollar and a half, and to-morrow not worth a half a dollar. Besides the three great periods of sudden excess and rapid curtailment, its whole career has been one series of experiments, more or less general, of inflation and exhaustion of the currency. And this is the institution, which now comes forward, and claims to be re-chartered, on the ground of having well performed the great offices for which it was created. It has failed in *all* its great ends. In its chief purpose, as a fiscal agent and assistant of the Government, one on which it might at all times securely rely, it has wholly failed. We have seen it interfering in the national politics, and endeavouring to rule the suffrages of the people, first by bribery and afterwards by compulsion. We have seen it place itself in open defiance to the Executive, and rank him in its official papers, with counterfeiters and robbers. We have seen it endeavouring to thwart the measures of his administration; collude with foreign creditors of the Government to defeat the avowed objects of the Treasury; refuse to give up the national funds at the commands of the competent authority; and finally turn a committee of congress with contumely from its doors, in violation of its charter, and in violation of every obligation of morality and every principle of public decency. This is the institution which now comes forward for a re-charter. If the people grant it they will deserve to wear its chains!

RIOT AT THE CHATHAM-STREET CHAPEL.

[*From the Evening Post of July* 8, 1834.]

The morning papers contain accounts of a riot at Chatham-street chapel last evening, between a party of whites and a party of blacks. The story is told in the morning journals in very inflammatory language, and the whole blame is cast upon the negroes; yet it seems to us, from those very statements themselves, that, as usual, there was fault on both sides, and more especially on that of the whites. It seems to us, also, that those who are opposed to the absurd and mad schemes of the immediate abolitionists, use means against that scheme which are neither just nor politic. We have noticed a great many tirades of late, in certain prints, the object of which appeared to be to excite the public mind to strong hostility to the negroes generally, and to the devisers of the immediate emancipation plan, and not merely to the particular measure reprehended. This community is too apt to run into excitements; and those who are now trying to get up an excitement against the negroes will have much to answer for, should their efforts be successful to the extent which some recent circumstances afford ground to apprehend. It is the duty of the press to discriminate; to oppose objectionable measures, but not to arouse popular fury against men; to repress, not to stimulate passion. Reason—calm, temperate reason—may do much to shorten the date of the new form in which fanaticism has recently sprung up among us; but persecution will inevitably have the effect of prolonging its existence and adding to its strength.

The riot at the Chatham-street chapel seems to have grown out of the following circumstances. The New-York Sacred Music Society have a lease of the chapel for Monday and Thursday evenings throughout the year. Some person, in behalf of the blacks, had obtained from the Secretary of the Music Society permission to occupy the chapel last evening. The blacks thereupon issued printed notices of their intended meeting, which it is said was called for the purpose of celebrating the postponed festival of the Fourth of July. In pursuance of this notice they met and commenced their exercises. Certain members of the Music Society also arrived, not knowing the disposition which had been made of the chapel; but being informed of the circumstances, agreed to postpone the purpose with which they had themselves assembled. Their number, however, being soon augmented by the arrival of other persons, they reversed their first peaceable and proper resolution, and concluded upon insisting that possession of the chapel should be given to them. The blacks, in the meanwhile, had prayed, sung a hymn, and had commenced reading the Declaration of Independence. They did not seem disposed, at that stage of the proceedings, to break up their meet ing and retire from the chapel One of their number rose and requested them to do so, but others called on the meeting to keep their seats. The Sacred Music Society then took forcible possession of the pulpit, and thereupon a general battle commenced, which seems to have been waged with considerable violence on both sides, and resulted in the usual number of broken heads and benches.

We have made up the foregoing statement wholly from the one-sided account of the Courier and Enquirer, the most inflammatory and unfair paper in the city on what relates to negroes, as on all other subjects. We have simply taken its facts, without their gloss; and we think readers of candid and temperate minds will perceive that the blame of this disgraceful transaction lies more with the white persons concerned in it, than with their coloured antagonists. Permission had been duly obtained to use the chapel on this occasion; and if it had not been, application should have been made to the civil authorities to expel the occupants. If there was any deception or concealment practised by Mr. Tappan in procuring permission to use the chapel, as is alleged, he made himself obnoxious to censure; but that circumstance furnished no warrant to eject the blacks by force of arms. That it was very wrong in them, and more particularly in the fanatical white persons who are leading them on, to meet there at all, for the purpose contemplated, or for any purpose, no one can deny, for it was obviously provoking a riot. That the whole scheme of immediate emancipation, and of promiscuous intermarriage of the two races, is preposterous, and revolting alike to common sense and common decency, we shall be ever ready, on all occasions, to maintain. Still, this furnishes no justification for invading the undoubted rights of the blacks, or violating the public peace; and we think, from the showing of those who mean to establish the direct contrary, that these were both done by the Sacred Music Society.

We are aware that we are taking the unpopular side of this question; but satisfied that it is the just one, we are not to be deterred by any such consideration. Certain prints have laboured very hard to get up an anti-negro excitement, and their efforts have in some degree been successful. It should be borne in mind, however, that fanaticism may be shown on both sides of the controversy; and they will do the most to promote the real interests of their country, and of the black people themselves, who will be guided in the matter by the dictates of reason and strict justice. The plans of the Colonization Society are rational and practicable; those of the enthusiasts who advocate immediate and unconditional emancipation wholly wild and visionary. To influence the minds of the blacks, then, in favour of the first, we must have recourse to temperate argument and authentic facts. Whatever is calculated to inflame their minds, prepares them to listen to the frantic ravings of those who preach the latter notions.

ABOLITION RIOTS.

[*From the Evening Post, July* 11, 1834.]

It is most earnestly to be hoped that the civil authorities will be prepared to act with all their strength, together with that of the military, if it should be necessary, to put down, this night, in the most effectual manner, any further attempt to make this city a scene of disgraceful riot and tumult. A mad spirit has gone abroad among our populace—a spirit excited in part, no doubt, by the proceedings and inflammatory publications of the Abolitionists, as they are called; but even in a greater measure by the violent tirades of certain prints opposed to the Abolitionists.

* * * * * * * *

Strongly as we are opposed to the doctrines and to the measures of the Abolitionists, both to those of the association, and those of a wilder and more deeply fanatical cast which are advocated in their journals, and in anonymous handbills and pamphlets, yet even greater is our opposition to all attempts to overthrow those doctrines by a resort to brute unauthorized force. Yet such force has been almost in terms appealed to, time and again, by the journal we have named, and bad as the conduct of the Abolitionists is, it has been represented in highly exaggerated colours, in order more strongly to inflame the public indignation against them.

Even now that these mobs have occurred, and their proceedings been characterized by a degree of lawless violence highly disgraceful to the city, the press, with two or three exceptions, has not the wisdom and independence to speak out boldly and energetically, and tell these rioters how madly they are acting. That a mob, composed more than half of boys, of wild, daring, undisciplined boys—and a very large proportion of the other moiety made up of the very dregs of society — that this mob, so composed, and actuated by no common sentiment or object, further than the mere love of disorder — should be treated as expressing the sentiments, and wreaking the vengeance of this great and moral community, is an insult on the character of the city. A mob attacking and destroying the private dwellings of citizens, and not stayed even at the threshold of the church, but with sacrilegious fury assailing even such an edifice, though held in respect by the common sentiment of mankind — such a mob ought to be treated with no honeyed words, but all good citizens ought to lend their assistance to maintain the supremacy of the laws, and put down this insurrectionary spirit.

No reader can for a moment suppose that we approve or would countenance in any degree the schemes of the Abolitionists. We have expressed repeatedly our deep abhorrence of a portion of their views, and our conviction that other portions are wholly visionary and impracticable. Even if their notions on the subject of abolition were proper in themselves, their conduct in attempting to propagate these notions is such that to ascribe it to fanaticism is the most charitable construction. But even these enthusiasts, while they transgress no law, are under the protection of the laws, and he who without legal warrant invades their houses and destroys their property, if he does it from any other motive than virtuous resentment against error, is an incendiary and robber; and if actuated by that feeling, is himself an example of fanaticism, though of an opposite kind. There are legitimate ways of expressing public opinion far more efficacious, as well as far more respectable, than a mob can ever be. We may call public meetings, and pass temperate but firm resolutions; we may expose through the press the absurdity and impracticability of the views of those who have been the objects of assault in this case; we may keep a vigilant eye upon them, and procure them to be indicted and visited with legal punishment whenever their proceedings become obnoxious to the law. But till then they are entitled to all the privileges and immunities of American citizens, and have a right to be protected in their persons and property against all assailants whatsoever. We trust that the authorities will this night show that this right is not a mere mockery; we trust that the rioters will be dealt with in a way that may long ensure the quiet of the city, if they dare again congregate to carry their incendiary purposes into further execution.

In making these remarks, we do not wish to be understood as intimating that there has been any remissness on the part of the civil authorities during the previous nights. On the contrary, last night in particular, they were exceedingly active, and took their measures with great promptitude and discretion. But it was evident that the disorders were far more extensive than had been anticipated, and the force under the direction of the Mayor was therefore not sufficient for the simultaneous protection of all the different points where the riot was expected to show itself.

ABOLITION RIOTS.

[*From the Evening Post, July* 12, 1834.]

The details which are published below, from the Journal of Commerce and the Daily Advertiser of this morning, are already on their way to every quarter of the country, to inform the whole people of the United States of the additional and deplorable blot which the events of last night have stamped on the character of this city. The fury of demons seems to have entered into the breasts of our misguided populace. Like those ferocious animals which, having once tasted blood, are seized with an insatiable thirst for gore, they have had an appetite awakened for outrage, which nothing but the most extensive and indiscriminate destruction seems capable of appeasing. The cabin of the poor negro, and the temples dedicated to the service of the living God, are alike the objects of their blind fury. The rights of private and public property, the obligations of law, the authority of its ministers, and even the power of the military, are all equally spurned by these audacious sons of riot and disorder. What will be the next mark of their licentious wrath it is impossible to conjecture.

* * * * * * * *

This night the trial is to be once again made whether the public authorities or a lawless mob are to be masters of the city; whether a motley assemblage of infuriated and besotted ruffians, animated with a hellish spirit, are to destroy and slay at the promptings of their wild passions and prejudices; or whether the true sentiments of this great community are to have their due preponderance. We accord to the city magistrates all the praise which their conduct hitherto deserves. But at the same time we must take leave to advise them, in the most serious manner, no longer to forbear resorting to stronger measures, to such measures as it is now evident can alone effectually quell the insurrectionary and destroying spirit which the proceedings of the Abolitionists, the indiscreet comments of certain prints, and most especially the seditious and inflammatory advice of that journal of whose tone and temper a specimen is given above, have aroused.* We call upon them not again to repeat the

* The extract here referred to is omitted for the reason stated in the Preface, that it is not the intention of this publication to re-

idle pageant of a military procession; not to add to the confidence of the rioters by an empty, ineffectual display of unused weapons. Let them be fired upon, if they dare collect together again to prosecute their nefarious designs. Let those who make the first movement towards sedition be shot down like dogs—and thus teach to their infatuated followers a lesson which no milder course seems sufficient to inculcate. This is no time for expostulation or remonstrance. Forbearance towards these rioters is cruelty towards the orderly and peaceable part of the community. Let us act with such promptness and decision now as to ensure that there will be no repetition of such outrages in time to come. Let us restore the dignity of the violated law. Let us not pause to parley when the foe is at the gate. Let us be brief when traitors brave the field. We would recommend that the whole military force of the city be called out; that large detachments be stationed wherever any ground exists to anticipate tumultuary movements; that smaller bodies patrol the streets in every part of the city, and that the troops be directed to fire upon the first disorderly assemblage that refuses to disperse at the bidding of lawful authority. This will restore peace and quietness to the city, and nothing short of this will do so.

---

vive the temporary controversies of the time when these articles were written.

ANTI-SLAVERY ASSOCIATION.

[*From the Evening Post, July* 22, 1834.]

It will be seen by the report of the proceedings of the Board of Aldermen last evening, published in another column, that the communication of the Executive Committee of the Anti-Slavery Association was treated with great contempt by that body. As the communication has been inserted, as an advertisement, in nearly all the newspapers, the public generally are probably pretty well apprized of its contents. It is a perfectly respectful document, prepared with the purpose of showing that the association above named had transcended none of those rights which are guarantied to its members, in common with all their fellow-citizens, by the Constitution of the United States; and that the objects of the society are not incompatible with the duties of its members as citizens under the existing institutions of this country.

With all due respect for the motives which actuated the Board of Aldermen in unanimously refusing to entertain this document, we must take the liberty to say that we think they did not act wisely in casting it out. An occasion was presented them for the expression of a calm and temperate opinion on the conduct of the abolitionists, as it affects the peace and order of society, which, properly embraced, might have been productive of much good, both on the minds of the enthusiasts in the cause of negro emancipation, and those, more especially, of the community at large. We would not have the Common Council throw itself in as a disputant in the fierce and inflammatory discussion which has already engaged so many fiery antagonists; but we should have been glad to see it treat the subject as a legislative body—as a body of municipal magistrates, charged with the framing and the enforcing of the laws. We should have been glad if this letter of Arthur Tappan and his associates had been referred to a discreet and intelligent committee, to the end that they might draw up a report, not controverting the abstract notions of the abolitionists on the subject of the emancipation and equal rights of the blacks, but proving by mild and judicious arguments, that even if the end they aim at is in itself proper, the time is ill chosen, and the means employed calculated, not merely to defeat their object, but to plunge the negroes into a far worse condition than that which they are now taught by their deluded guides to repine at.

The report might further have shown, that, even allowing the time to be well chosen for the work, and the means adapted to the end, they pursue a radically erroneous course in addressing their doctrines to the negroes themselves, whom they thus render discontented and wretched, but whose condition they cannot meliorate. To effect their object the minds of the whites must be convinced of its propriety; and all discourses addressed to the blacks meanwhile, to show them the degradation of their situation, and their natural right to an equal footing with the race of white men, must inevitably tend, at the best, to make them unhappy, and may lead to scenes of outrage which the mind shudders to contemplate.

In a report such as we are supposing, the committee might also have taken occasion to speak words of salutary counsel to those classes of the community most likely to be stirred up to acts of violence by the fanatical conduct of the abolitionists. They might have shown them that any insurrectionary movement, instead of effecting the object desired, would, by an invariable law of human nature, be followed by a very contrary result. They might have shown, that persecution is the very fuel that feeds the fire of fanaticism; that such men as the abolitionists are but fixed more firmly in their faith by the opposition that seeks to prostrate them ; that like the waves of the ocean, which swell from billows into mountains as the gale rages against them, their spirits but rise the higher when assailed by a storm of popular fury, nor subside again till the tempest is overpast. Fanaticism has ever flourished most exuberantly in the most intolerant countries; nor are there many minds in this community so ignorant of the history of nations as not to know, that, whether in religion or politics, enthusiasm gains strength and numbers the more its dogmas are opposed. The effort to put down the Roman Catholic religion by persecution has been tried, and with what result? The attempt to destroy the heresy, as it was deemed, of the Covenanters in Scotland, by hunting down its professors, was also thoroughly tried; but though the devoted peasantry were driven to caves and dens, and forced to subsist on the roots of the earth, the storm of religious persecution, instead of extinguishing, only fanned the fire of zeal into a fiercer flame.

These are views which, if the Common Council had embraced the opportunity of the letter of Arthur Tappan and his associates to put them before the community, in a report drawn up with ability and judgment, might, we think, have been productive of very considerable good. The Anti-Slavery Society, as the reader probably remarked, after stating that nothing had occurred to change their views on those subjects in relation to which they are associated, declare their determination not "to recant or relinquish any principle or measure they have adopted," but on the contrary, avow their readiness "to live and die" by the principles they have espoused. In this—however mistaken, however mad, we may consider their opinions in relation to the blacks—what honest, independent mind can blame them? Where is the man so poor of soul, so white-livered, so base, that he would do less, in relation to any important doctrine in which he religiously believed? Where is the man who would have his tenets drubbed into him by the clubs of ruffians, or would hold his conscience at the dictation of a mob?

There is no man in this community more sincerely and strongly opposed to the views and proceedings of the abolitionists than this journal is, and always has been. Our opposition was commenced long before that of those prints which now utter the most intemperate declamation on the subject, nor have we omitted to express it on any proper occasion since. But in doing this temperately, in employing argument and reasoning, instead of calling on the populace "to arm and strike a blow for liberty"—instead of painting disgusting portraits of the "blubber lips and sooty blood of negroes"—we think we are more effectually advancing the desired end, than we possibly could, by the most furious and inflammatory appeals to the angry passions of the multitude. Indeed, one of the reasons why we lamented the late violations of public order and private right, was, that the effect of such outrages would be to increase, instead of abating, the zeal of abolition fanaticism, and warm many minds perhaps, which were before only moderately inclined to those doctrines, to a pitch of intemperate ardour. The wildest fancies that ever entered into a disordered brain are adopted as truths when he who utters them meets with unreasonable persecution; while, if unnoticed, or noticed only by the proper tribunals, they make no harmful impression, even on the mind of credulity itself. "The lightning hallows where it falls," and so the bolt of persecution, in the eyes of thousands, sanctifies what it strikes.

SMALL NOTE CIRCULATION.

[*From the Evening Post of August* 6, 1834.]

Now that *real* money has come into circulation—now that the country is plentifully supplied with gold and silver—we trust the friends of a sound currency will take pains, and adopt all proper measures, to banish small notes from use. We call upon every man who professes to be animated with the principles of the democracy, to assist in accomplishing the great work of redeeming this country from the curse of our bad bank system. We never shall be a truly free and happy people while subject, as we now are, to Bank domination. No system could possibly be devised more certainly fatal to the great principle on which our government rests—the glorious principle of equal rights—than the Banking system, as it exists in this country. It is hostile to every received axiom of political economy, it is hostile to morals, and hostile to freedom. Its direct and inevitable tendency is to create artificial inequalities and distinctions in society; to increase the wealth of the rich, and render more abject and oppressive the poverty of the poor. It fosters a spirit of speculation, destructive of love of country—a spirit which substitutes an idol of gold for that better object which patriotism worships—a spirit which paralyzes all the ardent and generous impulses of our nature, and creates, instead, a sordid and rapacious desire of gain, to minister to the insatiable cravings of which becomes the sole aim of existence.

We do not expect and do not desire to overthrow our pernicious Banking system suddenly. We would not, if we could, do aught to infringe the chartered privileges of Banks already existing. Were they ten times worse in their effects than they are, we would not justify a breach of the public faith to get rid of the evil. But we desire most ardently that it may not be permitted to spread more widely. The legislatures may at least say, "Thus far shalt thou go and no further; here shall thy proud waves be stayed." They may refuse to grant any more charters of incorporation, and may take effectual measures to prohibit the small note issues. These measures constitute the proper first step in the great reformation for which we contend, and these measures the democracy of the country—if we do not strangely misinterpret their sentiments—will demand.

But in the meanwhile, the means are within the reach of the people themselves to do much—very much—towards the accomplishment of the desired object. Let employers provide themselves with gold to pay their hands; and let the hands of those employers who continue in the practice, which has been too extensive, of procuring uncurrent money to pay them, take such measures to remedy the evil as are within their reach, and not inconsistent with prudence. The practice is wholly unjustifiable, and stands, in a moral point of view, on a footing not very different from that of clipping coins. The law, however, which we all know is not always framed in the most perfect accordance with the principles of ethics, makes this important difference, that while to the one species of dishonesty it extends full protection, the other it visits with the most ignominious punishment. But though protected by the law, workmen may do much to rid themselves of the evils of this practise, and at the same time forward the great object of democracy—ultimate emancipation from the shackles of a detestable Bank tyranny. Let them remember, when paid in small uncurrent notes, that the longer they retain possession of those notes the greater is the profit of the Bank that issued them, and therefore let them take the best means within their reach of causing them to be returned to the Bank. Every dollar-note in circulation has displaced an equal amount of gold and silver, and, on the other hand, every dollar of gold and silver you keep in circulation, will displace twice or three times its amount in paper money.

Paper money is fingered by a great many hands, as may be easily perceived from the soiled and worn appearance of many of the bills. A cheap, and, to a certain extent, most effectual method of disseminating the principles of those opposed to incorporated rag-money manufactories, would be for them to write upon the back of every bank-note which should come into their possession, some short sentence expressive of their sentiments. For example—"No Monopolies!" "No Union of Banks and State!" "Jackson and Hard Money!" "Gold before Rags!" and the like. When it should become their duty to *endorse* a bill issued by a Bank, the charter of which was obtained by bribery and collusion, (as many such there be) it would be well to inscribe upon it in a clear and distinct hand, "*Wages of Iniquity!*"

What we have here recommended may seem to be but child's play; but we are satisfied that if the workingmen, upon whom the worst trash of Bank rags are palmed off, would only adopt such a practice, and persist in it for a short time, they would see the good result. The worst class of uncurrent notes would soon be plentifully endorsed, for it is the worst description of money which is generally *bought* to pay away to mechanics, in order that their employers may avoid paying them as large a proportion as possible of their just wages. Let them consider the hints thrown out in this article, and they can hardly fail, we think, to perceive, that if generally acted upon, they would have an important effect in assisting the introduction of gold as a currency, in the place of the small note circulation of which there is so much reason to complain.

RESOLUTIONS OF THE DEMOCRATIC REPUBLICAN COMMITTEE.

[*From the Evening Post, August* 12, 1834.]

Two advertisements, one from "the Democratic Republican Young Men's Committee," signed by MORGAN L. SMITH as Chairman, and the other from "the Democratic Republican General Committee," signed by ELDAD HOLMES, have been published regularly in the Times, the first articles in its columns, for the last eight or ten days past. These advertisements purport to be the proceedings of the Committees, at a meeting held by each on the evening of the fourth of this month. They each consist of three resolutions; both sets of resolutions have, *pari passu*, a corresponding object, and are expressed in language of great similarity; and both, we presume, may be ascribed to the same paternity. Being thus, as it were, twin-brothers, we shall save space by copying only the set that stands first, which will sufficiently acquaint the reader with the ground of the remarks we are about to offer. They are as follows:

"At a regular meeting of the Democratic Republican Young Men's Committee, held at Tammany Hall, on the evening of the 4th instant, the following resolutions were unanimously adopted:

"Resolved, That this Committee highly approve the political course of '*The New-York Times*,' a paper recently established, for the independent and fearless course it has pursued in support of the Democratic Republican principles of the present administra ion, and that we therefore confidently recommend it to the confidence and patronage of our Democratic Republican friends.

"Resolved, That the New-York Evening Post, the Truth Teller, and the other democratic papers, having been consistent and able labourers in the cause of Republican principles, are entitled to the continued confidence and support of this Committee.

"Resolved, That the above resolutions be printed in the Democratic Republican papers, and signed by the Chairman and Secretaries."

We certainly can have no objection that either of the General Committees, or both, should express their approbation of the course of the Times, *for its course*, or that they should *confidently* recommend it to *confidence* and patronage. There is nothing in this recommendation, except its tautology, at which any one has a right to feel offended. The Times is a new paper, was set up under peculiar circumstances, and may stand in need of such an endorsement. Its course has, certainly, so far, been as exactly and carefully squared by party rules as the most thorough-going party-man could desire, and it was therefore but reasonable that the Committees should be called together, and requested confidently to express their confidence in that print. If they had stopped there not one word of dissatisfaction should they have heard from us.

But so far as the Evening Post is made to figure in these resolutions, we must confess we are not exactly pleased. We have never presented ourselves, cap in hand, to either of the Committees, to beg their most sweet voices; we have never asked their aid, or their endorsement in any way or shape; and do not feel that our dignity or importance is increased now that it is voluntarily bestowed. For years we have maintained, with industry and zeal, the principles of democracy; we have been forward to engage in every contest in which we considered the rights or interests of the people were put to hazard ; we have been strenuous in asserting the great doctrine of equal rights ; we have utterly shut our eyes and turned a deaf ear to considerations of private interest ; we have hesitated not to speak in terms of severest truth to our misled and misdoing merchants, although they were the chief supporters of our journal ; we have been vigilant and active in season, and out of season ; and now, verily, we at last have our reward !—to be put at the fag-end of a resolution got up to glorify the Times !—a paper of yesterday ! a print which has all the gloss of newness yet upon it ; which, however sound in its doctrines, and firm in its principles, bears no marks of fight, can show no scars, has made no sacrifices.

We repeat, we have no objection that the Democratic Committee should glorify that paper, and recommend it to "patronage," (a most undemocratic word, by the way,) we have no objection they should laud its course,—(we also are gratified with its general tone and management,)—we have no objection that they should nod their heads in approbation, and thus give "the stamp of fate and signal of a god." But we do object to being ourselves lugged in to fill up the cry—we do object to being put in the same category with the Truth Teller and *all the other democratic papers.* It is a fortunate thing for us, by the way, that the Democratic Chronicle happened to expire a few days before this ovation to the Times, or the Evening Post might have found itself placed side by side with that disgusting dealer in filth and personalities, as an equally worthy champion in the same republican cause.

We do most sincerely and urgently request the two Committees that they will hereafter let us alone. This is a request they can scarcely refuse to grant, since it is the first we ever made of them. We request that, hereafter, when any one interested in a new paper, wishes them to stand its sponsors, that the Evening Post may not be required to swing the censer, or bear any other subaltern part in the ceremonial. As for their "patronage," or that of any other body, or individual, we never asked it, and never shall. The democrats who like our course will probably continue to take our paper, notwithstanding the unkind cut of the Committees in thus thrusting us into the train of the Times. And as for the Committees' own, direct "patronage," (which means advertising to the amount of some forty or fifty dollars a year,) they are at liberty, nay, they are desired to withdraw it, whenever they think they do not get their money's worth. It is on this footing that we wish to stand with all our subscribers and advertisers. We desire no man's "patronage," and no man's business, who does not receive from us a full and fair equivalent for all he renders.

REPLY TO THE "TIMES."

[*From the Evening Post, August* 13, 1834.]

The Times of this morning incorrectly represents the ground of the Evening Post's complaint against the two Committees which were called together a fortnight ago to endorse that paper. We assure the Times that we feel not the slightest jealousy towards it, nor do we in the least envy its good fortune in receiving a stamp of approbation from the two Democratic Committees. We hope that endorsement may effect the end which was intended, for while the Times continues its endeavours to forward the republican cause we shall be glad to see it sustained. We expressed yesterday our approbation of its general tone and management; and so far from wishing to supplant it in the affections of the general Committee, or of the Young Men's Committee, we only complained that the Evening Post, with *all the other democratic papers*, was lugged in to divide honours which we were quite willing should be conferred on the Times alone.

As to which is the leading paper, that is a question we are quite content to submit to the readers of the several journals, not thinking the matter by any means settled by the precedence given to the Times in the resolutions it refers to. It perhaps deserves that precedence; but though we do not claim to be a better soldier, we certainly are an older soldier than the Times, and bear some marks of the service we have passed through. Thus, for our course in support of the interests of the democratic party and in defence of the great principle of Equal Rights, we lost last year *several hundred mercantile subscribers*—and this is the first time we have ever breathed a syllable on the subject. Did we waver in our faith, did we falter in our struggle, did we slacken in our energy, when the merchants were running about, from counting-room to counting-room, and beseeching their brother merchants to stop the Evening Post? — when men who had taken our paper for thirty years, wrote us insolent notes, commanding its discontinuance?—when such persons as ——— ——— exerted themselves with might and main, to induce our subscribers to forsake us and take the Evening Star instead? — and when the news of a discontinuance was received in Wall-street with half-frantic cheers? Did we not, all the while, pursue the forward tenor of our way with unabated zeal, exposing the true nature of the conflict which the Rich were waging against the Poor—the Aristocracy against the Democracy? Did we utter a complaint? Did we ask the General Committee, or the Young Men's Committee, or any other Committee, or any person, for assistance? Did we not stand on our own resources, and look alone to the final triumph of truth for our reward?

We ask the Times, then, if we have not a right to complain, when we find ourselves thrust in at the tail of a proceeding got up to do honour and service to it? We have fought the battle of the Democracy for years, and were never made the subject of a special endorsement by the two Committees which have countersigned the Times. That troubled us not—we asked not their stamp—we desired it not. Nor does it trouble us that their stamp is now impressed upon the Times. That paper is welcome to the distinction, and we hope it may answer the end to give it greater currency. But that, to consummate its apotheosis, we should be mixed up in a batch with the Truth Teller and *all* the other democratic papers, and thrown in as a make-weight, is certainly a mark of "continued confidence and respect," of a very sinister description, to say the least of it.

Let it not be supposed that we mean aught we have here said to express disparagement of the Truth Teller, of the merits of which spirited and zealous weekly journal we are fully sensible. The Truth Teller itself has a right to complain of being kneaded into a common lump with a parcel of nameless prints — no one may say how many nor of what character. But if the Truth Teller, which is a weekly paper, and devoted but in part to American politics, has a right to feel displeased, how much more so have we, that for a long series of years have bent our undivided energies to one object, the promotion of the fundamental principles of the Republican party? But we do not complain; we confine our animadversions to a single request — that the Committees will hereafter let us alone, to pursue our own course, in our own way, and not drag us, against our will, to serve as torch-bearers or train-holders in any triumphant procession in honour of any new object of their glorification. If we cannot recommend ourselves to the democracy, we do not wish the Committees to do it for us. And as to being harnessed to the triumphal car of the Times, it is a piece of service we do not affect—we are somewhat restive, and might throw the train into confusion by kicking out of the traces.

THE PRESIDENTIAL CONTEST.

[*From the Evening Post of August* 19, 1834.]

The duties of our situation oblige us to study with more attention than mere taste might incline us to do, the indications of public sentiment and public policy, as furnished by the course and tone of political journals, and the proceedings of political meetings. From the survey we have taken of the movements of the opposition party, for the last few months, it seems to us quite evident that they are laying a scheme to cheat the people out of the election of President. They seem to act on a principle of settled distrust of the intelligence and patriotism of the great body of the people, and to have laid their plans to carry their object in defiance of the wishes of a majority. For this purpose, it is their present aim to bring together, and combine into one body, all the materials of opposition, however dissimilar and heterogeneous, with a view to return to the next Congress as many members as possible opposed to the present administration, no matter how contrariant and irreconcileable their respective grounds of opposition.

This object accomplished, their next step will be, not by mutual compromise and conciliation to name some candidate for the President on whom all the diversified sects of their composite party might unite; for they are sensible that such harmony of action is impossible, and that they are not more hostile to the present administration than they are to each other; but for each faction to set up its own candidate, and support him in his own particular district of country, in the hope that the sum of the votes thus scattered among the various chiefs of the opposition may be sufficient to defeat an election by the people, and carry the question into the House of Representatives. Should the question be between the candidate of the democracy, and any single candidate the opposition might name, they are well aware that the choice of the democratic party would be ratified by a very large majority of votes. They will therefore seek to distract the public mind by a multiplicity of candidates, to take the election out of the hands of the people, and submit it to a body where each state has only an equal voice, and where experience has shown that collusion and intrigue may obtain a decision in direct opposition to the clearly expressed will of the great body of the people of the United States.

That this is the game which the various united factions that compose the opposition intend to play off there can be no manner of doubt. It is a corrupt scheme, because it is devised with a manifest intention and desire of preventing a fair expression of the popular will; and the preliminary steps are corrupt, because in the industrious and almost incredible efforts which the combined parties of the opposition are now making to elect members to Congress opposed to the administration, great pains are taken to conceal from the people the ultimate object which they have in view. For this purpose the war is waged simply on the broad ground of hostility to the Executive and to Martin Van Buren. No definite principles of action or of public policy are avowed; because there are none on which this amalgamated body of political antipathies could agree. No name of a successor is breathed; because the utterance of such a name would dissolve the unholy spell which binds them together before the great end of the ill-assorted union is achieved. It is therefore opposition to the administration which they alone venture to declare as their motive of action, and to this motive they attempt to give a colour of patriotism by the iteration of certain sounding and illusory phrases, the ready resort of political knaves and demagogues in all countries and all ages of the world.

Among the catchwords on which they seem most to rely for success, are the shouts which they are forever bawling in our ears, of "Constitution and Laws!" and "Principles, not men!" As to their pretended veneration for the Constitution and Laws, it accords well with a party whose only hopes of success rest on the issue of a deliberate fraud upon the People! We say a fraud upon the People—and what can be a more positive and flagitious fraud, than this combination of political sects, as opposite as day and night in their doctrines and views, acting together, not with a view to establish any common and definite course of policy for the administration of the General Government, but simply for the preliminary purpose of pulling down a Chief Magistrate who enjoys the confidence and affections of the People—each leader of those opposite factions inwardly trusting to his own skill in the arts of collusion, intrigue, and corruption, to win over the partizans of the others in the House of Representatives, and thus secure the Presidential succession to himself?

When the country beholds the leaders of the most contradictory and irreconcileable political doctrines that were ever entertained under our confederacy leaguing together for a common purpose of hostility to the dominant party, and all joining with equal lustiness in the cry of *Constitution and Laws!* even Charity herself would whisper that their conduct and motives ought to be scrutinized with vigilantly inquiring eyes. Is it the leader of the sect which professes the nullification heresy whose fears are aroused for the safety of the Constitution and Laws? What! he who but a few months ago raised the standard of revolt, advised the South to spurn with contempt the revenue laws of the country, and to resist their enforcement to the death! What! he who talked of sundering the Union, of establishing a separate republic, and of shooting down like beasts that perish any such of his fellow-countrymen as, in pursuance of the orders of Government, should cross the borders of South Carolina to enforce the violated laws! Is he now one of the chief leaders of the opposition party against the Executive, on the ground of an invasion of the Constitution and Laws? A fit minister of vengeance for such an offence! Fellow-countrymen, watch him well!

Hand in hand with him, the next one of the league who attracts our notice is connected with reminiscences of a very different nature. In him we behold the author of that gigantic scheme of injustice and oppression, the object of which was to build up a manufacturing aristocracy, and enrich them out of the earnings of the hardy sons of commerce; that scheme, which under the sounding pretence of holding out protection to American industry, was intended to strengthen the General Government at the expense of the States, and to lay the foundation of an enormous and profligate system of public expenditure which would have resulted, at no distant day, in the total overthrow of the liberties of the American people; that scheme which was devised to advance his own ambitious views, in defiance of the provisions of the Constitution, and of the rights and interests of the South;

and the palpable injustice and cruel oppression of which led the Nullifier with whom he is now joined in a pretended fraternal embrace to those traitorous measures which, but for the inflexible patriotism and energy of our Chief Magistrate, would have eventuated in the dissolution of our inestimable union. He also is a fit one now to wage war against the administration on the ground of its violation of the "Constitution and Laws."

A third one in this unholy league has ever been distinguished by his opposition to the equal rights of the people, and to the fundamental principles of the democratic party. In him we behold a man in whom hostility to democracy is the only principle which he has never forsaken—a man who opposed with all his energy the measures of the Government when at war with Great Britain; who rejoiced in the victories of the enemy; who at one time was the opponent, and then the advocate, of the United States Bank; at one time a declaimer against the American System, and then its fast friend. This is the third member of the triumvirate of political rivals who join in proclaiming as their watchword and battle-cry, the *Constitution and Laws!*

Among the vague and ambiguous sentiments by which they profess to be governed, is the stale and unmeaning phrase, of "*Principles not Men.*" This is one of those juggling maxims with which sordid and selfish politicians have ever attempted to cheat mankind. It has an honest and taking sound, but is utterly without substance, a mere jingle of words, *vox et præterea nihil.* Not much discernment is requisite to detect the fallacy and emptiness of this dishonest invention of unprincipled demagogues; for surely any man must perceive that principles without men, are little better than men without principles. Do they mean to elect their principles to office? Do they mean to have us governed by abstractions? by a body of ethics? by a set of precepts? or will they, like every other party, be sooner or later obliged to hold forward some *man*, as the person who is governed by their principles, and who, if chosen, will carry them into exercise? This wretched sophistry of "*principles not men*," has been used, all the world over, as a cloak for political knavery—as a convenient shelter for those to fight behind, who had no principles at all, and who were endeavouring to elevate men so notoriously unworthy, that prudence forbade their being named. "It is an advantage to all narrow wisdom and narrow morals," says Burke, "that their maxims have a plausible air, and, on a cursory view, appear equal to first principles. They are light and portable. They are as current as copper coin; and about as valuable. They serve equally the first capacities and the lowest; and they are at least as useful to the worst men as the best. Of this stamp is the cant of *Not men but measures;* a sort of charm by which many people get loose from every honourable engagement." If the opposition party, or the "Whig party," as they prefer to call themselves, are one—one in their political doctrines and political objects—let them avow what their doctrines and objects are; let them name the person whom they desire to elevate that he may carry them into effect; let us see what are their principles and who are their men. "Unqualified and uncompromising hostility to Martin Van Buren," is but half a motive. Pulling down is but a moiety of the work they have to achieve; they must build up, also; and the People are curious to see what sort of a mixed and composite administration they propose to create out of the various materials of which their heterogeneous party is composed.

SMALL NOTES AND THE STATE BANKING SYSTEM.

[*From the Evening Post, August* 26, 1834.]

Every day adds to the number of the indications, which any man not blind must perceive, that the great body of the democracy of this state are radically opposed to the Banking System, as it exists in this country, and are determined to insist that their representatives in the legislature shall take the first great step towards a reformation, by prohibiting the issue of small notes. The Albany Argus has at last taken a decided stand on this subject, and we notice with great pleasure that several sound and influential country journals have likewise expressed themselves in favour of the prohibition, in manly and explicit terms. The Poughkeepsie Telegraph has the following sensible paragraph on the subject. [*Here follows extract.*]

The Albany Argus of last Saturday quotes the foregoing paragraph, with a remark, that it is "happy to perceive that the question of restricting the issue of bank notes of the smaller denominations is beginning to receive the notice of the republican press, as well as of the people in their primary meetings," and it avows its "full concurrence, both in the general expression, and in the extent of the restriction."

So far, so well. One step further, however, is demanded, both by the sentiments of a very large portion of the democracy, and by a due regard to the political principles on which the democratic party is founded. The Bank system is an insidious enemy of democracy. It is an essentially aristocratic institution. It has stolen upon us like a thief in the night. It has sprung up among us, before the people were aware of its true nature and its rapid growth. Either the Bank system, which, in other words, is an odious system of exclusive privileges, must be put down, or the days of democracy are numbered. We wish not this to be done by any sudden or violent means; but we look upon it as the bounden duty of all who really entertain republican sentiments; who would really grieve to see this country lapsing into aristocracy; who really desire to preserve the great and fundamental principle to the democratic party—the glorious principle of Equal Rights;—we look upon it as the bounden duty of all such to oppose, by all proper means, our most pernicious system of banking — a system which has grown up in this country so rapidly, and has acquired such formidable power, that we already present the degrading spectacle of a people professing to be self-governed, and yet completely held, in many respects, in the vile fetters of a host of exclusively privileged money monopolies.

We say, therefore, that one step further than the mere restriction of small bank-notes is necessary. The sentiment ought to be distinctly avowed that *no new bank charters shall be granted, and no existing charters extended, either in duration or amount.* Let the legislators be chosen with a full understanding that this is the wish of the people. Let them be told that they are to truck or bargain away no more exclusive money privileges, for any political or pecuniary consideration whatever, or for any other purpose, real or pretended. Let them understand, moreover, that these steps are but the beginning of a system of measures which will be steadily persevered in by the democracy, until every vestige of monopoly has disappeared from the land, and until banking — as most other occupations are now, and as all ought to be—is left open to the free competition of all who choose to enter into that pursuit.

We have already too many banks, viewing the subject without reference to the question of exclusive privileges. We have too many banks, merely considering them as instruments to supply a circulating medium. The banks which already exist cannot possibly do a profitable business, except by fostering a harmful, demoralizing spirit of overtrading and speculation. There is no good reason why a single additional charter should be granted, or why the capital of any bank should be enlarged. We therefore hope that the democracy, throughout the state, will be careful to let their sentiments on this interesting and important subject be fully and clearly expressed. In this city, we would in a particular manner call upon the people to give free and emphatic utterance to their wishes.

For our own part, this journal long ago voluntarily declared it would support no candidate for the legislature who is not understood to be unequivocally opposed to the granting of any new bank charter, or to the extending of any new one. This, and the determination to prohibit the issue of notes of a less denomination than five dollars, constitute a qualification, without which no candidate shall receive our support. The people have groaned and sweated under Bank tyranny long enough. It is time that they should rise in their strength, and assert their right to be freed from the petty yet galling despotism of money incorporations.

THE ELECTION.

[*From the Evening Post, Sept.* 24, 1834.]

The more we reflect on the recommendation of the Bank party at the meeting at Masonic Hall to the merchants of this city, to close their stores during the election, the more we are struck with the probable, nay almost certain consequences of such a rash and malignant procedure. Not that we apprehend any results injurious to our cause, or to those by whom it is supported. The hard hands, sturdy limbs, and honest hearts of the democracy of this city, are fully adequate to the defence of their sacred right of suffrage. Other considerations, therefore, have impelled, and will still impel us, to raise our voice against this second attempt to throw our city into confusion; to frighten our peaceable citizens into the innermost sanctuary of their dwellings; to invite to riot and bloodshed; and to bring disgrace on the name, the practices, and the principles of free government.

Hitherto, and until resort was had to this new expedient of letting loose upon the peaceful voters of this city, a host of mad-headed young men and half-grown men, for the purpose of marching out of their own peculiar wards into those where they had no business to go, for the purpose of surrounding the polls and insulting the democratic voters —until that pernicious example was set by the pretended supporters of order and decency, the elections of this country were the boast of our people, and the admiration of foreigners. Contrasted with the riots, the battles, and the broken heads of the English polls, they exhibited to the world the example of a decorous and peaceful struggle for power, honourable to the nation, and doubly honourable to the spirit of liberty. They afforded a full and unanswerable refutation of the vain assumption of aristocratic pride, that disorder and licentiousness will ever accompany a general diffusion of the right of suffrage, and deprived the enemies of freedom of their last argument against the equal rights of the people.

Hence, one of the great objects of the Bank party in adopting the measure which is the subject of these remarks, undoubtedly is, to goad on the young men and boys who are in a state of dependence, to provoke the people to acts of violence, by every means in their power, and then to proclaim to the world that these acts of just resentment are the boiling effervescences of the turbulent spirit of democracy. They intend to draw new arguments against equal rights and universal suffrage, from the consequences that may result from their own mad, malignant measures, and to charge the honest, industrious, upright, independent voters of this city with all the odium of acts forced upon them in their own defence. Such was the course they pursued during the last, such the course they are about pursuing in the coming election. In the former of these occasions, by the instrumentality of that dexterity in falsehood and misrepresentation which seems to be the main pillar of their principles and their practices, they metamorphosed the breakers of the peace into the conservators of the peace, and converted an attack on the property of the state, into a defence of the rights and property of the citizens. By the same adroitness at legerdemain, they will without doubt attempt to make the world believe, that a similar course of conduct on a future occasion resulted from the same disinterested regard to the public welfare, and the peace of the city.

If such is not the secret motive of this letting slip the dogs of war upon us, to what other motive shall we ascribe a measure so fraught with consequences such as they without doubt anticipate? Cannot these youngsters come quietly, one by one, and give in their votes, if they are entitled by age and residence, and go about their business when they have done so, like the rest of their fellow-citizens? To what purpose throng about the polls, day after day, except to impede others, insult their feelings, and provoke them to retaliation? Do they expect to gain any votes by this course of conduct? Certainly not. Their object is to prevent others from voting; to pry into the ballots of such tradesmen, mechanics, and labourers, as may be in the employment of the lordly master they themselves serve, and denounce them for future proscription, and finally, in the last resort, to invite the sturdy democracy to resent their impertinent interference.

But whatever may be the motives and the expectations of these "friends of order and decency," we earnestly hope, though we can scarcely in reason expect, they will be signally disappointed. We hope the manly and sedate democracy of our city, conscious of its superior strength, virtue, and independence, will content itself with laughing to scorn these puny insects, that come to buzz their impertinencies in their ears, and in the stern yet temperate spirit of utter contempt, treat them as spoiled children, invited to dangerous mischief, and ignorant of its probable consequences. Let them recollect that these misguided young men and beardless boys, are but the innocent puppets of violent and interested leaders, who send them forth as tools and cats-paws to provoke the men of the city, and bring upon their own heads the consequences of their own doings. We earnestly hope the parents of these indiscreet and deluded youth will make use of their authority, and enjoin them on their obedience and duty to keep away from these riotous meetings at Masonic Hall, and stay at home of evenings, under the sacred protection of their hearths and firesides. Finally, we call upon the ministers of the Gospel of Peace, in the spirit of pastors of their flocks, and advocates of social order, to adjure the aged to exert their influence to prevent their sons going forth thus to throw firebrands into the city.

What will be the probable result of this rabble of hot-headed young men and indiscreet boys, with their ships and their banners, intruding into the wards where they neither reside or have a vote? At first, perhaps, a contest of cutting jests, and bitter repartee, in which those who get the worst will become the most irrritated. From hard words to hard blows is but a single step. The madness will spread; the cudgel will be lifted; the paving-stones and brick-bats will fly; the concealed dirk will be drawn; blood will flow, and innocent lives pay the forfeit of the madness of youth, spurred on by smooth-faced hypocrites and reckless renegades. But this is not all, nor is it the worst. The civil authorities of the city being too weak to quell the fury of the multitude, will be obliged to call out a military force. But whence are they to obtain such a force? Those who compose the military would probably be engaged, on opposite sides, among the rioters. Yet let us suppose it practicable to obtain a military force for the purpose of restoring order. We shall then behold citizens with arms in their hands stand arrayed against those who have none. All other means failing to still the tumult and arrest the actors, it will become the painful duty of the Mayor to order the troops to fire into the multitude; or if he should refrain from so doing, a single missive not perhaps intended for that purpose, provokes one of the military to fire without orders. Who shall paint the consequences of such an act? We shrink from the anticipation. It is sufficient to refer to the thousand examples under similar circumstances. Who shall pretend to say that our city would not smoke in ashes and blood?

Such are the consequences likely to flow from this last and desperate resort of a baffled and twenty times defeated traitor. And all for what? That the Bank may triumph over the constitution, and money tyrannize over men.

THE STATE PRISON MONOPOLY.

[*From the Evening Post, Oct.* 1834.]

We are very sorry to see the opposition to the scheme of State Prison labour, or the State Prison Monopoly, as it is termed, showing itself in acts of violence, the effect of which must be to cool the friendship which men of correct principles entertain for that cause, if not to turn them wholly against it. We allude to the mutilation of edifices built of materials prepared at Sing-Sing Prison. A number of costly and beautiful houses in the upper part of the town have been defaced and mutilated by some misguided and unprincipled persons, for no other reason that can be conjectured than that they were constructed of materials procured at the State Prison. This journal is opposed — decidedly and strongly opposed — to any plan of convict labour, the effect of which is to interfere with the prosperity of upright citizen mechanics, or diminish the incentive to an honest and industrious pursuit of lawful vocations. But if any thing could induce us to withhold our assistance from the objects contemplated by those who are seeking to effect a radical change in the plan of prison labour, it would be the lawless and incendiary conduct to which we allude. A good cause can never need to be furthered by violence and outrage, and violence and outrage are in themselves *prima facie* evidence of a bad cause. While cut stone, or any other materials for building, can be procured cheaper at Sing Sing Prison than elsewhere, it would be expecting too much of contractors to ask them to forego the advantage thus extended to them. To buy where we can buy cheapest, and sell where we can sell highest, is the rule of all traffic, and it is putting men to too hard a test when they are required to correct, by individual forbearance, what should be provided for by a general law. Besides, even if those who erect buildings with materials purchased at the prison do wrong, and even if injury inflicted upon their private property be the best means of procuring redress (neither of which propositions is tenable) still it should be borne in mind that the houses which they build pass into other hands, and that, in mutilating them, instead of injuring those whom they consider justly obnoxious to anger, the opponents of the State Prison Monopoly may in reality be invading the the means of some citizen friendly to their cause.

THE DIVISION OF PARTIES.

[*From the Evening Post, November* 4, 1834.]

Since the organization of the Government of the United States the people of this country have been divided into two great parties. One of these parties has undergone various changes of name; the other has continued steadfast alike to its appellation and to its principles, and is now, as it was at first, the DEMOCRACY. Both parties have ever contended for the same opposite ends which originally caused the division—whatever may have been, at different times, the particular means which furnished the immediate subject of dispute. The great object of the struggles of the Democracy has been to confine the action of the General Government within the limits marked out in the Constitution: the great object of the party opposed to the Democracy has ever been to overleap those boundaries, and give to the General Government greater powers and a wider field for their exercise. The doctrine of the one party is that all power not expressly and clearly delegated to the General Government, remains with the States and with the People: the doctrine of the other party is that the vigour and efficacy of the General Government should be strengthened by a free construction of its powers. The one party sees danger from the encroachments of the General Government; the other affects to see danger from the encroachments of the States.

This original line of separation between the two great political parties of the republic, though it existed under the old Confederation, and was distinctly marked in the controversy which preceded the formation and adoption of the present Constitution, was greatly widened and strengthened by the project of a National Bank, brought forward in 1791. This was the first great question which occurred under the new Constitution to test whether the provisions of that instrument were to be interpreted according to their strict and literal meaning; or whether they might be stretched to include objects and powers which had never been delegated to the General Government, and which consequently still resided with the states as separate sovereignties.

The proposition of the Bank was recommended by the Secretary of the Treasury on the ground that such an institution would be "of primary importance to the prosperous administration of the finances, and of the greatest utility in the operations connected with the support of public credit." This scheme, then, as now, was opposed on various grounds; but the constitutional objection constituted then, as it does at the present day, the main reason of the uncompromising and invincible hostility of the democracy to the measure. They considered it as the exercise of a very important power which had never been given by the states or the people to the General Government, and which the General Government could not therefore exercise without being guilty of usurpation. Those who contended that the Government possessed the power, effected their immediate object; but the controversy still exists. And it is of no consequence to tell the democracy that it is now established by various precedents, and by decisions of the Supreme Court, that this power is fairly incidental to certain other powers expressly granted; for this is only telling them that the advocates of free construction have, at times, had the ascendancy in the Executive and Legislative, and, at all times, in the Judiciary department of the Government. The Bank question stands now on precisely the same footing that it originally did; it is now, as it was at first, a matter of controversy between the two great parties of this country—between parties as opposite as day and night—between parties which contend, one for the consolidation and enlargement of the powers of the General Government, and the other for strictly limiting that Government to the objects for which it was instituted, and to the exercise of the means with which it was entrusted. The one party is for a popular Government; the other for an aristocracy. The one party is composed, in a great measure, of the farmers, mechanics, labourers, and other producers of the middling and lower classes, (according to the common gradation by the scale of wealth,) and the other of the consumers, the rich, the proud, the privileged—of those who, if our Government were converted into an aristocracy, would become our dukes, lords, marquises and baronets. The question is still disputed between these two parties—it is ever a new question—and whether the democracy or the aristocracy shall succeed in the present struggle, the fight will be renewed, whenever the defeated party shall be again able to muster strength enough to take the field. The privilege of self-government is one which the people will never be permitted to enjoy unmolested. Power and wealth are continually stealing from the many to the few. There is a class continually gaining ground in the community, who desire to monopolize the advantages of the Government, to hedge themselves round with exclusive privileges, and elevate themselves at the expense of the great body of the people. These, in our society, are emphatically the aristocracy ; and these, with all such as their means of persuasion, or corruption, or intimidation, can move to act with them, constitute the party which are now strugling against the democracy, for the perpetuation of an odious and dangerous moneyed institution.

Putting out of view, for the present, all other objections to the United States Bank,—that it is a monopoly, that it possesses enormous and overshadowing power, that it has been most corruptly managed, and that it is identified with political leaders to whom the people of the United States must ever be strongly opposed—the constitutional objection alone is an insurmountable objection to it.

The Government of the United States is a limited sovereignty. The powers which it may exercise are expressly enumerated in the Constitution. None not thus stated, or that are not "necessary and proper" to carry those which are stated into effect, can be allowed to be exercised by it. The power to establish a bank is not expressly given; neither is incidental; since it cannot be shown to be "necessary" to carry the powers which are given; or any of them, into effect. That power cannot therefore be exercised without transcending the Constitutional limits.

This is the democratic argument stated in its briefest form. The aristocratic argument in favour of the power is founded on the dangerous heresy that the Constitution says one thing, and means another. That *necessary* does not mean *necessary*, but simply *convenient.* By a mode of reasoning not looser than this it would be easy to prove that our Government ought to be changed into a Monarchy, Henry Clay crowned King, and the opposition members of the Senate made peers of the realm ;

and power, place and perquisites given to them and their heirs forever.

THE CHARACTER OF THE PRESIDENT.

[*From the Evening Post, November* 4, 1834.]

The Aristocracy are exceedingly anxious to divert the attention of the people from the chief object of their warfare— the venerable and heroic old man who sits at the head of the Government. They protest that their efforts are no longer directed against General Jackson, but are now aimed against Martin Van Buren. But this pretence is so flimsy, that it would be almost insulting the sagacity of our readers to suppose they do not see through it. General Jackson is the object of the direst hatred of the Bank tories. It is his measures against the United States Bank which have excited them to such ferocious political warfare against him. It is his having declared the Bank to be unconstitutional, dangerous to our liberties, an oppressive burden to the great body of people, an aristocratic institution, hedging the rich round with exclusive privileges, and degrading the condition of the labouring poor—it is for having declared these opinions, and acted in conformity with them, that General Jackson is hated by the aristocracy, and termed a usurper and a despot, a cut-throat and a villain.

But when, in the course of his whole long and illustrious life, has Andrew Jackson ever shown the disposition to be a usurper or a despot? Was it in New Orleans, when, after having saved the city from sack and pillage, even in spite of itself, he appeared at the Bar of the Court, at one and the same moment to submit to its decision and to protect it against its consequences? Was it when, as the Judge was about to adjourn that Court, in apprehension of the just indignation of the people whom he had saved, the war-worn old veteran coolly exclaimed—"*There is no danger here; there shall be none. The person who protected this city from foreign invaders, can and will protect this Court, or die in the attempt.*" And the old veteran spoke the truth. The people were hushed, and suffered him to be fined one thousand dollars, which he paid on the spot, and for which he refused to be remunerated by the contributions of the community. Was this acting like a despot and usurper?

Was he a despot, when, elected by the people to the office of President, he recommended an amendment to the Constitution, giving to the people an immediate and direct voice in the selection of their Chief Magistrate, and that he should be eligible for only one term? Was this tyranny—was this usurpation? Was he the enemy of freedom, when, in the same communication to Congress he urged the passing of a law providing for the introduction of the principle of rotation in office, and securing its members from the dangers of Executive influence—his own influence!—by disqualifyng themselves from accepting office during the period they were elected to serve the people? Was this usurpation; or did it savour of a disposition to extend his prerogatives?

The whole life of General Jackson has been one of absolute uncompromising devotion to his country. He never was afraid of responsibility when he was in jeopardy. He did not stand mooting nice points of political orthodoxy, or questioning whether he was right or wrong, when the ravager was on her shores, and the knife at her bosom. He is not the man who, when he sees his friend, his wife, or his country, suffering violence or injury, will stop to inquire who is to blame, before he flies to the rescue. He thinks of saving them first, and in his honest delight of having succeeded, forgets to ask the particulars of the quarrel. Is it any wonder that the honest, warm-hearted, clear-headed people of the United States love, and trust, and venerate this noble old man, whose redeemed pledges they see every day before them; or that they shut their ears to the mingled yell of clamour that resounds from the Holy Alliance of discords; the union of chemical antipathies; the mixture of oil and vinegar, that compose the heterogeneous party now marshalled under "old Cacafoga and his money bags?"

And now he stands at the head of the Democracy of the world, fighting its battles, and stemming the tide of selfish interest combined with unprincipled ambition. He is there as the leader and champion of the people, and will the people desert him? He is now putting their virtue and their patriotism to the test. He is now trying the great experiment whether this government is in future to rest on the sordid principle of gain, or the sound principles of a free Constitution. Every appearance demonstrates that the present contest is one which will inevitably decide whether the rich or the labouring classes, the few or the many, are to rule this wide Confederation. This is the great cause in which the people are now called upon by every tie of interest and honour; by their present possessions and their future hopes; by the memory of their fathers and prospects of their children; by gratitude, by affection, by the still call of the dead, the voice of the past, the present, and the future—the cry of oppressed nations looking hitherward for the result of all their hopes—and by every other motive that can influence the actions of rational intelligent men, to rally round the old hero, and stand by him, as he has stood by them. One day more will decide whether or not these solemn appeals have been addressed to them in vain.

MONOPOLIES.

[*From the Evening Post, November* 20, 1834.]

Want of time, and other demands on our space, prevented us yesterday from extending our article on the subject of Corporations, so as to embrace a reply to those points in the remarks of the Times* which seemed to us worthy of answer. There is indeed not much in those remarks which absolutely requires notice; for, happily, the Times is as feeble in its arguments in favour of a certain class of monopolies, as it is unfortunate in the subject it has chosen on which to vent its malignity against the Evening Post. But as the question which that print, siding with the Courier and Enquirer, and echoing its heresies, has thought proper to moot, is one of great intrinsic importance, it may not be altogether without use and interest to take up its article of yesterday, as furnishing an occasion of some further exposition of the true democratic point of view in which charters of incorporation—the most insidious and dangerous form of monopoly—ought to be considered.

The Times has favoured us with a confession of faith on the subject of monopolies, and if its preaching were in accordance with its creed, there would be little ground of dispute, for it would seem by this that there is no great difference between us on general principles. The Times says:

"The Post is against all monopolies—so are we. The Post is for Equal Rights—so are we. The Post is for the suppression of small notes, and a reform of our banking system—so are we, for the last because it is needed, and for the first because the notes are an evil, and their extinction is essential to the success of one of our most important measures of public policy, the substitution of

* The Times newspaper has long since ceased to exist, and there is not therefore any particular reason for omitting this and some other articles attacking that Journal.

a specie currency. The Post is against legislating for the benefit of individuals, to the disadvantage or exclusion of others—so are we, and in this and on all these points, the party agrees with us."

So far, so good. We shall pass by the twaddle about "the party agreeing with us," which is mere harmless impertinence and coxcombry not worth reply. We shall pass by, too, the satisfactory and lucid reason stated by the Times for being in favour of "a reform of our banking system." We gather, then, from this confession of faith that the Times is opposed to *all* monopolies, is in favour of equal rights, believes that small bank-notes should be suppressed, the banking system reformed, and legislation for individuals, to the disadvantage or exclusion of others, should cease. One might naturally infer from all this that there is no real ground of controversy between us, and that, like many other disputants, we have been arguing about nothing. But when the Times comes to explain itself, we find, notwithstanding the apparent agreement in our premises, that we differ very widely in our conclusions. It is against all monopolies in the abstract, but for them in the concrete. It is opposed to charters of incorporation in general, but advocates them in particular. It is in short against exclusive privileges as monopolies, but in favour of them as means of effecting "great objects of public utility," "developing vast resources," "stimulating industry," and so forth, which is only a repetition of the stale cant which has been used, time out of mind, by those who desired to cheat the people out of their rights for their own selfish ends.

The Times is pleased to say that we ride the doctrine of monopolies as a hobby. We might retort by saying that the Times rides it only for convenience, and just as it suits its purposes. It is "ride and tie" with it. One moment it is on horseback, pricking its ambling steed along; the next it dismounts and turns him loose to graze on the common. For ourselves, we have only to say, that if opposition to monopolies, in every form and under every disguise, is our hobby, it is because we honestly believe them to be the most sly and dangerous enemies to the general prosperity that ever were devised by ingenious cupidity. It is on this ground we have opposed them earnestly—it is on this ground we mean to oppose them, with all our ability, until the evil is arrested, or we become convinced that opposition is vain.

Though the Times professes to agree with us in the opinion that all monopolies are infringements upon the equal rights of the people, and therefore at war with the spirit of our government and institutions, it differs widely with us in its definition. It separates monopolies from corporations, and its idea seems to be that monopolies must be entirely exclusive, or they are not monopolies. There are degrees of virtue and of vice; there are degrees in every thing; but according to the Times there are none in the nature and extent of monopolies. These consist in extremes, and have no medium.

Among its exceptions are railroad incorporations, which it does not consider as belonging to the great family of monopolies. It acknowledges that a railroad may be a monopoly—"a speculation for the profit of individuals, not required by, nor likely to promote the public interest;" but, on the other hand, to meet this case, it supposes another, in order to show that a railroad company may be incorporated without creating a monopoly. Extreme cases are but poor arguments; since by carrying any right or principle to an extreme, it may be made to appear vicious and unjust. But let us examine the supposititious case which the Times has manufactured to justify its insidious advocacy of monopolies. We copy the whole passage:

"Suppose Grand Island to be inhabited by twenty people, and that their only ferry is at one end of the island. Suppose that they have no good road, and that they want a railway to transport their produce from their farms down to the ferry. No one of them is rich enough to make it, but the whole together can, provided they have an act of incorporation for the management of the joint funds, and the direction of the work. Suppose the Post to be the legislature, and that these twenty isolated proprietors apply for a charter: how would the Post reply? It would say, "there is certainly nobody concerned in this matter but yourselves, and the work would benefit you vastly, but if no one of you is wealthy enough to construct it, you must do without—you cannot have a charter, *for* I oppose monopolies, *and* every act of incorporation *is a monopoly!*"

This is all very smart and very convincing, and we only wonder that the Times did not discover that it had trumped up a case which has no application whatever to the matter in dispute. The twenty inhabitants of Grand Island, according to the case here put, constituted a complete community, having one common interest in the contemplated railroad, and all sharing equally in its advantages. They are, so far as respects this question, *a whole people*, and being thus united in one common bond of interest, the rights of no one of them would be impaired by the whole body being incorporated for any common object. This supposititious act of incorporation bears a strong analogy to the very measure of legislation which we yesterday spoke of as the proper means of effecting those objects which are now attained by partial and unequal laws. Instead of Grand Island, let us read the State of New-York; and instead of an act of incorporation for a specific purpose including the whole population, let us suppose a law applicable to all purposes for which charters could be asked, under which any set of individuals might associate, and we have at once, a remedy for the evils of exclusive charters—we establish a system under which monopolies cannot exist.

But let us look a little closer at the railroad incorporation which the Times wishes to bestow on the twenty inhabitants on Grand Island. It is within the compass of possibilities that the population of Grand Island, particularly after "their resources should be developed," and "their industry stimulated," by an act of incorporation, might be increased by emigration, or in some other way. As the charter was conferred exclusively on the twenty original inhabitants, we suppose the new comers would be denied the benefits of the railroad, unless they paid a toll, or contributed an equal proportion with the original proprietors. Would not this railroad at once become a monopoly, and as such be open to all the objections to corporations of this kind?

But we are fighting shadows. Communities cannot be incorporated except under laws equally applicable to all their members; and the idea of giving society at large exclusive privileges is an absurdity. A law which is general in its operation cannot confer exclusive privileges. The fiction of a whole community requiring an act of incorporation to accomplish an object of public utility is equally fanciful and original.

The Times further maintains that the Evening Post is an enemy to every species of internal improvement, and that the position it has taken would exclude them altogether. The Post, it says, will allow no rich man to make a road because the Post upholds equal rights, and will not permit corporate bodies to do it; of course the people must go without roads. Now all this is gratuitous assumption both of facts and consequences.

There is no necessity for either the rich man or the

corporate company to make roads. The people will do it themselves; their own wants and convenience will impel them; and as their requirements and means increase, their modes of conveyance will advance accordingly. A rich man may hold all the property through which a road is to pass—but what of that? He cannot impose upon the people by making them pay to pass through it. The general law of the land points out the uniform mode of proceeding. He is remunerated by being paid the fair amount of his injury, and taxed his full share of the advantages derived from the improvement. There is here no monopoly, and there is no oppression, because every man's property is liable to similar contingencies.

But in order to justify this great system of monopoly in disguise, it is the fashion to proclaim from the house-tops that communities can do nothing in their combined capacity, and that general laws are insufficient for nearly every purpose whatever. We have special laws and contrivances interfering with and infringing the common rights of individuals. We must have societies of all kinds, for every special purpose, and corporate bodies of every name and device, to do what ought not to be done, or what the community can well dispense with, or what they could as well do for themselves. Nations, states, and cities can do nothing now-a-days, without the agency of monopolies and exclusive privileges. Nor can individuals "beneficially employ capital," unless they are inspired by an act of the legislature, and a prospect of exorbitant profits, such is "the progress of the age and the march of intellect."

We need not say again that we are not an enemy of public improvements—such as are equally beneficial to the whole of that community which bears an equal proportion of the expense which they cost. But we are for putting such improvements on the footing of county roads and other municipal undertakings. The people who are to be exclusively benefitted may make them if they please, and if they do not please they may let it alone. In our opinion it is paying at too dear a rate for quick travelling through New-Jersey to purchase it at the price of depriving the citizens of that state, not members of a certain railroad company, of the right to make another railroad from New-York to Philadelphia. By such a system of legislation, the sovereign people of a whole state are deprived of their equal rights.

But it is our custom to treat all great political subjects on broad and general principles, from which alone general conclusions can be derived. A superficial or partial comparison of the advantages and disadvantages of a certain course of legislation furnishes a poor criterion from which to strike the balance ; because it is wholly impossible for the ripest experience, aided by the most sagacious intellect to see and weigh everything connected with the subject of discussion. We must resort to general principles.

The question between the Times and the Evening Post, then, is not whether an act of incorporation may not be passed by a legislative body from the purest motives of public good, nor whether the public good may not in some instances be promoted by such an act. The true question is whether all history, all experience, nay, the very nature of man, does not support the position that this power of granting privileges, either wholly or partially exclusive, is not one that has always led, and, as we have thence a right to infer, will always lead, not only to corruption and abuse, but to either open or secret infringements of the sanctity of Equal Rights ? This is the only question worthy of a high-minded and patriotic politician. It is not whether the practice may not occasionally lead to public, or social, or individual benefit ;

but whether it has not in the past been made, and whether it will not in the future be made again, the fruitful source of those inequalities in human condition—those extremes of wealth and poverty, so uniformly fatal to the liberties of mankind.

Our pen has been often employed, and we trust not wholly without effect, in pointing out and illustrating the evil consequences of this system of bartering away the reserved rights of the great mass of the community, in exchange for public bonusses and *private douceurs*, either direct or indirect, or in furtherance of political views. This system has deranged the whole organization of society, destroyed its equilibrium, and metamorphosed a government the fundamental principle of which is equal rights to every free citizen, to one of EQUAL WRONGS to every class that does not directly share in its monopolies.

We neither wish to pull down the rich, nor to bolster them up by partial laws, beneficial to them alone, and injurious to all besides. We have repeated, again and again, that all we desire is, that the property of the rich may be placed on the same footing with the labours of the poor. We do not incorporate the different classes of tradesmen, to enable them to dictate to their employers the rate of their wages ; we do not incorporate the farmers to enable them to establish a price for their products; and why then should we incorporate moneyed men (or men having only their wits for a capital) with privileges and powers that enable them to control the value of the poor man's labour, and not only the products of the land, but even the land itself ?

If the Times will answer these questions, we are willing to discuss the subject, step by step, in all its important relations. But if it shall continue to lay down positions but to explain them away, like the boy who blows a bubble only for the pleasure of dissipating it by a breath, we shall not feel bound to pursue the subject in a controversial form. The weathercock must remain stationary for at least a moment, before we can tell which way the wind blows. The ship which, without rudder or compass, yaws and heaves about, the sport of every impulse of the elements, can scarcely be followed in her devious course by the most skilful navigator.

ASYLUM FOR INSANE PAUPERS.

[*From the Evening Post, Nov.* 28.]

We have received a copy of a circular letter on the subject of a recommendation made by Governor Marcy to the Legislature, at its last session, that an Asylum for Insane Paupers should be erected, at the expense of the State. A select committee was charged with the subject, which reported favourably on the project; but the legislature adjourned without acting upon it. We trust they will adjourn again without acting affirmatively on any such scheme.

The taking care of the insane is no part of the business of the state government. The erecting of such an Asylum as is proposed, and the appointment of the various officers to superintend it, would be placing a good deal more power—where there is already too much—into the hands of the state executive, to be used honestly or corruptly, for good or evil, as these qualities should happen to predominate in his character, or as the temptations to use his official patronage for his own aggrandizement or profit might be strong or weak. We are continually suffering, under one pretence or other, these pilferings of power from the people.

The circular to which we have alluded appeals strongly

to the sympathies of its readers. It presents a deplorable and harrowing picture of the miseries endured by insane paupers in the poor-houses of Massachusetts and New Hampshire, and intimates that their condition is no better in many counties of this state. If this is so, the evil ought to be investigated and remedied; but not in the method proposed, by the erection of a splendid state Asylum. The people ought not to suffer their judgment to be led away by their sympathies. They cannot be too jealous of the exercise of unnecessary powers by the state government. The nearer they keep all power to their own hands, and the more entirely under their own eyes, the more secure are they in their freedom and equal rights.

We would have destitute lunatics taken care of, but not under the charge or at the expense of the state government. It ought to be one of the leading objects of the democracy of this country for many years to come to diminish the power of the general and several state governments, not to increase it. On the subject of legislation for paupers they ought to be particularly vigilant. In nine cases out of ten, and we believe we might say ninety-nine out of a hundred, poor-laws make more poverty than they alleviate. If the reader has ever employed himself in tracing the history of the poor-laws in England, he will not require any proof of this assertion; if he has not, he could scarcely turn his thoughts to a subject more rife with matters of serious interest.

Lunatic paupers ought certainly to be taken care of. Both charity and self-protection require this. But we would remove this guardianship as far from government as possible. Each county should certainly provide for its own; each township would be better, and if it were practicable to narrow it down to the kindred of the insane persons, it would be better still. As a general rule, all public charities, except for the single purpose of promoting education, are founded on erroneous principles, and do infinitely more harm than good. See that the people are educated, and then leave every man to take care of himself and of those who have a natural claim on his protection. We have many large charities in this community, founded in the most amiable and benevolent motives, that annually add very largely to the sum of human misery, by ill-judged exertions to relieve it.

The picture of the wretched condition of lunatic paupers, as presented in the circular before us, is certainly very touching, but legislators must not be blinded by tears to the true and permanent interests of man. They must let their feelings of commiseration take counsel of the pauser judgment. They must look at the subject in all its bearings and aspects, before they saddle the people in their collective capacity with another tax, and place the revenue so instituted at the disposal of an executive officer, who may expend it with a view to advance his private ends.

We have said that the account given of the sufferings of these pauper lunatics is touching ; yet it would be easy to draw as touching a picture, and as true too, of the sufferings of sane paupers. Indeed, with many, what a horrible aggravation to their sufferings their very sanity must be,

> " Which but supplies a feeling to decay !"

The lunatics are by no means the most unhappy class of paupers, as a class. Insanity comes to many as a friend in their deepest affliction, to mitigate the tortures of a wounded spirit—to

> Pluck from the memory a rooted sorrow ;
> Raze out the written troubles of the brain,
> And, with a sweet oblivious antidote,
> Cleanse the stuffed bosom of the perilous stuff
> Which weighs upon the heart.

Those who are sick and desolate; who have fallen from a high estate — fallen by their own folly, perhaps, and therefore experience the gnawings of remorse, or fallen in consequence of the ingratitude or treachery of others, may easily be supposed to experience keener anguish than the demented inmates of the same abode; since the worst pain man suffers has its seat in the mind, not in the body; and from that species of affliction the crazy are exempt. If this scheme of a grand state lunatic asylum should be carried into effect, we see no reason why next we should not have a grand state poor-house, for the reception of all paupers who had not lost their wits. Other large state charities would probably follow, and one abuse of government would step upon the heels of another. The system is all wrong from beginning to end. *We are governed too much.* Let the people take care of themselves and of their own sick and insane, each community for itself. Let them, above all things, be extremely cautious in surrendering power into the hands of the government, of any kind, or for any purpose whatever, for governments never surrender power to the people. What they get is theirs "to have and to hold," ay, and to exercise too, to the fullest extent, nor is it often got back from them, till their grasp is opened with the sword.

Our remarks are cursory and loose, perhaps, as this article has been written in the midst of more than usual interruptions. Let the reader not thence infer, however, that we have taken ground on this subject hastily; for such is not the fact. The plan recommended by Governor Marcy last winter, has frequently occupied our thoughts, and in every light in which we have viewed it has appeared to us to deserve the opposition of the democratic members of the legislature. We are for giving as few powers to government as possible, and as small an amount of patronage to dispense. Let the aristocracy advocate a strong government; we are for *a strong people.*

MONOPOLIES.

[*From the Evening Post, Nov.* 29.]

"TO THE EDITORS OF THE EVENING POST.

"I have read attentively the views expressed in your paper on the subject of "monopolies," and I agree with you to some extent, but I am not certain that I understand how far the practical detail may interfere with the general principle. This may be tested by some cases in point. I take the first notice from the Journal of Commerce, and the others from the Albany Argus.

[*Here follow notices of applications for incorporations.*]

"You will perceive here are four distinct objects proposed to be accomplished. That the public may know how your theories are to be reduced to practice, I request that you will say how the members from this city, under their pledge as honourable men, are to vote on these general propositions; and secondly, how you would vote as a legislator without any pledge.

"AN HONEST INQUIRER."

We have witnessed with regret, and we may add with surprise, that, notwithstanding the recent clearly and strongly expressed sentiment of the great body of the democracy of this state against all monopolies, of every kind and degree, a number of notices, like those quoted by our correspondent, have already appeared in the public papers. There can be no sort of question that one of the chief points which the great body of the democratic voters meant to decide by their suffrages in the recent contest, was that there should be no more monopolies created by our legislature. And there can be no sort of question either, that in the term monopoly, according to the understanding of the democratic party, all acts of incorporation were included.

We do not mean to say that this was the universal understanding ; and perhaps it is never the case, in a political contest which turns on a variety of questions, that the whole body of voters are governed by absolute coincidence of sentiment on every particular subject. But we do mean to say, and we think no one will dispute, that those who gave the latitude of meaning to the word monopoly which we have here expressed, were at least much more numerous than the excess of votes in favour of Governor Marcy over Mr. Seward ; and further, that had it been announced, from any authentic source, previous to the election, that the candidates of the democracy for legislative office would, on being elected, vote for any act of incorporation whatever, they never would have had the opportunity of imposing any such contemplated additional fetters on the body politic.

The success of the democratic ticket in a majority of the republican counties, was clearly owing, in our view of the subject, to the belief that all exclusive and partial legislation would cease, if the democracy succeeded ; that laws would be made for the whole people, not for a part ; and that the great fundamental principle of our republic, the equal rights of all, would be their governing rule of action. It is to this conviction we owe our succcss ; and if this conviction had been destroyed by the promulgation of such sentiments before the election, as have since been expressed in certain degenerate prints, those who are now informed that the term monopoly applies only to such laws as no one ever dreamed would be passed, and are called upon to act accordingly in the legislature, would still have occupied a private station.

But independent of this consideration, we hold it to be demonstrable, (and we think we have not fallen far short of demonstration in our various articles on the subject,) that all acts of partial legislation are undemocratic; that they are subversive of the equal rights of men; are calculated to create artificial inequality in human condition; to elevate the few and depress the many; and, in their final operation, to build up a powerful aristocracy, and overthrow the whole frame of democratic government.

In this view of the subject, we consider it the duty of every democratic legislator, however much or little he may consider the disputed word monopoly to comprehend, to set himself firmly against every attempt to obtain new charters of incorporation, or to enlarge the term or conditions of old ones. Whether he thinks himself positively instructed or not, by the terms of his county resolutions, to oppose every bill of incorporation, no one will pretend that he has been instructed to advocate such a bill, and he is therefore certainly under the general obligation to oppose every measure of anti-democratic character or tendency. The man, then, who, pretending to represent democratic constituents, shall yet cast his suffrage, or exercise his influence, in favour of a single application for corporate powers, or shall refrain from exerting himself to defeat such an application, will be unfaithful to his trust, to his country, and to the principles of liberty, and will richly deserve to be held up, in the strongest language which indignant patriotism can use, to the scorn of his fellow-men. On such a gibbet we shall surely do all in our power to hang such a traitor, if any such there shall be found, which we hope and trust there may not.

Is our correspondent answered? As to the duty of our city delegation, there is not the slightest room for question. They are PLEDGED to oppose, with all their might, *all* monopolies; and happily the terms of the pledge have not left the word monopoly of dubious import. By specifying Insurance Corporations, which are as useful in their favourable features, and as little objectionable in their unfavourable, as any description of corporations whatever — by specifying these as one of the most obnoxious kinds of monopolies, the phrase clearly embraces corporate institutions of every kind and name. Should, then, any member of our city delegation, being thus pledged, vote for any monopoly within the comprehensive signification fixed by the obligation he subscribed, he would not only be unfaithful to his party and to republican principles, but a fore-sworn caitiff, worse even than Dudley Selden, if worse can be.

But we have no fear that the democracy of our metropolis have cherished any such viper in their bosom. We look not to see any of our delegates seek to escape from their honourable obligations through any flaw which the Times may try to discover in their pledge. We look not to see them skulk behind a quibble, or palter with their constituents in a double sense. We expect rather that they will exhibit a noble emulation in carrying into effect the spirit of that condition. We expect to see them all eager to identify themselves with the leading doctrines of the democracy in the present struggle with aristocratic opponents of equal liberty and laws, and each striving to outdo the others in the strenuousness of his hostility to exclusive privileges, partial legislation, or whatever endangers, in the slightest degree, the foundation principle of our political fabric, the equal rights of mankind.

MONOPOLIES.

[*From the Evening Post, Nov.* 29, 1834.]

The Journal of Commerce protests that it has not hauled down its flag, but joins its co-labourer the Times, in insisting we ourselves are *used up*. "We thought it unnecessary to proceed further with the discussion, because the whole ground had been gone over, and we believed the wrong doctrines of the Post sufficiently refuted." So says the Journal of Commerce. How complete this refutation is, our readers are qualified to judge, since we have placed its several articles before them, some in whole, and some in substance. The Journal admits that its "fifty dollar" argument "is just as good in relation to packeting as banking." It is just as good, then, in relation to any other business. For instance, one of the bubbles that accompanied the airy flight of the famous south-sea bubble, and exploded about the same time, though with less noise and devastation, was called "the Spanish Jackass Company." Now, by carrying out the idea of the Journal of Commerce, a New-York Jackass Company might be incorporated, and the Editor of the Journal of Commerce, by buying fifty dollars' worth of stock, might stand a fair chance to be chosen president. The stock of a company of that description might be expected to be very popular among a certain political party to which the Journal of Commerce, *in some measure*, belongs ; and it might all be taken up before one-tenth of the applicants were supplied. Would not the disappointed nine-tenths, as they wended their way homeward, with their fifty dollars apiece in their breeches' pockets, have reason to exclaim that there was something partaking of the character of exclusiveness in this Jackass Company ? And suppose the Editor of the Journal of

Commerce, despite his claims, should receive no apportionment of stock, would he not begin to think that there was some truth in the complaint against monopolies?

But badinage apart, we are surprised that the Journal of Commerce does not perceive that it makes no difference in the principle of the thing whether the stock of an incorporated Company is divided into fifty dollar shares, or five thousand dollar shares. Of whatever amount the subdivisions may be, but a small portion of the community can receive any at the original allotment, and but a small portion of them could receive any, if the Journal of Commerce's favourite plan of selling the shares by auction were adopted. When the pitcher is full it will hold no more; and when the shares were all apportioned or sold, disappointed applicants could not expect to get any. The corporation would then be a monopoly enjoyed by the successful applicants; and whether their number was five or five thousand, they would possess "exclusive privileges" nevertheless, and would be the beneficiaries of unequal legislation.

It is an error of the Journal of Commerce to say, that the practical operation of corporations is to "take privileges, which would otherwise be monopolized by the rich, and divide them into such small parts, that every one who has fifty dollars may be interested, upon equal terms of advantage with the most wealthy." In practice, the operation of the thing is quite the reverse. "Kissing goes by favour," in those operations. Large capitalists get all the stock they ask for, and poor men get but a part, if any, that they solicit. There are published lists of apportionments to which we can refer the Journal of Commerce. But the fact is notorious. And moreover, it is notorious, that this pretended division of stock has even much less of fairness and honesty about it than would seem by the face of things. Many of the applicants who get large apportionments are men of straw, mere catspaws, thrust forward to answer the purpose of some great capitalist, for whom the stock is really procured. We could name instances, if it were necessary. We have not come to this subject without being furnished with ample means of establishing our arguments. There is the very last bank that went into operation—was the stock of that incorporation divided to fifty dollar applicants? Is it not, on the contrary, a fact, that a controlling interest is in the hands of a single individual, who is represented by his puppets — we beg their pardon, his proxios—in the directory? Nor is that bank a solitary instance, as the Journal of Commerce well knows.

But if the argument were true, to the fullest extent, that "fifty dollar men" can become bankers, and life-insurers, and packet-owners, and so on, it would still not be a good argument in favour of special acts of incorporation for these several purposes; because these special acts would each embrace but a small portion of the community, and all special or partial legislation is, in its very nature, anti-republican and invasive of equal rights. Let capital and industry alone to find their own channels. This is the true principle to act upon. If any additional legislation is necessary, let it be legislation that shall embrace the whole body politic, and every variety of laudable enterprise. The "fifty dollar" argument of the Journal of Commerce might with much more propriety be put forward in support of a general law of joint stock partnerships, than in support of the everlasting iteration of special acts of incorporation, where every succeeding set of applicants are striving to get some privileges or advantages not conferred by previous charters, and, to effect their selfish and unjust ends, resorting to all the arts of collusion and corruption. Under a general law, not merely "fifty dollar men," but twenty dollar men, and one dollar men, might if they pleased place their means in the joint funds of an association to effect some great enterprise. Such a law would be the very measure to enable poor men to compete with rich. As it is, let the Journal of Commerce say what it may, acts of incorporation are chiefly procured by the rich and for the rich. What claims have your William Bards or your Nathaniel Primes on the country, that our legislature should spend their time in making laws for their exclusive or particular advantage? Did we cast our suffrages into the ballot-boxes to select legislative factors for those men, or such men? Let them have their equal rights, but let them have no more.

The Journal of Commerce seems to think our reasoning involves a contradiction, because we oppose special acts of incorporations or monopolies, and yet would extend incorporations indefinitely. We have not said we would extend *corporations indefinitely*; yet if corporations were extended indefinitely, there would be no monopoly; since when every member of the community has precisely the same opportunities of employing capital and industry given to him by the laws which every other member has, there is no exclusive privilege, and no invasion of equal rights. But it is an error in terms to say that we advocate the indefinite extension of corporations, since the very nature of a corporation, is to be endowed with special privileges. We shall not dispute about words, however, if we can bring the Journal of Commerce to agree with us about principles. The act of incorporation, then, which we should desire to see passed, would be an act incorporating the whole population of the State of New York, for every possible lawful purpose to which money or human labour, or ingenuity, is ever applied, with a clause admitting to a full communion of the benefits of the body corporate, every individual who should at any future time become a member of the body politic.

MONOPOLIES.

[*From the Evening Post, November*, 1834.]

What have the People, the Democracy, been struggling for in the last election? Was it merely to satisfy a personal predilection in favour of a few leaders, and to gratify a personal dislike to a few others; or was it for certain great principles, combined in the one great general term of Equal Rights? As to ourselves, and we believe we speak the sentiment of a great majority of those who acted with us, we answer unhesitatingly, not for men but principles; not for Messrs. Cambreleng, White, Moore, Morgan, McKeon, and others, whatever we may think of them as individuals, but because they have pledged themselves to the support of Equal Rights, and to an opposition to monopolies and exclusive privileges.

Yet the Times in effect denies and repudiates our doctrine, that every species of corporate body created for the purposes of gain, and gifted with privileges which others do not and cannot possess or exercise, is in its nature and consequences an infringement on the Equal Rights of the People. It advocates the system in all its prominent features of abuse and oppression, qualified indeed by certain restraints, which, being disguised in loose generalities, elude detection and defy argument. For ourselves, we have no concealments. On this subject we have heretofore opposed, and mean hereafter to oppose, with the utmost exertion of our powers, every new addition to this already overgrown and pernicious system of bartering away the sovereignty of the People to little bodies politic, fattening on the great body, and are satisfied that, but for the stand we took on this great constitutional ground, the late triumph of democracy would not have been so signal—in this great city at least. The majority of the People echoed our sentiments ; they rose in their might against monopolies and exclusive privileges ; and if their victory is not followed up by uncompromising opposition to the great source of monopolies, like the citizens of Paris, they will have fought the "three days" for nothing, or at least nothing worth gaining. They will have used their exertions only to drive away one swarm of flies, already gorged with their substance, to give place to another more hungry and insatiable. Again we ask, if we were not fighting against monopolies and exclusive privileges, what were we fighting for ?

That our readers may see the progress making in other portions of the Union, in this system of secret warfare against their Equal Rights, we lay before them an analysis of the privileges lately conferred on one of these corporate bodies in the state of Ohio. It is called a Life and Trust Company, and all these extensive powers are bartered away by the representatives of the people, under the specious pretext of enabling a few persons, having money to spare, to buy life annuities, and place their property in the safe keeping of a corporation ; a body without a soul ; an abstraction ; a remote circumstance ; a nothing tangible or responsible. In the opinion of these law-givers, the integrity of individuals and the general laws of the land are insufficient guarantees for the safety of property ; and nothing can secure it but the possession and the exercise of privileges founded on a perpetuity of property and a usurpation of rights.

The powers granted by the legislature of Ohio to their

most favoured bantling of legislative munificence, are as follows:

1. To make insurance on lives.

2. To grant and purchase annuities.

3. To make *any other contract* involving the *interest of money and the duration of life.*

4. To receive moneys on trust, and to *lend out the same at such rate of interest as may be agreed on.*

5. To accept and execute *all such trusts of every description as may be committed to them by any person, or by by any Court of Record.*

6. To receive and hold lands under grants with general and special covenants, *so far as may be necessary to their business or the payment of their debts.*

7. To buy and sell drafts and bills of exchange.

8. To hold an original capital of 2,000,000 of dollars.

9. *To vest said capital in bonds and mortgages on real estate valued at double the amount of the sums loaned.*

10. *To increase said capital to an* INDEFINITE EXTENT *by deposites at an agreed rate of interest.*

11. *To issue bank notes to double the amount deposited —not to exceed one million of dollars.*

12. To have twenty trustees, one-fifth elected every two years, so that ultimately each trustee remains in ten years.

Now we desire the people to look well at this delegation of their sovereignty to these twenty trustees. We ask them if there is any thing under heaven this corporation cannot do, except perhaps make war and peace; or any limits to its powers of accumulation? And as if to cap the climax of legislative folly or corruption, this corporation is permitted to *coin its own money,* to lend or to pay its annuities and the interest on its trusts. It receives pledges on land and real property, bonds and mortgages, on liens of its own paper, and charges interest for the same, thus exchanging rags for lands and houses, at a premium of interest "such as may be agreed on."

It is permitted "to increase its capital to an INDEFINITE EXTENT by deposites at an interest agreed on." In short it "can *make any contract involving the interest of money or the duration of life.*" This pledge covers every species of human dealing, and may be tortured by the ingenuity of cupidity into including all the business of life. In fact there is no limit to the powers which this minor sovereignty may exercise, as to its means of acquiring wealth and influence. Its duration is perpetual, and in less than one hundred years, it will swallow up the whole state of Ohio. Its proprietors of land will become tenants at will to the Life and Trust Company, and an independent yeomanry sink into a race of dependant slaves.

They have no remedy except a revolution; for according to the famous doctrine of "vested rights," one legislative body may barter away privileges which, however pernicious or fatal to the liberty and prosperity of the great mass of citizens, can never be reclaimed by its successors. The mill-stone once tied about the neck of the people, becomes a vested right, and cannot be unloosed, even to save them from drowning. If such is the settled principle, does it not hold up a warning to the depositories of the sovereignty of the peoole, against lightly giving way, or bartering for some pitiful consideration, privileges which, however dangerous or pernicious in their consequences, must either be perpetual or endured for a certain number of years? If the grant is irrevocable, how careful should they be in making it? Repentance cannot alleviate the consequences of the transgression; legislation can make no atonement. It is the fiat of fate, and to strive against it, is not only vain but blasphemous, according to the opinion of the champions of legislative omnipotence.

The people of this or any other country never contemplated bestowing on their government the power to inflict upon them evils which no subsequent exertion of that power could remove. They did not bestow upon their legislative bodies a portion of their sovereignty, to barter it away in exchange for the wages of corruption, or for political purposes. What they gave they expected would be received by those to whom it was given for the special benefit of the great majority, and not employed in forging for them fetters from which no after struggle could release them. This practice of frittering away the powers of the government, in themselves, not transferable, has divested that government of a great portion of what the people conferred on it, and it alone. It might just as well delegate to a corporation the rights of declaring war and concluding peace, as to bestow on it the exclusive right of giving a national currency. The one is an act of sovereignty as well as the other, and cannot be delegated.

Already we perceive the value of the privileges thus liberally bestowed on the Ohio Loan and Trust Company. It is scarcely yet in operation, and its stock is upwards of twenty per. cent above par. In a few years, it will in all probability, if managed with ordinary sagacity rise to one, nay, two hundred per cent. Other people are glad to get six or seven per cent. for their money and this is all the law allows them. But our legislatures make other laws, granting to a few what is denied to the many, and conferring on them the "vested right" of doubling their capital every few years. Not all the sophistries of interested cupidity, can now persuade the enlightened farmers and labouring classes, that such distributions of privileges are founded in the principles of Equal Rights.

The time we trust is at hand, when their pernicious inroads on the sanctity of individual independence will be arrested in their career, and that preparations must be made to retrace the path pursued for the last twenty or thirty years. The People have spoken, and they must be heard. For ourselves we mean to persevere in our endeavours to draw public attention to this most important of political subjects. Not all the clamours of aristocracy, nor the treacherous attacks of pretended friends, shall drive us from the stand we have made in behalf of the Equal Rights of the People. With them we have made common cause, and with them we mean to stand or fall.

THE MONOPOLY BANKING SYSTEM.

[*From the Evening Post, December*, 1834.]

It is a source of sincere pleasure to us to perceive that the attention of the people is seriously awakened to the subject of the Bank system, as it exists in this country. It seems to us quite evident that the sentiment is daily gaining ground that the whole system is erroneous—wrong in principle and productive of incalculable evils in its practical operation. Those who have been readers of the Evening Post, for the last six or eight months, have had this subject fully and freely discussed, not only in articles from our own pen, but in numerous excellent communications from able correspondents, and, more especially, in the clear, comprehensive, and unanswerable essays of Mr. Gouge, which, with the author's permission, we copied from his admirable work on American Banking. Those who perused these various productions, with the attention which the important and interesting nature of the subject required, have possessed themselves of sufficient materials for the formation of a correct opinion; and we have the satisfaction of knowing that very many of our readers concur fully with us in the sentiments we entertain with regard to our banking system.

We look upon that system as wrong in two of its leading principles: first, we object to it as founded on a species of monopoly; and secondly, as supplying a circulating medium which rests on a basis liable to all the fluctuations and contingencies of commerce and trade—a basis whieh may at any time be swept away by a thousand casualties of business, and leave not a wreck behind. There are many other objections incident to these, some of which present themselves in forms which demand the most serious consideration.

Our primary ground of opposition to banks as they at present exist is that they are a species of monopoly. All corporations are liable to the objection that whatever powers or privileges are given to them, are so much taken from the government of the people. Though a state legislature may possess a constitutional right to create bank incorporations, yet it seems very clear to our apprehension that the doing so is an invasion of the grand republican principle of Equal Rights—a principle which lies at the bottom of our constitution, and which, in truth, is the corner-stone both of our national government, and that of each particular state.

Every charter of incorporation, we have said, is, to some extent, either in fact or in practical operation, a monopoly; for these charters invariably invest those upon whom they are bestowed with powers and privileges which are not enjoyed by the great body of the people. This may be done by merely combining larger amounts of capital than unincorporated individuals can bring into competition with the chartered institution; but the end is more frequently effected by the more palpably unjust process of exonerating the chartered few from liabilities to which the rest of the community are subject, or by prohibiting the unprivileged individual from entering into competition with the favoured creature of the law.

When a legislative body restrains the people collectively from exercising their natural right of pursuing a certain branch of business, and gives to particular individuals exclusive permission to carry on that business, they assuredly are guilty of a violation of the republican maxim of Equal Rights, which nothing but the plainest paramount necessity can at all excuse. This violation is the more palpable, when immunities are granted to the few, which would not have been enjoyed by the people, had their natural rights never been restricted by law. In the case of Bank incorporations such is clearly true; since those who are thus privileged are protected by their charters both from the competition of individuals, and from loss to any greater extent than the amount of capital they may risk in the enterprise—a protection which would have been enjoyed by no member of the community, had the law left banking on the same footing with other mercantile pursuits. As a monopoly, then—as a system which grants exclusive privileges—which is at variance with the great fundamental doctrine of democracy—we must oppose Bank incorporations, unless it can be shown that they are productive of good which greatly counterbalances the evil.

A second objection to our banking system is that it is founded on a wrong basis—a basis that does not afford adequate security to the community; since it not only does not protect them from loss by ignorant or fraudulent management, but not even from those constantly recurring commercial revulsions, which, indeed, are one of the evil fruits of this very system. The basis of our banking business is specie capital; yet every body knows that the first thing a bank does, on going into operation, (if we suppose the whole capital to have been honestly paid in, which is very far from being always the case) is to lend out its capital; and the profits of the institution do not commence until, having loaned all its capital, it begins to loan its credit as money. No set of men would desire a bank charter merely to authorize them to lend their money capital at the common rate of interest; for they would have no difficulty in doing that, without a charter, and without incurring the heavy expense incident to banking business. *The object of a bank charter is to enable those holding it to lend their credit at interest,* and to lend their credit too, to twice, and sometimes three times, the amount of their actual capital. In return, then, for its capital, and for the large amount of promissory obligations issued on the credit of that capital, the Bank holds nothing but the liabilities of individual merchants and other dealers. It must be evident then that its capital is liable to all the fluctuations and accidents to which commercial business is exposed. Its integrity depends upon the ability of its dealers punctually to discharge their obligations. Should a series of commercial disasters overwhelm those dealers, the capital of the Bank is lost, and the bill holder, instead of money, finds himself possessed of a mere worthless and broken promise to pay.

Let us trace the progress of a new banking institution. Let us imagine a knot of speculators to have possessed themselves, by certain acts of collusion, bribery, and political management, of a bank charter; and let us suppose them commencing operations under their corporate privileges. They begin by lending their capital. After that, if commercial business is active, and the demand for money urgent, they take care to put as many of their notes in circulation as possible. For awhile this does very well, and the Bank realizes large profits. Every thing seems to flourish ; merchants extend their operations; they hire capacious stores, import largely from abroad, sell to country dealers on liberal terms, get the notes of those dealers discounted, and extend themselves still further. Others, in the meanwhile, stimulated by this same appearance of commercial prosperity, borrow money (that is notes) from the Bank, and embark in enterprises of a different nature. They purchase lots, build houses, set railway and canal projects on foot, and every thing goes on swimmingly. The demand for labour is abundant, property of all kinds rises in price, and speculators meet each other in the streets, and exult in their anticipated fortunes.

But by and by things take a different turn. The exports of the country (which furnish the true measure of business) are found to fall greatly short of the amount due abroad for foreign fabrics, and a large balance remains unpaid. The first intimation of this is the rapid advance in the price of foreign exchange. The bank now perceives that it has extended itself too far. Its notes, which, until now, circulated currently enough, begin to return in upon it in demand for specie ; while, at the same time, the merchants, whom it has been all along eager to serve, now call for increased accommodations. But the Bank cannot accommodate them any longer. Instead of increasing its loans, it is obliged to require payment of those which it had previously made; for its own notes are flowing in a continual stream to its counter, and real money is demanded instead. But real money it has none, as that was all lent out when it first went into operation. Here then a sudden check is given to the seeming prosperity. The merchants, unable to get the amount of accommodation necessary to sustain their operations, are forced to suspend payment. A rumour of the amount lost by the Bank in consequence of these failures, causes confidence in its solvency to be impaired, and being threatened with a run, it resorts to a still more rapid curtailment. Then follows wider derangement. One commercial house after another becomes bankrupt, and finally the Bank itself, by these repeated losses forced to discontinue its business, closes its doors, and hands over its affairs for the benefit of its creditors. Who are its creditors? Those who hold *its money*, that is, its "*promises to pay.*" On investigation it is discovered, most likely, that the whole capital of the institution has been absorbed by its losses. The enormous profits which it made during the first part of its career, had been regularly withdrawn by the stockholders, and the deluded creditor has nothing but a worthless bit of engraved paper to show for the valuable consideration which he parted with for what he foolishly imagined money.

What we have here stated can hardly be called a suppositititious case—it is a true history, and there are events within the memory of almost every reader of which it is a narrative almost literally correct.

The basis of our banking system, then, if liable to be thus easily dissipated, is certainly wrong. Banks should be established on a foundation which neither panic nor mismanagement, neither ignorance nor fraud, could destroy. The bill-holder should always be secure, whatever might become of the stock-holder. That which is received as money, and which is designed to pass from hand to hand as such, should not be liable to change into worthless paper in the transition.

A very important objection incident to the banking system of this country is the demoralizing effect which it exercises on society. It is a matter of the utmost notoriety that bank charters are in frequent instances obtained by practices of the most outrageous corruption. They are conceived in a wild spirit of speculation; they are brought into existence through the instrumentality of bribery and intrigue; and they exercise over the community the most unsalutary influence, encouraging men of business to transcend the proper limits of credit, and fostering a general and feverish thirst for wealth, prompting the mind to seek it by other than the legitimate means of honest, patient industry, and prudent enterprise. Let any man who has had an opportunity of observing the effect of introducing a banking institution, into a quiet country town, on the moral character of the inhabitants, answer for himself if this is not true. Let any man, whose knowledge enables him to contrast a portion of our country where banks are few, with another where they are numerous, answer if it is not true. Let any man whose memory extends so far back that he can compare the present state of society with what it was in the time of our fathers, answer if it is not true. The time was when fraud in business was as rare—we were about to say—as honesty is now. The time was when a failure was a strange and unfrequent occurrence; when a bankrupt excited the sympathy of the whole community for his misfortunes, or their censure for his rashness, or their scorn for his dishonesty. The banking system has made insolvency a matter of daily occurrence. It has changed the meaning of words, it has altered the sense of things, it has revolutionized our ethical notions. Formerly, if a man ventured far beyond his depth in business—if he borrowed vast sums of money to hazard them in doubtful enterprises—if he deluded the world by a system of false shows and pretences, and extended his credit by every art and device—formerly such a man was called rash and dishonest, but we now speak of him as enterprising and ingenious. The man whose ill-planned speculations miscarry—whose airy castle of credit is suddenly overturned, burying hundreds of industrious mechanics and labourers under its ruins—such a man would once have been execrated; he is now pitied; while our censure and contempt is transferred to those who are the victims of his fraudful schemes.

For its political effect, not less than moral, our bank system deserves to be opposed. It is essentially an aristocratic institution. It bands the wealthy together, holds out to them a common motive, animates them with a common sentiment, and inflates their vanity with notions of superior power and greatness. The bank system is maintained out of the hard earnings of the poor; and its operation is to degrade them in their political rights, as much as they are degraded in a pecuniary respect, by the accident of fortune. Its tendency is to give exclusive political, as well as exclusive money privileges to the rich. It is in direct opposition to the spirit of our constitution and the genius of the people. It is silently, but rapidly, undermining our institutions; it falsifies our grand boast of political equality; it is building up a privileged order, who, at no distant day, unless the whole system be changed, will rise in triumph on the ruins of democracy.

Even now, how completely we are monopoly-governed! how completely we are hemmed in on every side, how we are cabined, cribb'd, confined, by exclusive privileges! Not a road can be opened, not a bridge can be built, not a canal can be dug, but a charter of exclusive privileges must be granted for the purpose. The sum and substance of our whole legislation is the granting of monopolies. The bargaining and trucking away chartered privileges is the whole business of our law makers. The people of this great state fondly imagine that they govern themselves; but they do not! They are led about by the unseen but strong bands of chartered companies.

They are fastened down by the minute but effectual fetters of banking institutions. They are governed by bank directors, bank stockholders, and bank minions. They are under the influence of a power whose name is Legion—they are under the influence of bank monopolies, with a host of associate and subordinate agents, the other incorporated companies, depending on bank assistance for their means of operation. These evil influences are scattered throughout our community, in every quarter of the state. They give the tone to our meetings; they name our candidates for the legislature; they secure their election; they control them when elected.

What then is the remedy for the evil? Do away with our bad bank system; repeal our unjust, unsalutary, undemocratic restraining law; and establish, in its stead, some law, the sole object of which shall be to provide the community with security against fraud. We hope, indeed, to see the day when banking, like any other mercantile business will be left *to regulate itself;* when the principles of free trade will be perceived to have as much relation to currency as to commerce; when the maxim of *Let us alone* will be acknowledged to be better, infinitely better, than all this political quackery of ignorant legislators, instigated by the grasping, monopolizing spirit of rapacious capitalists. This country, we hope, we trust, is destined to prove to mankind the truth of the saying, that *the world is governed too much*, and to prove it by her own successful experiment in throwing off the clogs and fetters with which craft and cunning have ever contrived to bind the mass of men.

But to suit the present temper of the times, it would be easy to substitute a scheme of banking which should have all the advantages of the present one, and none of its defects. Let the restraining law be repealed; let a law be substituted, requiring simply that *any person* entering into banking business shall be required to lodge with some officer designated in the law, real estate, or other approved security, to the full amount of the notes which he might desire to issue; and to secure, that this amount should never be exceeded, it might be provided that each particular note should be authenticated by the signature of the comptroller, or other officer entrusted with the business. Another clause might state suitable provisions for having the securities re-appraised, from time to time, so that bill holders might be sure that sufficient unalienable property was always pledged for the redemption of the paper currency founded upon that basis. Banking, established on this foundation, would be liable to none of the evils arising from panic; for each holder of a note would, in point of fact, hold a title-deed of property to the full value of its amount. It would not be liable to the revulsions which follow overtrading, and which every now and then spread such dismay and ruin through commercial communities; for when bankers are left to manage their own business, each for himself, they would watch the course of trade, and limit their discounts accordingly; because if they extended them beyond the measure of the legitimate business of the country, they would be sure that their notes would return upon them in demand for the precious metals, thus forcing them to part with their profits, in order to purchase silver and gold to answer such demand.

But much as we desire to see the wretched, insecure, and, in a political view, dangerous banking system superceded by the more honest and equal plan we have suggested, we would by no means be considered as the advocates of sudden or capricious change. All reformations of the currency—all legislation, the tendency of which is to disturb the relations of value, should be slow, well considered and gradual. In this hasty and unpremeditated article, we have glanced at the system which we desire may ere long take the place of the present one, and have rapidly adverted to some of the reasons which render the change desirable. But as a first step towards the consummation, we should wish the legislature to do nothing more at present than restrain the issue of notes under five dollars, and refuse to charter any more banks. The people demand it, and we do not think that the public sentiment is in favour of any further immediate reformation. As to the prospective legislation which is proposed by some, we think it anti-republican and unwise. We would not take advantage of any present movement of the public mind to fasten a law upon the state, which public sentiment may not afterwards sustain. The same influence of public opinion which, is now about to lead to the long-desired *first step* in Bank reform, will be potent in carrying on the reformation to the desired conclusion. A good maxim, and one which it will be well to be governed by in this matter, is *festina lente.*

RICH AND POOR.

[*From the Evening Post of December* 6, 1834.]

The rich perceive, acknowledge, and act upon a common interest, and why not the poor? Yet the moment the latter are called upon to combine for the preservation of their rights, forsooth the community is in danger! Property is no longer secure, and life in jeopardy. This cant has descended to us from those times when the poor and labouring classes had no stake in the community, and no rights except such as they could acquire by force. But the times have changed, though the cant remains the same. The scrip nobility of this Republic have adopted towards the free people of this Republic the same language which the Feudal Barons and the despot who contested with them the power of oppressing the people, used towards their serfs and villains, as they were opprobiously called.

These would-be lordlings of the Paper Dynasty, cannot or will not perceive, that there is some difference in the situation and feelings of the people of the United States, and those of the despotic governments of Europe. They forget that at this moment our people, we mean emphatically the class which labours with its own hands, is in possession of a greater portion of the property and intelligence of this country, ay, ten times over, than all the creatures of the paper credit system put together. This property is indeed more widely and equally distributed among the people than among the phantoms of the paper system, and so much the better. And as to their intelligence, let any man talk with them, and if he does not learn something it is his own fault. They are as well acquainted with the rights of person and property, and have as just a regard for them, as the most illustrious lordling of the scrip nobility. And why should they not? Who and what are the great majority of the wealthy people of this city—we may say of this country? Are they not (we say it not in disparagement, but in high commendation) are they not men who began the world comparatively poor with ordinary education and ordinary means? And what should make them so much wiser than their neighbours? Is it because they live in better style, ride in carriages, and have more money—or at least more credit than their poorer neighbours? Does a man become wiser, stronger, or more virtuous and patriotic, because he has a fine house over his head? Does he love his country the better because he has a French cook, and a box at the opera? Or does he grow more learned, logical and profound by intense study of the day-book, ledger, bills of exchange, bank promises, and notes of hand?

Of all the countries on the face of the earth, or that ever existed on the face of the earth, this is the one where the claims of wealth and aristocracy are the most unfounded, absurd and ridiculous. With no claim to hereditary distinctions; with no exclusive rights except what they derive from monopolies, and no power of perpetuating their estates in their posterity, the assumption of aristocratic airs and claims is supremely ridiculous. To-morrow they themselves may be beggars for aught they know, or at all events their children may become so. Their posterity in the second generation will have to begin the world again, and work for a living as did their forefathers. And yet the moment a man becomes rich among us, he sets up for wisdom—he despises the poor and ignorant—he sets up for patriotism: he is your only man who has a stake in the community, and therefore the only one who ought to have a voice in the state. What folly is this? And how contemptible his presumption? He is not a whit wiser, better or more patriotic than when he commenced the world, a waggon driver. Nay not half so patriotic, for he would see his country disgraced a thousand times, rather than see one fall of the stocks, unless perhaps he had been speculating on such a contingency. To him a victory is only of consequence, as it raises, and a defeat only to be lamented, as it depresses a loan. His soul is wrapped up in a certificate of scrip, or a Bank note. Witness the conduct of these pure patriots, during the late war, when they, at least a large proportion of them, not only withheld all their support from the Government, but used all their influence to prevent others from giving their assistance. Yet these are the people who alone have a stake in the community, and of course exclusively monopolize patriotism.

But let us ask what and where is the danger of a combination of the labouring classes in vindication of their political principles, or in defence of their menaced rights? Have they not the right to act in concert, when their opponents act in concert? Nay, is it not their bounden duty to combine against the only enemy they have to fear as yet in this free country, monopoly and a great paper system that grinds them to the dust? Truly this is strange republican doctrine, and this is a strange republican country, where men cannot unite in one common effort, in one common cause, without rousing the cry of danger to the rights of person and property. Is not this a government of the people, founded on the rights of the people, and instituted for the express object of guarding them against the encroachments and usurpations of power? And if they are not permitted the possession of common interest; the exercise of a common feeling; if they cannot combine to resist by constitutional means, these encroachments; to what purpose were they declared free to exercise the right of suffrage in the choice of rulers, and the making of laws?

And what we ask is the power against which the people, not only of this country, but of almost all Europe, are called upon to array themselves, and the encroachment on their rights, they are summoned to resist? Is it not emphatically, the power of monopoly, and the encroachments of corporate privileges of every kind, which the cupidity of the rich engenders to the injury of the poor?

It was to guard against the encroachments of power, the insatiate ambition of wealth that this government was instituted, by the people themselves. But the objects which call for the peculiar jealousy and watchfulness of the people, are not now what they once were. The cautions of the early writers in favour of the liberties of mankind, have in some measure become obsolete and inapplicable. We are menaced by our old enemies, avarice and ambition, under a new name and form. The tyrant is changed from a steel-clad feudal baron, or a minor despot, at the head of thousands of ruffian followers, to a mighty civil gentleman, who comes mincing and bowing to the people with a quill behind his ear, at the head of countless millions of magnificent *promises*. He promises to make every body rich ; he promises to pave cities with gold ; and he promises to pay. In short he is made up of promises. He will do wonders, such as never were seen or heard of, provided the people will only allow him to make his promises, equal to silver and gold, and human labour, and grant him the exclusive benefits of all the great blessings he intends to confer on them. He is the sly, selfish, grasping and insatiable tyrant, the people are now to guard against. A CONCENTRATED MONEY POWER ; a usurper in the disguise of a benefactor ; an agent exercising privileges which his principal never possessed ; an impostor who, while he affects to wear chains, is placed above those who are free ? a chartered libertine, that pretends to be manacled only that he may the more safely pick our pockets, and lord it over our rights. This is the enemy we are now to encounter and overcome, before we can expect to enjoy the substantial realities of freedom.

REVOLUTIONARY PENSIONERS.

[*From the Evening Post of Dec.* 8, 1834.]

In the proceedings of the Board of Assistant Aldermen, on Monday evening last, as reported in the morning papers, and copied into this journal, there occurred the following passage:

"Assistant Alderman Tallmadge moved that the Board now take up the report of the special committee, relative to the relief of the surviving Revolutionary soldiers residing in the city and county of New-York. When the last Pension List was made out, the number amounted to one hundred and thirty-seven—but some, since then, had left the city, and others had joined the companions of their youth, in the cold and quiet grave, so that the number left is less than one hundred. He moved that one hundred dollars be paid out of the city treasury on the 1st January next, to every surviving officer and soldier of the revolution in the city and county of New-York, now receiving a pension, provided the number does not exceed one hundred. He accompanied it by an eloquent appeal, in which he showed, that while we are rejoicing at the victories of the revolution, we should not forget those in their old age who achieved them."

Mr. Tallmadge chose, beyond all question, a very fine theme, for the exercise of his oratorical powers, if he possesses any; and if we are to believe the reporters of the morning papers, there is not a stupid dolt in either board of the city council who does not evince the eloquence of a Tully every time he opens his mouth, and drawls and stammers out a few sentences of ungrammatical gibberish. Whether Assistant Alderman Tallmadge's oratory is of this stamp or not we do not profess to know, as we never had the happiness of hearing the gentlemen, or seeing him, or having any communion with him, direct or indirect, of any sort or kind whatever. We are bound to suppose, however, that his forensic powers are of a high order; for we do not know in what way else to account for the fact that his wild and unjustifiable proposition should have received, with a single exception, the unanimous support of the whole Board of Assistant Aldermen. The name of the man who voted in the negative ought to have been given. He deserves credit for his independence; he deserves credit for his fidelity to his constituents; he deserves credit for not suffering his common sense and common honesty to be swept away by the torrent of Assistant Alderman Tallmadge's "eloquent appeal!"

Let us reflect a moment what this proposition is which the Board of Assistant Aldermen have, with this single exception, unanimously adopted. Why to give away ten thousand dollars of the people's money to such of the revolutionary pensioners as reside in the city of New-York. Does not the plain good sense of every reader perceive that this is a monstrous abuse of the trust confided to our city legislators? Did we send them to represent us in the Common Council that they may squander away the city's treasures at such a lavish rate? Is it any part of their duty to make New-Year's presents? Have they any right under heaven to express their sympathy for the revolutionary pensioners at the city's cost? If they have, where is the warrant for it? Let them point their fingers to the clause in the city charter which authorizes them to lay taxes, that they may be expended again in bounties, rewards and largesses, to class any of men whatever.

Let no reader suppose that in making these remarks, we lack a proper appreciation of the eminent services rendered to this country, and to the cause of human liberty throughout the world, by those brave and heroic men who achieved our national independence. Doubtless many, very many of them, entered into that contest with no higher motives than animate the soldier in every contest, for whatsoever object undertaken—whether in defence of liberty or to destroy it. But the glorious result has spread a halo around all who had any share in achieving it, and they will go down together in history, to the latest hour of time, as a band of disinterested, exalted, incorruptible and invincible patriots. This is the light in which their sons, at least, the inheritors of their precious legacy of freedom, ought to view them; and they never, while a single hero of that band remains, can be exonerated from the obligations of gratitude which they owe. But we would not, on that account, authorize any usurpation of power by our public servants, under the pretence of showing the gratitude of the community to the time-worn veterans of the revolutionary war.—Every man ought to be his own almoner, and not suffer those whom he has elected for far different purposes, to squander the funds of the public chest, at any rate, and on any object which may seem to them deserving of sympathy. The precedent is a wrong one, and is doubly wrong, inasmuch as the general regard for those for whose benefit this stretch of power is exerted, may lead men to overlook the true character of the unwarrantable assumption.

Let ten thousand—let fifty thousand dollars be given by our city to the revolutionary veterans who are closing their useful lives in the bosom of this community; but let it be given to them without an infringement of those sacred rights which they battled to establish. If the public feeling would authorize such a donation as Mr. Tallmadge exerted his "eloquence" in support of, that same feeling would prompt our citizens, each man for himself, to make a personal contribution towards a fund which should properly and nobly speak the gratitude of New-York towards the venerable patriots among them. But the tax-payer, who would liberally contribute to such an object, in a proper way, may very naturally object to Mr. Tallmadge thrusting his hand into his pocket, and forcing him to give for what and to whom that eloquent gentleman pleases. If the city owes an unliquidated amount, not of gratitude, but of money, to the revolutionary pensioners, let it be paid by the Common Council, and let Mr. Tallmadge be as eloquent as he pleases, or as he can be, in support of the appropriation. But beyond taking care of our persons and our property, the functions neither of our city government, nor of our state government, nor of our national government, extend. We hope to see the day when the people will jealously watch and indignantly punish every violation of this principle.

That what we have here written does not proceed from any motive other than that we have stated, we trust we need not assure our readers. That, above all, it does not proceed from any unkindness towards the remaining heroes of the revolution, must be very evident to all such as have any knowledge of the personal relations of the writer. Among those who would receive the benefit of Mr. Tallmadge's scheme is the venerable parent of him whose opinions are here expressed. That parent, after a youth devoted to the service of his country, after a long life of unblemished honour, now, in the twilight of his age, and bending under the burden of fourscore years, is indebted to the tardy justice of his Government for much of the little light that cheers the evening of his eventful day. Wanting indeed should we be, therefore, in every sentiment of filial duty and love, if we could oppose this plan of a public donation, for any other than public and sufficient reasons. But viewing it as an attempt to exercise a power which the people never meant to confer upon their servants, we should be wanting in those qualities of which this donation is intended to express the sense of the community, if we did not oppose it. We trust the resolution will not pass the upper Board.

PROTECTION OF COMMERCIAL INTERESTS.

[*From the Evening Post, Dec.* 12, 1834.]

The resolution offered by Mr. Morgan, in the House of Representatives on Tuesday last, instructing the Committee on Commerce to inquire into the expediency of obliging all masters of vessels trading south of the equator to take at least two apprentices with them, does not embrace a sufficiently extensive range of inquiry. Ought not that Committee, or other appropriate ones, standing or special, to inquire into the expediency of obliging all shipwrights to have a certain number of apprentices, "as a means of benefitting the commercial interests of the United States?" The art of ship-building is certainly a very important one to our commercial interests, quite as much so as the art of navigating the southern ocean and catching whales and seals. Then again, there is the rope-making business, which is also important. If that art should be lost, our "commercial interests" would cut but a sorry figure. Ought we not, therefore, to guard against so great a calamity, oblige ropemakers to educate a certain number of apprentices? We should have few sailors if we had no ropes. The raising of hemp, and the manufacture of canvass, are both important to our "commercial interests." Congress had perhaps better look out that the race of hemp-raisers and canvass manufacturers do not become extinct by timely passing a law obliging all now engaged in these pursuits to take apprentices ; for we never heard of but one ship that could lie upon a wind and make headway without canvass, and there is not likely to be another, unless, indeed, steam might supply the place of canvass ; and then the law would only have to be modified so as to transfer the apprentices over to the steam engineer. If Mr. Morgan begins upon this forcing system, and is for doing everything by legislation, he must not stop at south sea ship apprentices. A wide field is open before him. When he comes to expatiate at large in it, however, he may chance to discover that he has started on a wrong principle,—that the old notions of government bounty, protection, prohibition and coercion in matters of trade, are totally exploded by the wisest men and deepest thinkers of the age,—that mankind have discovered at last that they are "governed too much ;—and that the true democratic principle, and the true principle of political economy, is "Let us alone." It may be proper to add that we do not mean, by our ironical mode of allusion to the subject, the slightest disrespect to Mr. Morgan, for whose character we entertain great regard.

THE FRENCH TREATY—PRESIDENT'S MESSAGE.

[*From the Evening Post, December* 15, 1834.]

We have heretofore remarked that a great number of the opposition prints, including some most distinguished for the bitterness of their hostility to the present Administration, fully approve of that portion of the President's message which relates to France. All of them, without exception, so far as we have observed, admit that his statement of the question at issue between the two governments is exceedingly lucid and accurate, and that the conduct of France deserves all the reprehension it has received. But constrained, either by the force of habit, or the force of political malignity, to oppose the Executive at all hazards and on all subjects, there are many prints that assail his proposed measure of reprisals with a bitterness which could hardly be exceeded if France were wholly in the right, and the mere suggestion of a course by no means belligerant were an actual declaration of war. The spectacle of so considerable a portion of the press of a free and enlightened country attacking the Chief Magistrate with the utmost vindictiveness, for simply recommending measures which he deems called for alike by regard for the long-deferred rights of plundered citizens, and by the claims of national honour, would create emotions of a painful kind, had not our vocation long since accustomed us to see partisan writers lose all sense of patriotism in the engrossing sentiment of hostility to the exalted man " who has filled the measure of his country's glory." As it is, we view the effervescence of their rancour with a feeling near akin to indifference; and indeed it is an employment not wholly without amusement to watch the straits to which they are reduced, in order to give some colour of reason to the violent invectives they pour out upon General Jackson's head.

One tribe of opponents, determined to consider the suggested measure of reprisals as tantamount to a declaration of war, straightway fall to counting the costs, and graduate the wickedness of the proposal by a scale of dollars and cents. These ready reckoners, with a facility of calculation surpassing that of Zerah Colburn, have ascertained the exact expense of war, which they set down at fifty millions of dollars; and hereupon they rail at the President for his enormous profligacy in proposing to spend fifty millions for the recovery of five! France, they acknowledge, has treated us very badly. Our national forbearance, they are obliged to confess, has been shown in an exemplary degree, throughout the whole course of a most protracted and perplexing negotiation; and when that negotiation at last terminated in a treaty, by which the spoiler of our commerce and the plunderer of our citizens agreed to pay us back simply the amount rifled from us many years before, and not even that amount without the concession, on our part, of commercial advantages which she had no right to claim, they admit that to violate such a treaty, in the face of all the honourable obligations which can bind one nation to keep faith with another, is a degree of perfidy that it would be difficult to characterise by too strong a term. But fifty millions of dollars!—there is the rub. The phantom of that large sum of money haunts their imaginations and appals their understanding! To spend fifty millions to coerce France into the payment of one tenth of that sum is a proceeding for which they can find no rule in their political arithmetic. If we could compel France to pay us the debt at an expense of two or three millions, so that we might pocket one or two millions by the operation, these patriotic journals would applaud the undertaking. If we could make money by fighting, they would be the first to cry havoc! and let slip the dogs of war. But the idea of throwing money away for the mere "bubble reputation," seems to them exceedingly preposterous. National honour is a phrase to which they can attach no import by itself; it must be accompanied by the expression, *national profit*, to give it any significancy in their eyes.

We should like to know what opinion these worthies

entertain of the conduct of those men who "plunged this country in all the horrors of war" on account of a preamble, to use Mr. Webster's explanation of the matter. We allude to the authors of our revolution. It has never been supposed that they counted on making a great deal of money by the enterprise. They pledged their lives, their fortunes and their sacred honour on the issue—and life and fortune many of them forfeited; but none of them their honour! They entered into that contest expecting to endure great hardships, to make great sacrifices, to expend vast treasures, and for what? Not for the purposes of acquiring fifty millions of dollars from England, or five millions; but for the simple acknowledgment of an abstract principle. It was enough for them that the principle of liberty was invaded. They did not wait until the consequences of the aggression should call for resistance. They thought, as Mr. Webster has truly and eloquently represented (though for an unhallowed purpose!) that "whether the consequences be prejudicial or not, if there be an illegal exercise of power, it is to be resisted."

"We are not to wait" (let us borrow the language of a man whose words have the weight of law with the opponents of the President) "till great public mischiefs come; till the government is overthrown; or liberty itself put in extreme jeopardy. We should not be worthy sons of our fathers, were we so to regard great questions affecting the general freedom. Those fathers accomplished the Revolution on a strict question of principle. The Parliament of Great Britain asserted a right to tax the colonies in all cases whatsoever, and it was precisely on this question that they made the Revolution turn. The amount of taxation was trifling, but the claim itself was inconsistent with liberty; and that was, in their eyes enough. It was against the recital of an act of Parliament, rather than against any suffering under its enactments, that they took up arms. They went to war against a preamble. They fought seven years against a declaration. They poured out their treasures and their blood like water, in a contest, in opposition to an assertion, which those less sagacious, and not so well schooled in the principles of civil liberty, would have regarded as barren phraseology, or mere parade of words. On this question of principle, while actual suffering was yet afar off, they raised their flag against a power to which, for purposes of foreign conquest and subjugation, Rome, in the height of her glory, is not to be compared; a Power which has dotted over the surface of the whole globe with her possessions and military posts; whose morning drum-beat, following the sun, and keeping company with the hours, circles the earth daily with one continuous and unbroken strain of the martial airs of England."

Such was the cause for which our fathers fought, and such the power with which they battled. They were of that metal that on a question of honour or right they did not stop to count the cost. Their minds were thoroughly imbued with the sentiment, that

> Rightly to be great
> Is, not to stir without great argument,
> But greatly to find quarrel in a straw,
> Where honour's at the stake.

A portion of their descendants seem to be animated with very different principles. Those who but recently were ready for civil broil, who proclaimed that we were on the eve of a revolution, and on questions which involved mere difference of political opinion—questions which the peaceful weapon of suffrage was fully adequate to decide,—now start back with well-painted horror from the prospect of strife with a foreign nation, which, after having despoiled our citizens, and trifled with our government, through long years of patient intercession, has at last capped the climax of indignity by the grossest insult which can be offered to a sovereign people; namely, by the causeless violation of a solemn international pact. But it is discovered that a war with that nation would be attended with expense, and therefore it ought not to be undertaken! Money, according to these journals, is of more value than honour. Let a foreign nation tread on you and spit on you, and bear it meekly, if it will cost you money to avenge the insult! Such at least is the precept to be inferred from their remarks.

It is for the purpose of enforcing this precept, we presume, that the public have been treated, in various journals, with highly coloured pictures of the evils of war. Our merchants have been represented as prostrated, our ships rotting at the wharves, our shores lighted with conflagrations, and the ocean incarnadined with slaughter. The tears of widows have streamed through the pens of these pathetic gentlemen, and the cries of orphans have been heard in the clatter of their presses. Pirates and marauders infest every line they write, and the thunders of a naval conflict roar in every paragraph. It is fortunate, however, that the reader can turn from these dismal forebodings to the sober pages of history, and learn how far the truth, in relation to the past, sustains these fancy sketches of the future. What is the fact? We have passed through two wars with the most formidable power on earth, and yet survive, to prove to France, by force of arms, if it should be necessary, that while we ask nothing that is not clearly right, we will submit to nothing that is wrong.

But this extremity will not be necessary. France has trifled with us, but she will repair the wrong. Should she not—should she, through the duplicity of her king, or the misapprehension of her deputies, or wilful slight, or any other cause, persist in denying us our right, we even yet propose to pursue only the mildest and most pacific course. The nature of reprisals is too clearly established to need newspaper elucidation. It is unnecessary to load our columns with extracts from Grotius or Puffendorf, from Burlemaqui or Vattel, for the laws of nations rest on the plain principles of equity ; and what can be more obviously just than our right to detain the property of France for the purpose of defraying her acknowledged debt, should she adhere to her strange refusal to comply with her own promise of payment? Such seizure and detention of property affords a nation no ground for war ; any more than an individual, whose property has been taken by due course of law to satisfy his debts, is furnished by that proceeding with a justification for murder. They, therefore, who treat the proposed measure of reprisals as equivalent to a declaration of war, do great injustice to the character of France ; as if that nation were governed by so unfriendly a feeling towards this young republic, that she would eagerly seize any pretext to fight with us, though all the world must perceive that our Government has claimed nothing but its rights.

That the conduct of France will be so contrary to that liberal spirit which animates her people we can not believe, and shall not, till some stronger evidence is afforded than the predictions of those who are even eager to fortell "war, pestilence, and famine" as the necessary consequences of the administration of a man who has done more to elevate our character abroad, promote our prosperity at home, and revive and secure the great principle of equal liberty than any other man that ever lived in the tide of time. But if war must come of our asserting our rights, let it come! Much as we should regret, on various accounts, any collision with France, we would not avoid strife even with that country at the expense of national honour or justice. We are prepared for any event. True, certain members of Congress exclaimed with affected horror, "What! plunge into war with an empty treasury!" But heaven grant that we may never have a full treasury. We desire to see no surplus revenue at the disposal of the Government, to be squandered in vast schemes of internal improvements, or prove an apple of discord to rouse the jealousy and enmity of different sections of the country. If we have not the money in the treasury, we have it in the pockets of the people. Our wide and fruitful territory is loaded with abundance. Plenty smiles in every nook and corner of the land. The voice of thanksgiving ascends to heaven from the grateful hearts of millions of happy freemen. Our Government owes not one dollar of public debt, and its credit is unbounded, for its basis is the affections of the people, and its resources are coextensive with their wealth. Let it become necssary again for that Government to maintain its honour at the hazard of war, though it should even be "against a preamble," and we shall again find that a people thoroughly imbued with the principle of liberty are ever ready to pledge their lives, their fortunes, and their sacred honour in support of such a quarrel.

But another objection is found to the Presidenets proposal, that it will build up a national debt. A national debt is certainly a national evil; but it is not the worst evil that can befal a nation. And the argument that we should waive on just claims for indemnity from France, rather than incur the hazard of debt, comes with an ill grace from that party of which it has always been a leading maxim that a national debt is a blessing instead of a curse. This sentiment is entwined with the very heartstrings of aristocracy—if, indeed, aristocracy has a heart. Its doctrine has always been that a public debt gives solidity to the Government, creates in the bosoms of a vast number of people a strong personal interest in its welfare, consolidates in its favour all the moneyed influence of the country, strengthens its power, and gives permanence to its duration. For the disciples of this school now to cry out against measures which involve the possibility of war, because war would create a public debt, is a degree of hypocrisy and inconsistency which scarcely deserves reply.

There is another ground of objection which strikes us as equally preposterous. They deprecate war lest the power of conducting it should fall into the hands of General Jackson! And into whose hands, in the name of common sense and common honesty, could such a power be so wisely and advantageously entrusted? Why, the whole sum and substance of the opposition clamour against the Chief Magistrate, has been on the ground that he is a Military Chieftain—that he was qualified to rule in the camp or battle-field, but was too dictatorial to preside over the peaceful councils of the nation. His talents as a soldier have never been disputed. His sagacity, bravery, alertness, energy are qualities notorious to the world. What! the war power not to be trusted into the hands of Andrew Jackson! a soldier almost from his cradle; a champion who has contended alike against the native savages of our forest and the most disciplined troops of Europe; who has encountered all sort of foes, and always with success. What, not trust the war-power with the Hero of New-Orleans? Put up with a gross affront from France, rather than confide our quarrel to a a man who, of all men living, is best entitled to the confidence of the people, best qualified to conduct the strife to a prosperous result! Nothing can exceed the utter absurdity of this objection.

But let it not be lost sight of that all the objections to the suggestions of General Jackson relative to our relations with France, are founded on false assumptions. No "war power," no "discretionary power" is asked. No proposition of a belligerant kind is offered. No menace is held out. His allusions to France are in the kindest and most conciliatory spirit, and the most lively regret is manifested that the failure of that country to perform its solemn covenant has forced upon the Chief Magistrate of this the necessity of adverting to the measures which may become necessary, in case she should show no disposition to redeem her violated faith. The spirit of General Jackson's message is the spirit which we trust this Government will always display to the Governments of other nations. It is neither dictatorial nor submissive; neither boisterous nor wheedling. Calm, temperate, firm, it affords to France no excuse for resentment, and will command the respect and admiration of other foreign nations. We wish that journalists, who, beneath all the scum and crust of party prejudices and passions have the true interest and glory of their country at heart, would adopt a similar tone—

> "Let us appear not rash nor diffident:
> Immoderate valour swells into a fault,
> And fear admitted into public counsels,
> Betrays like treason: let us shun them both."

UTOPIA—SIR THOMAS MORE—JACK CADE.

[*From the Evening Post, December* 18, 1834.]

Not many days ago we placed before our readers some pregnant reasons for thinking that the epithet of *Utopian*, which has been applied to the doctrines advanced by this journal on the subject of corporations and other cognate matters, is not, after all, the worst name with which the efforts of a zealous advocate of equal rights may be branded by the aristocratic enemies of that principle. We showed that the word is derived from the title of a speculative work, written by a man of great powers of mind, great purity of life, and great love for the best interests of his fellow-men. Those who are familiar with the history of Sir Thomas More cannot but admire his character. He was a man whose doctrines and whose life were coincident. His very first public act was to place himself in prominent and uncompromising opposition to the rapacious demands of a powerful monarch, though by doing so he brought down on his own parent the most rigorous punishment that unbridled tyranny dared to inflict. He subsequently, with equal boldness and integrity, incurred the resentment of the haughty Wolsey, by strenuously opposing his oppressive measures. Again, when afterwards elevated, under the imperious and licentious Henry the Eighth, to the office of Lord Chancellor of England, he relinquished the seals and retired from that high station, provoking the lasting enmity of the king, rather than consent to his divorce from Catharine of Arragon. And finally, persecuted by the vindictive monarch under various pretences, he at length yielded up his life on the scaffold, preferring death to violating the dictates of his conscience.

Such was the man whose admirable work on Governments, veiled under a thin disguise of fiction, has given to the language a word, which monarchical and aristocratic writers are fond of bandying as expressive of the wildest dreams of visionaries and lunatics. Whether the production deserves such a character from republicans, let those judge who are acquainted with its contents, or who perused the extracts which we placed before our readers. It is a work replete with political truth and wisdom. Many of its doctrines have since been adopted by the wisest statesmen; many of them have a conspicuous place in the democratic theory of our Government; and many others are destined yet to force their way, in spite of the opposition of aristocratic selfishness and pride, not only in this young republic, but in the king-governed nations of the old world.

Reason there is that despots and the parasites of despots should treat such views as the impracticable theories of dreamers and enthusiasts. But in this country, blessed with freedom above all others; blessed with a Government founded on the broad basis of Equal Rights; in this country, where the people are the sole source of power, and their equal good its sole legitimate object; where there are neither lords nor serfs, masters nor bondmen, but where rich and poor, learned and unlearned, proud and humble, move and mingle on one unvarying plane of political equality—in this country we ought to reject the prejudices and cant of other lands, and think, and reason, and act for ourselves.

That all the views of Sir Thomas More are practicable we by no means contend; and strange indeed would it have been if one living at his time, and under such a constitution of society, could so far have outsoared mankind, as to prefigure a government in all respects adapted to the rights, wants and capacities of man in a state of absolute political and religious freedom. But if his theory of Government is not in all respects sound, it is at least full of important truths; and the aristocratic abuses which prompted his meditations are accurately and vividly delineated, as are the hydra evils, political and social, of which they constitute the prolific source.

The lesson which his work teaches, then, is highly important, if no other than to guard with sleepless vigilance the great palladium of freedom, the principle of equal rights; to guard it against the first insidious approaches of that spirit which is ever seeking to subject the many to the will of the few; which comes with professions of zeal for the public good on its lips, and with its heart topful of schemes of self-aggrandizement and ambition. Let the people examine well into the true designs of those who betray this suspicious ardour of philantropy, caring all for the public, and nothing for themselves. When they hear the oft-repeated cant about "stimulating the industry of the country," "developing its vast resources," and the like, let them inquire how much this stimulus is to cost, and let them remember, if it is to be purchased by the surrender of one jot or tittle of their equal privileges, the price is infinitely too dear. These are the sentiments which they will derive from a perusal of Sir Thomas More's excellent work, and let them not fear to entertain and act upon these sentiments, though by doing so they should incur from the aristocracy the epithet of Utopian.

But the opponents of the doctrines we advocate, as if calling names were a certain method of overthrowing our arguments, are not content with stigmatizing our views as Utopian, but bestow the appellation of Jack Cade upon ourselves. Thus an article in the Courier and Enquirer of this morning, after grossly misstating the objects for which we contend, and indulging in much groundless abuse, at last closes with what the writer may have supposed the very climax of invective, by designating us as "*the Jack Cade of the Evening Post.*"

Here again we see the readiness of our opponents to adopt the aristocratic cant of those countries, the Governments of which repudiate the principle of equal liberty, and exert their powers to concentrate all wealth and privilege in the hands of a few. It is heart-sickening to see men, citizens of this free republic and partakers of its equal blessings, thus assume without examination, and use without scruple, as terms of reproach, the epithets with which lying historians and panders to royalty have branded those, whose only crime was their opposing, with noble ardour and courage, the usurpations of tyranny, and setting themselves up as assertors of the natural and inalienable rights of their oppressed fellow-men.

Have the editors who use the name of Cade as a word of scorn looked into the history of that heroic man? Have they sifted out, from the mass of prejudice, bigotry and servility, which load the pages of the old chroniclers, the *facts* in relation to his extraordinary career? Have they acquainted themselves with the oppressions of the times; the lawless violence of the nobles; the folly and rapacity of the monarch; the extortion and cruelty of his ministers; and the general contempt which was manifested for the plainest and dearest rights of humanity? Have they consulted the pages of Stow, and Hall, and Hollingshed, who, parasites of royalty as they were, and careful to exclude from their chronicles whatever might grate harshly on the delicate ears of the privileged orders, have yet not been able to conceal the justice of the cause for which Cade contended, the moderation of his demands, or the extraordinary forbearance of his conduct? Have they looked into these matters for themselves, and divesting the statements of the gloss of prejudice and servility, judged of the man by a simple reference to the facts of his conduct, and the nature and strength of his motives? Or have they been content to learn his character from the scenes of a play, or the pages of that king-worshipper, that pimp and pander to aristocracy, the tory Hume, who was ever ready to lick absurd pomp, and give a name of infamy to any valiant spirit that had the courage and true nobleness to stand forward in defence of the rights of his fellow-men?

Let those who use the name of Cade as a term of reproach remember that the obloquy which blackens his memory flowed from the same slanderous pens that denounced as rebels and traitors, and with terms of equal bitterness, though not of equal contumely, the Hampdens and Sydneys of England—glorious apostles and martyrs in the cause of civil liberty! Let them remember, too, that, as the philosophic Mackintosh observes, all we know of Cade is through his enemies—a fact which of itself would impress a just and inquiring mind with the necessity of examination for itself, before adopting the current slang of the aristocracy of Great Britain.

The very name of Jack Cade, if we take the pains to look into contemporary historians, is but a nick-name conferred upon the leader of the Kentish insurrection, in order to increase the obloquy with which it was the policy of Henry the Sixth and his licentious nobles to load the memory of that heroic and treacherously-murdered man. But whatever was his name or origin, and whatever might have been his private motives and character, if we judge of him by the authentic facts of history alone, we shall find nothing that does not entitle him to the admiration of men who set a true value on liberty, and revere those who peril their lives, their fortunes, and their sacred honour to achieve it from the grasp of tyrants, or defend it against their encroachments. Nothing can exceed the grossness of the oppressions under which the people laboured when Cade took up arms. Nothing can exceed the arbitrary violence with which their property was wrested from their hands, or the ignominious punishments which were causelessly inflicted on their persons. The kingdom was out of joint. An imbecile and rapacious monarch on the throne; a band of licentious and factious nobles around him; a parliament ready to impose any exactions on the commons; and all the minor offices of

Government filled with a species of freebooters, who deemed the possession of the people their lawful prey—in such a state of things, the burdens under which the great mass of Englishmen laboured must have been severe in the extreme.

If Cade was the wretched fanatic which it has pleased the greatest dramatic genius of the world (borrowing his idea of that noble rebel from old Hollingshed) to represent him, how did it happen that twenty thousand men flocked to his standard the moment it was unfurled? How did it happen that his statement of grievances was so true, and his demands for redress so moderate, that, even according to Hume himself, "the Council, observing that nobody was willing to fight against men so reasonable in their pretensions, carried the King for safety to Kenilworth?" How did it happen, as related by Fabian, that the duke of Buckingham and the archbishop of Canterbury being sent to negotiate with him, were obliged to acknowledge that they found him "right discrete in his answers; howbeit they could not cause him to lay down his people, and to submit him (unconditionally) unto the king's grace." But we need not depend upon the opinions of historians for the reasonableness of his demands. Hollingshed has recorded his list of grievances and stipulations of redress; and let those who think the term Jack Cade synonymous with ignorant and ferocious rebel and traitor, examine it; let them compare it with the grievances which led our fathers to take up arms against their mother country, nor lay them down until they achieved a total separation; let them look at it in reference to what would be their own feelings under a tithe part of the wrongs; and, our life on it, they will pause before they again use the word in such a sense. Nay more: let them follow Cade through his whole career; let them behold him in the midst of insurrection, checking the natural fierceness of his followers, restraining their passions, and compelling them by the severest orders to respect private property; see him withdrawing his forces each night from London, when he had taken possession of that city, that its inhabitants might sleep without fear or molestation; mark him continually endeavouring to fix the attention of the people solely on those great ends of public right and justice for which alone he had placed himself in arms against his king: let them look at Cade in these points of view, and we think their unfounded prejudices will speedily give way to very different sentiments.

Follow him to the close of his career; see him deserted by his followers, under a general but deceitful promise of pardon from the Government; trace him afterwards a fugitive through the country with a reward set upon his head, in violation of the edict which but a few days before had dissolved him of the crime of rebellion on condition of laying down his arms; behold him at last entrapped by a wretch and basely murdered; weigh his whole character as exhibited by all the prominent traits of his life and fortune, remembering too that all you know of him is from those who dipped their pens in ink only to blacken his name! and you will at last be forced to acknowledge that instead of the scorn of mankind, he deserves to be ranked among those glorious martyrs, who have sacrificed their lives in defence of the rights of man. The derision and contumely which have been heaped on Cade, would have been heaped on those who achieved the liberty of this country, had they been equally unsuccessful in their struggle. It ill then becomes republicans, enjoying the freedom which they achieved, admiring the intrepidity of their conduct, and revering their memory, to use the name of one who sacrificed his life in an ill-starred effort in defence of the same glorious and universal principles of equal liberty, as a by-word and term of mockery and reproach.

Cade was defeated, and his very name lies buried underneath the rubbish of ages. But his example did not die;

> For freedom's battle once begun,
> Bequeathed from bleeding sire to son,
> Though often lost is ever won.

Those who are curious in historical research may easily trace the influence of the principles which Cade battled to establish, through succeeding reigns. If they follow the stream of history from the sixth Henry downwards, they will find that the same sentiments of freedom were continually breaking away from the restraints of tyranny, and that the same grievances complained of by the leader of the Kentish insurrection, were the main cause of all the risings of the Commons, till at last the cup of oppression, filled to overflowing, was dashed to the earth by an outraged people, the power of the throne was shaken to its centre, and the evils under which men long had groaned, were remedied by a revolution.

Let readers not take things upon trust. Let them not be turned away from doctrines which have for their object the more complete establishment of the great principle of equal rights, by the reproachful epithets of aristocratic writers. Let them, above all, not take the worn out slang of other countries as equivalent to argument; but subjecting every thing to the touchstone of good sense and candid examination, try for themselves what is current gold, and what is spurious coin. If they look well into the true meaning of words, they will discover that neither Agrarian nor Utopian is a term of very deep disgrace; that to be called a Jack Cade is rather complimentary than discreditable; and that even the dreaded name of Jacobin has not half so odious a meaning as people are apt to suppose. In studying the histories of other countries, he shows a true American feeling, who separates facts from the prejudices of the writer, and forms conclusions for himself as to character and events in the great drama of existence.

TO WILLIAM L. MARCY,

GOVERNOR OF THE STATE OF NEW-YORK.

[*From the Evening Post, Dec*, 24, 1834.]

Recent events have fixed the eyes of the Democracy of this State with great interest upon you. They await your Message with much anxiety. Not even the admirable and truly democratic state paper lately addressed to Congress by the National Executive was perused with greater eagerness and attention, than will be that communication which your duty will soon require you to lay before the Legislature. Circumstances have arisen to create a very extensive apprehension that the will of the people, on a question deeply interesting in its nature, and one on which their sentiments have been clearly expressed, will be disregarded by their servants; and to you, as their chief servant, they look with fear and trembling, lest that confidence which they have expressed by their suffrages in your intelligence and integrity should prove to have been misplaced. We shall not, in a false spirit of courtesy, or unrepublican strain of adulation, affect to deny that we largely partake of these fears; nor shall we hesitate, with that freedom and frankness which become democrats, looking upon you, not as their master, but as their representative, to lay before you such views as we think ought to govern your conduct on the subject to which we allude.

It is a truth, susceptible of the clearest demonstration that the great body of the people of this state have expressed themselves decidedly opposed to the incorporation of any new banks, and as decidedly in favour of the withdrawal of all bank-notes of a less denomination than five dollars from circulation. A very cursory reference to the proceedings of town and county meetings, previous to the late election, must satisfy any candid mind that this was one of the leading favourite objects of the democracy. Situated where you are, and having necessarily some knowledge of the mode by which those who assume to be "leading politicians" sometimes contrive to stifle the expressions of the people, or weaken their force, or perplex them with ambiguities, you may readily conclude that public sentiment is in reality much more adverse to banks and a small note currency, and the desire for the speedy extinction of the latter is much stronger and urgent than would even appear by the tone of the published proceedings of democratic meetings.

It may not be known to you, however, that, by a fraud of so atrocious a character that no name of infamy would be too strong to apply to it, some of those who take upon themselves the task of guiding and regulating public opinion, have had the hardihood, in certain important instances, to forge resolutions on the subject of banks and currency, and put them forth as a part of the proceedings of Democratic Conventions, though entirely different in their tenor from the resolutions which were really adopted. It may not be known to you, for example, that the proceedings of the Young Men's Herkimer Convention underwent, in very important respects, this audacious mutation. That Convention consisted of a very numerous body of the delegated representatives of by far the largest and most active class of the democracy of this state; and it comprised as much intelligence, patriotism and discretion, as any assembly of political delegates which was ever convened on any like occasion in our country. What must have been the feelings of those honourable delegates, when the published account of their proceedings was placed in their hands, to perceive resolutions ascribed to them which they never adopted? to see other resolutions, on important subjects, so changed by interpolations and omissions, as to have lost all the force and efficacy of their original tenor? and to find, also, that resolutions, expressing the sense of the meeting on questions of great and pervading interest, had been wholly expunged?

Such was literally the fact! The proceedings of that Convention, as published, were not the proceedings which took place! The account was a forgery! The hand of political knavery had been employed upon it, and had changed the sentiments of the convention to sentiments in accordance with what the "party leaders" had then, no doubt, laid out as the course to be pursued by our legislature on those great questions of state policy which have agitated the public mind for a long time past. We desire to express ourselves explicitly. We distinctly charge that the proceedings of the Young Men's Herkimer Convention *were materially altered in Albany*. We charge, in particular, that the resolution on the subject of the suppression of small notes, and the substitution of a metallic currency, was so transformed, in Albany, by additions and omissions, as to be of very different and far feebler and more qualified import, than was the resolution as passed by the Convention, and transmitted to that place for publication. We charge, also, that another resolution, on a cognate subject, in which the sense of the Convention was strongly expressed against all monopolies whatever, was, by the Albany junto, wholly suppressed.

These are some of the facts which authorize us in saying that the sentiments of the democracy of this State, are much more hostile to banks and a small note currency than might be inferred from the language of their published proceedings. We by no means mean to be considered as intimating that you have had any share in the gross frauds which have been practised upon the people, or that you have been in any degree accessory to them. But it is a fact susceptible of proof, that these frauds have been committed.

Taking it as a point conceded, then, that the sentiments of a vast majority of the people of this state are in favour of the suppression of all bank notes of a smaller denomination than five dollars, let us ask what reasonable pretence can be urged why this measure should be postponed to a future day? Was there ever a time in this country when this reform in our currency could be so easily effected as now? Was there ever a time when such a vast quantity of gold and silver was accumulated in our banking houses, and only restrained from filling up the channels of circulation, and flowing in healthful currents through the country by every vein and artery being previously occupied with the sickly, worthless trash which has so long supplied the place of constitutional money? Our country contains, at this moment, twenty millions of dollars in specie more than it did a twelvemonth ago, and the most exaggerated calculation of the amount of our small note currency does not make it more than fifteen millions. The specie which we now have within our control will desert us soon, unless it be detained by the legislative reform which the public voice demands. Paper and gold cannot circulate together. The banks are discounting freely, and the spirit of speculation, recovered from the shock which it received a year ago, is already engaged in hazardous enterprizes. Bank notes are the aliment on which speculation subsists, and there is something in the quality of that nutriment which seems fatal to caution and prudence. Already our merchants are importing largely. Stocks have risen in value, and land is selling at extravagant rates. Every thing begins to wear the highly-prosperous aspect which foretokens commercial revulsion. If nothing should occur to check the "liberality" of the banks, our gold and silver must soon desert us, to pay for the excess of our importations over the amount of our exports. Upon this there will follow rigorous curtailments of discounts on the part of those institutions which are now lavish of their favours. After having pampered the public into commercial extravagance, they will suddenly withdraw their aid, careful to shelter themselves from the evils which their own selfish liberality has occasioned. Deserted in their utmost need, men who have ventured far beyond their depth on the flood of bank credit, will find themselves suddenly overwhelmed, and we shall again see many goodly a merchant stranded on the shore, or lying broken wrecks, on the shoals and quicksands of that treacherous sea. Such will be the inevitable course of things, if nothing occurs to check the dangerous generosity of our banks. If the proposed prohibition of notes of less than five dollars is postponed eighteen months, it will not take place at all. The commercial business of the country in the intermediate time will change the face of affairs. Before eighteen months shall have elapsed, the gold and silver, which have flowed so copiously into our country, in payment of that balance in our favour which the panic of last winter, by checking importation, has so happily occasioned, will have left us by the natural reflux of trade. When we buy more of foreign nations than our cotton, tobacco and flour will pay for, we must discharge the balance of debt with specie. The only way to keep the necessary quantity of the precious metals among us, is to abolish the small note currency at once. No injustice will be done to the banks by carrying this measure into immediate effect. They have had long warning that the sentiments of the people demanded this reformation, and they know that the wishes of the people are—or rather ought to be—the supreme law. It is to be feared, however, that bank influence will prove stronger than the popular will. It was that influence, and the pretext of the panic, which prevented a law being passed last winter to restrain the banks from issuing the smaller denominations of notes. That influence, and some other groundless pretext, there is too much reason to apprehend, will again be found more potent with our legislators than their duty to their constituents, and to the great and permanent interests of the state. It was our intention to include a summary of the reasons which render it imperative that the State Government should abstain from adding any more banks to our already almost innumerable host; but interruptions which we did not anticipate oblige us to put a hasty end to this article. We shall take the liberty of resuming the subject on an early day.

MONOPOLIES.

[*From the Evening Post, December* 30, 1834.]

This day week the Legislature will convene at Albany. Seldom has it happened that the meeting of that body has been looked forward to with so much general interest. The Message of Governor Marcy will probably be communicated to both Houses of the Legislature on the first day of the session, and we expect to be able to place it before our readers on the following Thursday. By the sentiments of that Message, will Governor Marcy be tried. They will either raise him in our estimation, and in the estimation of all who are animated by truly democratic principles, to a most enviable height, or sink him to the level of the gross herd of petty, selfish, short-sighted and low-minded politicians. The rare opportunity is presented to him now, by one single act, to inscribe his name among those of the greatest benefactors of mankind. If he should stand forth as the honest, bold, unequivocal asserter of the great principle of Equal Rights, and strenuously recommend to the Legislature to pursue such measures only as are consistent with that principle; if he should urge upon their attention the evil effects of the partial and unequal system of legislation which we have been pursuing for years; if he should illustrate the incompatibility of all acts of special incorporation with the fundamental principle of our Government, and show their tendency to build up a privileged order, and to concentrate all wealth and power in the hands of the few; if he should sternly oppose all further extension of exclusive or partial privileges, and earnestly recommend, instead, the adoption of a general law of joint stock partnerships, by which whatever of truly valuable is now effected by private incorporations might be done by voluntary associations of men, possessing no privileges above their fellow-citizens, and liable to the same free competition which the merchant, the mechanic, the labourer, and the farmer are, in their vocations—if he should take such a stand, his name would go down to posterity inseparably associated with that of the patriotic and democratic man, who, at the head of the National Government, has done so much to restore to the People their violated rights, and check the course of unequal, aristocratic legislation. If, on the contrary, Governor Marcy should listen to the suggestions of selfish interest or short-sighted policy ; if, through timidity of character or subserviency to the views of unprincipled demagouges, who assume to be the "leaders" of the democracy, and claim a right to legislative rewards, he should recommend "a middle course," or should cloak his sentiments in ambiguities, or fetter them with qualifications that take from them all force and meaning ; if he should either approve a continuance of the fatal course of legislation which has done so much to oppress the people, or express disapproval of it in such mincing, shuffling, evasive terms as to pass for nothing ; if he should object to the incorporation of more banks, *except in places where more banks are asked for*, and should suggest the propriety of prohibiting the small note currency, *at some future and indefinite period :* if Governor Marcy, instead of realizing the expectations of the honest democracy of the state, should pursue such a trimming, paltry, time-serving course, most completely will he forfeit the high prize of fame which is now within his reach, most blindly will he turn aside from the proud destiny which it is in his power to achieve. We await his message with anxiety, but not without strong hopes.

JOINT-STOCK PARTNERSHIP LAW.

[*From the Evening Post, December* 30, 1834.]

The charters of several incorporated companies in this city are about to expire, and we have several times been asked if this paper, in pursuance of the doctrines we profess, would feel called upon to oppose the renewal of those charters. To this our answer is most unequivocally in the affirmative. We shall oppose, with all our might and zeal, the granting or renewing of any special charter of incorporation whatever, no matter who may be the applicants, or what the objects of the association.

But at the same time, we wish it to be distinctly understood, that we do not desire to break up those incorporated associations the charters of which are about to expire. How so? You would refuse to re-charter them, and thus they would inevitably be broken up. Not at all; as we shall explain.

It is not against the objects effected by incorporated companies that we contend; but simply against the false principle, politically and politico-economically, of special grants and privileges. Instead of renewing the charters of Insurance Companies, or any other companies, about to expire, or granting charters to new applicants, we would recommend the passing of one general law of joint stock partnerships, allowing any number of persons to associate for any object, (with one single temporary exception, which we shall state in the proper place) permitting them to sue and be sued under their partnership name, to be secure from liability beyond the amount of capital invested, to conduct their business according to their own good pleasure, and, in short, to possess all the powers defined by the revised statutes as belonging to corporations. There is nothing not perfectly equitable in the principle which exempts men from liability to any greater amount than the capital actually invested in any business, provided proper notoriety be given of the extent and circumstances of that investment. If such a law were passed, the stockholders in an insurance company, or the stockholders in any other chartered company, when their corporate privileges were about to expire, would have merely to give the proper public notification of their intention to continue their business in the mode specified in the general joint-stock partnership law, and they might go on precisely the same as if their special privileges had been renewed. The only difference would be that those privileges would no longer be special, but would belong to the whole community, any number of which might associate together, form a new company for the same objects, give due notification to the public, and enter into free competition with pre-existing companies or partnerships; precisely as one man, or set of associated men, may now enter into mercantile business by the side of other merchants, import the same kinds of goods, dispose of them on the same terms, and compete with them in all the branches of their business.

There has been a great deal said about our ultraism and Utopianism; and this is the extent of it. By a general law of joint-stock partnerships all the good effects of private incorporations would be secured, and all the evil ones avoided. The humblest citizens might associate together, and wield, through the agency of skilful and intelligent directors, chosen by themselves, a vast aggregate capital, composed of the little separate sums which they could afford to invest in such an enterprise, in competition with the capitals of the purse-proud men who now almost monopolize certain branches of business.

The exception to which we have alluded above, is the business of banking. Our views on this subject were fully stated yesterday. We would not have banking thrown open to the whole community, until the legislature had first taken measures to withdraw our paper money from circulation. As soon as society should be entirely freed, by these measures, from the habit of taking bank-notes as money, we would urge the repeal of the restraining law, and place banking on as broad a basis as any other business whatever.

OBJECTS OF THE EVENING POST.

[*From the Evening Post, January* 3, 1835.]

Those who only read the declamations of the opponents of the Equal Rights of the people, may be induced to believe that this paper advocates principles at war with the very existence of social rights and social order. But what have we asked in the name of the people, that such an interested clamour should be raised against them and us? What have we done or said, that we should be denounced as incendiaries, striking at the very roots of society and tearing down the edifice of property? It may be useful to recapitulate what we have already done, in order that those who please may judge whether or not we deserve these reproaches, from any but the enemies of the equal rights of person and property.

In the first place, in designating the true functions of a good government, we placed the protection of property among its first and principal duties. We referred to it as one of the great objects for the attainment of which all governments were originally instituted. Does this savour of hostility to the rights of property?

In the second place, we maintained that all grants of monopolies, or exclusive or partial privileges to any man, or body of men, impaired the equal rights of the people, and was in direct violation of the first principle of a free government. Does it savour of hostility to the rights of property to maintain that all property has equal rights, and that exclusive privileges granted to one class of men, or one species of property, impair the equal rights of all the others?

As a deduction from these principles, we draw the conclusion that charters conferring partial or exclusive monopolies on small fractions of society, are infringements on the general rights of society, and therefore that the system ought to be abandoned as soon as possible, as utterly at war with the rights of the people at large. It is here that the shoe pinches, and here the clamour against us will be found to originate. Thousands and tens of thousands of influential individuals, at the bar, on the bench, in our legislative bodies, and everywhere, are deeply interested in the continuance of these abuses. Law-makers, law-expounders and law executors, have invested either their money or their credit in corporations of every kind, and it is not to be wondered at that they should cry out against the abandonment of a system from whence they derive such exorbitant gains.

We are accused of violating vested rights when we ask, in the name of the people, that no more be created, and that all those possessing the means and the inclination, may be admitted, under general regulations, to a participation in the privileges which hitherto have been only enjoyed through the caprice, the favour, the policy, or the corruption, of legislative bodies. We never even hinted at touching those vested rights, until the period to which they had been extended by law had expired, and till it could be done without a violation of legislative faith. We defy any man to point out in any of our arguments on this subject a single idea or sentence that will sustain the charge of hostility to actually vested rights.

Our opposition was prospective, not retroactive; it was not to present, but to future vested rights.

In attacking a course of policy in the future, do we make war on the past? In pointing out what we believe errors in former legislation, and recommending their abandonment in future, do we violate any right of property, or recommend any breach of puplic faith? Or, in advocating the equal rights of all, do we impair the constitutional rights of any? It might be well for the clamourous few who assail our principles and our motives with opprobious epithets, which, though they do not understand their purport themselves, they mean should convey the most dishonourable imputations—it might be well for them to answer these questions before they resort to railing.

One of the greatest supports of an erroneous system of legislation, is the very evil it produces. When it is proposed to remedy the mischief by adopting a new system, every abuse which has been the result of the old one becomes an obstacle to reformations. Every political change, however salutary, must be injurious to the interests of some, and it will be found that those who profit by abuses are always more clamourous for their continuance than those who are only opposing them from motives of justice or patriotism, are for their abandonment. Such is precisely the state of the question of monopoly at this moment.

Under the abuses of the right to grant exclusive privileges to the few, which is a constructive, if not a usurped power, a vast and concentrated interest and influence has grown up among us, which will undoubtedly be seriously affected in its monopoly of gain from that source, by the discontinuance of their chartered privileges, when they shall expire by their own limitation. The admission of all others having the means and the inclination to associate for similar purposes, by destroying the monopoly at one blow, will in all probability diminish the prospect of future gains; and these will be still further curtailed, by at first restricting banks in their issues of small notes and in the amount of notes they are permitted to put into circulation, and finally by repealing the restraining law, and throwing banking open to the free competition of the whole community. These may prove serious evils to the parties concerned; but it is a poor argument to say that a bad system should be persevered in, least a small minority of the community should suffer some future inconvenience. The magnitude of the evlis produced by an erroneous system of legislation, far from being a circumstance in favour of its continuance or increase, is the strongest argument in the world for its being abandoned as soon as possible. Every reformation may in this way be arrested, under the pretence that the evils it will cause are greater than those it will cure. On the same principle the drawing of a tooth might be opposed, on the ground that the pain is worse than that of the tooth-ache, keeping out of sight the fact that the one is a lasting and increasing, the other a momentary evil.

It is the nature of political abuses, to be always on the increase, unless arrested by the virtue, intelligence and firmness of the people. If not corrected in time, they grow up into a gigantic vigour and notoriety which at length enables them to wrestle successfully with the people, and overthrow them and their rights. The possessors of monopolies and exclusive privileges, which form the essence of every bad government, pervert a long perseverance in the wrong, into a political right; abuses grow venerable by time; usurpation matures into proscription; distinctions become hereditary; and what cannot be defended by reason, is maintained on the ground that a long continuance of wrongs, and a long possession of rights, are equally sacred.

REFUSAL OF THE U. S. BANK TO PRODUCE ITS BOOKS.*

[*From the Evening Post, May*, 13, 1834.]

The resolution adopted by the popular branch of Congress to appoint a Committee of Investigation to inquire into the affairs and conduct of the United States Bank was passed by a vote of 174 to 41. There has scarcely a question of any kind arisen during the present session which has received the approbation of so large and signal a majority of the House. Rumors have been in circulation for some days past, from the purport of which it was surmised that the managers of the United States Bank were determined to defeat all attempts to investigate the concerns of that corrupt institution, and refuse to remove the veil which conceals their iniquitous transactions. These rumors, however, could not gain entire credit from those who bore in mind how strong was the vote of the House in favour of appointing the Investigating Committee, how explicit were the instructions given them, and how ample the powers with which they were clothed.

It seems, however, that these reports were but too well founded. The Bank has added another act of audacious wickedness to those which had already made it the object of unappeasable detestation and abhorrence to the great body of the People of the United States. It has given another evidence of its determination to rule the country; and as it lately undertook to withhold the public funds from the executive department charged with their custody, and to dictate the law to the President of

* Several pieces are inserted here out of the order of date.

the United States; so now it refuses obedience to a resolution of Congress, framed in strict accordance with the terms of its charter, and shutting its books against the Committee of Investigation, sends them back to Washington no wiser than when they left.

We learn this fact from various sources. The Pennsylvanian says, "After a tedious and protracted attempt to induce the Bank to submit amicably to an investigation legally ordered and emanating from the direct representatives of the people, it was found necessary at last to serve a *subpœna duces tecum* upon the President, Directors, &c. of the United States Bank, to bring them and the requisite books and papers of the institution before the committee, then sitting at the North American Hotel. The officers so summoned made their appearance before the committee, and FORMALLY REFUSED EITHER TO TESTIFY, OR TO PRODUCE THE BOOKS AND PAPERS, IN EFFECT DENYING THE AUTHORITY OF THE COMMITTEE AND DISCLAIMING ALL RESPONSIBILITY TO THE REPUBLIC AND ITS SERVANTS! The refusal being peremptory, the only course left to the committee was an immediate adjournment."

The proceedings referred to in the foregoing paragraph took place on Saturday last. The committee of Investigation adjourned, we understand, to meet again in Washington, on Thursday next, when, it is presumed, a full official report of their whole proceedings and those of the Bank will be submitted to Congress and laid before the people of the United States.

Nothing has occurred in the whole history of this powerful and dangerous monopoly which equals in arrogance this high-handed and startling proceeding. Its bribery and corruption, extensively as it has been practised, was meant to operate in secret. Its resistance to the Executive authority, in the matter of the pension fund, was offered under the pretence of obedience to the law. But in its refusal to submit to the investigations of the Committee of Congress, there is no plea to justify or extenuate its audacity; and we can look upon this instance of monstrous and unheard of arrogance in no other light than as the result of a conviction entertained by the Bank that the power of its gold has at length prevailed, and that what with direct bribery, what with indirect corruption, and what with pecuniary coercion, it has obtained the mastery over the American people. We shall be greatly mistaken, however, if this last exhibition of autocratic arrogance does not arouse the indignation of the people to the highest pitch. We have miscalculated the moral sense of our fellow-countrymen if they can tamely brook the audacious conduct on the part of a money corporation, thus openly and insolently setting all law and all authority at defiance.

The clause in the charter of the Bank, by which Congress reserved to itself the power to examine into the affairs and management of that institution is clear and explicit. The twenty-third section of the act of 1816 chartering the United States Bank, is in the following words: "That it shall, at all times, be lawful for a committee of either House of Congress, appointed for that purpose, to inspect the books, and examine into the proceedings of the corporation hereby created, and to report whether the provisions of this charter have been, by the same, violated or not."

With regard to the particulars of the conduct of the President and Directors of the United States Bank towards the Investigating Committee we have heard several verbal reports, of which the following paragraph, given in a postscript of the Albany Argus, contains the substance. The extreme arrogance of the bank, and the unlawfulness of the pretence it set up, may be inferred from the course adopted by the Committee, who would not have relinquished the investigation and returned to Washington, had the Bank attempted to prevent their investigation by no other means than those which its charter authorizes it to use.

"The Committee soon after their appointment," says the Albany Argus, "assembled in Philadelphia, and demanded the usual convenience of a room in the Bank for the examination of the books and accounts of the bank. This was refused, except upon the condition that a committee of seven of the directors should be present at all examinations of the books, and it was also refused to allow copies or extracts to be taken. The committee then adjourned to a room in one of the hotels, and demanded that the books be sent thither. This was also refused; but a proposition made on the part of the Bank to allow an examination of the books in the bank and in the presence of the officers of the institution. The committee, anxious to fulfil the duties of their appointment, accepted the proposition, and proceeded to the Bank; when Mr. Biddle refused to allow an examination of the books, unless the object of such examination of the particular books were stated in writing. A compliance with such extraordinary terms, was of course inadmissible; and the committee returned to their room, and directed subpœnas to issue for the appearance before them of the president and directors, with the books of the bank. The subpœnas were served by the marshal, and the president and directors appeared, but refused the books, and refused to be sworn or to give evidence. The committee of course, had no alternative but to return to the seat of government which they were to do, we learn, on Monday."

Nothing but the consciousness of damning guilt—nothing but the fear that practises of the most enormous and flagitious corruption would be detected—nothing but the apprehension that its vast and wicked schemes were about to be laid before the American People, could have prevailed upon the Bank of the United States to act as it has done towards the Committee of Investigation. If its conduct had been pure—if its business had been honestly conducted—if its condition was solvent—if it had acted in conformity with the provisions of its charter—what need was there to shun investigation? Guilt shrinks in holes and corners, but an upright man stands boldly forth in the light of day. The course which the Bank has adopted must alienate those (if any there were) who have hitherto believed in its integrity. This effect, indeed, is said already to have taken place.

REFUSAL OF THE U. S. BANK TO PRODUCE ITS BOOKS.

[*From the Evening Post of May* 31, 1834.]

" Button button, who's got the button ?"

Our readers will doubtless recollect an old play of this name among the amusements of their youthful days, but probably never anticipated it would be played by such dignified personages as the President and Directors of the Bank of the United States. It will be seen by a perusal of the documents accompanying the Report of the Committee of Investigation, that they were as much puzzled to find out who had the custody of the Bank books, as we have often been to find who had the button. The books of the ancient sibyls were not more difficult of access than those of the Bank of the United States. When application was made by the Committee to the President, it was found they were not in his custody. When asked what clerks had charge of particular books, it was replied none; and when the Directors had a similar question put to them, they could not be brought to confess that these books were in their possession, or under their control. In reading this correspondence, we are strongly reminded of the fable of the two corporate gentlemen, who went into a butcher's shop and stole a piece of beef, and can scarcely refrain from adopting the same opinion with the honest butcher.

But it not only appears that no person has charge of the books of the Bank, but there are moreover strong indications in this correspondence that nobody represents the Bank itself, or is responsible for its proceedings. The committee address a letter to Mr. Biddle, and are answered by Mr. Sergeant. They write to Mr. Sergeant, and presto! Mr. Biddle responds, or in default of Mr. Biddle, Monsieur Jaudon volunteers. In this way the committee are bandied about from one to another, until they become as much puzzled to find out the rogue, as the honest butcher in the fable. All that they, or we, can gather from this inextricable jumble is, that nobody has the custody of the books, and that nobody represents the Bank or is responsible for its proceedings. Whether the President, the Cashier, the Directors, or the Clerks, constitute this extraordinary body corporate, is a profound mystery. The President, we all know, wields the whole power of the Bank, but the responsibility for its exercise is, for all we know, in the man of the moon. They have got the button among them, that is certain, but the fortunate possessor has not yet been detected.

The Bank reminds us, in truth, of that race of mischievous amphibious animals, called water rats, which are neither amenable to the laws of the land, nor the laws of the sea. When detected in rifling the house they take shelter in the docks; and when routed thence ensconce themselves in the cellar. The very best mousers are at fault, and the rats escape with impunity. Whether they have any learned counsel to aid or abet them, we cannot say, but rather apprehend that such is the case, since all experience verifies the fact, that no rogue will ever lack a pettifogger, who has discretion enough to steal a cheese for a fee.

The truth is, that such corporate bodies as the Bank of the United States, being founded on no general principle of law, are in fact amenable to none, and always escape the responsibility of their illegal acts by the aid of shuffling chicanery, stimulated by the ample means of remuneration in their possession. Legal opinions may be bought like any other commodity, and so may the men who sell them, if the price is proportioned to the dignity and value of the purchase. Having neither souls nor bodies, corporations cannot be brought to a sense of shame by exposure, nor to a sense of justice by the fear of punishment. They can neither feel disgrace nor smart under corporeal infliction. They belong to no genus of animals; are subject to none of the laws of nature and society; and when justice seeks to lay hold of them, it finds that it has grasped at a shadow. Even High Constable Hays, the terror of all evil doers, would be at fault in hunting such game. They are private citizens, one moment asserting their natural and constitutional rights; the next a corporate body, sheltering itself in the obscurity of its equivocal being, and claiming the privilege of exemption from the duties and responsibilities of private individuals. Thus dodging about from side to side, and availing itself of pettifogging subtilties, a full purse, and a brazen face, the Bank of the United States has hitherto baffled the scrutiny of the public inquest, defied the constituted authorities of the nation, and triumphed in the impunity of detected yet unpunished guilt.

But there is one great and omnipotent tribunal it cannot evade—the tribunal of the sovereign people of the United States. To that tribunal it must come at last, and by that tribunal it will be condemned to annihilation.

You cannot FEE THEM—they are too virtuous to be corrupted by bribes, and if they were not so, too numerous to be bribed. A few of their leaders may be seduced by the temptations of ambition and avarice combined; but a nation of freemen, never yet bowed their necks to the yoke, even though it were of solid gold. The doom of the Bank of the United States is sealed; the condemnation is in the mouths and hearts of the American people; and the evils inflicted upon them by that powerful, unprincipled corporation, will be amply repaid by the deep detestation they will ever afterwards feel for such a dangerous and unconstitutional monopoly.

THE BANK PARTY.

[*From the Evening Post of June* 12, 1834.]

WHOEVER is an observer of the signs of the times must have noticed the earnest and painful efforts of the Bank party to rid themselves of that appellation. They have recently been endeavouring with great zeal to persuade the world that they are not partizans of the United States Bank; that the re-charter of that institution is a matter of secondary consequence with them; and the chief object of their warfare with the democracy of the country is to rescue the Constitution from the hands of a despot and usurper; to correct the evils of Executive misrule; and to retrieve the land from the ruin which is laying it waste and desolate. The question to be decided, they say, is not *Bank or no Bank*, but *Laws or no Laws*. If they are sincere in these professions, then must the strife of parties cease at once; for surely the democracy will never be found warring against those who avow the same principles, and aim at the same objects with themselves. To prevent usurpation, repress tyranny, and maintain a system of equal and just laws, have always been the great aims of the democratic party. These form at all times, and under all circumstances, the main precepts of their doctrine, and furnish the battle-cry of their political contests. If those with whom we have been hitherto contending are animated by the same sentiments, and directed by the same motives, let us at once drop our weapons, clasp each others' hands in fellowship, and proceed hereafter in a united band, like brothers, not disputing each inch of ground, like foes. But before we cast aside our arms and offer tokens of amity, it may be well to scrutinize these pretensions, and compare them with the conduct of those by whom they are avowed.

The despotism and usurpation of the chief magistrate, as far as any specific accusation can be inferred from the vague charges uttered against him, consists in the removal of the Government deposites from the United States Bank. The Senate, it is true, in passing their verdict against him, were careful to exclude from it all specification of particular offences. While they pronounced him guilty of high crimes and misdemeanors, they left it to conjecture to discover the transgression, with no narrower limit to circumscribe its search than the vague phrase of "late executive proceedings in relation to the public revenue." But though that extraordinary sentence is thus indefinite in its description of the particular act it condemns, there are circumstances which point to the removal of the deposites as the measure which has given occasion to such a world of denunciations against infringements of the constitution, and such pious horror of executive despotism and usurpation. This is the particular act of the administration against which the slings and arrows of an outrageous party are incessantly discharged. The removal of the deposites is the theme of their newspaper tirades; it is the burden of all their petitions to Congress; it is the topic on which Bank orators in that body have exhausted their eloquence, and well nigh exhausted the English language of its terms of invective and reproach. We take it then, that the removal of the deposites is the measure which is relied upon to prove the Executive a tyrant and usurper.

It is not necessary to the purpose of this article that we should establish either the policy or the constitutionality of that measure. Let us first examine if our opponents are sincere in alleging that their warfare is in defence of a violated Constitution, not in defence of the United States Bank. If they are really not a Bank party, but a Constitutional party; if their object is not to perpetuate a huge moneyed institution, too powerful for a free people to risk, and too corrupt for a virtuous people to endure; but to re-establish the Constitution in its original strength and simplicity, before the spirit of expediency had strained any of its provisions to larger issues than its framers designed, and before the fatal precedent had been pleaded to justify subsequent perversions—if our opponents are governed by such motives, no wonder that they reject with scorn the appellation of Bank party.

But if we look back to the history of their hostility to the Executive, shall we find that it commenced with the removal of the deposites? Shall we find that before that act they yielded him their support, joined with him in censuring the corruptions of the Bank, and manifested no desire for the renewal of its charter? Shall we not on the contrary, find that a large portion of those who now fight against the administration under a common banner, and shout a common war-cry, were as decidedly opposed to Andrew Jackson before he was elected chief magistrate as they are at this moment? Shall we not find that they misrepresented his actions, maligned his motives, and even slandered his dead wife, while she lay yet hardly cold in her grave? And on his being chosen by the People to preside over them, did the enmity of these champions of the Constitution cease? Did they not embarrass his administration by every art that ingenuity could devise, and shower on his head every reproach that slander could invent? Did they not deride his public measures, and traduce his private conduct—at one moment denouncing him as a military chieftain ruling with the sword, and the next as a superannuated imbecile, blindly led by flatterers and favourites? Did they not receive his very first suggestion to Congress relative to the United States Bank with jeers and hisses? Did they not defend the conduct of that institution in all its successive steps of wickedness and corruption?—its interference in elections, its infidelity to its trust in the business of the three per cent. stock—its corruption of the press—its enormous over-issues, inducing ruinous speculation—its rapid curtailments, causing wide-spread ruin and distress—and finally its audacious violation of its charter, by turning a Committee of Congress from its doors? To these questions every man not deaf or blind, physically or mentally, must return an answer in the affirmative.

The other portion of this patriotic party, which is now waging fight in defence of the Constitution and laws against the usurpations of a despot, is composed of those true lovers of their country and its happy institutions who, a little while ago, showed their devotion for the constitution by raising the standard of rebellion—by arming themselves against the laws—and threatening to cut to pieces the officer who should attempt to carry them into execution. The tyranny and usurpation of the Chief Magistrate were then shown in his preserving the Union against their parricidal assaults and taming their fiery spirits to obedience. Their foiled leader, moved by restless ambition and implacable hatred, now stands among the foremost champions of the Bank—he who but a few months since was ready to drown the country in blood in defence of state rights, is now the advocate of an institution, which has not a word of warrant in the Constitution, and the inevitable effect of which, sooner or later, must be to melt this confederation into one vast consolidated empire, and place an aristocracy at its head.

These are the materials of which the party opposed to the administration is mainly composed. There are joined with them, a certain class of men in the mercantile cities, who are such pure and intelligent patriots, that no question, of whatever importance to the country, could bring them into the field of politics, unless it directly affected their personal and pecuniary interest—men whose hearts are in their money-bags—whose patriotism rises and falls with the rates of exchange and the price of stocks—whose constitutional scruples are so nice, that it is a sufficient answer with them to all the objections to the United States Bank, that it furnishes a convenient medium for the management of domestic exchanges. These men join in the cry of executive tyranny and usurpation, and complain that the national faith is violated by the removal of the deposites!

This then is the party which claims to be called Whigs, and repudiates the name of the Bank party. Yet what are they contending for but the re-charter of the United States Bank? What has the Senate of the United States been doing for six months past, but reading and making speeches about memorials praying for the restoration of the deposites and the renewal of the Bank charter? What is the burden of every harangue from the opponents of the administration, but a declaration that the country cannot prosper without a national Bank? What is the object of every journal of their party, but to obtain a re-charter of the Bank? Bank! Bank! Bank! is their constant theme—it is the prayer of their meetings —the topic of their newspaper declamation—and the beginning, middle and end of the violent philippics of the partizans of that institution in Congress. The Bank is the band which holds this ill-assorted party together—it is the magazine which furnishes them with weapons—it is the treasury which supplies them with means. It is by the aid of the Bank that they hope to pull down the administration.

The cry of Executive usurpation and despotism is mere declamation to mislead the unwary—it is mere dust and smoke to hide the real object. The Bank is the real object of the warfare; for it is only through the Bank that any leader of the desperate faction can hope to succeed. Yet aware of the honest indignation felt by the People at the contemplation of the numerous acts of corruption and audacity practised by that institution—and particularly afraid of the effect of its last daring and unprecedented step—they now seek to cast off the name of Bank party, and to be known only by their stolen appellation of Whigs. Whigs, indeed! What right have they to that title, inseparably associated as it is with the memory of patriotism and valour and manly worth? What right have they—tories in all that distinguished tories in the revolution—to a name which implies love of freedom and the equal rights of mankind? No, let us not lose sight of their proper—their *only proper designation.* They are not whigs, and from this hour forth shall never be so styled in this journal. They are the BANK PARTY—a name significant of infamy—a name with which they will go down in history, and

"Stink in the nose of all succeeding time,—"

a name which they have richly earned by their unprincipled support of an unconstitutional, dangerous, most corrupt and usurping institution. Let that name stick to them. The democracy ought to call them by no other.

CONDUCT OF THE BANK.

[*From the Evening Post, June* 9, 1834.]

THE Bank of the United States desires to carry on its business in secret and hide the record of its corruptions from every eye, and the Senate of the United States, some of whose members are doubtless governed in the matter by strong reasons, are determined to gratify that desire. The Bank has now been more than six months wholly free from the supervision of Government Directors. The Senate have made the office of Government Director so unpleasantly conspicuous, and the honest exercise of its duties a subject of such reproaches and abuse, that there are few men willing to accept the unenviable trust, and those who do are turned away from the Bank on the ground of their not having been *invited!* The reader ought not to lose sight of the fact that the conduct of the Board of Directors of the Branch Bank in this city to Saul Alley, *was in pursuance of orders from Nicholas Biddle!* The two checks provided by the cautious framers of the Bank charter, to prevent it from abusing its enormous money power—namely the right of the Government to be represented by five directors at its Board, and of either House of Congress to appoint a Committee to look into its affairs, are completely destroyed by the high-handed conduct of that guilty institution, and its collusory assistants in the United States Senate. How much longer will this audacious monopoly be allowed to abuse the patience of the People?

TRUE FUNCTIONS OF GOVERNMENT.

[*From the Evening Post, Nov.* 21, 1834.]

"There are no necessary evils in Government. Its evils exist only in its abuses. If it would confine itself to *equal protection*, and, as heaven does its rains, shower its favours alike on the high and the low, the rich and the poor, it would be an unqualified blessing."

This is the language of our venerated President, and the passage deserves to be written in letters of gold, for neither in truth of sentiment or beauty of expression can it be surpassed. We choose it as our text for a few remarks on the true functions of Government.

The fundamental principle of all governments is the protection of person and property from domestic and foreign enemies; in other words, to defend the weak against the strong. By establishing the social feeling in a community, it was intended to counteract that selfish feeling, which, in its proper exercise, is the parent of all worldly good, and, in its excesses, the root of all evil. The functions of Government, when confined to their proper sphere of action, are therefore restricted to the making of *general laws*, uniform and universal in their operation, for these purposes, and for no other.

Governments have no right to interfere with the pursuits of individuals, as guarantied by those general laws, by offering encouragements and granting privileges to any particular class of industry, or any select bodies of men, inasmuch as all classes of industry and all men are equally important to the general welfare, and equally entitled to protection.

Whenever a Government assumes the power of discriminating between the different classes of the community, it becomes, in effect, the arbiter of their prosperity, and exercises a power not contemplated by any intelligent people in delegating their sovereignty to their rulers. It then becomes the great regulator of the profits of every species of industry, and reduces men from a dependence on their own exertions, to a dependence on the caprices of their Government. Governments possess no delegated right to tamper with individual industry a single hair's-breadth beyond what is essential to protect the rights of person and property.

In the exercise of this power of intermeddling with the private pursuits and individual occupations of the citizen, a Government may at pleasure elevate one class and depress another ; it may one day legislate exclusively for the farmer, the next for the mechanic, and the third for the manufacturer, who all thus become the mere puppets of legislative cobbling and tinkering, instead of independent citizens, relying on their own resources for their prosperity. It assumes the functions which belong alone to an overruling Providence, and affects to become the universal dispenser of good and evil.

This power of regulating—of increasing or diminishing the profits of labour and the value of property of all kinds and degrees, by direct legislation, in a great measure destroys the essential object of all civil compacts, which, as we said before, is to make the social a counterpoise to the selfish feeling. By thus operating directly on the latter, by offering one class a bounty and another a discouragement, they involve the selfish feeling in every struggle of party for the ascendancy, and give to the force of political rivalry all the bitterest excitement of personal interests conflicting with each other. Why is it that parties now exhibit excitement aggravated to a degree dangerous to the existence of the Union and to the peace of society? Is it not that by frequent exercises of partial legislation, almost every man's personal interests have become deeply involved in the result of the contest? In common times, the strife of parties is the mere struggle of ambitious leaders for power; now they are deadly contests of the whole mass of the people, whose pecuniary interests are implicated in the event, because the Government has usurped and exercised the power of legislating on their private affairs. The selfish feeling has been so strongly called into action by this abuse of authority as almost to overpower the social feeling, which it should be the object of a good Government to foster by every means in its power.

No nation, knowingly and voluntarily, with its eyes open, ever delegated to its Government this enormous power, which places at its disposal the property, the industry, and the fruits of the industry, of the whole people. As a general rule, the prosperity of rational men depends on themselves. Their talents and their virtues shape their fortunes. They are therefore the best judges of their own affairs, and should be permitted to seek their own happiness in their own way, untrammelled by the capricious interference of legislative bungling, so long as they do not violate the equal rights of others, nor transgress the general laws for the security of person and property.

But modern refinements have introduced new principles in the science of Government. Our own Government, most especially, has assumed and exercised an authority over the people, not unlike that of weak and vacillating parents over their children, and with about the same degree of impartiality. One child becomes a favourite because he has made a fortune, and another because he has failed in the pursuit of that object; one because of its beauty, and another because of its deformity. Our Government has thus exercised the right of dispensing favours to one or another class of citizens at will; of directing its patronage first here and then there;

of bestowing one day and taking back the next; of giving to the few and denying to the many; of investing wealth with new and exclusive privileges, and distributing, as it were at random, and with a capricous policy, in unequal portions, what it ought not to bestow, or what, if given away, should be equally the portion of all.

A government administered on such a system of policy may be called a Government of Equal Rights, but it is in its nature and essence a disguised despotism. It is the capricious dispenser of good and evil, without any restraint, except its own sovereign will. It holds in its hand the distribution of the goods of this world, and is consequently the uncontrolled master of the people.

Such was not the object of the Government of the United States, nor such the powers delegated to it by the people. The object was beyond doubt to protect the weak against the strong, by giving them an equal voice and equal rights in the state; not to make one portion stronger, the other weaker at pleasure, by crippling one or more classes of the community, or making them tributary to one alone. This is too great a power to entrust to Government. It was never given away by the people, and is not a right, but a usurpation.

Experience will show that this power has always been exercised under the influence and for the exclusive benefit of wealth. It was never wielded in behalf of the community. Whenever an exception is made to the general law of the land, founded on the principle of equal rights, it will always be found to be in favour of wealth. These immunities are never bestowed on the poor. They have no claim to a dispensation of exclusive benefits, and their only business is to "*take care of the rich that the rich may take care of the poor.*"

Thus it will be seen that the sole reliance of the labouring classes, who constitute a vast majority of every people on the earth, is the great principle of Equal Rights; that their only safeguard against oppression is a system of legislation which leaves all to the free exercise of their talents and industry, within the limits of the GENERAL LAW, and which, on no pretence of public good, bestows on any particular class of industry, or any particular body of men, rights or privileges not equally enjoyed by the great aggregate of the body politic.

Time will remedy the departures which have already been made from this sound republican system, if the people but jealously watch and indignantly frown on any future attempts to invade their equal rights, or appropriate to the few what belongs to all alike. To quote, in conclusion, the language of the great man, with whose admirable sentiment we commenced these remarks, "it is time to pause in our career—if we cannot at once, in justice to the interests vested under improvident legislation, make our government what it ought to be, we can at least take a stand against all new grants of monopolies and exclusive privileges, and against any prostitution of our Government to the advancement of the few at the expense of the many."

CORPORATIONS.

[*From the Evening Post, November* 22, 1834.]

In reading the lucubrations of the advocates of monopolies and incorporations, one might be induced to wonder how other countries, not favoured with the marvelous expedients for "the proper development of enterprise," and "the employment of capital," managed not only to exist, but to enjoy a reasonable degree of prosperity. According to their doctrine, the people, in their capacity of a body politic, can do nothing; individual capital, except aided by exclusive privileges, can do nothing in the way of public improvements. Without incorporations we can have no roads; without incorporations we can have no canals, or any other public improvements; without incorporations we can have no money; and, by and by, we shall perhaps be told that unless the bakers be incorporated we shall have no bread. In order to have public improvements, "a proper development of enterprise," and "a beneficial employment of capital," it would seem, according to these writers, that it is indispensable that the great mass of the people should be divested of the Equal Rights guarantied to them by the constitution.

Did these advocates of incorporations ever read of the great Roman acqueduct for conveying water from Tusculum to Rome? Did they ever hear of the Appian way, both the work of one single man? Or did they ever hear of the Flaminian way, also the work of one magnificent Roman? These works, like the Egyptian pyramids, seem destined to be coeval with the duration of the earth which supports them. Some twenty centuries have elapsed since their construction, and almost a hundred generations have availed themselves of these great public benefits, and still they remain the almost eternal monuments of individual public spirit. Will any of our railroads, or incorporated bridges, last as long? For a period of near two thousand years, the inhabitants of Rome, and all the world that flocked to Rome, have enjoyed the benefits of these great public improvements, without paying a single cent in tolls, or for a drink of water, and without the grant of a single exclusive privilege to any man or association of men. Neither Appius Claudius, nor Titus Flaminius, nor their heirs, ever levied contributions on the people of Rome for the water of the acqueduct, or the use of the road. We never heard that either Appius or Flaminius was incorporated ; transmuted into irresponsible nonentities, above the laws, or so slippery as to evade their operation. They were mere simple individuals—one an orator, the other a soldier who fell in defending his country against Hannibal. Actuated by a noble spirit of patriotism, they gave to their countrymen, as a free gift, what it seems can now only be attained in this modern republic by grants of exclusive privileges, and by a perpetual tax upon the people.

All the ancient world is filled with instances of these noble benefactions for public purposes ; and is there any reason why this new world should not emulate the example ? A few Stephen Girards might in a similar spirit of munificence confer equal benefits on this country. But we do not rely upon individual wealth or patriotism to do all that is salutary in the way of public improvements. We look to the wants of the people, and to the great interests of the community at large for such purposes. Is the hope fallacious, or have we no examples to encourage us ?

Let us see what the People, through the agency of their representatives, have already done in this and other States of the Union ; and let us look what they and their rulers have done elsewhere. Was the great canal of Languedoc the work of an incorporated company ? Was that system of canals in China, to which the old world affords no parallel, the work of an incorporated company or companies ? Are the great system of internal improvements, in operation in Pennsylvania and Ohio, the work of incorporated companies, or are they the work of the people of those states through the agency of their common representatives, and by means of their common resources ? And last, though not least, have not the greatest works of this age, the Erie and Champlain canals, been achieved by the people, the great body politic of the state, after an incorporated company had totally failed in completing one small section of this noble enterprise? Nay, let us go further, and ask whether in nine cases in ten incorporated companies for great national objects, have not failed, and been obliged at last to throw themselves on the charity of the state for support? Have we forgotten the Delaware and Hudson Canal Company, and the loans of state credit? And is it not notorious that at this moment the Ohio and Chesapeake Canal Company is dependent on Congress for the ability to pay the interest on its Dutch loan? Instances might be multiplied to tediousness were it necessary, but the recollection of every man will supply them.

In the face of these undeniable facts, we are not to be told, that we are for putting an end to all future public improvements, because we are opposed to incorporations. The imputation is as weak as it is unfounded, for the examples we have adduced, and could adduce by scores, sufficiently prove that incorporated companies are not indispensable, not even safe agents to depend upon for our public improvements.

We will suppose, however, for the sake of argument, that the canals of New York had been the work of incorporations, and not of the great body politic acting through its representatives. The charter being perpetual, the tolls would of course be also perpetual, and thus the people of this and other states making use of these conveniences, would have paid a perpetual tax to the company, long after it had been amply remunerated for all the expense and risk of constructing them. Being however the work of the people the case is far otherwise. The tolls are now rapidly extinguishing the canal debt; in a few years it will be entirely paid, and the people will then enjoy this great public benefit, at the trifling cost of keeping it in repair. On the other hand, the company would enjoy a perpetuity; it would accumulate millions upon millions of the money of the people, and every attempt to diminish its exorbitant gains, would be resisted as an innovation on the sacred principle of "vested rights."

Here then is exhibited a complete and fair exemplification of the relative advantages of a system of public improvements prosecuted by the people themselves, and one exclusively confined to incorporations. In the one case the people after paying for the improvement, enjoy it ever afterwards free of all taxes, except for repairs; in the other they are saddled with a perpetual burden, and condemned to pay for it ten times over to the corporation. It may be said, that there is no advantage in this exemption from toll to the state, by the state, since the money is paid by one hand and received by the other. But this is a view of the case entirely fallacious. The doctrine would equally apply to every species of taxation, and it might be asserted with equal truth, that the amount of public burdens is a matter of no sort of consequence, provided the money is again distributed among the people. This we know is one of the favourite fallacies of a particular school of political economists, but it will not do here we trust. According to them, every thing moves in a circle; the money taken from the people is distributed among them again, and the circulation like that of the blood, gives life and vigour to the body politic. The mischief however is, that there is no certainty that the same man who pays five dollars, will ever receive it back again; and that if he does, it is so long in coming, that "while the grass grows the steed may starve." Generally speaking, every man's money is safest in his own pocket, and he does not require the aid of government in its distribution.

LITERARY CORPORATIONS.

[*From the Evening Post, November* 26, 1834.]

WHEN, a few days ago, we expressed the opinion, that so contrary to the principle of equal liberty is the principle of corporations, that a legislature, governed by sincere and enlightened sentiments of democracy, would refuse to incorporate even a college or a church, an exclamation of pious horror was raised by certain opposition prints, which were very glad, no doubt, to seize the pretext of regard for the institutions and best interests of learning and religion, as an occasion for defending their favourite aristocratic system of monopolies and exclusive privileges, through the instrumentality of which alone can they ever hope to break down the power of the people, and reduce the many into subserviency to the few. That what we said did not proceed from any want of veneration for the vast benefits to society of religion and learning, our readers will readily believe; and, indeed, this might be inferred from the very ground on which we assail the principle of corporations, as hostile to the principle of equal freedom; since we think it will not be denied that a free country, of all others, is most favourable to the cause of religion and virtue, and to the development of the human mind. But if we look at the subject of corporate institutions of learning merely in a politico-economical point of view, we think it will be easy to discover that the interests of society are not promoted by giving charters of incorporation to seminaries of education. We shall make this the subject of our leading article this afternoon; and in the first place let us propose the following questions.

Have the charters of incorporation bestowed on our colleges contributed, in general, to promote the ends of their institution? Have they contributed to encourage the diligence, and to improve the abilities of the teachers? Have they directed the course of education towards objects more useful, both to the individual and to the public, than those to which it would naturally have gone of its own accord? It would not seem very difficult to give at least a probable answer to each of these questions

In every profession, the exertion of the greater part of those who exercise it, is always in proportion to the necessity they are under of making that exertion. This necessity is greatest with those to whom the emoluments of their profession are the only source from which they expect their fortune, or even their ordinary revenue and subsistence. In order to acquire this fortune, or even to get this subsistence, they must, in the course of a year, execute a certain quantity of work of a known value; and where the competition is free, the rivalship of competitors, who are all endeavouring to justle one another out of employment, obliges every man to endeavour to execute his work with a certain degree of exactness. The greatness of the objects which are to be acquired by success in some particular professions, may, no doubt, sometimes animate the exertions of a few men of extraordinary spirit and ambition. Great objects, however, are evidently not necessary in order to create the greatest exertions. Rivalship and emulation render excellency, even in mean professions, an object of ambition, and frequently occasion the very greatest exertions. Great objects, on the contrary, alone and unsupported by the necessity of application, have seldom been sufficient to occasion any considerable exertion. Success in the profession of the law leads to some very great objects of ambition; and yet how few men, born to easy fortunes, have ever, in this country, been eminent in that profession!

One of the effects of the charters of corporation bestowed on colleges, is to give to those institutions the facility of acquiring, in their corporate capacity, and holding from generation to generation, a large amount of property. Out of the revenue of this property the salaries of professors are paid, either in whole or in part. Only a portion of the expenses of the institutions, in most cases, at least, is defrayed from the sum received for tuition. The subsistence of a professor, then, so far as it is defrayed out of the permanent revenue of the corporation, is evidently derived from a fund altogether independent of his success and reputation in his particular profession. His interest is, in this case, set as directly in opposition to his duty as it is possible to set it. It is the interest of every man to live as much at his ease as he can ; and if his emoluments are to be precisely the same whether he does or does not perform some very laborious duty, it is certainly his interest, at least as interest is vulgarly understood, either to neglect it altogether, or, if he is subject to some authority which will not suffer him to do this, to perform it in as careless and slovenly a manner as that authority will permit. If he is naturally active and a lover of labour, it is his interest to employ that activity in any way from which he can derive some advantage, rather than in the performance of his duty, from which he can derive none.

If the authority to which he is subject resides in the body corporate, the college, or universitv, of which he himself is a member, and in which the greater part of the other members are, like himself, persons who either are or ought to be teachers, they are likely to make a common cause, to be all very indulgent to one another, and every man to consent that his neighbour may neglect his duty, provided he himself is allowed to neglect his own.

If the authority to which he is subject resides, not so

much in the body corporate of which he is a member, as in some other extraneous persons, in the governor, for example, or in a board of regents, it is not indeed in this case very likely that he will be suffered to neglect his duty altogether. All that such superiors, however, can force him to do, is to attend upon his pupils a certain number of hours, that is, to give a certain number of lectures in the week, or in the year. What those lectures shall be, must still depend upon the diligence of the teacher; and that diligence is as likely to be proportioned to the motives which he has for exerting it. An extraneous jurisdiction of this kind, besides, is liable to be exercised both ignorantly and capriciously. In its nature it is arbitrary and discretionary; and the persons who exercise it, neither attending upon the lectures of the teachers themselves, nor perhaps understanding the sciences which it is their business to teach, are seldom capable of exercising it with judgment. From the insolence of office, too, they are frequently indifferent how they exercise it, and are very apt to censure or deprive of office wantonly and without just cause. The person subject to such jurisdiction is necessarily degraded by it, and, instead of being one of the most respectable, is rendered one of the meanest and most contemptible persons in society. It is by powerful protection only that he can effectually guard himself against the bad usage to which he is at all times exposed; and this protection he is most likely to gain, not by ability and diligence in his profession, but by obsequiousness to the will of his superiors, and by being ready at all times to sacrifice to that will the rights, the interest, and the honour of the body corporate of which he is a member. Whoever has attended for any considerable time to the administration of a French university, must have had occasion to remark the effects which naturally result from an arbitrary and extraneous jurisdiction of this kind.

Whatever forces a certain number of students to any college or university, independent of the merit and reputation of the teachers, tends more or less to diminish the necessity of that merit and reputation.

The privileges of graduates in arts, &c. when they can be obtained only by residing a certain number of years in certain universities, necessarily force a certain number of students to such universities, independent of the merit and reputation of the teachers. The privileges of graduates are a sort of statutes of apprenticeship, which have contributed to the improvement of education, just as the other statutes of apprenticeship have to that of arts and manufactures.

The discipline of corporate colleges is in general contrived, not for the benefit of the students, but for the interest, or more properly speaking, for the ease of the masters. Its object is, in all cases, to maintain the authority of the master, and, whether he neglects or performs his duty, to oblige the students in all cases to behave to him as if he performed it with the greatest diligence and ability. It seems to presume perfect wisdom and virtue in the one order, and the greatest weakness and folly in the other. Where the masters, however, really perform their duty, there are no examples, I believe, that the greater part of the students ever neglect theirs. No discipline is ever requisite to force attendance upon lectures which are really worth attending, as is well known wherever any such lectures are given.

Force and restraint may, no doubt, be in some degree requisite in order to oblige children, or very young boys, to attend to those parts of education which it is thought necessary for them to acquire during that early period of life ; but after twelve or thirteen years of age, provided the master does his duty, force or restraint can scarce ever be necessary to carry on any part of education. Such is the generosity of the greater part of young men, that, so far from being disposed to neglect or despise the instructions of their master, provided he shows some serious intention of being of use to them, they are generally inclined to pardon a great deal of incorrectness in the performance of his duty, and sometimes even to conceal from the public a good deal of gross negligence. Those parts of education, it is to be observed, for the teaching of which there are no public institutions, are generally the best taught. Schools have no exclusive privileges. In order to obtain the honours of graduation, it is not necessary that a person should bring a certificate of his having studied a certain number of years at a public school. If upon examination he appears to understand what is taught there, no questions are asked about the place where he learnt it.

In the attention which the ancient philosophers excited, in the empire which they acquired over the opinions and principles of their auditors, in the faculty which they possessed of giving a certain tone and character to the conduct and conversation of those auditors; they appear to have been much superior to any modern teachers. In modern times, the diligence of public teachers is more or less corrupted by the circumstances, which render them more or less independent of their success and reputation in their particular professions. Their salaries too put the private teacher, who would pretend to come into competition with them, in the same state with a merchant who attempts to trade without a bounty, in competition with those who trade with a considerable one. If he sells his goods at nearly the same price, he cannot have the same profit, and poverty and beggary at least, if not bankruptcy and ruin, will infallibly be his lot. If he attempts to sell them much dearer, he is likely to have so few customers that his circumstances will not be much mended. The "privileges" of graduation, besides, can be obtained only by attending the lectures of the incorporated institutions. The most careful attendance upon the ablest instructions of any private teacher, cannot always give any title to demand them. It is from these different causes that the private teacher of any of the sciences which are commonly taught in universities, is in modern times generally considered as in the very lowest order of men of letters. A man of real abilities can scarce find out a more humiliating or a more unprofitable employment to turn them to. The endowments of schools and colleges have, in this manner, not only corrupted the diligence of public teachers, but have rendered it almost impossible to have any good private ones.

Were there no public institutions for education, no system, no science would be taught for which there was not some demand; or which the circumstances of the times did not render it, either necessary, or convenient, or at least fashionable to learn. A private teacher could never find his account in teaching, either an exploded and antiquated system of a science acknowledged to be useful, or a science universally believed to be a mere useless and pedantic heap of sophistry and nonsense. Such systems, such sciences, can subsist no where, but in those incorporated societies for education whose prosperity and revenue are in a great measure independent of their reputation, and altogether independent of their industry. Were there no public institutions for education, a gentleman, after going through, with application and abilities, the most complete course of education which the circumstances of the times were supposed to afford, could not come into the world completely ignorant of every thing which is the common subject of conversation among gentlemen and men of the world.

But in placing these speculations before our readers, do we not run some risk of being again called "a little free-trade crazy?" Let those who cannot controvert the views and arguments ascribe them to lunacy, or idiocy, if they please. They are at all events the views and arguments, ay, and the very language, too, of Adam Smith, from whose immortal work on the Wealth of Nations we have borrowed these paragraphs, having copied them literally, with the exception of two or three slight verbal changes.

CHARACTER OF MR. VAN BUREN.

[*From the Evening Post, January* 19, 1835.]

DURING the session of the national and state legislatures, so many subjects crowd upon our attention and occupy our columns, that we are frequently obliged to dismiss, with a very cursory and imperfect notice, matters which intrinsically deserve careful and particular comment. This was the case with the letter of Mr. Benton to the Democratic Convention of the State of Mississippi, declining their nomination of him as a candidate for Vice President, which we recently had the pleasure of laying before our readers. That letter so highly creditable to Mr. Benton's mind and heart, so illustrative of his intelligence, firmness, candour, and sincerity, contained matters well worthy of being recommended to the consideration of the democracy in every part of the Union, by frequent and earnest editorial comments.

The great object which Mr. Benton had in view, was to impress upon the attention of the people of the United

States, the necessity of harmony and concert in relation to the candidates for the two highest offices of the Government, if they wish to succeed in those cardinal objects of the republican party which are of incalculably more importance than ever can be, under any circumstances, the gratification of mere personal preferences or sectional pride. To ensure this harmony, as far as lay in his own power, Mr. Benton did not merely exercise his eloquent pen in delineating the consequences which would almost inevitably flow from divided councils, but gave the strongest proof of his disinterestedness and magnanimity, by positively declining the high compliment which had been paid him, and refusing to suffer his name to be used as a candidate for Vice President, thus removing one circumstance which he feared might prove an obstacle to the desired concord. In thus doing, though sinister objects are of course imputed to him by those whose business and pleasure it is to revile all the prominent champions of democratic principles, yet no person of the least candour can help feeling, in his secret heart, that Mr. Benton has exhibited an evidence of singleness of motive and nobleness of character which entitle him to the increased admiration and respect, not only of every true republican, but of every man, whatever his political creed, who can appreciate the sacrifices of disinterested patriotism.

It would have been highly pleasing to us, we are free to confess, if it had been considered quite compatible with the important end of a perfect union and harmony of purpose and action among the democracy in all parts of the country, to have seen Mr. Benton placed before the people as the republican candidate for Vice President. Well has he deserved such a mark of honour. His consistency, industry and zeal in the cause of the people; his vigilance in detecting the arts of the aristocracy; his fearlessness in exposing them; his readiness to stand forward, at all times, as the champion of democratic principles; his eloquence; his blunt and manly independence of character; and the honest boldness with which his indignant feelings have always led him to rebuke those who seek personal aggrandizement at the expense of the equal rights of man: these are qualities which have won for Mr. Benton the general regard of the democracy, and have caused many to desire that he might be nominated as the successor of Martin Van Buren in the place which the latter now so worthily fills.

We do not know, however, whether the true interests of the people are not better answered by the course Mr. Benton has determined to pursue. Much as he deserves to be elevated to a higher post, we do not know whether he could well be spared from that where he is now stationed. His talents, his firmness, his assiduity, his unshrinking courage, his powerful eloquence, are needed in the Senate chamber. We do not question that he would adorn other stations; but for that of Senator he seems peculiarly adapted. His masculine understanding, his resolute heart, his diligent and unwearied application, are now exerted in their proper sphere. To him public business seems not a task, but a pleasure; and if he has ambition (as no great mind is without it) his recent noble act of self-denial sufficiently proves that his at least is not the ambition which begins and ends and centres all in self, but that nobler kind which seeks to win its way through the laborious gradations of public service, and achieve its object by promoting the real good of his fellow-men.

Those who duly consider Mr. Benton's letter, will find in it a conclusive answer to the clamorous objections which the aristocracy urge against Martin Van Buren. Most of these objections consist of the catchwords of party declamation, and do not deserve reply, until they can be shown to rest on some more substantial basis than the mere imputations of political hostility. The epithets of magician and intriguer have been reiterated against him, for may years, with all the earnestness of vituperative malice ; but we are not aware that any proof has yet been exhibited, or even attempted, that he either practices "arts inhibited," or that he winds his way to his object through the devious and covert mazes of subtlety and intrigue. We have been attentive readers, for a long time past, of the charges against Mr. Van Buren, and close observers of his public conduct ; and our respect for his talents, his integrity, and his patriotism, for the purity of his motives, and the wisdom of his proceedings, has increased the more we have read and observed. Mere denunciation, however often reiterated, is not likely to injure a public man in the estimation of the intelligent citizens of this country. Had it been otherwise, we should have lacked the executive services of the illustrious Jefferson ; the reins of Government would never have been swayed by the patriot Jackson ; and Martin Van Buren would long since have been consigned to infamy or oblivion. But happily "curses kill not ;" and till something more relative than gibes and anathemas of a factious aristocracy can be uttered against Mr. Van Buren, he stands in little danger, we think, of losing his strong hold on the affections of the democracy of the United States.

The brilliant passage in Mr. Benton's letter, in relation to the oft-repeated charge, that Mr. Van Buren is of the *non-committal school,* "a flippant phrase got by rote and parotted against him," must stand as a most triumphant and unanswerable vindication of his character from whatever is derogatory in the imputation. Never in any instance, where the obligations of honour or patriotism required that he should *commit* himself, has Mr.

Van Buren hesitated to speak or act. The public have not been left to guess his views on important questions. He has not, it is true, obtruded himself, uncalled for, before the nation, and hastily volunteered opinions which he was afterwards glad to retract. He has not *committed* himself, like the leading demagogues worshipped by those who raise this senseless cry, for and against the United States Bank, for and against the American System, and for and against a dozen other important national measures. His first care has been to acquaint himself thoroughly with the merits of all great questions ; and once satisfied of the right, he has taken his ground boldly and openly, and maintained it firmly to the end. Hence the extraordinary consistency of his career. No politician in this country has pursued a more even and undeviating course. And this very consistency, amidst all the fluctuations of opinion and policy, and all the vicissitudes of public events, is as strong an evidence as can be adduced of the soundness of his motives, and the boldness of his character.

Had Mr. Van Buren been distinguished by that species of timidity which is implied in the phrase *non-committal*, instead of pursuing his straight-forward course through good report and through evil report, he would have accommodated himself to the variations of public sentiment ; he would have trimmed his sail to the popular breeze ; he would have veered and tacked, now steering to this point, and now to that, until his course was as mazy as that of Mr. Webster or Mr. Clay. But timidity, or at least that species of timidity which springs from selfish ambition, is no part of the character of Mr. Van Buren. If he has ever hesitated, it has only been until he could satisfy himself what was demanded by the true interests of his country. "Interested timidity," says Burke, "disgraces as much in the cabinet, as personal timidity does in the field. *But timidity, with regard to the well-being of our country, is heroic virtue.*" This is the extent of Mr. Van Buren's timidity—this is the only sense in which the cry of "non-committal" has any truth.

There is another point in the Letter of Mr. Benton, to which we take pleasure in inviting the attention of our readers. It comes in here as an appropriate illustration of the absurdity of the charge to which we have just referred. We allude to the brief exposition it contains of Mr. Van Buren's views on the subject of the Bank system. What Mr. Benton says on that subject, must be looked upon as authentic. The nation has a right to consider it as said by Mr. Van Buren himself; for the circumstances under which this Letter was written, would have required of that gentleman, if his sentiments on any great question of public policy were inaccurately stated, to correct the error in as public a form as that in which it was made. The silence of Mr. Van Buren cannot therefore be cited as an instance of "non-committal;" but, on the contrary, he must be looked upon as having early and decidedly taken his stand on a question already of exceeding interest in several states, and destined ere long to become a chief touchstone of democratic principles throughout the Union. We have great pleasure, then, in begging our readers to take note that Mr. Van Buren "is a real hard-money man; opposed to the paper system; in favour of a national currency of gold; in favour of an adequate silver currency for common use; against the small note currency; and in favour of confining bank notes to their appropriate sphere and original functions, that of large notes for large transactions and mercantile operations."

Much has been said and written on the subject of the claims of New-York to supply an incumbent of the Presidential chair. Our paper, not a great while ago, contained a most excellent article from the Harrisburg Reporter, in which the propriety of nominating Mr. Van Buren on that ground was urged with singular eloquence and force. The article in question, as we have access to know, came from the pen of a disinterested and enlightened man, whose sentiments were the result of a broad and patriotic view of the whole subject, and had no other object than to advance the best interests of our common country. For our own part, we do not place our advocacy of Martin Van Buren on sectional grounds. It is the least of his claims, in our sense, that he drew his first breath on the soil of the Empire State. Show us a worthier man; a man whose career has been more consistent, whose services have been more useful, whose principles have been more democratic, whose character has been freer from reproach; show us a man more entitled to the confidence of the democracy, possessing a larger share of their esteem, and more likely to carry out those great republican principles which have guided the administration of Andrew Jackson; show us such a man, and we will to-morrow withdraw our support from Martin Van Buren and transfer it to that other and worthier one. But the nation contains no such man; and we therefore advocate him, not as the favourite son of New-York, but, after General Jackson, as the foremost champion of the democracy of the United States, and the candidate intrinsically best entitled to unite all their suffrages.

These are our sincere sentiments, governed by no personal considerations, by no sectional pride. Were we a denizen of the south or of the west, Martin Van Buren would still be our choice. And the south and the west and the east will unite with the "great middle" in this preference, and, with one accordant voice, will call him to preside over the republic. Aristocratic railers may continue to shower their abuse on his head, but in vain. It is the fate of all prominent asserters of democratic principles to be maligned; and if their rancour is fiercer towards Martin Van Buren than any other, it is only because he is more strongly fixed in the affections of the people. Their attachment rests on the strong basis of his real worth. They look through the aspersions of his enemies, and read the truth for themselves, and the truth in relation to that distinguished man, needs only to be known to insure him general regard. And it is known. The people of this country are too clear-sighted to be misled by the mere clamour of calumny and detraction, and there is a quality in truth itself which is sure eventually to triumph over mirepresentation.

> Truth, though it trouble some minds,
> Some wicked minds that are both dark and dangerous,
> Yet it preserves itself, comes off pure, innocent,
> And like the sun, though never so eclipsed,
> Must break in glory.

THE JOINT-STOCK PARTNERSHIP LAW.

[*From the Evening Post, January* 23, 1835.]

The Attorney General of this State, in his report on the subject of Corporations, which we published yesterday, says, "In the interpretation of the constitution, we ought, as far as possible, to enter into the mind and intention of those who framed the instrument, and *adopt that construction which will best fulfil the end for which it was made.*" We are very willing that the ninth section of the seventh article of the Constitution, which "makes the assent of two-thirds of the members elected to each branch of the legislature requisite to every bill creating, continuing, altering, or renewing any body politic or corporate," should be interpreted by this rule. The end for which that section was framed was distinctly explained by Mr. King, chairman of the committee that introduced it. "The common law abhorred *monopolies*," he said, and the object of the section was "not to increase them, but diminish them as far as we can consistently with the preservation of vested rights." He therefore had reported a clause requiring a two-thirds vote, not only for the creation of any new corporation, but for altering, continuing, or renewing any old one. But while he was desirous of placing this difficulty in the way of granting special charters of incorporation, on the ground that they were monopolies, he did not seek to abrogate or limit those general laws, then existing, under which voluntary corporations, for certain purposes, and to an indefinite number, might be formed by whomsoever chose to enter into them. Corporations, no matter for what purposes, which derived their existence from direct special legislation, were monopolies, and those the Constitution sought to diminish as far as was consistent with vested rights ; but corporations formed under laws which were of equal applicability and equally open to the whole community, were not considered monopolies, and therefore no change or modification of those laws was proposed.

We think the reader who carefully peruses the Report of the Convention which framed the Constitution, and strives "to enter into the mind and intention of those who framed the instrument, and adopt the construction which will best fulfil the end for which it was made," will agree with us in the view we have here taken. The grand general aim of the Constitution, also, to protect the community in their equal rights of person and property, ought to be kept constantly in sight ; as well as the grand democratic maxim of equality of political and civil rights, on which the Constitution and the laws all are founded.

The Attorney General is of opinion that, according to the Constitution, "the legislature cannot now provide by general laws for the incorporation of voluntary associations, but must act directly on every grant of corporate privileges, creating some one or more corporations in particular." Yet he is of opinion, at the same time, that "the legislature may, by one act, create two or more corporate bodies." That is to say, they may create ten thousand corporations by one act, if they please, only naming each particular set of individuals incorporated, but cannot pass a law establishing the general principles on which any set of individuals may form themselves into a corporation. The Constitution says, "the assent of two-thirds of the members elected to each branch of the legislature shall be requisite to every bill creating, continuing, altering, or renewing any body politic or corporate." If *every bill* creating *any body politic*, may mean a bill creating *a myriad of bodies politic*, it may mean any thing. The object of the two-thirds provision was to insure separate and careful deliberation on every particular application for a special grant of corporate privileges. If a thousand applications may be huddled together, and one bill passed granting a corporate franchise to all, the intention of the framers of the Constitution is more effectually overleaped than it possibly could be by a bill establishing the general principles and conditions under which any association of men might assume and exercise corporate powers. But the Constitution, in the Attorney General's plastic hand, is a mere nose of wax, and is moulded into what shape he pleases.

The thirteenth section of the seventeenth article of

the Constitution continued in force all laws then existing which were not repugnant to any of its provisions; but all laws or parts of laws repugnant to the Constitution were by that instrument abrogated. At the time the Constitution went into effect, general laws were in operation, under which corporations, for a variety of purposes might be created, without the direct intervention of the legislature. The Attorney General says, "the several laws providing for the creation of corporate bodies, without a special grant from the legislature, have been acted upon for the twelve years which have elapsed since this part of the Constitution went into operation, and it is believed that the validity of those laws, or the right to form associations under them, has never been seriously questioned." If those laws are valid, which we do not doubt, it is because they are not repugnant to the Constitution. But it seems, by the Attorney General's reasoning, that a law now passed, though by a two-thirds vote, and for precisely the same objects, and expressed in the same terms, would be repugnant to the Constitution. That is to say, a principle which was perfectly consistent with the Constitution in 1828, is totally contrary to it in 1834. For example, if the legislature, at its present session, should repeal one of those laws under which corporations may now be formed without a direct act, and the next legislature, convinced that the law had been useful, and that the repeal of it was unwise, should repass it by a vote of two-thirds of each House, it would not be valid, because it would be repugnant to the Constitution. It had been quite constitutional a year before, but though the Constitution in the meanwhile had undergone no change, and the law was revived in precisely the same words as before, it would be wholly null and void. We confess we cannot give our judgment up to such reasoning as this.

The general laws under which corporations were formed without special legislation prior to the adoption of the Constitution, were abrogated by that instrument, if they were repugnant to any of its provisions ; and if they were not repugnant to any of its provisions, neither would a law at this day be, framed on the same principles and in corresponding terms. The Constitution makes a vote of two-thirds necessary to create any body politic, that is any one body politic, on the ground that partial legislation, giving special privileges to particular individuals, partakes of the character of *monopoly ;* but it does not even make a two-thirds vote necessary to pass a law, general in its provisions, and calculated for the equal good of the whole community. A general law of joint-stock partnerships would not be a law "creating *a* body politic." But when A, B, and C, wish to be erected into a corporation, and have particular privileges conferred upon them, the legislature are hindered by the constitution from granting their prayer, unless two-thirds of the whole number elected think it worthy of their assent.

If we "enter into the mind and intention of those who framed the instrument," we shall find that this condition of the assent of two-thirds was stipulated for the express purpose of preventing special acts of incorporation from being passed, except where the reasons for them were very cogent. If we then examine the acts of the very first session of the legislature after the Constitution went into effect, we shall find that so ineffectual was this provision for the purpose intended, that there were thirty-nine new private companies incorporated, and numerous acts passed amending and enlarging previous charters. But while this two-thirds check (which proved in effect to be no check at all) was established for the reason that "the multiplication of corporations was an evil," and that it was the duty of the Convention "not to increase them but diminish them," no step was taken to limit the number of voluntary corporations which the spirit of enterprise and competition might cause to spring into existence under the general laws. The reason was, no doubt, that these were not considered an evil. A grant of special privileges to a particular set of men was considered an "abhorred monopoly;" but a general law of joint-stock partnerships, for the mere facilitation of certain pursuits, of which all men alike might avail themselves, was not a monopoly. Those who "enter into the mind and intention of the framers of the Constitution," will arrive, we think, at a very different conclusion from that of the Attorney General. It would be a singular circumstance, truly, if the Convention had fastened, eternally and irremediably, a most odious and oppressive system of monopolies on the free people of this state, by the very provision which they framed with the avowed purpose of *diminishing these monopolies as far as they could consistently with the preservation of vested rights.*

THE JOINT-STOCK PARTNERSHIP LAW.

[*From the Evening Post, January* 26, 1835.]

THERE was one point in our argument, on Saturday, in relation to the Constitutional power of the legislature to pass a general joint-stock partnership law which we wish to modify; namely, that it is competent for the legislature to pass such a law without the concurrence of two-thirds of the members elected to each branch. This slipped from us inadvertently, and in positive, instead of hypothetic language. More mature deliberation has satisfied us that a vote of two-thirds would be requisite to pass either a general or partial law.

The great object of the section in the Constitution, indeed, was very evidently to establish the necessity of the concurrence of two-thirds of the members elected on the subject of corporations. It was not to change the previous practise in any other respect than as regards the extent of the majority. It was to secure upright and deliberate legislation; to diminish the chances of corruption; to throw a strong impediment in the way of the log-rolling system.

If the language of the Constitution required the assent of two-thirds of the legislature for every bill creating any body, *or bodies*, politic or corporate, we fancy that the competency of the legislature to pass a general law, defining the principles and establishing the conditions on which bodies politic or corporate might be formed, could not for a moment be doubted. Yet the Attorney General admits that the present phraseology, though in the singular number, presents no bar to the creation of a plurality of corporations by one legislative act. He admits that the legislature may incorporate any number of associations, even to the extent of including the whole population of the State, by a single bill. It seems to us that this admission gives up the whole question. If "every bill creating any body politic," is equivalent to "every bill creating any number of bodies politic," it may surely also mean "every bill defining the terms on which any association of men may possess themselves of corporate powers."

If the legislature is not required to act separately on every single question of creating a body politic, but may by one vote, provided it has the requisite majority, create a million of bodies politic, it is not easy to perceive how the powers of the legislature on the subject of granting corporate privileges are at all modified or restrained by the present Constitution, except simply as to what shall constitute a valid majority on such questions. Indeed, the Attorney General seems so naturally to have come to this conclusion, that he expresses it in so many words. He says, the Constitution only prescribes the number of votes necessary to every bill, "leaving all other questions about the passing of such laws as they stood before, to the discretion of the legislature." The legislature have a right now to pass any law whatever respecting corporations by a vote of two-thirds of all the members, which it before had by a simple majority of the members present. Whenever we have a vote of two-thirds the Constitutional requirement is complied with; and if a general law of joint-stock partnerships is objectionable, it is on grounds distinct from those presented by the language of the ninth section of the seventh article of the Constitution.

That objections of this kind existed in the Attorney General's mind is plainly to be inferred from some of his remarks. Thus he argues that if the legislature can provide by general laws for the incorporation of such persons as shall associate for any particular purpose, though "both useful and harmless," "it can, in like manner provide for the incorporation of such persons as may associate for the purpose of carrying on the business of banking, insurance, or receiving and executing trusts." This, we apprehend, is the grand difficulty. A general law of joint-stock partnerships would do away with all necessity or excuse for interested applicants assembling at Albany every winter to use *that peculiar species of argument* with legislators and "leading party men" in favour of their schemes, which it is notorious has heretofore been used to a prodigious extent, and which, with very many men, constitutes the main ground of their desire to get into the legislature.

The Attorney General devotes a portion of his report to a eulogy on corporations, and repeats the old cant about their furnishing "the best means for aggregating the necessary amount of capital for the *rapid and full development* of the resources of the State." If this rapid development is really so desirable an object, is it more likely to take place through the agency of special corporations, or through the means of a law which opens the the field of competition to the whole community? But the Attorney General admits that "there is an admixture of evil in almost every grant of corporate privileges." And what is this admixture of evil? It is, chiefly, that, under the present system of granting charters, they partake of the character of monopoly—they confer powers on a few privileged individuals which are taken, or at any rate withheld, from the great body of the people. Create a general law, under which any set of men may form themselves into a body corporate, and you at once take from such associations the chief admixture of evil.

The Attorney General admits, that, on the subject of Colleges the legislature has not acted upon his doctrine, and that the Revisers do not seem even to have dreamt of his construction. With all deference to the Attorney General, the Revisers are much higher legal authority than he can with any sort of propriety claim to be. But let us try his views on their own merits, and to do so, we may test the applicability of his rule to other subjects. Abundant opportunities of testing its soundness in this way are presented by the Constitution. The very section under consideration requires the assent of two-thirds of the legislature "to every bill appropriating the public moneys or property for local or private purposes." Now, what is more common than, after deciding on the whole principle of an appropriation, to refer the matter to Commissioners, to the Comptroller, or to some other public officer, to expend and apply the money in a certain manner, to take bonds for its payment, and even proofs of its amount. We do not say that such legislation is not sometimes improper, but we apprehend it will hardly be called unconstitutional. Laws making appropriations for private purposes, on general principles, necessarily leave something to the discretion of the Commissioners to whom the carrying those laws into effect is entrusted; but in the case of a law fixing the principles and conditions on which any set of individuals might become a body politic, nothing need be left to discretion. Under such a law, individuals give notification of their intention in a certain specified way, file certain papers with a specified officer, and straightway they become a corporate partnership. The legislature has the undoubted power to create those individuals a body politic absolutely and unqualifiedly. It is apprehended that those who have the power to do any thing absolutely and unqualifiedly, have the power to do it on conditions. The greater power includes the less, or if the Attorney General pleases, a power to sell includes a power to mortgage.

If this doctrine is unsound—if the views of the Attorney General are right throughout, then that officer has the merit of abrogating, by a single exercise of his pen, the corporate powers, not only of all the colleges and academies which have gone into exercise under the Revised Statutes, but also nearly all our banks and other moneyed corporations, for their charters have been generally granted on certain conditions relative to opening their books, distributing the stock, paying in the capital, and filing an affidavit that the capital had been paid in. The appointment of Commissioners may very well come within the Attorney General's rules, which prohibit the legislature from delegating any discretionary power.

The Attorney General, in attempting to break down our anti-monopoly doctrines, may get into more difficulty than he seems to be aware of. His arguments against a general law of joint-stock partnerships, on the ground that such a law would be a delegation of power to others to do what the Constitution requires should be done directly by the legislature, and by a two-thirds vote, bear with greater force against the system he applauds than that which he condemns. He says, in effect, chartered privileges must be distributed by the legislature itself to a *favoured few*, and cannot be granted to *all* by a general law, because the legislature cannot delegate its power. But at the same time the legislature does delegate its power, in every charter of incorporation it passes, to distribute the stock among such favoured individuals as certain Commissioners may select, and the power delegated is rendered great by reason of these legislative favours being withheld from the great body of the people. These inconsistencies will not tend to convince the people that a general joint-stock partnership law is not needed, though it may satisfy them that there is some occasion for a better expounder of the laws already in existence.

REPLY TO THE CHARGE OF LUNACY.

[*From the Evening Post, Jan.* 30, 1835.]

The Bank tory presses originated the imputation of lunacy against the conductors of this journal, and the echoes of the Albany Argus have caught up the cry, and rung the changes upon it, until very possibly many of their readers, who do not read the Evening Post, may suppose it has some foundation in truth. One good-natured editor in Connecticut, we perceive, has taken the matter up quite seriously in our defence, and seeks to prove that we are not crazy in the full sense of the word, but only partially crazy, or suffering under a species of monomania on the subject of monopolies. We are infinitely obliged to our benevolent defender, and in return for his courtesy beg leave to assure him, that if our views on the subject of banks and corporations are evidence of the malady he imputes to us the disease is endemic in this state, and not even Governor Marcy's proposed magnificent lunatic asylum would be capable of containing one hundredth part of the monomaniacs who now go at large, and are generally supposed to be in the full enjoyment of their senses.

The charge of lunacy against an antagonist whose arguments are not refutable is neither a very new nor very ingenious device. Its novelty is on a par with its candour. It is a short and wholesale method of answering facts and reasonings, of which weak and perverted minds have ever been ready to avail themselves, and it has ever been especially resorted to against such as have had the boldness to stand forward as the asserters of the principles of political and religious liberty. Those who are unable to refute your arguments, can at least sneer at their author; and next to overthrowing an antagonist's doctrines, it is considered by many a desirable achievement to raise a laugh against himself. To be laughed at by the aristocracy, however, (and there are too many aristocrats who, to answer selfish purposes, rank themselves with the democracy) is the inevitable fate of all who earnestly strive to carry into full practical operation the great principle of equal political, civil, and religious rights. To escape "the fool's dread laugh," is therefore not to be desired by those who are ardent and determined in the cause of true democratic principles. Such derision they will consider rather as evidence of the soundness of their views, and will be inclined to say with John Wesley, "God forbid that we should not be the laughing-stock of mankind !"

But we put it to every reader seriously, whether, in all they have seen against the doctrines maintained by this paper on the subject of banks and corporations, they have yet found one single argument addressed to men's reasons, and tending to show that our views are wrong. They have read, doubtless, a deal of declamation about our ultraism and our Jacobinism ; they have seen us called a Utopian, a disciple of Fanny Wright, an agrarian, a lunatic, and a dozen other hard names. They have seen it asserted that we are for overthrowing all the cherished institutions of society ; for breaking down the foundations of private right, sundering the marriage tie, and establishing "a community of men, women, and property." But amidst all this declamation—amidst all these groundless and heinous charges, have they yet found one editor who had the candour fairly to state our views, and meet them with calm and temperate argument ? If they have found such a one, they have been more fortunate than we.

While the principles which we maintain are subject to such constant and wilful misrepresentations, it may not be without use frequently to repeat, in a brief form, the real objects for which we contend. All our agrarian, utopian and anarchical views, then, are comprehended in the following statement of the ends at which we aim.

First, with regard to corporations generally: we contend that it is the duty of the legislature, in accordance with the principle of equal rights, on which this government is founded, to refrain, in all time to come, from granting any special or exclusive charters of incorporation to any set of men, or for any purpose whatever; but instead, to pass one general law, which will allow any set of men, who choose to associate together for any purpose, (banking alone temporarily excepted,) to form themselves into that convenient kind of partnership known by the name of corporation.

Second, with regard to banking: we contend that suitable steps should be immediately taken by the legislature to place that branch of business on the same broad and equal basis: that to this end, no more banks should be created or renewed; that existing banks should be gradually curtailed of their privilege to issue small notes, until no bank notes of a smaller denomination than twenty dollars should be in circulation; and that then the restraining law should be repealed, and the community left as free to pursue the business of banking, as they now are to pursue any business whatever.

We are not in favour of pulling down, or overthrowing, or harming, in any way, any existing institutions. Let them all live out their charters, if they do nothing in the meanwhile to forfeit them; and as those charters should expire, the very same stockholders might, if they chose, associate themselves together in a voluntary corporation, under the proposed general law, and pursue their business without interruption, and without let or hinderance.

The grand principle which we aim to establish is the principle of equal rights. The only material difference between the present system, and the system we propose, is that instead of exclusive privileges, or particular facilities and immunities, being dealt out to particular sets of individuals by the legislature, all kinds of business would be thrown open to free and full competition, and all classes and conditions of men would have restored to them those equal rights which the system of granting special charters of incorporation has been the means of filching from them.

All our Utopianism, Jacobinism, Agrarianism, Fanny Wright-ism, Jack Cade-ism; and a dozen other *isms* imputed to us, have this extent, no more. It would argue that there was something very rotten in the democracy of the present day, if for entertaining and strenuously asserting such views, the conductors of a public journal, whose business and pride it is to maintain democratic principles, should be generally supposed to labour under mental derangement. If this is lunacy, it is at all events such lunacy as passed for sound and excellent sense in Thomas Jefferson. The sum of a good government, as described by that illustrious champion of democracy, is all we aim at—"a wise and frugal government, which shall restrain men from injuring one another; shall leave them otherwise free to regulate their own pursuits of industry and improvement; and shall not take from the mouth of labour the bread it has earned."

THE SENATE OF THE UNITED STATES.

[*From the Evening Post, February* 3, 1835.]

It is a good old republican custom, sometimes, nay often, to call the attention of the people to the conduct of the different branches of their Government, legislative, as well as executive and judicial. The people, whose province and whose duty it is to stand sentinel over their rights, and over that Constitution which was devised solely for their security, should never sleep on their posts, for the encroachments of power are like the pestilence, that walketh in darkness, and no one can tell when they will come.

The present organization and late course of the Senate of the United States are, in our opinion, serious subjects for the deep consideration of all who value the representative principle in its purity, or who look to the true spirit of the Constitution. A majority of the states and the people is represented by a minority of that body, the majority of which is acting in defiance of both. This majority is enabled to carry its measures by the aid alone of those members who are acting entirely independent of any other impulse than that of their own sovereign will. While these Senators are pretending to stickle for the rights of the states, they are setting at naught the authority of those very states, and in the language of Mr. Madison, instead of "giving to the State Governments such an agency in the formation of the Federal Government as must secure the authority of the former," are depriving them of all agency whatever, except that which is directly contrary to their instructions.

This bold defiance of the public will, it is believed, is stimulated and sustained by the influence of a combination of political enemies, who, while they differ, in their fundamental principles, agree in one point, that of opposing the public voice and thwarting the wishes of the people. Living upon the reputation acquired by former services and trading on a stock of integrity long since exhausted, these distinguished men, for distinguished they certainly are by political arts, if not by political wisdom, despairing it would seem of rising to the summit of their ambition on the billows of popular applause, are determined to revenge their disappointment by opposing the public will. Certain little men around them, seduced by their example, or probably deluded by their eloquence, have caught the contagion of disobedience, and masking their personal insignificance behind the shield of sturdy independence, crow defiance in the teeth of their constituents with all the arrogance of ill-founded self-sufficiency. They neither, forsooth, represent the states nor the people; they represent the Constitution of the United States, and like watchful guardians, prey upon the treasure they affect to guard.

Under the scattered banner of these independent politicians, who trade on their own bottom, the majority of the Senate so constituted as we have stated, is gradually taking the lead of the House of Representatives, the peculiar guardian of the people. Not content with assuming the right of impeachment, which is exclusively the constitutional prerogative of the House of Representatives, it has constituted itself the grand inquest of the nation, which it no longer represents. It delegates its authority to itinerant committees, which travel about during the recess of the Senate taking ex parte testimony against public and private individuals. It forestalls the action of the House of the people, the proper organ of the popular will, and contrary to established custom as well as obvious propriety, takes the lead in all those great national questions which it was evidently the design of the Constitution should be first proposed and decided in that body which most immediately emanates from the sovereign power. There might be sufficient grounds of justification for the majority of the Senate representing a minority of the states, were they to confine themselves to assuming the lead in questions purely constitutional. But they have widely overstepped the bounds of this, their peculiar province, and every day exhibit an unseemly ambition to go foremost in very thing. The Constitution, for example, says that "all bills for raising revenue shall originate in the House of Representatives." This provision is in strict accordance with the first and best principles of liberty. It constitutes one of the great safeguards against the encroachments of power on the part of the less popular branches of government, because it leaves it entirely to the immediate and peculiar representatives of the people to withhold appropriations for all purposes of which they do not approve. They are the proper guardians of the money of the people, and, being possessed of the exclusive right of originating revenue bills, can, as they ought to do, entirely control the ambition or prodigality of the other branches of Government.

The reasons which govern in the case of raising, apply to the expenditure of the public money, or the voting of any moneys whatever, either out of the existing public funds or in anticipation of them. The vote for raising a revenue, and that for expending it, either before or after it is raised, seem so analagous in their application to the principles just laid down, that it appears difficult to separate them. Both should originate in the House of Representatives, and be sanctioned by it, before being taken up by the Senate, whose example and influence operating on the former, might improperly control its action, and cause it to lose sight of its responsibility to the people. In one word, we doubt the right of the Senate to vote any appropriation of the people's money, except it be first sanctioned by the House of Representatives.

The Senate has consumed a considerable portion of the present session in debating a bill for the appropriation of five millions of the public money, to be raised from the people, for the payment of certain unliquidated demands on the French Government. The question of national obligation to pay this money is of no consequence to this argument, and therefore we pass it by. We would only ask whether a bill to pay money, which, if paid at all, must be raised by a revenue bill, is not, if not a revenue bill, at least its legitimate father? So far as the sanction of the Senate goes, it is an application of the public money which can be raised in no other way than by a revenue bill. It seems to us that if the Senate can originate the one, they can the other with quite as much reason. The principle is much the same, and there is strong ground for believing that the spirit, if not the letter of the Constitution, includes both the raising and the expenditure of the public revenues.

What would be the use of this provision otherwise? Had it been entirely omitted in the Constitution, the Senate could no more have raised a revenue without the assent of the other House than it can now. The object was, that as the people pay the revenue, their immediate representatives, acting it is to be presumed in conformity with their will, should have the first say in the business. It was to secure to the people, as far as possible, a direct controul over the expenditures of the government, by giving them a right of first deciding on their propriety or necessity. Do not precisely the same reasons apply to the assumption of the Senate to appropriate five millions of the money of the people, which can only be provided for by a revenue bill? Has the voice of the people, or of their representatives been heard, or their opinions ascertained through the medium of their appropriate organs? Certainly not. Yet the bill is jogging on in the march of wild legislation, and so far as the decision of the Senate can be anticipated, and so far as that decision is to go, the people are to be saddled with five millions of debt at the present time besides ten times that sum in future, by a bill originating in the Senate, which, though not a revenue bill, involves the direct necessity of "raising a revenue!"

We have no idea that any thing we or the people may say on this or any other encroachment of the Senate, will have any influence on the majority of these lordly contemners of the popular will. Under pretence of vindicating the Constitution, they may violate its letter and spirit at pleasure, and during six years at least, enjoy the enviable satisfaction of "defending the people from their own worst enemies, themselves." Still there may be some little use in agitating the subject of senatorial assumption—we will not call them by so harsh a name as usurpations—if it be only that of awakening the sleeping dignity of the House of Representatives to a recollection of its ancient precedence in all money matters at least. We take it that this is a popular government, and that all questions in which the people are deeply and extensively interested, and most especially all those involving expenditures of money, should be first passed upon by those most likely to feel and obey the impulse of the popular will.

GOVERNOR McDUFFIE'S MESSAGE.

[*From the Evening Post, February* 10, 1835.]

Governor McDuffie, in his late message to the Legislature of South Carolina, has promulgated various errors in relation to the views and principles of the democracy of the middle and northern states, which might excite astonishment at his ignorance, or regret at his insincerity, did we not know that they are founded on the misrepresentations of the Bank tory organs of this part of the world. Great pains have been taken by these to persuade the people of the south, that all the violent anathemas uttered against the system of slavery, by enthusiasts and fanatics in this quarter, and all their dangerous zeal for immediate emancipation, originate with the democracy. The charge of agrarianism, also, which has with such marvellous propriety been urged against this journal, because it supports the doctrine, not of an equalization of property, which is an impracticable absurdity, but because it maintains the principle of equal political rights, seems to have excited the sensitive apprehensions of the Governor of South Carolina, and prompted him to the utterance of sentiments which we are sorry to see avowed on such a public and grave occasion, as that of addressing the legislature in his official capacity.

We must beg leave to set Governor McDuffie right on these points. In the first place, what is called agrarianism by the Bank tory presses is nothing more than the great principle which has always been maintained with peculiar earnestness by the southern states, and most especially by Virginia and South Carolina. It is simply an opposition to all partial and exclusive legislation, which gives to one profession, one class of industry, one section of the Union, or one portion of the people, privileges and advantages denied to the others, or of which, from the nature of their situation and circumstances, they cannot partake. It is opposition to bounties, protections, incorporations, and perpetuities of all kinds, under whatever mask they may present themselves. It is neither more nor less in short, than a denial of the legislative authority to grant any partial or exclusive privileges under pretence of the "general welfare," the "wants of the community," "sound policy," "sound action," "developing the resources and stimulating the industry of the community," or any other undefinable pretence, resorted to as a subterfuge by avarice and ambition. This is what the whig papers, as they style themselves, hold up to the South as a dngerous doctrine, calculated to unsettle the whole system of social organization, and subject the rights of property to the arbitrary violence of a hungry and rapacious populace!

We would ask Governor McDuffie if this is not, to all intents and purposes, the doctrine of those who maintained the independent authority of the states, in all points where it was not voluntarily and specifically surrendered to the Federal Government? Did they not repudiate and deny the power of that government to grant charters of incorporation? And when the Convention which formed the Constitution of the United States rejected the plan of a national or consolidated government, was it not mainly on the ground that it would place the states, and what is the same thing, the people of the states, wholly at the mercy of a power, which might, if it pleased, under the specious pretext of the "public welfare," sacrifice the interests of one state, or one section, to those of another, and thus introduce a system of partial and exclusive legislation? If such a system, adopted by the Federal Government, would be injurious to the rights of the states; so is it now when adopted by a state legislature towards the people of a state just as injurious to the rights and liberties of the great majority, because it is the very essence of such privileges, that, to be worth having, they must of necessity be confined to a small minority. Governor McDuffie cries out against the oppressions inflicted on a minority of the states, by a partial system of federal legislation, and the democracy of the north exclaim against a similar system adopted by our own legislatures to the prejudice of the rights of a majority of the people. Which has the broadest ground of action, he who maintains the rights of the few or he who maintains the rights of the many, in a government the first principle of which is, that within the limits of the Constitution, the majority of the poeple must and ought to govern?

Governor McDuffie is still more misled in his ideas of the part taken by the democracy of this and the eastern states in the mad and violent schemes of the immediate abolitionists, as they are called. He may be assured that the abettors and supporters of Garrison, and other itinerant orators who go about stigmatizing the people of the south as "men stealers," are not the organs or instruments of the democracy of the north, but of the aristocracy—of that party which has always been in favour of encroaching on the rights of the white labourers of this quarter. It is so in Europe, and so is it here. There, the most violent opponents of the rights of the people of England, are the most loud in their exclamations against the wrongs of the people of Africa, as if they sought to quiet their consciences, for oppressing one colour, by becoming the advocates of the freedom of the other. Daniel O'Connell is one of the few exceptions, and even he, in one of his speeches, with the keenest and most bitter irony, taunted these one-sided philanthropists with perpetuating the long enduring system of oppression in Ireland, while they were affecting the tenderest sympathy for the blacks of the West Indies. Was Rufus King, the great leader on the Missouri question, a representative of the democracy of the north? and were not the interests of the planters of the south sustained by the democracy alone?

Governor McDuffie may make himself perfectly easy on the score of the democracy of the north. They are not agrarians, nor fanatics, nor hypocrites. They make a trade neither of politics, nor philanthropy. They know well that admitting the slaves of the south to an equality of civil and social rights, however deeply it might affect the dignity and interests of the rich planters of that quarter, would operate quite as injuriously, if not more so, on themselves. The civil equality might affect both equally, but the social equality would operate mainly to the prejudice of the labouring classes among the democracy of the north. It is here the emancipated slaves would seek a residence and employment, and aspire to the social equality they could never enjoy among their ancient masters. If they cannot bring themselves up to the standard of the free labouring white men, they might pull the latter down to their own level, and thus lower the condition of the white labourer by association, if not by amalgamation.

Not only this, but the labouring classes of the north, which constitute the great mass of the democracy, are not so short-sighted to consequences, that they cannot see, that the influx of such a vast number of emancipated slaves would go far to throw them out of employment, or at least depreciate the value of labour to an extent that would be fatal to their prosperity. This they know, and this will forever prevent the democracy of the north from advocating or encouraging any of those ill-judged, though possibly well-intended schemes for a general and immediate emancipation, or indeed for any emancipation, that shall not both receive the sanction and preserve the rights of the planters of the south, and, at the same time, secure the democracy of the north against the injurious, if not fatal consequences, of a competition with the labour of millions of manumitted slaves.

If any class of people in this quarter of the Union have an interest in this question, independent of the broad principle of humanity, it is the aristocracy. It is not those who labour and have an interest in keeping up its price, but those who employ labour and have an interest in depressing it. These last would receive all the benefits of a great influx of labourers, which would cause the supply to exceed the demand, and consequently depress the value of labour; while the former would not only experience the degradation of this competition, but become eventually its victims.

If we look back to the political history of this country, it will be found that the true democracy of the north has always supported the southern policy. They sustained every republican candidate for the Presidency from that section of the Union (for such we considered General Jackson) and their uniform co-operation distinctly indicates a near affinity of interests and principles between the republicans of the south and the democracy of the north. The latter will probably, at the ensuing Presidential election, put forward a candidate identified with these interests and principles, and will the former desert their old friends, who never deserted them? Will they aid in dividing and distracting the republican party by multiplying candidates, and thus by throwing the decision upon Congress, pave the way for a successful intrigue that may again cheat the people of their choice, and restore the ascendancy of an aristocratic faction which has always been arrayed in opposition to their interests.

Again we assure Governor McDuffie, and all those who imagine they see in the democracy of the north, the enemies to their rights of property, and the advocates of principles dangerous to the safety and prosperity of the planters of the south, that they may make themselves perfectly easy on these heads. The danger is not in the democratic, but the aristocratic ascendancy. The whole is a scheme of a few ill-advised men, which certain whig politicians have used to set the republicans of the south against the democracy of the north, and thus, by dividing, conquer them both.

THE FERRY MONOPOLY

[*From the Evening Post, February* 18, 1835.]

We have received from Albany a copy of the Report of the Select Committee of the Assembly on the several petitions addressed to that body, relative to the establishment of additional ferries between this city and Brooklyn. The petitioners ask that an intelligent and impartial board of commissioners may be appointed, with full powers to establish ferries between New-York anu Long Island, and that the present rates of ferriage be reduced. The fact that additional means of communication between the cities of New-York and Brooklyn are very much needed, that the present rates of ferriage are exorbitantly high, and the accommodations none of the best, is too notorious for any one to deny. It is also a well-known fact, that numerous responsible persons have frequently and vainly petitioned the corporate authorities of this city for permission to establish another ferry, offering to bind themselves to furnish suitable accommodations, and to pay too a large sum for the desired "privilege." In consequence of the rejection of all these applications, resort has at last been had to the State Legislature.

The power of establishing ferries over the East River is claimed by the corporate authorities of this city as a franchise conferred upon them by the ancient charters, and confirmed by various subsequent acts of state legislation.

The Report before us contends that "the authority to establish ferries, granted to the city of New-York by charter, is to be considered, not as a monopoly for the purpose of revenue to the city, but as a delegated legislative power, to be exercised with the same regard to the convenience of the public, as the legislature themselves would exercise it." They further argue that "although the charter declares that the Common Council shall have the *sole* power of establishing ferries, yet that this only means that this power, *as a delegated authority*, should be possessed by them, *to the exclusion of any other office, tribunal, or public body*," and that the power may be altered modified, repealed, or resumed, at the discretion of the legislature, always taking care, of course, it is to be presumed, not to violate the public faith, as pledged by the acts of the Common Council in the exercise of the authority delegated to them.

In the difficulties which citizens now experience to obtain reasonable facilities of communication between New-York and Brooklyn, a forcible illustration is afforded of the absurd and oppressive nature of monopolies. The question how far the power to regulate this matter has been granted to the Common Council of New-York, and how far it yet resides in the legislature of the State is one which we have not qualified ourselves to answr. It seems to us, however, from an attentive perusal of the Report, and a reference to some of the authorities there mentioned, that the positions assumed in that document are sound, and that the Legislature have a primary, unalienated and supreme control over the whole matter in dispute.

Be this as it may, the common sense view of the subject plainly teaches that there ought to be no further legislative or municipal interference with the business of ferriage, than is demanded by a simple regard for public safety and convenience. We have not time to go into any argument to-day ; but on this subject, as on all others, we are the advocates of the principles of *free trade*. We would put no hinderance in the way of any man, or set of men, who should choose to undertake the business of ferrying people across the river. The public interests would be best served by leaving the matter to regulate itself—or rather leaving it to be regulated by the laws of demand and supply. Free competition would do more to insure good accommodations, low prices, swift and safe boats, and civil attendants, than all the laws and charters which could ever be framed. The sheet of water which separates New-York from Brooklyn ought to be considered as a great highway, free to whomsoever should choose to travel on it, under no other restriction than complying with certain regulations for the mutual safety and convenience of all: such regulations as are now enforced with regard to private vehicles in the streets and public roads. Yet since the corporate authorities choose to turn every business that they possibly can into a source of revenue to the city, they might make a license necessary for ferry-boats, as is now done with regard to the Broadway and Bowery omnibusses. Even this tax is an infringement of those sound principles of political economy which ought to govern in the matter; but it could not be objected to in the case of ferries, while it is recognized in that of stage coaches.

In making these remarks, we are by no means forgetful of the "chartered rights" of those who now have the "exclusive privilege" of carrying people to and fro between New-York and Brooklyn. Much as we detest the principle of such monopolies, we would by no means justify any invasion of the rights duly granted to them. The public faith is pledged, and, at the expense of any temporary inconvenience, let it be preserved inviolate. But though the Corporation ought not to invade the rights which have been foolishly granted, yet as far as they still retain any control over the subject, they might restore to the community their natural rights, and leave those who wish to establish other ferries to make the best terms they can with the existing monopolies. Such a course is in reality dictated as well by selfish and local interests as by an enlarged and liberal view of the whole question. Every additional facility of access to this metropolis increases its general prosperity. We are aware that pains have been taken to create a belief that the establishment of more ferries would injuriously affect the prices of property in the upper part of the city, and that narrow and selfish opposition has been thus engendered. But we think it could be demonstrated that every additional means of communicating with Long Island will add to the prosperity of New-York. Be this as it may as respects owners of real estate, there can be no question that it is true with regard to the great body of the people.

THE OPPOSITION IN THE SENATE.

[*From the Evening Post of Feb.* 24, 1835.]

THE Senate of the United States occasionally presents a spectacle calculated to excite wonder, if not ridicule, at the inconsistencies of many of its distinguished leaders. On the one hand we see Mr. Calhoun, who has carried the doctrine of State Rights to the very verge of the greatest possible extreme, proposing a scheme of reform, which, if adopted, will place the states on the pension list of the United States for eight years to come at least. Of all the plans we have yet seen propounded by great statesmen to increase the influence of the federal government, and to impoverish the people at the same time, that of raising a revenue only to distribute it again, minus the deduction the expenses of collecting and distributing, appears to us the most preposterous. Besides this inevitable loss to the people, they will of necessity lose the use and the interest of this surplus revenue, which Mr. Calhoun calculates at nine millions per annum, during the whole period which elapses from the time of paying to that of receiving it back again. The scheme of the honourable Senator from South Carolina for enriching the States, reminds us of the honest trader who always sold his goods below cost, and lived by the loss.

But there is no danger that those who pay the surplus of nine millions per annum for seven or eight years will ever see their money again. The current of taxation is like that of the Mississippi: it always runs one way; it flows into the great ocean of public expenditure, and is lost in oblivion. The money returned to the States will never find its way into the pockets of its old owners again. It will come into the hands of certain officers of the State Governments, who will infallibly apply it to "the public good," that it to say, "supplying the wants of the community," "giving energy to public enterprise," "providing new avenues for the surplus products of the country," &c. &c.; all which, done into plain practical English, means nothing more or less than distributing the money contributed equally by the whole community in political bribes, or to further the schemes of a few speculating politicians, who make a trade of patriotism, and apply the confidence of a deceived people solely to their own interested purposes.

In the midst of these extraordinary schemes of reform, supported by arguments equally extraordinary, we see a system of most extravagant expenditures adopted by these original reformers, for the encouragement of printing and bookmaking it would seem. The reformers are determined that the people of the United States and their representatives shall be enlightened. They have from time to time voted a few hundred thousands of dollars for printing vast numbers of speeches and reports which would take the people years to read, and ages to comprehend. In order to make sure of the people becoming thoroughly enlightened, they have distributed only the arguments on one side of the question, from a just apprehension that if the other was presented they might be placed in the situation of a certain animal between two bundles of hay, and suffer an intellectual starvation in the midst of too great plenty.

In addition to this expedient of economy, the reformers in the Senate have voted a few hundred thousands more for the double purpose of supplyihg themselves with books, and, as has been surmised, of enabling certain meritorious printers of newspapers to employ the money of the people in opposing the administration of their choice. Thus they kill two birds with one stone. They supply themselves with a library comprising a vast accumulation of useless knowledge, and thus enable themselves to legislate to the greatest advantage, and they at the same time foster the spirit of literature by multiplying books that nobody reads. Now, for our humble selves, we think this mode of fitting legislators for the performance of their duties, *after* they are chosen, is putting the cart before the horse. In our opinion they should by all means be qualified beforehand, as in all other trades, in which a man serves his apprenticeship before he sets up in business. This *extempore* education reminds us of the story of an honest Frenchman, who, having occasion for spiritual advice called several times on his bishop, but was always put off with the excuse that he was at his studies. Upon which, getting at last out of all patience, he exclaimed, "I wish to heaven our king would send us a bishop who had finished his education."

We see no special propriety in legislators finishing their education at the expense of the people; or if they will do this, it seems but just that the other functionaries of the government should be put on the same footing. It was a terrible infraction of the great precept of doing as we would be done by, to refuse the Attorney General an ap-propriation for law books, while Congress is every day voting itself a supply of books of legislation. It is ru-moured that more than one of the honourable members has set up a book store at the seat of government, and that others who have been overlooked by the people at the last election, intend commencing business at home, on the stock in trade acquired by a few years of services to the people.

On the other hand, we see Mr. Clay and *his* band of reformers, strenuously opposing the increase of executive patronage, by advocating the principle of appointments for life, or at least during good behaviour. Does it not strike the honourable Senator that, if, as he presumes, the whole body of public officers are "the supple tools of Exe-cutive power," that these men, being entirely governed by motives of self-interest, will make much greater sacrifices for an appointment for life, or during good behaviour, than for one of four years, subject to the will of the Exe-cutive, or the vicissitudes of political changes? If he looks into history, he will find the atrocities committed by kings and nobles to secure themselves the possession of hereditary honours and hereditary power, beyond all comparison greater than those of men struggling only for a temporary superiority. The greater the boon the greater the sacrifice; and a great man who would thwart the wishes of the people for the sake of a temporary office, might be tempted to plunge his country into all the horrors of a revolution to render the possession perma-nent.

But what right does Mr. Clay brand the whole class of office holders, with being "the supple tools of Execu-tive power?" Does he speak from his own experience, or is this high charge the result of his exalted opinion of human nature? That distinguished person is himself at this moment in office, and has been nearly all his life seeking offices. We do not urge this as a reproach; for situations of honour, emolument and trust, are objects not unworthy of the highest character in this country, and if they are gained by means and exertions becoming a man of principle and independence, they are badges of honour, not of disgrace. A gentleman once standing so high, and still standing high in the estimation of a considerable portion of this Union, ought to be above repeating the miserable slang about office holders, with which every petty disappointed demagogue solaces his miseries, and assuages the aggravated inflammation of his political buffetings. It is unworthy of him, and is an extravagant assumption. One great fault in the system of political ethics acted upon by Mr. Clay and his whig partizans, is that of underrating the virtue and intelligence of the people. They ascribe that to the influence of office holders, which is in reality the result of public intelligence and feeling, and stigmatize as the corrupt instrument of "the supple tools of Executive power," what in reality is nothing more than enlightened perception of their own rights and interests on the part of the people. Mr. Clay and his partizans have been defeated by the free people of the United States, and not by a combination of "supple tools of Executive power." His own party once had the same means of corruption in their hands. Were they too pure to use them; or were the people incorruptible? Again we repeat, the slang is unworthy the high source whence it emanated on this occasion. It is in fact a general and sweeping charge against the character of the people of the United States, because it directly intimates that they are all equally assailable by corruption, or that they are instruments in the hands of "the supple tools of Executive power."

But while expressing our just reprehension of this most illiberal denunciation, we cannot forbear a burst of unfeigned pleasure at the assertion of the honourable Senator which follows. Mr. Clay insisted that, "Responsibility was as essential an ingredient of a free government, as the vital air which surrounds us was necessary to animal life. Every officer was responsible to the people; all were public servants." We should like to have seen how the "responsible" Senators from New-Jersey, Alabama, Mississippi and North Carolina looked at receiving such a lecture as this. It was a most unkind cut thus to tell them to their faces that they had been existing for so long a time without the "vital air," which was "absolutely necessary for animal life," and that of consequence they "smelt of mortality." If they, or any one of them, except Mr. Frelinghuysen, ever forgive him, they are better Christians than we supposed.

In the midst of these scenes, which are calculated to create a surmise that frequent disappointments, like too much learning, are apt to make men mad, we turn with great pleasure to the manly, consistent, and straightforward course of the distinguished Senator from Missouri, Colonel Benton. Vigorous, intelligent and indefatigable; without fear and without reproach; equally remarkable for the sagacity and clearness of his intellect, and the unfaltering industry of his research; always ready, always profound, and always irresistible, he marches straight forward, right into the trenches of his adversaries, and routs them from every fancied strong-hold they occupy. The Republic owes him much, and we trust that it will not be found ungrateful.

[*From the Evening Post, March* 6, 1835.]

We devote the entire reading portion of our paper to-day, together with some additional columns borrowed from advertisements, to the proceedings of Congress on the two last days of the session. It will give our readers great pleasure to perceive that the protracted discussion in the House of Representatives on the subject of our differences with France, at last terminated in *the unanimous adoption of a resolution that the treaty with France ought to be maintained, and its execution insisted on*. Mr. Cambreleng has entitled himself to the greatest credit for his able, conciliatory and truly American course on this question. And of Mr. Adams we must say, also, that though not entirely free from his old trick of "dodging," he behaved on this question, on the last day of the discussion, in a manner which, if it more frequently characterized his conduct, would very materially increase his claims to the respect of his countrymen.

That our readers may have before them the means of ascertaining what has been done and what left undone by Congress, we publish to-day a list of the bills which have received the assent of both branches of that body, and now only require the signature of the President to be laws of the land. A glance at this list will serve, more forcibly than any thing we can say, to show how shamefully the National Legislature have trifled away the session. But few of the important measures which the country looked for at their hands have been attended to. The hour of their dissolution arrived without their having consummated a tenth part of the business for which they convened. Never, since the adoption of the Constitution, was there a more utterly unprofitable session of

Congress. The Senate, governed to the last by its factious spirit—its ruling passion of hostility to the President and to the democracy of the country, strong even in death—did all in its power to embarrass the other House, and defeat those measures which are imperatively demanded by the posture of our Foreign affairs.

It will be seen that in this venomous and spiteful temper that body voted against the appropriation of three millions to put the country in a posture of defence, and voted against it on the shallow pretence that such an appropriation was placing both the sword and purse in the hands of the Executive! A factious majority—among which we are glad to see the name of but one of those who have hitherto supported the administration, and sorry that that one is Judge WHITE — have dared to take upon themselves the responsibility of defeating a bill absolutely indispensable in the present emergency to the safety of our country. We shall be mistaken, indeed, if public sentiment do not brand this proceeding with the name of infamy which it deserves. We look on each individual who voted against that most just and wise and necessary appropriation, as guilty of little less than treason. We ask on this subject, attention to the article from the Globe of yesterday, giving some account of the factious conduct of the Senate.

The Judiciary bill, the prime object of which was to defeat the nomination of Mr. TANEY, as a Judge of the Supreme Court, did not receive the concurrence of the House of Representatives. The debate on this subject will be found interesting. The National Intelligencer remarks that the nomination of Mr. TANEY was indefinitely postponed by the Senate in Executive session, on Tuesday evening.

We rejoice that the insulting clause added by the Senate, on motion of DANIEL WEBSTER, to the General Appropriation bill, was indignantly rejected by the House. Mr. Adams did himself great credit by the spirit which he displayed on that occasion. We do not agree with him in the position that it is within the constitutional power of the President to fill the vacancy in the mission to England without the advice and consent of the Senate, but on the contrary we are at a loss to perceive how any intelligent mind can find a shadow of authority for such a proceeding in the language of the Constitution, which to us seems most plainly to withhold the power of appointment from the President, without the concurrence of the Senate, except in a case which, as regards the embassy to England, does not now exist. But whether the President has or has not the constitutional right toappoint a minister during the recess, the clause added to the appropriation bill was equally improper. and deserved the pointed condemnation which it received from the House. If the President has a right to appoint, the Senate have no business to limit the exercise of his constitutional powers: if he has not the right to appoint, they have no business to insert a clause of limitation under the presumption that he would exceed his constitutional powers.

We have left ourselves room barely to ask the attention of our readers to the exposition made by the Washington Globe of Tuesday respecting the unworthy conduct of the majority in the Senate on the subject of Mr. Benton's expunging resolution. This ignoble triumph, obtained by legislative trickery, will be of short duration.

THE SENATE AND THE FRENCH QUESTION.

[*From the Evening Post of March* 9, 1835.]

All parties and all men in this country must unite in the opinion that the omission, on the part of Congress to provide for the national defence, in the present posture of public affairs, is deeply censurable. Fall the blame where it may, this is an instance of remissness which all must alike condemn. Difference of opinion may exist in alloting the censure, but there can be no difference as to the fact of the censure being deserved. Our relations with France are now in such a situation that it may be considered an even chance whether we shall have peace or war. Some of our best informed citizens, who have resided much abroad, and are intimately acquainted with the sentiments and temper of many of the leading members of the French Government on the subject of the indemnity due to this country, consider war as more probable than we have stated. But whatever may be the degree of probability, no one can shut his eyes to the fact that our relations with France are such as imperatively require that we should be prepared for hostilities. Our minister at Paris, in an official communication to his Government, has stated it as his deliberate opinion, that if the French Chamber of Deputies should again reject the bill of indemnity, it is highly probable *that France would anticipate our reprisals by the seizure of our vessels in her ports, and an attack on our ships in the Mediterranean with a superior force.* Her hostile measures in such an event would not be limited to these acts. We might hourly expect to hear of a French fleet upon our coast; and the first intelligence of their approach might be the booming of their cannon, as they poured their volleys into our unarmed fortresses ,and sweeping by them, entered unresisted into our very harbours. Where then would be our forces to beat them back? Where would be our navy, to meet them midway on the seas, and guard our shores from the ravages of the foe? Where would be our coast defences, to bar the entrance of hostile fleets? Shall such a state of things arrive, and find us without an army; with our ships of war dismantled at the docks, and our fortresses delapidated and unmanned? Is the country to be thus taken by surprise, unprepared to strike a single blow for the maintainance of its vaunted freedom, and subject to be overrun and harried by an insolent foe? And why must we run the hazard of this incalculable evil?

The obvious and only answer to this question is, because the Senate of the United States did not choose to trust the spending of three millions of dollars for the national defence to the discretion of the Chief Magistrate of the nation! We see at the head of our Government a man recently elected to that exalted station by an overwhelming majority of the free suffrages of the people; a man of unequalled military experience and sagacity; a man who, since his first elevation to the highest office of the country, in all the difficult and trying questions on which he has been called to act, has so borne himself as to command, more and more, at each successive exhibition of his character, the admiration, the esteem and the gratitude of the people. This is the man whom the Senate would not trust with the expenditure of three millions of dollars, to put the country in an attitude of defence, if events should occur before the next session of Congress to render defence necessary. This is the length and the breadth and the depth of the question. The Senate have left the country defenceless, rather than trust the ordering of its defence to the wisdom and patriotism of a Chief Magistrate who possesses, and has nobly earned, the people's unlimited confidence. Partizan newspapers and partizan orators may fume and vapour as they please ; but this is the naked simple fact. The Senate have incurred this tremendous responsibility ; and no art of sophistry, and no device of misrepresentation can shift it from their shoulders to those of the other branch of the national legislature.

The very eagerness of the National Intelligencer to throw the blame of this most parracidal conduct on a distinguished member of the House of Representatives, shows the prophetic consciousness of guilt on the part of those Senators whose mouthpiece that unprincipled journal is, that the people will judge rightly where the censure belongs. It is all in vain to attempt to throw the odium on Mr. CAMBRELENG. Throughout the whole of this affair, that gentleman's conduct has been dictated by the truest patriotism and the most enlightened policy. From the first to the last, he evinced the strongest desire to merge considerations of party in the higher considerations of what was due to his entire country. Never did he speak in a loftier, more liberal, more conciliatory tone. He laboured earnestly, assiduously, successfully, to have such measures adopted as might properly speak the sentiments of this great nation. To unite as many as possible in such measures, he voluntarily and cheerfully gave up his resolution and adopted in place of it the language of an opponent. When that opponent then cavilled at his own terms, he modified them to obviate the new objection. He seemed not to care on whom the honour of the proceeding should rest, so that the honour of the nation was asserted. In the same spirit, he introduced the proposition to appropriate three millions of dollars to provide for the national defence. This proposition was carried by an immense majority, and among those who voted for it (to their honour be it spoken) were several prominent opponents of the administration. The Senate rejected the appropriation—rejected it positively, entirely—suggesting no amendment, proposing no alternative. The House again considered it, and again, by an undiminished majority, declared in favour of the measure. Again the Senate, *by a party vote*, rejected it!—and still that body offered no substitute, and intimated no midway course. The House once more took up the subject, and after discussion, a third time decided, by a large majority, to adhere to the appropriation, and appointed a Committee to confer with the Senate. Before that Committee and the Senate's Committee had come to any agreement on the question, the hour had passed on which the functions of the twenty-third Congress expired, and when the Committee of the House of Representatives returned to the Representative Chamber, they found that there was not a quorum present, and that several members who were present refused to vote on any question on the ground that their legislative functions had ceased. This is a brief statement of undeniable facts. Can there be any difficulty, then, in deciding where the censure of the people of the United States ought to fall? By whose act has their country been left in a defenceless situation at a time when it is threatened with a foreign war, and when even now, perhaps, a French fleet is on its way to our shores? No man, who regards truth, and whose mind is not darkened with the worst of prejudices, can fail to ascribe our deplorable situation to the conduct of the factious majority of the United States Senate. Thank heaven, the reign of terror is over!

UNCURRENT BANK NOTES.

[*From the Evening Post, March*, 10, 1835.]

We wish some public spirited man who has access to data that would afford a reasonable basis for a conjectural calculation, would furnish us with an estimate of the immense amount of money which is annually lost in this city, by the labouring classes, in the discount upon uncurrent bank notes in circulation. Do the mechanics and the labourers know, that every dollar which is paid in the discounting of uncurrent notes in Wall-street, is filched out of their pockets? That such is the fact is susceptible of the clearest demonstration.

In the first place, the circulation of uncurrent bank notes is chiefly kept up by a direct and infamous fraud upon the working classes. It is a common practise with employers when they pay off their hands on Saturday, to go into Wall-street and purchase of some broker for the purpose, a lot of notes of depreciated value, varying from half to one and a half per cent. below par. These notes they palm off upon their workmen as money. If a master mechanic has a thousand dollars a week to pay to his hands, it is clear that he pockets every week by this operation some ten or fifteen dollars; and it can be shown with equal clearness that those in his employment are defrauded out of this sum. If a man hesitates to take this depreciated paper, he is told that it passes as currently as silver in payment of any thing he may wish to purchase; and so, in truth, it does. Yet he could not exchange it for silver, without paying the broker a discount, and let him not imagine, though he may seem to pass it away to his grocer or his baker at par, that he does not lose this discount all the same. Nay, the mechanic and labouring man whose employers are conscientious enough to pay them their wages in real money, bear their full proportion of the loss on the uncurrent notes in circulation, equally with those to whom the depreciated paper is paid. *The entire sum paid for the discount of depreciated bank paper falls on the mechanics and labourers, and is wrung out of their sweat and toil. Nay more: they not only lose the amount which is actually paid for discount to the money changers, but they also pay a per centage on that amount equal to the average rate of profit which merchants charge on their goods.* We can make this plain to the dullest apprehension.

The labouring man, when he returns home of a Saturday evening, with his week's wages in his pocket, in this depreciated paper, stops at his grocer's, and pays him the amount of his weekly bill. The grocer in the course of a few days pays this money away into the hands of the wholesale merchant from whom he purchases his commodities. The merchant, when a certain amount of this kind of paper has accumulated on his hands, sends it into Wall-street, and sells it to the brokers, and when his clerk returns, an entry is made in his books of the amount paid for discount. The sum total paid in the course of a year for the discount of depreciated paper forms an item of expense which is calculated as one of the elements in the cost of his goods. To pay for his goods he is obliged to buy bills of exchange, or in other words, to remit specie to Europe. Whatever this specie costs him, his goods cost him; and he therefore looks upon the amount he had to pay to turn the uncurrent paper received from his customers into specie as a constituent part of the first cost of his merchandize. Upon the whole sum of the cost, thus ascertained, he puts a certain per centage profit, and fixes his prices accordingly. The retail trader then buying a lot of goods of him, pays him not only a proportional part of the discount which the wholesale merchant actually paid on his uncurrent paper, but a profit thereon. This, however, makes no difference to him, for he has only to put his own profit on above all, and let the loss fall on the labourer, when he comes for his tea and sugar and other little necessaries and comforts for his family. That this is a true, though homely exposition of the case, any body must see who will only give himself the trouble to think about it.

The whole amount of uncurrent notes which pass through the broker's hands annually may be stated at a given sum, and the discount thereupon amounts, on an average to a given per-centage. This sum, whatever it is, (and it must be immense) is a tax on the business of the community, which each individual shuffles off his own shoulders on those of the persons next beneath him, and so it descends by gradation till it reaches the broad backs and hard hands of the mechanics and labourers, who produce all the wealth and bear all the burdens of society.

But the mechanics and labourers have it in their power to rid themselves of this imposition. The task is very easy: it is only to learn the efficacy of the word COMBINATION. There is a magic in that word, when rightly understood and employed, which will force the scrip nobility to do them justice, and yield them, without drawback and without cheatery, the full fruits of their toil. Let them inquire by what means it is that this immense amount of depreciated paper is kept in circulation. They will find it is chiefly through the instrumentality of master-workmen and others having mechanics and labourers in their employment. They will find that this wretched substitute for money is bought, for the express purpose of palming it off upon them as real value, while their task-masters and the brokers share the spoils between them. A mechanic dare not refuse to take the wretched trash; because, if he does, he will be turned away to starve. But what a single mechanic may not be able to compass alone, could be easily effected by *combination.* Will the mechanics and labourers wait for eighteen months, in the hope that the juggling law now before the legislature will by that time go into operation, and rid them of *the paper money curse?* Let them not rest in any such belief. Let them *know their own strength and resolve to be imposed on no longer.* Why are the producers of all the wealth of society the poorest, most despised and most down-trodden class of men? Because they submit to be the dupes of the scrip nobility—because they are ignorant of their own strength. Let them combine together to demand whatever the plain principles of justice warrant, and we shall see what power there is which can deny them.

THE LEGISLATION OF CONGRESS.

[*From the Evening Post, March* 11, 1835.]

We have been at the pains to count the number of acts passed by Congress at its last session. If we have made no mistake in our enumeration, they amount, in all, to one hundred and fifteen. Of these no less than eighty-four are of a private or local character, and in the remaining thirty-one we do not perceive what there is of so intricate or difficult a character as to have required Congress to continue its legislative functions several hours beyond the period of its constitutional existence. Indeed, we do not know but that body would have continued making laws, or rather making speeches, until this time, had not the indecency of any further violation of the constitution been prevented by the want of a quorum, which at last forced it to adjourn.

We are not aware of any particular clause in the Constitution which ordains that Congress shall be the grand political arena of the country; yet it seems, by the common consent of all the members, to be so considered, and their whole conduct is squared accordingly. It happens as one of the consequences of this construction, that the legislative business of the nation is generally put off to the latést period, and then huddled through and "slubbered o'er in haste," in the last three or four days of the session. This remark was particularly illustrated by the last Congress. Every thing was crowded into the last few hours, when, owing to the absolute necessity of members attending to their private arrangements, and to agencies committed to them by their constituents, it was difficult to procure the attendance of a quorum, and it continually occurred that, when questions were taken, it was found necessary to move a call of the House, in order to muster the requisite number of members.

By examining the votes given on a large portion of the questions, it will be found that they were decided by a bare majority of the whole number of the representatives of the people, and consequently the constituency of the United States was not properly represented on these occasions. Indeed it has long been notorious that there is great laxity on the part of members in their attendance on Congressional debates, and it is only on great party questions that they can be rallied. Hence, in most cases of a private nature—which it will be seen by our statement constitute nearly three-fourths of the whole—the money of the people is disposed of without the consent or knowledge of their immediate representatives. Thus the great principle of representation is practically frittered away to nothing, and the people are virtually deprived of their voice and influence in the disposal of their own money, and in the assertion of their own rights.

The greater part of every session of Congress is wasted in unprofitable debate. A few great party questions occupy nearly the whole time; and when, at the close of the term, it becomes indispensably necessary to act, the hours, days, and weeks consumed in talking without acting are redeemed by action without debate or consideration. They fly from one extreme to the other. The favourite maxim of the Albany Argus, *in medio tutissimus ibis*, is no part of the wisdom of Congress. Laws, involving important principles and vast expenditures, are hurried along on a torrent of impetuous legislation, with a precipitancy that defies reflection or analysis, and finally passed, perhaps in the dead of night, by a Rump Congress, consisting of a bare quorum of members, worn out with fatigue, and some of them probably half asleep.

The last days of a session are not the proper period for important acts of legislation, not only for the reasons already stated, but for others of equal weight and importance. The passions, engendered by months of argument, rivalry and contention, always break forth at that period, and produce a state of mind utterly incompatible with calm, temperate consideration. It is the last round of a long fight, and each party summons all its energies to give the decisive blow. In such a state of things it may well happen—as it often has happened—that measures of the greatest importance are debated and decided in a spirit wholly at war with the interests and honour of the nation. Scenes are exhibited calculated to impair that respect which is indispensable to the exercise of authority in a free government. Law-givers become objects of contempt or derision, and the people at last lose that confidence in the representative system, without which there is no security for the permanency of our Government. That confidence once wholly lost, and they will be ready to throw themselves into the arms of despotism as a refuge from doubt and despair.

Either the present number of representatives in Congress is necessary, or it is not. If the former, then a regular and general attendance is demanded of the members. If the latter, then it is an abuse to saddle the people with the expense of these supernumerary legislators, who spend their time in gallanting the ladies about the city of Washington, or flirting with them in the galleries of the two Houses. If their wisdom is essential to the welfare of the people, then the people who pay them have a right to its exercise : if it is not, it might better be emyloyed on their own account at home.

The close of every session of Congress, whether short or long, invariably exhibits a vast mass of public business either not acted upon, or left unfinished, consisting not unfrequently of questions of great and general importance to the whole Union. This lamentable result may be partly owing to the annual increase of private claims not susceptible of judicial decision, and therefore brought before Congress as the only resort. If so, it would seem to be high time to make such a disposition of these matters as may allow ample time to the proper affairs of the nation ; to those general laws which are of universal concern, and the neglect of which is felt in every part of the country.

The cause of this neglect of more important affairs, in the first instance, and this precipitate legislation on them afterwards, will be discovered in the unlimited indulgence of the rage for speech making—the *cacoethes loquendi*, which is the prevailing epidemic in Congress—added to that propensity to private, partial, and local legislation, which is becoming the curse of this country. Almost every member has his budget of matters of this sort, in which the great mass of the nation has no concern whatever, and which he cannot die in peace without thrusting upon the attention of Congress, and urging with a pertinacity and verbosity precisely in proportion to their insignificance. In this way the people are borne down to the earth with public benefits and harrassed with legislation, and there is some reason to fear that it will be discoverea ere long that they cannot breathe without a special act of Congress.

"DO NOT GOVERN TOO MUCH," is a maxim which should be placed in large letters over the speaker's chair in all legislative bodies. The old proverb, "too much of a good thing is good for nothing," is most especially appli cable to the present time, when it would appear, from the course of our legislation, that common sense, common experience, and the instinct of self-preservation, are utterly insufficient for the ordinary purposes of life; that the people of the United States are not only incapable of self-government, but of taking cognizance of their individual affairs; that industry requires protection, enterprize bounties, and that no man can possibly find his way in broad day light without being tied to the apron-string of a legislative dry-nurse. The present system of our legislation seems founded on the total incapacity of mankind to take care of themselves or to exist without legislative enactment. Individual property must be maintained by invasions of personal rights, and the "general welfare" secured by monopolies and exclusive privileges.

The people of the United States will discover when too late that they may be enslaved by laws as well as by the arbitrary will of a despot; that unnecessary restraints are the essence of tyranny; and that there is no more effectual instrument of depriving them of their liberties, than a legislative body, which is permitted to do anything it pleases under the broad mantle of THE PUBLIC GOOD—a mantle which, like charity, covers a multitude of sins, and like charity is too often practised at the expense of other people.

WHO PAYS FOR UNCURRENT BILLS?

[*From the Evening Post, March* 11, 1835.]

A RETAIL grocer receives from his customers in the course of a week say a hundred dollars in uncurrent bills. He cannot take up his promissory note in the bank without getting these uncurrent bills exchanged. He takes them to a broker, and receives ninety-eight dollars in bankable money for them. If this operation is repeated every week, it amounts to say fifty dollars in the course of a year. Out of whose pocket is this paper-money tax paid? Does the grocer incur the loss? Certainly not; he pays it in the first instance, but who indemnifies him? It forms one of the items of his annual expenses, which he is obliged to calculate in putting a profit on his goods. Those who deal with him pay the tax, and who are they? The carpenter, the bricklayer, and the labourer, when they buy a pound of tea, or cheese, or butter, or any other article in his line, to take home to their families. If the currency of the city were specie, or even paper convertible into specie without a discount, the prices of all commodities would undergo a sensible reduction. Every article of consumption is now charged from two to three per cent. higher than it ought to be, in consequence of the depreciated currency in circulation. This tax falls almost exclusively on the mechanics and labourers. The profit goes into the pockets of the bankers and brokers. Why should the mechanics and labourers be burdened to support banks? Are they in the habit of getting discounts? Do they live by bank-favours? No, quite the reverse. The men who live on bank credits are not labourers. "They toil not, neither do they spin;" or if they work at all, it is head-work, the end and aim of which is to supply themselves with luxuries at other people's expense. Is it not a little hard that they who receive none of the benefits dispensed by banks, should be saddled with all the burdens? If they will suffer the scrip nobility to mount them, however, and spur them, like horses, or we might more properly say like asses, it is their own fault, since they have it in their power to throw them off whenever they please. But if they would rather have depreciated paper than real money, though we may wonder at their choice, we shall not quarrel with it. *De gustibus non est disputandum.* Perhaps they prefer, as a matter of taste, a small loaf to a large one. It may be a thing of no consequence to them whether they have to pay ten pence or only eight pence a pound for beef; and to be caught now and then with a few dollars of broken bank notes in their pockets may be considered a capital joke. We should think their relish of this joke would be keener, however, if they had not purchased those notes by several days of hard toil.

THE BANK OF THE UNITED STATES.

[*From the Evening Post, March* 12, 1835.]

Most seriously and earnestly do we ask the attention of the public to the subjoined abstract of the Report of the United States Bank for the first of the present month. In our view of the subject, beyond all shadow of doubt, that huge moneyed institution is acting on a deliberate and settled design to make one last and desperate effort to perpetuate its existence by again shaking the foundations of credit, and spreading a financial panic through the land. They are fatally mistaken who imagine that the Monster has received its death-blow ; it but recoiled for a moment paralysed from the stroke, and is now spreading itself out for a more desperate struggle.

Examine, we beseech you, readers, the present condition of that hateful money power, as exhibited in the statement we subjoin. In the last four months the Bank has extended its loans MORE THAN TWELVE MILLIONS OF DOLLARS! What a warning this single fact speaks! That institution, which, eight months ago, enormously curtailed its business to the ruin of thousands of prosperous citizens, and the dismay of the whole land, on the pretext that it was compelled to prepare for the final dissolution of its charter, now, when there are no extrrordinary occasions for money, swells itself out, of its own voluntary act, to a greater degree of distension than it ever did before. The Branch Bank in this city never at any period of its existence had as much money loaned out as at this moment. Its loans now exceed those of the mother bank in Philadelphia, which was never the case before. Every indication shows, not only that a pecuniary pressure and panic is in preparation, but that this city is to be the chief scene and centre of operations. Another desperate effort will be made to break down our local institutions, and spread dismay and financial devastation through the state. And yet the local banks are extending themselves as confidentially if this slumbering volcano were not ready to explode beneath them, and scatter their foundations to the winds.

It requires no extraordinary perspicacity to perceive that another panic, and more dreadful than the first, is in preparation. The approach of the next session of Congress is the season chosen for carrying this design into execution. The forcing a recharter is the main object in view, and the secondary to defeat the democracy in the election of President. We beg men capable of reflection to ponder on this subject. We beg those having influence to use their efforts to avert the evil. The local banks, unwittingly, are lending themselves to the designs of the great money power. They are discounting with a freedom almost unparalleled. There never was before such a constant and copious flood of small country bank notes pouring into this city as at the present moment. Shall nothing be done to avert this evil—to check and roll back this tide of ruin?

Earnestly did we hope that the Legislature would do what a regard to the public wishes, and a regard to the public interests without respect to their wishes, imperatively required in relation to the small note currency. If all notes under five dollars had been prohibited at once (and the currency was never better able to sustain such a measure) the calamitous state of things which we foresee might at least be obviated in a degree. One important part of the materials of panic would have been deficient. These were the views which governed us in the Letter which we addressed to Governor Marcy through our paper of the 24th of December last. For those views we have been bitterly reviled. They who reproached us for them we live to see how true were our predictions.

Come what may, it is a satisfaction to us to know that it at least cannot be said that our warning voice was not timely raised. If the statement which we subjoin do not rouse the people, they would slumber in apathetic indifference to the future, though one should rise from the dead to put them on their guard. Have the fearful lessons of experience taught them by the events of last winter been already forgotten? Here is something then to freshen their recollections:

ABSTRACT OF THE

REPORT OF THE UNITED STATES BANK

For the first of March, 1835.

Loans on Personal Security	$31,152,368.22
do. on Bank Stock	862,566.12
Other Security	3,935,370.13
	$35,956,304.47
Domestic Bills of Exchange	21,864,100.18
	$57,814,404.65
In London and Paris	$2,754,244.65
Specie	16,567,893.36
Redemption of Public Debt	699,999.89
Treasury United States	690.704.37
Public Offices	1,192,723.02
Individual Depositors	8,903,807.35
Circulation	19,519,777.90
Due from other Banks	2,261,477.10
Due to . . do	5,011,634.24
Notes of States Banks	2,173,925.41
Loans at New York Branch.	
On Personal Security	$5,505, 365.05
On Bank Stock	134,950.00
On other Security	483,574.07
Domestic Exchange	2,328,906.83
	$8,452,797.95
At Boston	2,774,318.75
At Philadelphia	8,067,899.79
At Baltimore	1,634,155.80

THE AUCTION MONOPOLY.

[*From the Evening Post, March*, 13, 1835.]

THE American of last evening does us the honor to address its leading article particularly to this journal; and we lay aside other matters of pressing importance to extend to it the courtesy of an immediate reply. With regard to the law restraining the right to sell by auction, we have no hesitation to state, in the most explicit language, that we consider it unwise, unjust, at variance with the fundamental principles of our government, and constituting a monopoly, not merely in the popular, but in the strict legal sense of that term. Our "incessant assault upon monopolies," the American may have noticed, has been aimed rather against general principles than particular institutions. When we have adverted to particular institutions, it has been more with the view to illustrate the operation of general principles, than to give a particular direction to public sentiment. The restraining law in regard to auctions we consider quite as unsound as the restraining law in regard to banking; though the effect of restrictions on banking are more deeply and extensively pernicious than those on auctions. We earnestly desire the repeal of both, but with this difference: the first we would repeal immediately, while the latter we would desire to see maintained, until certain preliminary measures should have guarded the public against those evils which would result from throwing banking open to the whole community in the present state of our currency.

This answer we trust the American will find sufficiently explicit, so far as the auction law is concerned. But we will go a step further, and advert to the tax which the state imposes on auction sales. We look upon this tax as unequal, unjust, and oppressive, and are not without strong doubts that it is a positive, as it most assuredly is a virtual, violation of the Constitution of the United States. If we have not commented on this subject before, it has not been because we had not reflected maturely on it, and deliberately formed those opinions which we now express; but because we were unwilling to waive the discussion of general principles, for the sake of directing our energies against a single and not the most important branch of the subject of monopolies. We consider it a nobler and more useful object to strive to do away those false notions on which the whole system of restrictions and exclusive privileges rest, than to attack particular abuses in detail. We have striven to lay the axe to the root of the tree, not to cut off its branches one by one. If the trunk perishes, the boughs must needs wither.

With regard to the complaints which the American prefers in behalf of those individual auctioneers whose commissions have not been renewed, we are likewise free to state that if, as that journal avers, they have been refused a renewal of their commissions for no other reason than "because they are not for Martin Van Buren as President of the United States," Governor Marcy has acted towards them in a most proscriptive, narrow, and contemptible spirit, and his conduct deserves the scorn of all honourable men. But as we have abundant reason to believe that Governor Marcy is controlled by no such spirit, we must be excused from yielding entire credit to the assertion of the American, while it remains wholly unsupported by proof, particularly as it is wholly at war with some facts which are within our own positive knowledge. But it is not only on the score of those to whom commissions have been denied that the American finds grounds of complaint; those on whom they have been conferred afford equal ground of censure.

Again we say, if the statement made by that journal is correct, and these new auctioneers are indeed "wretched political retainers and hacks—men without credit, and unworthy of it," Governor Marcy, by appointing them, has entitled himself to severer reprehension than the American expresses. But we must join issue on the fact. It is again within our knowledge that the American is incorrect. With some of the auctioneers newly appointed we have a personal acquaintance, and others we know well through the representations of men in whom we have the fullest confidence ; and we must take leave to say, that the American is misinformed as to their characters, and does those men cruel injustice. We assert with the utmost positiveness that in every moral and intellectual quality they are, *to say the least*, quite equal to those whose places they have been appointed to fill ; that they are as honest, respectable and capable, and we do not doubt will discharge the duties of auctioneers quite as much to the satisfaction of the public and the advantage of the state.

The American, however, in bewailing the fate of the superceded auctioneers, and pouring its scorn on the heads of their successors, quite loses sight of the admirable anti-monopoly principles with which it commenced its article. That journal should recollect that it censured the auction law as "a universal abridgement of a natural right"—"a monopoly injurious and unjust ; " and spoke of those appointed under it as "a privileged class created at once." To limit their tenure then, and subject them to the operation of that principle of equal rights which requires rotation in office, is certainly diminishing the odiousness of the monopoly. And if we must have privileged classes, we ought to thank Governor Marcy for not recognizing their pretensions to be privileged for life; but by requiring them to return, after a certain term, to the level of the mass of the people, reduce the evil of aristocratic distinctions as near to the simplicity of the republican system as possible. We agree with the American that the auction law creates an odious monopoly; and the American will surely agree with us that to give "a favoured few" a perpetuity of the "privileged and valuable offices" created by that law would be to render the monopoly more exclusive and unquestionable, and add a still darker hue to its character.

There is another point of view in which the American must permit us to express our satisfaction at the course pursued by Governor Marcy; since we esteem ourselves indebted to it for the valuable assistance of that journal against monopolies. If the sympathies of the American had not been excited by the non-renewal of the "valuable offices" of certain of its friends of the privileged class, and its disgust provoked by those offices being filled with men of a different political stamp, it is impossible to say how long a time might have elapsed before that paper would have discovered that the auction law is a monopoly and the auctioneers a privileged order.

We might adduce other arguments in support of the course Governor Marcy has pursued; but unwilling to give our space to supererogative disquisitions, we shall take the liberty of referring the American to its own forcible approval of the course of the present Whig Common Council, in dismissing the democrats whom, on their being elected, they found incumbents of the various minor municipal offices.

FREE TRADE POST OFFICE.

[*From the Evening Post*, *March* 23, 1835.]

The party newspapers, both for and against the administration, contain, every now and then, statements exposing individual instances of gross abuse of the franking privilege. There can be no doubt that the franking privilege is a prolific source of many of those evils in the Post-office department which are complained of on all hands, and that a reformation of the laws on this subject is very mnch needed.

It is but a few days since we had occasion to mention a circumstance calculated to show in a strong light the grievous burdens which are imposed on the mails by those having the power to send their communications free of postage. This was the transmission, from Washington to Connecticut, by a single individual, and in the course of three days, of franked packages, weighing in all nearly two hundred pounds! These packages were said to be made up of the majority report of the Post-office committee of the United States Senate, exposing the alleged corruptions of the Post-office Department, and were doubtless sent into Connecticut at this particular time, and in such extraordinary numbers, for the purpose of being used for political effect, to influence the result of the approaching election in that state.

Though this particular instance exhibits, perhaps, a somewhat unusual excess in the use of the franking privilege, it is a fact perfectly notorious that similar impositions on the public mails are daily practised, and probably as much by the members of one party as of the other. Post masters, as well as members of Congress, exercise a most unjustifiable latitude of construction in the use of their franking privilege. Not only communications on the business of their office, and in relation to their own private affairs, are sent free from one extremity of the country to another, but in very many cases they seem to act as the general agents of their neighbourhood, and employ their franking privilege, as charity does its mantle, to cover a multitude of sins. Many particular agencies seem to be done almost entirely through the country post-masters at the expense of the Government. Nothing is more common, for example, than their gratuitous agency between the subscribers of a newspaper and its publishers. We believe we speak within bounds when we assert that full one-half of the country subscribers to the Evening Post are received through the franked letters of village post-masters. They forward to us both the names of subscribers and the payment for the paper. These facts abundantly show that a reform of the franking system is absolutely needed.

But at the hazard of giving a new occasion for the charge of ultraism against this journal, we shall take the liberty to express an opinion, which we have long entertained, that the source of the evils in our Post-office system lies far too deep to be reached by any regulation or abridgement of the franking privilege, or even by its total abolition. It lies too deep, in our opinion, also, to be reached by any possible organization of the Post-office Department which it is in the power of the General Government to establish. There are five words in the Constitution of the United States which we look upon as the grand primary source of all the evils of which the people have so much just cause to complain in relation to that particular department of the Government. We allude to the clause which gives to Congress the power "*to establish post-offices and post-roads.*"

These words, in our view of the subject, ought never to have formed a part of the Constitution. They confer a power on the General Government which is liable, and almost inevitably subject, to the grossest political abuse. The abuse is one which will necessarily increase, too, from year to year, as population increases in numbers and spreads over a wider surface. The Post-office, controled and directed by the General Government, will always be conducted with a vast deal of unnecessary expense, and, what is a consideration of far more serious importance, will always be used, to a greater or less extent, as *a political machine.*

It is not probable that the history of this Union, should it stretch out for ages, will ever exhibit to the admiration of mankind an administration under the guidance of a more faithful, energetic, intrepid and patriotic spirit, than that which happily now rules the executive councils of the nation. Yet even under the administration of a man whose integrity no arts can corrupt, whose firmness no difficulties can appal, and whose vigilance no toils can exhaust—even under the administration of such a man, what a sickening scene does the mismanagement of the Post-office not present! Remove Mr. Barry and appoint another in his place, and you will not correct, and most likely you will not even mitigate the evil. Abolish the franking privilege, and the essential defects of the system would still remain. Re-organize the whole department, and introduce all the guards and checks which legislative ingenuity can devise, and still you will not wholly remove the imperfection. The Post-office will still be a government machine, cumbrous, unwieldy, and liable to the worst sorts of abuses.

The Post-office is established by the Government for the purpose of facilitating intercourse by letter between distant places. But personal intercourse between distant places is as necessary as epistolary, though not, perhaps, to the same degree. Why then should not the Government take upon itself the support and regulation of facilities for carrying passengers as well as letters from place to place? The transmission of packages of merchandise from one part of the country to another is no less necessary, than intercourse by letter or person. Why should not Government go a step further, and institute transportation lines for the conveyance of our goods? But we shall be answered, that these objects may safely be left to the laws of trade, and that supply will keep pace with demand in these matters as in other commercial and social wants of man. Might not the laws of trade, and the power of demand to produce supply through the activity of private enterprise, be safely trusted to, also, for the carriage of letters from place to place?

If the mail establishment, as a branch of the United States Government, should be abolished this hour, how long would it be before private enterprise would institute means to carry our letters and newspapers from city to city, with as much regularity as they are now carried, and far greater speed and economy? But the objection may be raised that inland places and thinly settled portions of the country would suffer by such an arrangement. There is no place on the map of the United States which would not soon be supplied with mail facilities by paying what they were worth, and if it gets them for less now, it is only because the deficiency is levied from the inhabitants of some other place, which is contrary to the plainest principles of justice.

There are very many considerations which might be urged in favour of *a free trade view of this subject.* The curse of office hunting, which is an incident of our form of Government, and is exerting every year, more and more, a demoralizing influence on the people, would undergo a check and rebatement by the suggested change. But would you withdraw—some one may ask—the stimulus which the present post-office system furnishes to emigration, by extending mail routes through the wilderness, and thus presenting inducements for population to gather together at points which would otherwise remain unimproved and uninhabited for years? To this we answer, unequivocally, yes. We would withdraw all Government *stimulants;* and let no man suppose that the progress of improvement would be retarded by such a withdrawal. The country would grow from year to year, notwithstanding, as rapidly and more healthily than now. It would only be changing the hot-bed system to the system of nature and reason. It would be discontinuing the force-pump method, by which we now seek to make water flow up hill, and leaving it to flow in its own natural channels. It would be removing the high-pressure application of Government facilities from enterprise and capital, and permitting them to expand themselves in their own proper field. The boundaries of population would still continually enlarge, circle beyond circle, like spreading rings upon the water; but they would not be forced to enlarge this way and that way, shooting out into strange and unnatural irregularities, as it might please land speculators, through the agency of members of Congress, to extend mail facilities into regions which perhaps God and nature meant should remain uninhabited for ages to come.

There are various other points of view in which the subject deserves to be considered. But we must reserve these for another occasion.

STOCK GAMBLING.

[*From the Evening Post, March* 25, 1835.]

In the bill now before the legislature of this state to regulate the sales of stocks and exchange, we behold another beautiful illustration of the benefits which the community derive from our wretched system of special and partial legislation. The professed object of this bill is to prevent stock-gambling ; and stock-gambling, according to our humble opinion, is a species of speculation which our law-givers, by the whole course of their legislation for years past, have done all in their power to foster and promote. If they desire now, really and sincerely, to do away with the evils of this desperate and immoral kind of enterprise, which daily displays itself to a frightful extent in Wall-street, let them adopt a more effectual method than that proposed by the bill under their consideration. Let them address their efforts to correct the cause of the evil, and the effect will be sure to be removed. Let them apply the axe to the root of the tree, and the branches will needs wither, when the source from which they derive their nourishment is destroyed.

The whole course of our legislation, in regard to financial matters, has had a direct tendency to excite a feverish and baneful thirst of gain—gain not by the regular and legitimate operations of trade, but by sudden and hazardous means. Every body has been converted into a stock speculator by our laws. Every body is seeking to obtain a charter of incorporation for some purpose or other, in order that he may take his place among the bulls and bears of the stock-market, and play his hand in the desperate game of Wall-street brag. What is the true nature of the spectacle which is presented to the contemplation of sober-minded men, every time any new company of scrip gamblers is created? Do we not see persons not worth a hundred dollars in the world, running with all speed to put in their claims for a division of the stock—persons who are not able to raise even the instalment on the amount of stock which they ask, and who, in point of fact, are the mere agents of brokers and other speculators, selling the use of their names for a certain rate of premium per share on the division of stock which may be awarded to them?

A gaming spirit has infected the whole community. This spirit is the offspring—the deformed and bloated offspring—of our wretched undemocratic system of exclusive and partial legislation. To destroy the effect, and leave the cause untouched, would be as easy a task for our legislature, as to restrain an impetuous torrent while you yet leave wide the flood-gates which presented the only barrier to its course. The legislature might pass a law commanding the stream to keep within certain limits; but we doubt if its waves would recede, notwithstanding the terrors of the law—

> "They rolled not back when Canute gave command."

It is time the legislature made the discovery that there are some things which cannot be done by law. They cannot prevent the thunder from following the lightning's flash, however carefully they may word their statute, or whatever penalty they may affix to its violation. They cannot change the whole nature of man by any enactment. We doubt very much whether even the famous Blue Laws wholly deterred men from kissing their wives on occasions, particularly in the first part of their matrimonial connexion; nor do we believe they prevented beer from working on Sundays during the season of fermentation. As easy would it be, however, to effect such objects by law, as to repress the yearnings of cupidity and avarice, or stay the adventurous spirit of wild speculation which has been excited, by the penalties of a bill to regulate the sales of stock and exchange. The whole scope and tendency of all the rest of our legislation is to inflame the feverish thirst of gain, which afflicts the community ; and how vain, how worse than vain, while our law-makers hold up the lure in every possible form of attraction before the public, to bid them, shut their eyes, and not attempt to grasp it !

As to the particular project before the legislature, if we understand its provisions, it is not only inadequate to the end proposed, but unjust in its bearing, and impolitic on various grounds. It proposes to destroy the use of credit in the transactions of the stock-exchange, which is much such a cure for the evil it aims to abolish as amputation of the leg would be for a gouty toe. The gout might attack the other foot, or the stomach, notwithstanding ; nor would its victim be more able to resist its influences with a frame weakened by the barbarous and uncalled for mutilation he had suffered. There is no earthly reason why credit should not be used in the purchase and sale of stocks, as well as in any other species of traffic. There is no kind of business intercourse which may not be made the means of gambling, and were it even within the competency of the legislature to check the public propensity to traffic on speculative contingencies, so far as one particular species of business is concerned, the ever active disposition would immediately indulge itself in some other form of hazardous and unreal enterprise. For the real *bona fide* transactions in stock and exchange, the employment of credit is as intrinsically proper, as the employment of credit in foreign commerce, in the purchase of real estate, or in any of the various modes and objects of human dealing. The legislature might as well pass a law forbidding the citizen to deal or credit with his tailor, hatter, or shoemaker, to run up a score with his milkmen or baker, or postpone the payment for his newspaper, as to fordid a man to employ his legitimate credit in the purchase and sale of stocks.

The mere business of dealing in stocks is as respectable and useful as most others : the crime of gambling in stocks is the inevitable result of the wild and speculative spirit which springs from unsalutary legislation. When we look into the statute books, and see that more than two-thirds of all the laws passed in our state are for the creation of specially incorporated joint-stock companies ; when we learn that two-thirds of these joint-stock companies were created originally, not with strict reference to their professed ultimate object, but for purposes of intermediary speculation : we must perceive that the evil to be remedied is in the legislature, not in the community ; that the fountain is turbid at its head, and that it will be vain and foolish to attempt to purify it by straining the waters of a distant branch through a clumsy, filtering contrivance of the laws.

There is another view of this subject which it is important to take. By abolishing the use of credit in stock operations, you would not abolish stock-gambling, but only confine it to the more wealthy operators, and put additional facilities of fortune into the hands already favoured overmuch. You make a concession to the spirit of aristocracy. You lay another tribute at the feet of riches. You join your voice in its exaltation. You exclude from the magic circle the poor man whose capital consisted in his skill, industry, and character for sagacity and integrity, and you give it to the millionary to lord it there alone, as if his gold were better than the poor man's blood.

That we are opposed to stock-gambling and gambling,

in all its forms, we need not say. But we are equally opposed to those false notions of Government which so extensively prevail in this country, and which seem to consider that every thing is to be done by law, and nothing by common sense and the inevitable operation of the laws of trade. For gambling, public opinion is the great and only salutary corrective. If it cannot be suppressed by the force of the moral sense of the community, it cannot be suppressed by statutes and edicts, no matter how comprehensive their terms, or how heavy their penalties. We have our laws against gambling now, yet establishments fitly denominated *hells* are notoriously conducted in different parts of the city, and there are various neighbourhoods where the dice-box and the roulette wheel rattle and clatter all night long. We have our laws against lotteries, too, yet what do they avail? The history of a recent instance of a man convicted of trafficking in the forbidden pursuit must convince any mind that those laws are a little more than a dead letter. And such would be the law to suppress stock operations on time. It would not do away with either the proper or improper part of the business; but it would diminish the respectability of the honest and prudent dealer, and give a more desperate character to the reckless adventurer.

REGISTRATION OF VOTERS.

[*From the Evening Post, April* 3, 1835.]

The Veto of the Mayor of this city on the proceedings of the Common Council, relative to the proposed law for the registering of voters, was confined, we understand, to the constitutional objection, and did not object to the measure on the ground that it was not competent for the municipal legislature to take any steps to procure a statute at all changing or modifying the basis of the right of suffrage, as fixed by the State Convention. We presume Mr. Lawrence restricted himself to the constitutional argument, and pretermitted the other ground of objection, because the first afforded abundant justification of the course he pursued in declining his signature. Had the constitution, however, presented no impediment to the passing of such a law as the Common Council proposed, it might still be a matter of grave consideration how far our city authorities could, consistently with their legitimate functions under the City Charter, take part in procuring an important restriction on the right of suffrage. As the Mayor, however, has not touched on this topic in his late message returning to the Common Council their resolution and other proceedings in relation to the registry law, we shall confine our attention, in the following paragraphs, to a consideration of the constitutional question, whether the legislature has or has not the power to pass such a law.

In the Constitution of this state, as adopted by the Convention in 1821, the first section of the second article established numerous qualifications for voters. The right of suffrage, by that section, was extended to every male citizen of the age of twenty-one, who should have been an inhabitant of the state for twelve months, and of the town or county where he offered his vote six months next preceding the election; *provided,* he had paid a tax, or was by law exempted from taxation, or had performed military duty in the state, or was by law exempted from military duty, or had laboured on the highway, or paid an equivalent for such labour, &c. &c. After stating these various qualifications, two other brief sections were added, one empowering the legislature to pass laws excluding from the right of suffrage persons convicted of infamous crimes; and the other to pass laws "for ascertaining by proper proofs, the citizens who shall be entitled to the right of suffrage *hereby established.*"

It is under this last clause that the power is claimed for the legislature to pass a law requiring the inhabitants of this city to register their names, before they can be entitled to vote in an election. Yet that the power conferred by the clause is not so extensive, must be perfectly apparent to all who will take the pains to examine the proceedings of the Convention which framed the Constitution. It was intended to apply, probably, only to the qualifications as established by the first section of the second article, which, as they were numerous and somewhat complex, might require the enactment of a law to provide one uniform mode of proof. If this was so, that clause became a dead letter, when the qualifications were stricken out, as they were by an amendment of the Constitution in 1826.

Be this as it may, the Journal of the Convention contains abundant proof that the section, empowering the legislature to pass laws for ascertaining, by proper proof, the persons entitled to suffrage under the Constitution, never conferred the power of passing a law requiring a registry of voters. The section, as originally reported to the Convention, by "the Committee appointed to consider the right of suffrage, and the qualifications of persons to be elected," was in the following words:

"Laws shall be made for ascertaining, by proper proofs, the citizens who shall be entitled to the right of suffrage, hereby established. *The legislature may provide by law, that a register of all citizens entitled to the right of suffrage, in every town and ward, shall be made at least twenty days before any election; and may provide, that no person shall vote at any election, who shall not be registered as a citizen qualified to vote at such election.*"

On the eighth of October, nearly a month afterwards,

and when the subject had probably received the mature consideration of every member of the Convention, a motion was offered by Mr. Root, "*to strike out the third section, relating to a registry of votes.*" This motion underwent a long and animated discussion. It was finally modified, with the consent of the mover, by excepting the first sentence, and extending the motion to strike out only to the residue of the sentence—namely, to that part which, in the above quotation, we have printed in italics. But in permitting the first sentence to stand, it was clearly the intention of the Convention that the power to require that the names of all voters should be registered should not be conferred on the legislature. The motion, thus amended, passed by a vote of 60 to 48. If we adopt the generally received maxim, which was eloquently enforced by Mr. Madison on a memorable occasion, that "*in a controverted case, the meaning of the parties to the instrument, if to be collected by reasonable evidence, should be considered a proper guide,*" there can be no doubt or hesitation as to the propriety of the stand which the mayor has taken on this question of the registry of voters. But if we even turn our backs on the proceedings of the Convention, and insist on understanding the Constitution without the help of any lights not furnished by its own text, still, we think, an answerable argument might be maintained against the constitutionality of the power which the common council are desirous that the legislature should exercise. We may embrace some other opportunity to turn our attention to that branch of the discussion.

WEIGHMASTER GENERAL.

[*From the Evening Post, April* 10, 1835.]

THE report of the proceedings of the Legislature on Wednesday, which is copied into our paper of to-day, shows to our readers that there was a decided majority in the Assembly in favour of the bill providing for the appointment of a Weighmaster General for this city, with power to name his own deputies. This measure was passed by a strict party vote; and for the sake of creating another office to be supported out of the means of this overburdened community, those members of the legislature who were elected by the democracy, and call themselves democrats, have concurred in fastening another shackle on the limbs of trade.

There is probably not one man in our legislature so totally destitute of all knowledge of that magnificeut science which is revolutionizing the world, as not to be aware that the bill now before that body to regulate the weighing of merchandise, is an indirect tax on the people, is a violation of the principle of equal rights, is another link in that chain which folly and cunning have combined to fasten on the body politic, and by which the pupular action is already so much restrained, that, notwithstanding we enjoy universal suffrage, our elections, for the most part, are rather a reflection of the wishes of the banks and of the office-holders, than of the free, unbiassed will of the people. The effect of the present bill, besides imposing an additional tax on the community, and placing harmful checks and limitations around trade, will be to institute a band of placemen in the city, who will doubtless endeavour to show themselves worthy of their hire by exerting their lungs in shouts and pæans in praise of those to whom they owe their situations.

To a certain extent exertions of this kind guide the course of public sentiment, and increase its force. Independent, then, of the politico-economical objections to legislative interference of the sort now under consideration, a more momentous objection exists in the fact that such measures are directly calculated to place government on a basis other than that of the spontaneous sentiments of the people, and draw a cordon of placemen around it, more powerful than the lictors and prætorian cohorts which hedged in the abuses and corruptions of the licentious rulers of Rome.

Earnestly did we hope that our present legislature, instead of rivetting new fetters on the people, would have broken and cast away a portion, at least, of those disgraceful bonds with which the craft and ignorance of their predecessors had loaded us. But the fact is not to be disguised that our legislature, though called democratic, and elected by democrats, are in reality anything but true friends to the equal rights of the people. They represent banks, insurance companies, railroads, manufacturing establishments, high-salaried officers, inspectors of raw-hides, sole-leather, beef, pork, tobacco, flour, rum, wood, coal, and, in short, almost every necessary and comfort of life. To state this more briefly, they represent monopolies and office-holders; and no wonder, therefore, that the whole course of their legislation is at the expense and to the detriment of the people at large, as they on all hands seem to be considered lawful prey.

WEIGHMASTER GENERAL.

[*From the Evening Post, April* 16, 1835.]

It will be seen by the report of the proceedings of the legislature yesterday afternoon, that Governor Marcy has returned to the Senate the bill providing for the appointment of a Weighmaster General for this city, together with his objections; that the bill was subsequently reconsidered and rejected, one person only dissenting, and a new bill for the same purpose as the former, but framed so as to avoid the objections stated by the Governor, was thereupon introduced by Mr. Macdonald. We hope, against hope, that there will be good sense enough in the legislature to defeat this new attempt to impose additional fetters on the body politic. We perceive with pleasure that Mr. Young, who has been absent for some days past in consequence of a domestic affliction, has resumed his seat in the Senate. We trust he may be induced to exert his powerful mind in exposing the true nature and utter folly of the proposed law.

The real motive of those who are pushing this measure is as well understood in this city as in Albany. It is perfectly well known here that the object is to create an office for a young politician from this city, who, for several years past, has been an active partizan, and who, during the past winter, has strenuously represented that it is time he had his reward. We have not the slighest objection that the individual alluded to should be provided with an office; for we believe he is quite as honest and capable as nine-tenths of the office seekers, and have no doubt that his exertions have been of service to the democratic cause. But we have objection that an office should be especially created for his benefit, one for which there is not the slightest public need, which would operate as an indirect tax on the community, and would present another and strong impediment in the way of that total emancipation of trade from the restrictions and impositions which have been placed upon it by crafty and foolish legislation.

The weighing of merchandise is a matter with which legislation has nothing to do: the laws of trade would arrange that business much more to the satisfaction of all parties concerned than the laws of the state can ever do. When the Government has supplied its citizens with a measure of value, of weight, of length, and of quantity, it has done all in the way of measuring which properly belongs to Government. All your inspectors, your guagers, and your weighers, after that, with their whole host of deputies and subalterns, are but adscititious contrivances of political cunning, to provide means for rewarding those who assisted in its elevation, or to establish a phalanx to guard it in the height it has attained.

It was our hope that our present legislature—chosen under so distinct an expression of the public sentiment against all monopolies and all infringements of the principle of Equal Rights—would exert themselves to do away the restrictions on trade and the thousand subtle contrivances for indirectly extorting taxes from the people to support useless officers; or at all events that they would not add to the number of those impositions. If we go on for many years to come, strengthening, and extending the artificial and unequal system we have for years past been building up, we shall at length find, perhaps too late, that we have erected around us an enormous, unseemly, and overshadowing structure, from which the privileged orders will have the encircled community wholly at their control, and which we cannot hope to demolish without bringing the whole fabric down with ruin on our heads.

DIRECT TAXATION.

[*From the Evening Post of April* 22, 1834.]

No reflecting mind can consider the mode of raising revenue in this country for the support of the Government, in connexion with the great principle on which that Government is founded, without being struck with the anomaly it presents. The fundamental principle of our political institutions is that the great body of the people are honest and intelligent, and fully capable of self-government. Yet so little confidence is really felt in their virtue and intelligence, that we dare not put them to the test of asking them, openly and boldly, to contribute, each according to his means, to defray the necessary expenses of the Government; but resort, instead, to every species of indirection and arbitrary restriction on trade. This is true, not only of the General Government, but of every State Government, and every municipal corporation. The General Government raises its revenue by a tax on foreign commerce, giving rise to the necessity of a fleet of revenue vessels, and an army of revenue officers. The State Governments raise their funds by a tax on auction sales, bonuses on banks, tolls on highways, licenses, excise, &c. The municipal corporations descend a step in this prodigious scale of legislative swindling, and derive their resources from impositions on grocers, from steamboat and stage-coach licenses, and from a tax on beef, wood, coal, and nearly every prime necessary of life. This whole complicated system is invented and persevered in for the purpose of deriving the expenses of Government from a people whose virtue and intelligence constitute the avowed basis of our institutions! What an absurdity does not a mere statement of the fact present?

Has any citizen, rich or poor, the least idea of the amount which he annually pays for the support of the government? The thing is impossible. No arithmetician, not even Babbit with his calculating machine, could compute the sum. He pays a tax on every article of clothing he wears, on every morsel of food he eats, on the fuel that warms him in winter, on the light which cheers his home in the evening, on the implements of his industry, on the amusements which recreate his leisure. There is scarcely an article produced by human labour or ingenuity which does not bear a tax for the support of one of the three governments under which every individual lives.

We have heretofore expressed the hope, and most cordially do we repeat it, that the day will yet come when we shall see the open and honest system of direct taxation resorted to. It is the only democratic system. It is the only method of taxation by which the people can know how much their government costs them. It is the only method which does not give the lie to the great principle on which we profess to have established all our political institutions. It is the only method, moreover, in consonance with the doctrines of that magnificent science, which, the twin-sister, as it were, of democracy, is destined to make this country the pride and wonder of the earth.

There are many evils which almost necessarily flow from our complicated system of indirect taxation. In the first place, taxes fall on the people very unequally. In the second place, it gives rise to the creation of a host of useless officers, and there is no circumstance which exercises such a vitiating and demoralizing influence on politics, as the converting of elections into a strife of opposite parties for place instead of principles. Another bad effect of the system is that it strengthens the government at the expense of the rights of the people, induces it to extend its powers to objects which were not contemplated in its original institution, and renders it every year less and less subject to the popular will. The tendency of the system is to build up and foster monopolies of various kinds, and to impose all sorts of restrictions on those pursuits which should be left wholly to the control of the laws of trade. We are well satisfied, and have long been so, that the only way to preserve economy in government, to limit it to its legitimate purposes, and to keep aroused the necessary degree of vigilance on the part of the people, is by having that government dependent for its subsistence on a direct tax on property.

If the fundamental principle of democracy is not a cheat and a mockery, a mere phrase of flattery, invented to gull the people—if it is really true that popular intelligence and virtue are the true source of all political power and the true basis of Government—if these positions are admitted, we can conceive no possible objection to a system of direct taxation which at all counterbalances any of the many important and grave considerations that may be urged in its favour.

For our own part, we profess ourselves to be democrats in the fullest and largest sense of the word. We are for free trade and equal rights. We are for a strictly popular Government. We have none of those fears, which some of our writers, copying the slang of the English aristocrats, profess to entertain of an "unbalanced democracy." We believe when government in this country shall be a true reflection of public sentiment; when its duties shall be strictly confined to its only legitimate ends, the equal protection of the whole community in life, person, and property; when all restrictions on trade shall be abolished, and when the funds necessary for the support of the government and the defence of the country are derived directly from taxation on property—we believe when these objects are brought about, we shall then present to the admiration of the world a nation founded as the hills, free as the air, and prosperous as a fruitful soil, a genial climate, and industry, enterprise, temperance and intelligence can render us.

STATE PRISON MONOPOLY.

[*From the Evening Post, April* 28, 1835.]

The legislature, it will be seen, have at last taken up, in good earnest, the state prison question. As this is a subject which both parties have tried their utmost to turn into a mere political gull-trap, it is not probable that any measure will be finally acted upon, before members have baited the trap with a deal of mawkish oratory, and, in so doing, expose, most thoroughly, their ignorance of the first principles of political economy.

This journal has never said much in relation to the state prison monopoly, as it is called, because a degree of importance had been given to the subject entirely disproportioned to its real merits, and demagogues had made it the theme of their vehement harangues, until an excitement was produced among the mechanic classes so strong and general, that it swallowed up almost every other question, and pervaded almost every vocation. We are as decidedly opposed to the *principle* of state prison labour as any person can be; yet we believe that the *practical evil* of the present system, on any branch of productive industry, is exceedingly trifling, and indeed almost below computation, while the result to society at large is decidedly beneficial. Nevertheless, as the fundamental principle of the system is, in our view, totally erroneous, we have never hesitated to oppose it when we deemed that the occasion called on us to speak.

One of these occasions was furnished by the publication of the report of the State Prison Commissioners, which was a weak, inaccurate, shuffling document, and was the more calculated to provoke indignation, as one of its authors is well known to have ridden himself into office on the hobby of the state prison monopoly question. It seemed to us a barefaced piece of treachery for this person, after having won the suffrages of the mechanics by the incessant and superior loudness of his vociferation against the employment of convict labour in competition with honest industry, to turn round and immediately present to the legislature such a deceptive hocus-pocus report as that to which his name was subscribed.

The suggestions of the report made by the Commissioners have been embodied in the bill now before the Assembly. By this plan the prisoners are to be employed in branches of industry not yet introduced among our citizens, and among these the culture and manufacture of silk occupy a conspicuous place. We are surprised that sensible men in the legislature should not perceive that in principle, it is the same thing whether the convicts are employed in callings in which free citizens are already engaged, or are turned to others to which free citizens would naturally direct their attention in the course of a short time.

The question of the state prison monopoly, in our view, reduces itself to this : it is the exclusive employment, by Government, of a labour-saving machine, in competition with a certain portion of citizens who have no such advantage. Has Government a right to set up a labour-saving machine, and to enter into competition with any class of its citizens in any pursuit of industry? Government, it will be admitted, is instituted for the equal protection of all, in person, life, and property. These are its only legitimate objects. The confinement of criminals, so as to restrain them from perpetrating their outrages against society, is an object in which all are equally interested. The support of them in confinement is a contingent evil, and ought to be borne in the ratio of benefit conferred—that is, equally. But when the criminals are made to earn their own support by manufacturing a class of articles which a certain portion of citizens also manufacture for their livelihood, it is obvious that a fundamental principle of government is violated, since equal protection is no longer extended to all.

But the political economist may contend that the evil in this case is but temporary; that the supply will soon adjust itself to the demand; that a certain number of citizens, driven from their occupation by the introduction of convict competition, will only be obliged to turn themselves to other branches of industry; and that in a short time, the matter equalizing itself through all the callings of active life, a permanent benefit will accrue to society, in the aggregate, by reason of the increased production and diminished price of all the articles created by human labour.

If we admit this statement to be true, is it not at best an argument in favour of the state prison system on the ground that *all is well that ends well?* or that *it is right to do evil in the first instance, that good may follow?* These are principles which ought never to be countenanced in our system of political ethics. The cardinal object of Government is the equal protection of all citizens. The moment the prisoner is set to work, and the products of his labour sold, some free citizen is unequally and oppressively burdened. If this citizen is induced to forsake his now overstocked calling, and engage in some other, the competition in this new branch will operate injuriously to those already engaged in it; and this will continue to be the case, though in a gradually diminishing ratio, through all the various pursuits of active industry, until the displaced particles of society, so to speak, diffuse themselves evenly over the entire surface.

The aggregate of products manufactured by convict labour in the United States bears so small a proportion to the sum of the products of free labour, that the practical evil of state prison competition on any mechanic class is, as we have already stated, exceedingly and almost incalculably light. The final result of all labour-saving machinery (and the operation of our penitentiary system is precisely analogous with that of such a machine) is beneficial to society. An individual citizen has a perfect right to introduce labour-saving machinery, and however hard may be the effect temporarily on any number of citizens, the good of the greatest number is immediately promoted, and eventually the good of all. But when a state government sets up such a labour-saving machine, it oppresses temporarily a class of citizens, for the immediate benefit of the rest, and though the whole community will be eventually benefitted, the state has obviously, to produce this result, violated the fundamental principle of equal rights.

STATE PRISON LABOUR.

[*From the Evening Post of April* 29, 1835.]

THE Albany Argus gives the following outline of the bill on the subject of state prison labour whichis now under discussion in the legislature of this state:

"The bill reported by Mr. Wilkinson from the majority provides that the state prisons at Auburn and Mount

Pleasant shall each be under the direction of five inspectors, three to be residents of those places respectively, who shall have the appointment of assistant keepers and all other powers now vested in them, except as otherwise provided by the bill. After prescribing the duties, compensation, &c., of the inspectors, chaplains, assistant keepers, &c., the bill provides that no mechanical trade shall hereafter be taught to convicts in the state prisons, except for the making of those articles, the chief supply of which for the consumption of the country is imported from foreign countries—that the inspectors shall have power to employ artizans from abroad for the purpose of teaching new branches of business in the prisons which are not pursued in the state—that no contract for the services of the convicts shall be made for a longer period than six months, without the sanction of the inspectors at a regular meeting, that two months' notice of the time and place of letting such contracts shall be published in the state paper and such other papers (not exceeding four) as the inspectors shall direct—the notice to specify the branch of business in which the convicts are to be employed and their number applied for, the length of time for which the contracts are to be made (which are not to exceed five years); such convicts only to be employed in such branches of business which chiefly supply domestic consumption, as had learned that particular trade before coming to the prison. Nothing in the act is to prevent the teaching of mechanical business in the prisons as far as may be necessary to fulfilling existing contracts; but it is made the duty of the inspectors and agents to avail themselves, as fast as the interest of the prisons will permit, of every opportunity to change the present contracts, so as to make them conform to the principles of the act, and they are authorized to negotiate with the present contractors, for the abandonment of their contracts, at such times and on such terms as they may deem proper. It is also made their duty to cause the manufacture of silk goods, from cocoons, to be introduced, as soon as it can be conveniently done, and for that purpose, to purchase as well cocoons raised in the country, as the raw material imported, and to extend such business as fast as in their opinion, it can with a prospect of ultimate profit. The inspectors and agents of Mount Pleasant Prison are also directed as soon as practicable to cause so much of the state farm at Sing Sing, as they may think proper, to be planted with and applied to the raising of the white mulberry tree, and other approved varieties, to be by them gratuitously distributed or sold at moderate prices, for the production of cocoons and the manufacture of silk. The agents of both prisons are also directed to procure a supply of the white mulberry seed, which shall be furnished gratuitously to the keepers and superintendents of the several county poor houses, who shall apply for it, with the view of raising mulberry trees on the several poor house farms."

No mechanical trades, according to this bill, are hereafter to be taught the prisoners in our state prisons, except for the making of such articles as are *chiefly* imported from other countries. The ground on which a change in our penitentiary system is asked is, that it is unjust and inconsistent with the principle of equal rights that the State Government, which is established for the equal protection of the whole people, should become the competitor of any portion of the people in their lawful callings. The Government being established for the equal protection of all, it is proper that the necessary expenses of that protection should be equally defrayed by all, in the proportion of their several means. When the expenses are defrayed from the profits of prison labour, the burden manifestly falls most heavily on those whom that labour competes with in their lawful callings. This would be true, if the State Government came into the competition only on equal terms; since the excess of the supply over the demand would necessarily, according to the invariable operation of the laws of trade, occasion a diminution of price, and consequently of profit to the free citizen whose vocation was interfered with by this degrading rivalry. But it is true in a more striking manner when the State Government, entering into competition with any portion of its own citizens, employs facilities of which it enjoys the exclusive use. The state prison turned into a mechanical institute is, in effect, a labour-saving machine, for the labour costs nothing. All beyond the cost of raw materials is profit to the state. The state can therefore well afford to sell articles of prison manufacture at a price which would not supply the free mechanic with bread. A certain number of free citizens are thus necessarily driven from their callings, and obliged to find employment in others, or to depend on charity, public or private, for their support.

We have admitted that though this is a grievous temporary evil to a few persons, it operates as a benefit to the community at large, and finally to the very calling which was at first interfered with. But the argument is that this eventual good is obtained by the previous violation of a fundamental principle of democratic government—the great principle of Equal Rights. The extent of the evil, be it greater or less, does not change the aspect of the question. If the equal rights of one citizen are trampled on by our state prison system, there is ground to require a reformation of it: if the profits of any class of mechanics or tradesmen are diminished, though but in the proportion of a mill on the dollar, or the hundred dollars, they have a right to demand redress. Nay, we go further: it not merely a right, but a duty; for if you once admit the principle, who can fortell for what evils and abuses the "fatal precedent" may not plead?

We are of the number of those who believe that the practical evils of our penitentiary system are very inconsiderable and restricted, and the practical benefits great and widely diffused. Yet we are opposed to that system; because it is founded on a violation of a fundamental principle of our Government. We do not perceive that the bill now before the legislature does away this objection. It lessens the practical evil, but does not vary the principle. If the prisoners are to be turned to the production of articles chiefly imported from foreign countries; yet as long as some portion of those articles is made here, certain mechanic classes, however small, would experience injurious competition from a Government which they have a right to look to for protection, not for opposition. The rights of a small class of mechanics are as dear to them as are those of the most numerous class to its members. But there is another class of persons besides mechanics, whose equal rights the proposed measure will invade. Those citizens whose capital and enterprise are engaged in foreign commerce, importers of the articles which the state prisons are hereafter to be set to work to manufacture, the retailers who deal with them, and all subsidiary callings, are to be deranged, to a greater or less degree, by the proposed bill. Here still, the erroneous principle, which is the only thing in the question worth contending about, is quite as manifest as ever.

There is one thing quite certain in regard to this matter: namely, that the bill now under discussion, cannot become a law without a majority of two-thirds of both houses should vote in its favour. *Governor Marcy will veto it.* On this point there is no room for doubt. We have before us a statement under his own hand tantamount to such a declaration. In a letter addressed to Mr. Rudolph Snyder, Chairman of the Corresponding Committee of the Convention of Mechanics which met at Utica last autumn, Governor Marcy says, "That the labour of convicts in our state prisons, as now conducted, is injurious to several branches of mechanical business, is generally conceded, and the only diversity of opinion on the subject is as to the extent of the injury and the practicable means of removing it. *The evil being admitted, it is the imperative duty of the legislature to apply a corrective, and I shall exert my influence, in whatever situation I may be, in favour of all proper measures for the attainment of that end. That any class of citizens who yield obedience to the laws, and contribute to the support of government, should be injured by the means used for the punishment of malefactors, is manifestly unjust; a system of prison discipline which necessarily produces such a result is clearly wrong; and a government which sustains it, neglects one of its obvious duties, the duty of protecting the equal rights of all.*"

Those who are engaged in importing the articles which it is proposed that prison labour shall be employed in making hereafter, are a "class of citizens who yield obedience to the laws and contribute to support the government;" for the state to enter into competition with them in their business and undersell them, thus either forcing them to seek some other employment for their capital, or to be content with diminished profits, would obviously be "to injure them by the means used for the punishment of malefactors;" and as this is declared by Governor Marcy to be "manifestly unjust," it is plain that the bill must receive his veto. He is publicly pledged to this course, and Governor Marcy is not a man to violate a pledge or shrink from a duty.

THE COURSE OF THE EVENING POST

[*From the Evening Post, May* 18, 1835.]

Saturday last was the semi-annual dividend day of this office. It is presumed that a majority of the subscribers of the Evening Post feel sufficient interest in its prosperity to justify our adverting, for a single moment, and in the most general terms, to the private affairs of this office. It is with satisfaction, then, we have it in our power to state, that the business of our establishment, during the past six months, has been flourishing and profitable, and was never more thoroughly and soundly prosperous than at the present moment. The number of subscribers to our journal is larger than at any previous period; the amount received for advertising is undiminished; and the total receipts of the establishment greater than they ever were before,

This result is exceedingly gratifying to us for considerations of a higher kind than those which merely relate to the success of our private business. It furnishes us with an evidence of the public sentiment in relation to those cardinal principles of democratic government which this journal, for a long time past, has laboured zealously to propagate and defend. That evidence is in our favour, and animates us to fresh exertions. We start afresh, then, from this resting-place on our editorial road, invigorated with renewed confidence of ultimately attaining the goal for which we strive, the reward for which we toil, the victory for which we struggle—the establishment of the great principle of Equal Rights as, in all things, the perpetual guide and invariable rule of legislation.

It is now about two years since the Evening Post—having at length seen successfully accomplished one of the great objects for which it had long and perseveringly striven, namely, the principles of free-trade in respect of our foreign commerce—turned its attention to a kindered subject, of equal magnitude, in our domestic policy, and began the struggle which it has ever since maintained in favour of the principles of economic science, as they relate to the internal and local legislation of the country. We had long seen with the deepest regret that the democracy, unmindful of the fundamental axiom of their political faith, had adopted a system of laws, the inevitable tendency of which would be to build up privileged classes and depress the great body of the community. We saw that trade, not left in the slightest respect to the salutary operation of its own laws, had been tied up and hampered in every limb and muscle by arbitrary and unjust statutes; that these restrictions furnished employment for an almost innumerous army of office-holders; and that the phalanx of placemen was yearly augmented by the multiplication of unequal and oppressive restrictions and prohibitions on the body politic. We could not help seeing, also, that this multitude of unnecessary public offices, to be disposed by the Government, was exercising a most vitiating influence on politics, and was constantly degrading, more and more, what should be a conflict of unbiassed opinion, into an angry warfare of heated and selfish partisans, struggling for place.

But besides the various and almost countless restrictions on trade, for the support of a useless army of public stipendiaries, we saw our State Governments vieing with each other in dispensing to favoured knots of citizens trading privileges and immunities which were withheld from the great body of the community. And to such an extent was this partial legislation carried, that in some instances, a State Government, not content with giving to a particular set of men valuable exclusive privileges, to endure for a long term of years, also pledged the property of the whole people, as the security for funds which it raised, to lend again, on easy terms, to the favoured few it had already elevated into a privileged order. These things seemed to us to be so palpable a violation of the plainest principles of equal justice, that we felt imperatively called upon to make them objects of attack.

Of all the privileges which the States were lavishing on sets of men, however, those seemed the most dangerous which conferred banking powers; authorized them to coin a worthless substitute for gold and silver; to circulate it as real money; and thus enter into competition with the General Government of the United States, in one of the highest and most important of its exclusive functions. There was no end to the evils and disorders which this daring violation of the fundamental principle of democratic doctrine was continually occasioning. It was placing the measure of value (the most important of all measures) in the hands of speculators, to be extended or contracted to answer their own selfish views or the suggestions of their folly. It was subjecting the community to continual fluctuations of prices, now raising every article to the extremest height of the scale, and now depressing it to the bottom. It was unsettling the foundations of private right, diversifying the time with seasons of preternatural prosperity and severe distress, shaking public faith, exciting a spirit of wild speculation, and demoralizing and vitiating the whole tone of popular sentiment and character. It was every day adding to the wealth and power of the few by extortions wrung from the hard hands of toil; and every day increasing the numbers and depressing the condition of the labouring poor.

This was the state of things to reform which, after the completion of the tariff compromise, seemed to us an object that demanded our most strenuous efforts. We have consequently sought to draw public attention to the fact that the great principle on which our whole system of government is founded, the principle of Equal Rights, has been grossly departed from. We have sought to show them that all legislative restrictions on trade operate as unjust and unequal taxes on the people, place dangerous powers in the hands of the Government, diminish the efficiency of popular suffrage, and render it more difficult for popular sentiment to work salutary reforms. We have sought to illustrate the radical impropriety of all legislative grants of exclusive or partial privileges, and the peculiar impropriety and various evil consequences of exclusive banking privileges. We have striven to show that all the proper and legitimate ends of Government interference might easily be accomplished by general laws, of equal operation on all. In doing this, we necessarily aroused bitter and powerful hostility. We necessarily assailed the interests of the privileged orders, and endangered the schemes of those who were seeking privileges. We combated long rooted prejudices, and aroused selfish passions. In the midst of the clamour which our opinions provoked, and the misrepresentations with which they have been met, to find that our journal has not merely been sustained, but raised to a higher pitch of prosperity, is certainly a result calculated to afford us the liveliest pleasure, independent altogether of considerations of private gain. We look on it as a manifestation that the great body of the democracy are true to the fundamental principles of their political doctrine; that they are opposed to all legislation which violates the equal rights of the community; that they are enemies of those aristocratic institutions which bestow privileges on one portion of society that are withheld from the others, and tend gradually but surely to change the whole structure of our system of Government.

Animated anew by this gratifying assurance that the people approve the general course of our journal, we shall pursue with ardor the line we have marked out, and trust the day is not distant when the doctrines we maintain will become the governing principles of our party.

CHARACTER OF ANDREW JACKSON

[*From the Evening Post, May* 21, 1834.]

THE epithets, Usurper and Tyrant, have been freely bestowed upon the President of the United States, by grave Senators, in the course of debate. If he is a usurper and a tyrant, it is right the people should be informed of it; though it may be questioned whether the angry use of these opprobrious terms in the Senate Chamber is the best method of communicating that information. These charges are of the most momentous import; and if they be true, it must be easy to cite the acts which justify them. The history of the eventful life of Andrew Jackson, from his boyhood upwards—from the time when, at fourteen years of age, he was found battling with the enemies of his country, to the present hour, which sees him engaged in a not less important struggle, and with an equally dangerous foe—is known to his countrymen. His course has not been run in secret. His deeds have not been done by stealth. His acts, his motives, his ends, are all known: which one is it that stamps him a usurper and tyrant?

He has filled many important offices: he has been Attorney General of the south-western Territory—a member of the Convention that framed the Constitution of

Tennessee—a Representative of that state in Congress, first in one house, and then in the other—a Judge on her supreme bench—a leader of the army of his country—and finally her Chief Magistrate, elected, and re-elected, by a most overwhelming majority of the free suffrages of his fellow citizens. In which one of all these situations have his acts proved him a usurper and a tyrant?

Was he a usurper and tyrant when he fought the battles of his country against the Indians on the south-western frontier—that dark and perilous struggle, when, in addition to the efforts of a ferocious and formidable foe, he had to contend with famine, sickness, mutiny, and every ill than can beset a discontented and undisciplined army, which he conducted notwithstanding, with an undaunted spirit, to a glorious result?

Was he a tyrant and usurper at Fort Strother, when, deserted by his famishing troops, he exclaimed, "If only two men will remain with me, I will never abandon this post!" Or afterwards, when his forces broke out into open mutiny, and moved off in a body towards their homes, "he seized a musket, and resting it on the neck of his horse, (for he was disabled by a wound from the use of his left arm) he threw himself in front of the mutinous column, and declared that he would shoot the first man who should venture to advance?"

Was he a tyrant and usurper at New Orleans, when his military achievements furnished the incidents of one of the brightest pages in our history? and where his honourable and courteous conduct is attested in warm terms by his foes?

Was he a tyrant and usurper when, dragged before a court, and fined for those very acts which had secured the safety of New Orleans, he bowed with proud submission to the decree, and interposed his own influence—the only influence that could have availed—to repress the indignation of his countrymen, and induce them to respect, as he did, the decisions of a competent legal tribunal, however arbitrary and unjust?

Was he a tyrant and usurper in those acts of his administration which have resulted in such a successful and advantageous termination of the long pending negotiations between our Government and foreign powers? Or, on his being chosen Chief Magistrate of the nation, was it tyranny and usurpation to recommend that the constitution should be so altered as to make any President ineligible for more than one term, in order that there might be greater security that the measures of the executive would always be devised with single reference to the good of the People and his own permanent glory?

Was he a tyrant and usurper in recommending that an ample district of country in the far west should be given to the poor Indians who were discontented with their situation within the limits of Georgia? Was he a tyrant and usurper in the noble stand which he took in preservation of the Union against the mad assaults of a faction at the South?

Was his refusal to sanction unconstitutional schemes of internal improvement usurpation and tyranny? or his conciliatory recommendations with regard to the oppressive tariff? What single act of General Jackson's, in short, deserves so foul a name?

Was the removal of Mr. Duane usurpation? Surely not, for no one, at this time of day, will risk his reputation by asserting that the President has not unlimited constitutional power of removal. Was the removal of the deposites by Mr. Duane's successor usurpation? Surely not, for the power was expressly reserved to him in the charter of the United States Bank. Where then, again we ask, is the evidence of General Jackson's tyranny and usurpation? If he is a usurper, he is the strangest, the most anomalous one that ever drew the breath of life. A usurper has hitherto been considered one who seizes that to which he has no right; but if the term is to be applied to General Jackson, it must undergo a wide change of meaning, since all his usurpations are committed within the limits of the Constitution. We defy any adversary of that noble and heroic patriot to cite a single act of his administration that violates, in the slightest degree, a single provision in the Constitution of his country. He is a usurper then of the power with which he was already clothed by the unbought suffrages of a nation of freemen—he seized what he already lawfully possessed—he is a tyrant, because he discharges those duties which the people imposed upon him when they raised him to the Chief Magistracy—he is a despot who shows his own indomitable will by scrupulously obeying the Constitution and the laws! Well would it have been for mankind if all tyrants and usurpers had confined themselves within similar limits!

But let us look for a moment at the character of those who lavish these hard epithets on General Jackson. Is the Senate of the United States entirely above the liability to have these charges retorted upon itself? Was it not a member of that body who declared that he never would consent to an adjournment till a national bank was established and the deposites restored? And is there not something that savours of tyranny and usurpation in this coercive threat, intended to control the action of a co-ordinate and independent department of the Government? Was it not that body that rejected the nomination of certain persons as directors to represent the government in the board of the United States Bank, because, in pursuance of what they deemed their duty, they had reported the mal-practices and corruptions of that institution to the Executive? And was there no tyranny and usurpation in this? Again, did not the Senate of the United States, in defiance of the rights of the Chief Magistrate as secured by the Constitution, in violation of their own oaths to obey that instrument, and in manifest infringement of those inalienable rights which belong to every American citizen, condemn the President of the United States of high crimes and misdemeanors, without a trial, and without a hearing? And when that aged and venerable man, whose whole life has been spent in the service of his country; whose bosom is scarred with the wounds he has received in its defence; who stands alone of all his family, having seen his brothers shed their lives for that freedom he has done so much to preserve, and his wife sink into the grave the mark of vile political slanderers—when that aged and venerable man, thus unjustly sentenced, and stung to the quick that his conduct should be thus maligned, respectfully asked that his solemn protest against the decision of the Senate might be entered on their journal along with the condemnation, was he not refused—refused with added insult? And was this conduct not usurpation and tyranny?

Verily, a factious Senate, the majority of which is composed of desperate political leaders, united by no common tie but that of hate to the war-worn hero who presides at the helm of state—governed by no common motive but indomitable ambition—verily, such a body is a fit source for such aspersions on the character of the man who has filled the measure of his country's glory.

DESPOTISM OF ANDREW JACKSON.

[*From the Evening Post, May* 22, 1834.]

HITHERTO despotism has assuredly been considered as the concentration of all power in one man, or in a few privileged persons, and its appropriate exercise the oppression of the great majority of the people. But the Presidential Bank candidates in the Senate of the United States, and the bribed tools of the Bank who preside over the Bank presses, have lately discovered, or rather invented, an entire new species of despotism. They have found out that pure republican despotism consists in administering the Constitution and laws with an express reference to, and entirely for, the benefit of the people at large.

If we examine the whole course of that extraordinary despot, the President of the United States, it will be found that the very essence of his usurpation consists in interpreting the Constitution, and administering the laws, for the benefit of the many instead of the few. This is the true character of his despotism, and for this is he denounced by those who wish to free the people from this original and extraordinary tyranny, by reversing the picture, and placing the rights and interest of the many at the mercy of the few. In order more clearly to exemplify the character of General Jackson's despotism, we will pass in brief review the prominent acts of his administration.

If we comprehend the nature and principles of a free government, it consists in the guaranty of EQUAL RIGHTS to all free citizens. We know of no other definition of liberty than this. Liberty is, in short, nothing more than the total absence of all MONOPOLIES of all kinds, whether of rank, wealth, or privilege. When Gen.

eral Jackson was elected by a large majority of the people of the United States to the first office in their gift, he found in successful operation a system calculated, if not intended, to sap the whole fabric of equal rights, because it consisted of little else than monopolies, either open and palpable, or in some flimsy disguise or other calculated to cheat the people into a quiet acquiescence.

The first was an oppressive tariff, a system of bounties in disguise, under the operation of which the consumers of domestic manufactures were obliged to pay from twenty-five to two hundred per cent. more for certain indispensable articles of consumption than he would have paid had things been suffered to take their natural course. The consumers of an article always constitute a much greater number of the people than the manufacturers, simply because one man can supply the wants of many. Hence this bounty was a device to tax the many for the benefit of the few. It operated exclusively in favour of the smaller class, and exclusively against the most numerous. It was, therefore, not only destructive of the principle of Equal Rights, but it was a sacrifice of the rights of a great majority in behalf of a small minority.

The first act of General Jackson was to set his face against this anti-republican principle of protecting one class of labour at the expense of the others. He made use of his personal and political influence to bring down the rate of duties on importations to their proper standard, namely, the wants of the government, in which all were equally concerned; and that influence, aided by the good sense of the people, was on the point of being successful, when, by a juggle between Messrs. Clay and Calhoun, the measure was transferred to the Senate. That body passed a bill similar to one on the eve of passing the House of Representatives, which was sent to the latter as an amendment to their own bill, and adopted with wonderful docility. The object of this most excellent legerdemain was to give to Messrs. Clay and Calhoun the credit of an adjustment of the tariff, which but for General Jackson would have remained a subject of heart burning and contention, in all probability to this day. By this notorious assumption Mr. Clay sought to gain credit for his disinterestedly sacrificing his friends on the altar of Union, while Mr. Calhoun was delighted with so capital an excuse for postponing his plan of nullification to a more favourable opportunity. It was a cunning manœuvre; but, cunning is not wisdom, any more than paper money is gold. Notwithstanding the absurd pretensions of these two gentlemen to the honour of adjusting the tariff, there is probably not a rational man in the United States who is not satisfied that the real pacificator was General Jackson, and that Mr. Clay only assented to what he could not prevent. He found the current going strongly against him, and was nothing more than honest King Log, floating with the tide.

This was General Jackson's first act of despotism. He interfered to relieve the many from those burthens which had been imposed on them for the benefit of the few; he restored, in this instance, the EQUAL RIGHTS of all, and for this he is denounced a despot and usurper.

When General Jackson came into office he found another system in operation, calculated not only to undermine and destroy the principles and independence of the people, but to trench upon the sacred republican doctrine of EQUAL RIGHTS. We allude to Mr. Clay's other grand lever by the aid of which he hoped to raise his heavy momentum to the height of his lofty ambition —his system of national internal improvement. Besides the constitutional difficulty arising from the necessary interference with state jurisdictions, there were other powerful objections to this system. It placed the whole revenues of the people of the United States at the disposal of Congress, for purposes of political influence. It enabled ambitious politicians to buy up a township with a new bridge; a district with a road, and a state with a canal. It gave to the General Government an irresistible power over the elections of the states, and constituted the very basis of consolidation. In addition to all this, it was a direct and palpable encroachment on the equal rights of the citizens. It was taxing one state for the exclusive benefit of another; nay, it was diverting money contributed by one state to purposes injurious to the interests of that state. It was appropriating the funds contributed by New-York for the general benefit, to the Ohio and Chesapeake Canal, the successful completion of which it was boasted would be highly injurious to her own internal navigation. In short, it was a system of favouritism entirely destructive to Equal Rights, inasmuch as it was entirely impossible that all should partake equally in its benefits, while all were taxed equally for its expenditures.

To test the firmness of the old patriot, the great champion of Equal Rights, a bill was concocted by the combined ingenuity of the advocates of internal improvement, combining such powerful temptations, and appealing to so many sectional interests, that it was hoped General Jackson either would not dare to interpose his constitutional prerogative to arrest its passage, or that if he did, the consequences would be fatal to his popularity. But the old patriot was not to be frightened from his duty, and besides has a generous confidence in the intelligence and integrity of his fellow-citizens. He knows by glorious experience that the true way to the affections and confidence of a free and enlightened people, is to stand forth in defence of the Equal Rights of all. He vetoed this great bribery bill and the people honoured his firmness, and sustained him in the great effort he had made in their behalf. This is the second great usurpation of General Jackson, and the second great example of his despotism. He interposed to protect the people from a system which afforded a pretext for applying the means of the many to the purposes of the few, and furnished almost unbounded resources for corrupting the people with their own money.

We shall continue the history of the despotism of Andrew Jackson in our paper of to-morrow.

DESPOTISM OF ANDREW JACKSON.

[*From the Evening Post, May* 23, 1834.]

THE next text on which the Bank coalition have rung the changes of " tyranny," " despot," and " usurper," is the veto on Mr. Clay's bill for distributing the public lands among the respective states. The people should understand that these lands are their exclusive property. They contribute a general source of revenue common and equal to all. But the bill of Mr. Clay, no doubt for the purpose of raising the popularity of that permanent candidate for national honours in the west, established a distinction in favour of certain states, of either twelve or fifteen per cent.—we cannot just now be certain which—on the plea that a large portion of these lands were within their limits, although they were the property of the people of the United States.

General Jackson justly considered this preference of certain states over others as not only unconstitutional, but unjust, and for these and other cogent reasons, to which the coalition has never been able to fabricate an answer, declined to sanction the bill. Here, as in every other act of his administration, he stood forward the champion of the Equal Rights of the people, in opposing an unequal distribution of their common property. Yet for this, among other acts equally in defence or vindication of these rights it has been thundered forth to the people that he is a tyrant and usurper.

But it is in relation to his course with regard to the Bank of the United States, that he appears most emphatically as the champion of the Constitution and the Equal Rights of the people. Fully aware of the great truth, that monopolies, whether of rank or privilege, whether possessed by virtue of hereditary descent or conferred by legislative folly or legislative corruption, were the most sly and dangerous enemies to equal rights ever devised by the cunning of avarice or the wiles of ambition, he saw in the vast accumulation of power in that institution, and its evident disposition to exercise, as well as perpetuate it, the elements of destruction to the freedom of the people and the independence of their government. He, therefore, with the spirit and firmness becoming his character and station as the ruler of a free people, determined to exercise his constitutional prerogative in arresting its usurpations, and preventing their being perpetuated.

The child, the champion, and the representative of the great democracy of the United States, he felt himself identified with their interests and feelings. He was one of themselves, and as such had long seen and felt the oppressions which a great concentrated money power, extending its influence, nay, its control, over the currency, and consequently the prosperity of the country throughout every nook and corner of the land, had inflicted or might inflict upon the people. He saw in the nature, and in the acts, of this enormous monopoly, an evident tendency, as well as intention, to subjugate the states and their government to its will; and like himself, and in conformity with the whole tenor of his life, he resolved to risk his place, his popularity, his repose, in behalf of the EQUAL RIGHTS of the people.

He saw, moreover, as every true democrat must see, who interprets the Constitution upon its true principles, that the creation of a Bank with the privilege of establishing its branches in every state, without their consent, was not delegated by the states to the general government ; and he saw that by one of the first declaratory amendments of the Constitution, that "*The powers not delegated to the United States by the Constitution, nor prohibited to it by the states, are reserved to the states respectively, or to the people.*"

But there is, unfortunately, a clause in the Constitution, which is somewhat of the consistency of India rubber, and by proper application can be stretched so as to unite the opposite extremes of irreconcileable contradictions. It is somewhat like the old gentleman's will in the Tale of a Tub, about which Lord Peter, Martin and Jack disputed so learnedly, and which at one time was a loaf of brown bread, at another a shoulder of mutton. It admits of a wonderful latitude of construction, and an ingenious man can find no great difficulty in interpreting it to suit his own particular interests. We allude to the following, which will be found among the enumeration of the powers of Congress :

"To make all laws which shall be *necessary and proper* for carrying into execution the foregoing powers, and all other powers vested in the government of the United States, or in any department or officer thereof."

The sticklers for state rights in the Convention which adopted the Constitution, and in the State Conventions to which it was referred for acceptance or rejection, did not much relish this saving clause. They imagined they saw in it a sort of Pandora's box, which, if once fairly opened, would cast forth a legion of constructive powers and constructive usurpations. They thought they perceived in these two little words "NECESSARY AND PROPER," a degree of elasticity which might be expanded so as to comprehend almost any thing that a majority of Congress might choose to ascribe to them. They were, in our opinion, not much mistaken in their anticipations, although probably they scarcely dreamed that the constructive ingenuity of the times would find *that* to be indispensably "necessary" which the country was enabled for many years to dispense with, during which time it enjoyed a degree of prosperity which excited the envy and admiration of the world!

However this may be, the people of the United States will do well to bear in mind, when they hear General Jackson denounced as a tyrant and usurper for the course he has pursued in relation to the Bank, that this institution has no other legs in the Constitution to stand upon than those two little words "necessary and proper." If it is necessary and proper, then it *may* be re-chartered under the Constitution; but it has no right to demand a re-charter. If it is not necessary and proper, then it ought never to have been chartered, and ought not to be continued one moment longer than the faith of the nation is pledged.

As this is one of those points which rests on the nice interpretation of words, it naturally depends for its decision on the general bias of the two parties in the controversy. The party attached by habit, education, interests, or prejudice, to a consolidated or strong government, will interpret "necessary and proper" one way, and the party opposed to any accumulation of constructive powers in the federal government, will interpret them the other way. General Hamilton, for example, considered a Bank of the United States "necessary and proper," while Mr. Jefferson believed, and has repeatedly denounced it, to be the most dangerous infraction of the constitution ever attempted under the cloak of constructive power. Such has always been the opinion of the great leaders of the democracy of the United States, although some of them have yielded to the voice of a majority of Congress, mistaking it for that of the people.

We have premised thus much in order to show that the course pursued by General Jackson, in regard to the Bank of the United States, is in perfect consonance with the known principles of the democrocy, the people of the United States. When the Democratic Party had the ascendency, they took the first opportunity that offered to put an end to the first Bank of the United States, and now they avail themselves of a similar occasion to give a like demonstration of their settled principles and policy. General Jackson would not have been re-elected by tha party, against all the corruptions of the Bank, combined with the whole force of all the disjointed, incongruous elements of opposition, *after* he had placed his *Veto* on its re-charter, had he not acted in this instance in strict conformity with the sentiments of a great majority of the democracy of the United States. Here as in every other act of his administration, they saw in him the great opponent of monopolies, the stern, inflexible champion of EQUAL RIGHTS.

With regard to the other alleged acts of despotism charged upon this true unwavering patriot, such as the removal of Mr. Duane from office, and the appointment of one of the very ablest and purest men of this country in his stead; the subsequent removal of the deposites from the Bank of the United States, and the protest against the *ex-parte* condemnation of the "Independent Aristocratic Body," more has already been said in his defence than such charges merited. We do not believe the Senators making them believed one word they themselves uttered on the subject, because, though tainted to the core by personal antipathies and personal ambition, they are men of too clear intellect, seriously to cherish such ideas of the constitution as they have lately put forth to the people. These speeches and denunciations, like those on the subject of universal distress and bankruptcy, were merely made for effect. They certainly could not believe that what the constitution expressly delegates was intended to be withheld; that what was expressly conceded by the charter of the Bank of the United States was intended to be denied; or that the exercise of a privilege inherent in human nature, to wit, that of self-defence, was an outrage on the privileges of the Senate. Real honest error may sometimes be combated successfully by argument; but we know of no way of convincing a man who only affects to be in the wrong in order to deceive others, and shall therefore spare ourselves and our readers any further discussion with opponents who are not in earnest, but who have so high an opinion of the sagacity of the people, that they think they can make them believe what they do not believe themselves.

It will be perceived from this brief analysis of the leading measures of General Jackson's administration, that all his "tyranny" has consisted in successfully interposing the Constitution of the United States in defence of the EQUAL RIGHTS of the people; and that all his "usurpations" have been confined to checking those of the advocates of consolidation, disunion, monopolies, and lastly a great consolidated moneyed aristocracy, equally dangerous to liberty from the power it legally possesses, and those it has usurped. Yet this is the man whom the usurpers themselves denounce as a usurper. This is the man against whom the concentrated venom of disappointed ambition and baffled avarice is vainly striving to contend in the heads and hearts of the American people, and to bury under a mass of wilful calumnies. This is the very man whose whole soul is wound up to the great and glorious task of restoring the EQUAL RIGHTS of his fellow-citizens, as they are guarantied by the letter and spirit of the constitution. May Providence send us a succession of such USURPERS as Andrew Jackson, and spare the people from such champions of liberty as Henry Clay, John C. Calhoun, Daniel Webster, George Poindexter, and Nicholas Biddle!

[*From the Evening Post, May* 26, 1835.]

THE AMERICAN INDEMNITY BILL PASSED *By the French Chambers,* PRINCIPAL AND INTEREST.

THE Bill of Indemnity is at length passed, principal, interest, and all, in exact compliance with the Treaty; but accompanied with a condition, which, if it be any thing more than mere French gasconading, puts the prospect of restitution to this country for the outrages long since committed on our commerce further off than ever. The President of the United States, it will be seen, is required to make an apology to France for the terms of his last annual message, before we can be paid our just and too long deferred debt! He is to offer a satisfactory explanation! He is to refine away all that true republican grit which it seems made his communication to Congress too rough for the delicate nerves of Frenchmen. He is to emasculate his proposition of reprisals of all its virulity, and to go on his kness and beg pardon for daring to intimate that, if further insulted by France again refusing to perform her violated promise, it would become the duty of America to take the redress of her grievances into her own hands, and pay herself her admitted claim. This is the ground on which the French Government demands the explanation of the President of the United States, as the condition on which she will pay her too long deferred debt. If General Jackson complies with this condition, we have much mistaken the character and temper of that heroic man. And we have much mistaken the spirit of the American people if they would not cast him off from their affections for so doing, deeply fixed as he is in the hearts of his countrymen. The very proposition by France is an additional insult, and compliance with it would be degradation far greater, than would have been, a year ago, the total remission of the debt due from that country.

But there is not the slightest reason to apprehend that this insolent demand will in any degree be complied with. If the President makes any communication at all on the subject, it will be one which France may consider an apology or explanation, if she pleases, but which will receive a very contrary interpretation from all the rest of the world. The truth is no explanation is expected. The whole proposition is a mere last ineffectual splutter to turn attention from the sorry attitude in which the French Government has placed itself by its bad faith, and by lending a too credulous ear to the representations of M. Serrurier and others, that the United States might be fobbed off, from time to time, as long as it suited the pleasure of France to temporise. The energetic message of General Jackson rudely awakened that Government from its delusion. They suddenly found that they were dealing with an Administration which would "ask nothing that was not clearly right, and submit to nothing that was wrong." They saw that this Administration possessed the unbounded confidence of a vast majority of the American people, and that its noble rule of action in its foreign relations met with their cordial approval. They saw that there was a fixed determination on the part of this Government and this people to obtain our just and acknowledged debt from France, "peaceably if we could, forcibly if we must." Seeing this, the tone of France was at once wonderfully lowered, and the silly measures of bravado that Government has adopted to hide its real sentiments and motives of action do but add to the ludicrousness of the unfortunate posture in which it has placed itself. The United States will get the indemnity, principal and interest in full, according to the Treaty negotiated by Mr. Rives; and France will get no apology—nothing bearing even such a remote resemblance to one, that it can be palmed off upon the world as such by all the vaunting and gasconading of sputtering Frenchmen. To such luckless straits a nation is reduced that has not sense enough of right to redeem its faith, nor might enough to maintain its perfidy.

The Bill of Indemnity it will be seen was passed by a vote of 289 to 137.

CORPORATION PROPERTY.

[*From the Evening Post, June* 3, 1835.]

THE property belonging to the corporation of this city is estimated, in the Message of the Mayor which we had the pleasure of presenting to our readers a few days since, at ten millions of dollars. Of the property which is valued at this sum, a very small portion is actually required for the purposes of government. A large part of it consists of town lots, wholly unproductive. Another part consists of lots and tenements leased or rented for a trifling consideration. That part which is in the actual occupancy of the corporate authorities for public uses, is comparatively small, and smaller still that part which is actually needed in the exercise of the legitimate functions of the government.

That our municipal government should possess no property, except what is really required for the performance of its duties, seems to us so plain a proposition as scarcely to require an argument to support it. We elect our city authorities from year to year to supervise the affairs of the body politic, pass needful municipal regulations, enforce existing laws, and attend, generally, to the preservation of public order. Adequately to fulfil these trusts, a building set apart for the meetings of the city authorities is necessary. A place of detention for the city criminals is necessary, and, under the present system, a place for the city paupers. These, and a few other buildings, occupying grounds of a suitable location and extent, constitute all the real estate required for the due administration of the functions of our municipal government. If our authorities, then, purchase more property than this, they either waste the money of their constituents, or buying it on credit, or paying for it with borrowed funds, they waste the money of posterity.

The government of our city is nothing more nor less than a certain number of persons chosen from year to year, by the suffrages of a majority of the citizens, to attend to those affairs which belong to all in common, or, in other words, the affairs of the community. They represent the aggregate will of the existing community in relation to those affairs ; and their functions, by the very tenure of their offices, are confined within the circle of the year. It is plain, then, viewing the subject on principles of abstract right, that a government so constituted, ought do nothing which would not be approved by those from whom it derives its powers. The accumulation of unnecessary property, to the amount of millions of dollars, can never have been intended by any considerable number of voters of this city, as a duty which the city government ought to perform; and having accumulated it, to retain it seems equally averse to the plainest principles of sound policy and right.

To whom does this property belong? Not to the authorities of the city, surely, but to the citizens themselves—to those who chose those authorities to manage their affairs. If it belongs to them, and government is not a permanent existence separate from the will of the people, but the mere breath of their nostrils, their mere representative, renewed at their pleasure from year to year, it must be obvious that there can be no good reason for having that property retained in the possession of the government. It would be much better in the possession of the people themselves, since every body knows that as a general and almost invariable rule, men attend to their private affairs much better than agents attend to their delegated trusts.

Let no reader be startled at the idea we have here put forth, and suppose he sees in it the ghost of agrarianism,—that bugbear which has been conjured with for ages to frighten grown-up children from asserting the dictates of common sense in relation to the affairs of government. We have no agrarian scheme in contemplation. We are not about to propose a division of public property, either according to the ratio of taxation, or equally by the poll list, or in any other objectionable mode. But our citizens are every year called upon to pay taxes. The last legislature passed a law authorizing our corporate authorities to levy a tax greatly increased since last year. We have also our public debt, for which the property of our *posterity* is pledged, and this debt was lately swelled one million of dollars by money borrowed to be paid in 1860. Now it strikes us as somewhat unreasonable to call upon the citizens to pay taxes to defray the current expenses of the government, and to saddle posterity with an enormous debt, when the unnecessary and disposable public property now in the hands of our municipal government would wipe off the whole amount of the debt which was contracted on the credit of posterity, and defray the current expenses of the city besides for several years to come.

We would by no means dispose of our City Hall, or our Park, or our Battery, any more than we would dispose of Broadway or the Bowery. These are for the public use, for their present, daily, and hourly use, in various respects. But in the public property which the Mayor estimates at an aggregate of ten millions of dollars there will be found much which is not necessary for the purposes of Government or the health and convenience of the people. All such we would sell, and apply the proceeds to the liquidation of the public debt, and to the payment of those expenses for which taxes are now assessed. Let not the argument be used that this property will be far more valuable in a few years, and may then be disposed of to much greater advantage. If we admit the validity of this argument, it is one which may be urged to postpone the sale for half a century, and of what benefit would be the augmented amount, fifty years hence, to the present people, to whom the property in truth belongs? Society is daily, hourly, momently, changing its constituent individuals. The particles which compose the stream of life are continually passing away, to be succeeded by other particles, and the transition of these human atoms is nowhere so rapid as in the whirlpool of a great city. Many of those whose votes elevated the present municipal officers to their places, will never cast a suffrage again—some have gone to other states, some to distant lands, some to that bourne from whence no traveller returns. But others will push into their places. The social tide will still rush on. The young man will pass his probationary period and acquire the rights of citizenship; foreigners will be adopted; brethren from other portions of the confederacy will take up their abode among us. No matter, therefore, how rapidly increasing in value any portion of this surperfluous public property may be, we who own it now and who next year may own it no longer, have a right to demand that it should be disposed of for our benefit, and to liquidate those debts which we have no right to leave for posterity to pay.

But we deny that there is any validity in this argument founded on the conjectural or probable rise of price. If the property improves in price, we ask whether is it better that the increase should be in the hands of the government or of individual citizens? Should the government continue to hold this property for years, through its annual successions, it is at last to be appropriated to some public purpose. If the property had been disposed of, its increased value would necessarily have been in the hands of citizens, whose capacity would in the same measure have been increased to contribute to the public expenses. The property of the citizens is at all times abundantly able to sustain any legitimate expenses of government, and all property, not required for such purposes, should remain in the people's own hands.

There is one species of public property to which we have not adverted in this article, because it does not probably enter into the Mayor's estimate, but which we could well wish were also disposed of by the public authorities, and suffered to go into the hands of private citizens. We allude to the wharves, piers and public docks, with the exception of the slips at the end of streets. Those in our view ought to be as free as the streets themselves, and the rest ought to be left in private hands. We cannot undertake to argue this subject to-day ; but let those who are disposed to differ from us, reflect that we only propose to put the wharves on the same footing with houses and stores, and that the same competition, the same laws of supply and demand, which regulate the rent of the one description of property, would equally regulate the wharfage of the other.

APOLOGY TO FRANCE.

[*From the Evening Post, June* 16, 1835.]

WE copy with exceeding pleasure the following patriotic remarks on the French question from the Pennsylvanian. They are of a similar tenor with those which we copied on Saturday from the Gloucester Democrat. It gives us great satisfaction to perceive that the sound democratic journals throughout the country are taking, as with one mind, the true *American* view of this subject. For our own part we say, MILLIONS FOR DEFENCE, BUT NOT ONE WORD IN EXPLANATION.

If Mr. Livingston, as we do not doubt, left instructions with Mr. Barton, the American *Chargé d' Affaires* in Paris, to follow him immediately to the United States, in the event of the bill of indemnity being passed by the Chamber of Peers as sent to that branch of the French legislature by the other Chamber, he acted, in our view, as became the representative of this Government, and established an additional claim to the respect of his countrymen. We do not see how, among men who have a sincere regard for the honour and dignity of their country, there can be any difference of opinion as to the question of the demanded explanation. If the bill should finally become a law, the very demand is an insult to us, of a far more aggravated character than the pecuniary wrong of which we before complained. We before demanded payment of a debt withheld from us by a simple refusal to perform a treaty. The payment was then withheld on the ground that the legislative branch of the French Government did not consider the amount claimed to be due, and maintained that the treaty was not binding until it should have received their sanction. But by the present law the amount claimed is acknowledged to be due to us ; yet compliance with the treaty is positively forbidden unless the American Government shall in the first place make satisfactory explanations to heal the wounded honour of France. To state this in equivalent but briefer phrase, France refuses to pay us our debt, unless we in the first place beg her pardon for having dared to demand it.

It does not affect the question in the slightest degree, according to our judgment, to say that this explanation is a mere matter of form which two diplomatic agents may arrange in a friendly interview, and without the slightest difficulty. If it is reduced to a mere form, it is still a form degrading to us. If the explanation shall be acknowledged to lie in the bow with which the representative of the American Government salutes the French Minister on entering his apartment, or in his shake of the hand ; if it is recognised in any act, word, or look, it is a compliance nevertheless with an insolent law—it is losing sight of our own honour to appease the wounded pride of vain-glorious France. Never be it said in our history, that to obtain the paltry sum of five millions of dollars, we consented to any stipulations inconsistent with the dignity of a nation of freemen.

We have seen with lively regret, that some papers

which profess to be democratic, take a contrary view of this subject, and urge the propriety of some explanation being made by the President to soothe the ruffled feelings of France, or in other words to coax the Frenchmen into good humour. The Albany Argus, followed as usual by its "gentle echo," but in fainter sounds of response than heretofore, seems to think that General Jackson might comply with the demand of France, by assuring her, either by the repetition of a passage of his last Message, or by words of equivalent import, that no threat or menace was intended. It would be the first instance in our national experience of the Chief Magistrate of this great country having complied with the demand of a foreign Government to make any explanation of any message, which, in his Executive capacity, he had seen proper to communicate to a co-ordinate branch of the federal Government. We fear it would not be the last. We fear we should be doomed to hear many iterations of the same insulting demand. "What do you mean by this, sir?" and "What do you mean by that, sir?" would be interrogatories to which, under the penalty of war, the President of the United States would have to stand ever ready to answer. To avoid such a disagreeable liability, instead of free, ingenuous, and unreserved communications from the head of our Government to the national legislature, in which all subjects of general interest are frankly and fully discussed, and the opinions of the Chief Magistrate candidly stated, we should soon see short, vague, unsatisfactory addresses, like those of the King of England to Parliament, in which the few words that are employed seem used rather to conceal than express the writer's meaning.

We may be wrong in the view we take of this subject, and if we are, we are very wrong, since it seems to us the question does not admit of doubt. It seems to us that

France has no right to ask, much less demand, an explanation of the message, since it is a mere expression of the views of one branch of the Government to another, and not an act or expression of the Government at all. It seems to us that she has no need of an explanation, since the message, so far from being obscure, was so plain that he who runs might read it, and was as decorous and temperate, in all that related to France, as any document which ever recounted the wrongs which one nation had experienced from another, or proposed any mode of final redress. If we consider the case as between individuals under analogous circumstances, we shall clearly see the gross impropriety of yielding submission to the law of France, and entering into degrading explanations, in order that it may please his High Mightiness, the King of the French, to pay his debts. Let our readers suppose that a subscriber of this journal had put off our collector for twenty years by various excuses and evasions; that he had then entered into a solemn covenant to pay us our money by a given time; had subsequently violated that obligation, and after several additional delays, again agreed to pay it, but only on condition that we should first appease his wounded honour by making a satisfactory explanation—let our readers suppose such a case, and each answer for himself what ought to be our reply. To make the case more analogous, it should be supposed that the debt, in this instance, had not been incurred by the mere accumulation of subscription dues, but had been created originally by a forcible entry into our office, and a wanton destruction or seizure of our property.

With the Pennsylvanian, we entertain the utmost confidence that the President of the United States will act in the matter now about to come before him in the same spirit of lofty patriotism and independence which has distinguished him all his life long, and most conspicuously and gloriously in his illustrious administration of the American Government. We entertain no single misgiving of fear that he will ever do an act to sully the bright page which he has written in our country's history. Age has not chilled his spirit, nor abated one jot the ardour of his patriotism. The honour of this people in his hands is safe, and will not be surrendered to the audacious demand of France.

We have hopes, we confess, that the French Government will before this have come to their senses, and expunged the insolent condition from their law. Should it be otherwise, however, much as we should regret hostile measures on many accounts, there are paramount reasons why we should desire to see them promptly resorted to. For our own part, we could wish that war, immediate war, might be the alternative. We trust that we have not been vainly boasting all this while, that while we would ask nothing not clearly right, *we would submit to nothing that is wrong*. We trust there is spirit enough in the country yet to maintain our character, at whatever expense of treasure or of blood. Our fathers went to war for a three-penny tax on tea. Their sons have suffered a worse wrong. They have been smitten on the right cheek: will they turn the left also?

OUT OF DEBT.

[*From the Evening Post, June* 20, 1835.]

It is the peculiar boast of the people of the United States that the nation is now out of debt. We hear it repeated every day with an exultation which would be just, if the boast were true. But as it is not true, it may be worth while to apprise our fellow-citizens of the real state of the case. The *People* of the United States are not out of debt, and never will be, while the present system of banking and borrowing continues to subsist.

The General Government it is certain owes nothing. Thanks to the policy of General Jackson, it has redeemed all its obligations. But what shall we say of the States individually? Are they out of debt? On the contrary, are they not, almost without exception, every day plunging deeper and deeper into the bottomless pit of unredeemed and irredeemable obligation? Some are borrowing millions for public improvements; others pledging the credit of the States, or in other words the property of the citizens, for millions; and others are becoming subscribers to banks, and canals, and railroads, to the amount of millions more. Under this system, the individual States at this moment owe more money than did the United States, at the close of either of the wars of Independence. Yet we boast of being out of debt!

Who pay the piper for all this political and speculating dancing? Who pay the interest by the sweat of their brow, and who must pay the principal, by the sweat of their brow, or transmit the everlasting burden from the backs of one generation to another? The same people who boast of being out of debt. What difference, we would ask, is there between the debts we owe as citizens of the United States and citizens of a State? Must we not equally labour and sweat under their weight? Must we not pay them at once, or we and our posterity pay them ten times over in interest? Unquestionably. Yet for all this, faster, ten times faster, are the legislatures of the states plunging the people over head and ears in debt, than the Federal Government is relieving them from their burdens. There is not a legislative session held in any state of the Union in which some new debt is not contracted, some new weight laid on the backs of the people and their posterity. The latter unhappily can say nothing against all this ; but we will tell the former, that if they do not say something to the purpose, and say it soon, never poor ass, not even the ass of all asses, old England, was so laden with wealth, the burden of which he bears without sharing in the spoils, as will be the labouring classes of this country. Instead of leaving freedom and competency to their posterity, they will leave them nothing but their debts to pay, and receive in return nothing but curses.

But the debts created by loans for public improvements and pledges of state credit, are not the only blessings to be conferred on posterity. There are in the United States upwards of six hundred Banks at this moment with an issue of paper probably amounting to two hundred millions of paper money. Who pays the piper for this mode of dancing? Who pays the expenses of banking houses, salaries of officers and other contingencies? Who paid a million and a half for the marble palace in which the great paper Mammon is worshipped in Philadelphia? And who will be obliged to pay all these through all time to come, so long as they exist and crush us to the earth? The people ; the labouring classes of the United States, and their foredoomed posterity.

Let us go on. Who has paid the penalty of all the millions which the failure of hundreds of paper banks left unredeemed? The people ; the labouring classes of these United States. And who is now actually responsible for the two hundred millions of paper money now circulating in every house, and from hand to hand in every nook and corner of the land? Out of whose pockets, out of the sweat of whose brow, come the dividends of these banks ; and whence will be derived the means of redeeming these two hundred millions, if they are ever redeemed? From the pockets of the people ; from the sweat of the labouring classes. And who will pay both interest and principal of these enormous issues of paper money, resting on paper promises? We answer again, the labouring classes of the United States. If this paper is ever redeemed it must be by the profits of these institutions squeezed out of the People; and if it is not, the same People must pay the penalty, by losing the whole amount in circulation. It will die on their hands.

Thus it will be seen, as clear as the light of day, that these two hundred millions of paper money operate as actual debts on the People of the United States. *They* pay the interest, and *they* must redeem the principal, if it is ever redeemed. Happy people! to be *so* out of debt, and thrice happy posterity to inherit so many blessings!

EDWARD LIVINGSTON.

[*From the Evening Post, June* 23, 1835.]

The Constitution has at length arrived. We bid Mr. Livingston welcome back to that country, whose honour he has shown himself so ready and so able to maintain abroad. The attention of this community has been earnestly fixed upon Mr. Livingston through the whole course of the difficult and unpleasant controversy with France; and the regard before entertained for him, as a worthy son of New-York, as a man whose distinguished talents had always been exerted to advance the great principles of democratic government, and whose whole life indeed had been passed in the discharge of various important public trusts, has been increased and strengthened by the firm yet moderate, and dignified yet conciliatory manner in which he has conducted himself through the responsible and delicate circumstances in which he has been placed.

Mr. Livingston seems truly to have adopted, as his rule of action, the noble sentiment of General Jackson, to ask nothing that is not clearly right, and submit to nothing that is wrong. He seems to have borne constantly in mind, too, that he was the representative of his country, and to haye merged, on more than one irritating occasion, the feelings of the man in those which were proper to the nation. We have hence beheld him acting with the most temperate and lofty forbearance, in circumstances which were calculated to stir ordinary minds to violence, and by which there are few men, even of deliberate judgment, who would not have been urged into some hasty measure or expression of asperity. But Mr. Livingston kept his eyes steadily fixed on the real interest and dignity of his country, determined not to sacrifice, under the influence of any private motive, or by yielding to any natural suggestion of personal resentment, the slightest portion of that weight which the American cause possesses, as well by the moderation and calmness with which it has been urged through every stage of the protracted negotiation, as by the intrinsic justice of the original claim.

We are sure that we but speak the universal sentiment of the democracy of this community and of the country, when we express the warmest approbation of the course pursued by Mr. Livingston, while the minister of the American Government in France. He may rest assured that his countrymen have fully appreciated the embarrassing circumstances in which he has been placed; that they have keenly felt the sa rcasms and contumelious expressions which were aimed at him ; and have admired the equanimity with which he withstood the petty malice of gasconading assailants, whose dearest object would have been achieved, could they have disturbed that evenness and dignity which made their own vehemence and bravado so contemptible in the sight of nations.

That the sentiments we have here expressed are entertained by the democracy of this metropolis we have good reason to know, and suitable measures were already on foot, before the Constitution arrived, to testify to Mr. Livingston, in an unequivocal manner, the respect and entire approbation which his conduct abroad has created. New-York, though the commercial centre of this great empire, and having consequently a deep stake in the preservation of amity with foreign nations, will be prompt to support the administration in any step proper to assert the honour of the country. New-York insists upon a strict, unconditional fulfilment of the French treaty, at all hazards, and will never consent that the Republic shall be degraded, through its Chief Magistrate, by yielding any explanations in compliance with the insolent demand of France.

The elevated and firm, yet calm and assuasive conduct of Mr. Livingston at the French Court, with whatever satisfaction it has been viewed by our fellow-citizens, yet adds but one claim to the many he before possessed on their liveliest regard. A native of the Empire State; a man whose talents, from an early period of his life for a long series of years, were constantly exerted to promote the best interest of this community; who has served it, and served it faithfully, in various official capacities; who has presided over this metropolis as its chief magistrate, and represented it in Congress: such a man, returning to his birth-place from a foreign mission, which has been embarrassed with unusual difficulties, and conducted with unusual ability and dignity, has an irresistible title to the most cordial reception.

The names of few men are recorded in our history whose lives have been of more real service to the republic than that of Mr. Livingston. Identified from his youth upward with the party which professes the political principles of Jefferson, the whole tenor of his public conduct has been to illustrate and advance those principles. Early selected to represent this city in Congress, he was one of the sturdiest and ablest advocates of the doctrine of democratic equality, at a time when the opposite opinions were upheld by the most formidable array of talent which has ever contended, in this country, under the banner of aristocracy. The learning of Mr. Livingston, the force of his eloquence, and the comprehensive reach and unanswerable cogency of his writings, did much to accomplish the ultimate triumph of democratic principles, a result so auspicious to the cause of equal freedom. His patriotic efforts did not stop here ; but in the legislature of his adopted state, and in the celebrated "Code," for which she is indebted to the vast erudition, vigorous intellect, sound judgment, and fervent patriotism of that distinguished man, he still exerted all his powers to promote the happiness of his countrymen and erect a strong foundation for their rights. In consonance with his whole career has been the course of Mr. Livingston as the diplomatic representative of his Government in France. After experiencing the contumelies of insolent Frenchmen for calmly but strenuously asserting the rights and honour of his country, he is once more among us, on that soil where he drew his first breath, and among that people for whom he exerted his earliest efforts. It is for his countrymen to say what shall be his reception.

THE O'CONNELL GUARDS.

[*From the Evening Post, June* 25, 1835.]

THE incendiary papers continue their efforts to inflame the minds of such native citizens as they can influence against our citizens of Irish birth :

"THE O'CONNELL GUARDS.—No greater insult was ever offered the American People than the arrangements now being made for raising in this city an *Irish* regiment to be called the '*O'Connell Guards.*' Such a corps would soon attempt to enforce with the bayonet what too many of the misguided and ignorant of the foreign voters already boast of—the complete subjection of the *Native* citizens to their dictation. We know Governor Marcy too well to believe it possible that he will sanction such an outrage upon society, notwithstanding its being got up under the auspices of that *creature* CAMBRELENG and his associates ; and trust this infamous proceeding is destined to recoil upon the unprincipled Party which originated it."

The first observation we have to make is to repeat, in the most earnest manner, the hope we have heretofore expressed that our fellow-citizens of Irish birth will continue to exhibit, in the trying circumstances in which they are placed, that moderation and forbearance which distinguished their conduct when they were made the object of mob assaults in the spring of 1834, and which has no less distinguished them in the recent disorders. Could they be excited, by the inflammatory paragraphs of those prints which are endeavouring to array the community against them, to commit any act of violence—to become the aggressors in any tumultuary movement—a leading object of their unprincipled opponents would be accomplished; and that single retaliatory act would be used against them with all the zeal and industry of the most bitter political hatred. Should they continue, on the other hand, to rely upon the civil authorities for protection in their rights, the inflammatory arts of their opponents must react upon themselves. It is not possible that any considerable number of citizens can long be misled by the wicked efforts of those unprincipled newspapers which, by the most unfounded calumnies, and the most inflammatory appeals to the worst passions of their readers, have provoked this temporary ebullition of popular feeling against the Irish.

With regard to the pretended "insult offered to the American people" in the proposition to raise a regiment under the title of the O'Connell Guards, let any American citizen, of whatever lineage, examine the subject dispassionately for a moment, and he will plainly see that the only insult offered to the community lies in the conduct of the prints which have opposed the formation of this regiment, not in that of the authors of the undertaking. Our institutions must be frail or rotten indeed, if they stand in any danger from a militia regiment composed of citizens, no matter from what country they may have sprung. A truly intelligent mind can entertain no apprehensions of any undue or untoward influence being exercised in this country by those who have come among us from foreign nations. Emigrants from every quarter of the globe, landing upon our shores, are assimilated by the principles of liberty, and form a part of one harmonious people, all equally interested in the preservation of those institutions, which, like the dews of heaven, shed equal benefits upon all. If it is a quality inherent in the very nature of a free government thus to incline all hearts in its favour, with what double cordiality and devotedness must the Irish emigrant feel enlisted in its support, with whom a love for liberty has been the main principle of action from the cradle, and to escape from political oppression his sole motive in abandoning the land of his birth, and making this the land of his adoption. The bayonets of Irish citizens will never be raised against the breasts of native Americans, unless, indeed, political fanaticism and persecution—shall have recourse to arms to effect their unhallowed purposes, and render an armed defence necessary.

It will be well for our citizens, when they read the articles intended to excite in their minds feelings of jealousy and unkindness towards the Irish, to remember that there is no portion of our society more devotedly attached to the principles of human liberty than those against whom it is now sought to direct popular hostility. Indeed, the true and only motive of these attempts lies in this very circumstance. Had a majority of the Irish citizens supported the United States Bank in its audacious war upon the Government and the rights of the people, the minions of the Bank, the purchased slaves who conduct the Courier and the Star, would never have sought to stir up the popular enmity against them, and make them the victims of riot and violence.

That Mr. Cambreleng has had any thing to do, directly or indirectly, with the proposed regiment of O'Connell Guards, is wholly untrue — a malicious fabrication of a print destitute of the principle of truth and of every sentiment of honour. If it were otherwise, however, we do not know that he would be particularly obnoxious to censure; for we have not forgotten that a regiment of Irish citizens, under the title of "the Irish Greens," long existed in this city, were noted for the excellence of their discipline, and the propriety of their conduct, and when the war with Great Britain broke out, volunteered their services to go upon the frontier, and demeaned themselves with the most distinguished gallantry, and the most ardent devotion to the best interests of their adopted country.

A COLLECTION

OF THE

POLITICAL WRITINGS

OF

WILLIAM LEGGETT,

SELECTED AND ARRANGED,

WITH A PREFACE,

BY

THEODORE SEDGWICK, Jr.

IN TWO VOLUMES.

VOL. II.

NEW-YORK:

TAYLOR & DODD.

1840.

H. LUDWIG, PRINTER,
72, Vesey-street, N. Y.

A COLLECTION

OF THE

POLITICAL WRITINGS

OF

WILLIAM LEGGETT.

CHIEF JUSTICE MARSHALL.

[*From the Evening Post, July* 28, 1835.]

We perceive with pleasure that public and spontaneous demonstrations of respect for the character and talents of the late Judge Marshall have taken place in every part of the country where the tidings of his death have been received. These tributes to the memory of departed excellence have a most salutary effect on the living; and few men have existed in our republic who so entirely deserved to be thus distinguished as examples, by a universal expression of sorrow at their death, as he whose loss the nation now laments. Possessed of a vast hereditary fortune, he had none of the foolish ostentation or arrogance which are the usual companions of wealth. Occupying an office too potent—lifted too high above the influence of popular will—there was no man who in his private intercourse and habits, exhibited a more general and equal regard for the people. He was accesible to men of all degrees, and " familiar, but by no means vulgar" in his bearing, he was distinguished as much in the retired walks of life by his unaffected simplicity and kindness, as in public by the exercise of his great talents and acquirements.

The death of such a man, of great wisdom and worth, whose whole life has been passed in the public service, and whose history is interwoven with that of our country in some of its brightest and most interesting passages, furnishes a proper occasion for the expression of general respect and regret. In these sentiments we most fully join; but at the same time we cannot so far lose sight of those great principles of government which we consider essential to the permanent prosperity of man, as to neglect the occasion offered by the death of Judge Marshall to express our satisfaction that the enormous powers of the Supreme tribunal of the country will no longer be exercised by one whose cardinal maxim in politics inculcated distrust of popular intelligence and virtue, and whose constant object, in the decision of all constitutional questions, was to strengthen government at the expense of the people's rights.

The hackneyed phrase, *de mortuïs nil nisi bonum*, must be of comprehensive meaning indeed, if it is intended that the grave shall effectually shelter the theoretic opinions and official conduct of men from animadversion, as well as the foibles and offences of their private lives. In this sense at least we do not understand the precept, and if such were its obvious purport we should refuse to make it our law. Paramount considerations seemed to us to demand that, in recording the death of Judge Marshall, and joining our voice to that of general eulogy on his clear and venerable name, we should at the same time record our rooted hostility to the political principles he maintained, and for the advancement of which he was able to do so much in his great office.

Few things have ever given us more disgust than the fawning, hypocritical and unqualified lamentations, which are poured out by the public press on the demise of any conspicuous political opponent. Of the man whom the day before it denounced in terms of the most unmeasured bitterness, let him but shuffle off his mortal coil, and the next day it is loud in undiscriminating, unlimited praise. We would not have journalists wage their political dissentions over the grave, and pour the ebullitions of party hostility on the dull cold ear of death. Neither would we have them stand aloof in dogged silence, refusing to join in the tribute to the memory of a great man who had made his exit from this theatre of perpetual strife, because, while he lived, they were found in the ranks of his opponents. But if there is any sincerity in the political doctrines they profess; if they are not mere jugglers in a game of cheatery and fraud; if they are really contending, with their whole heart and soul, in behalf of certain great principles, the success of which they consider of vital importance to the best interests of man: then not even the death of an opponent—and more especially of one whose mind was so vigorous and enlightened, whose heart was so benignant, and whose whole life had been so pure and exemplary as that of Judge Marshall—not even the death of such an opponent, we say, should restrain them from accompanying their tribute of respect with an expression of dissent from his political opinions.

There is no journalist who entertained a truer respect for the virtues of Judge Marshall than ourselves; there is none who believed more fully in the ardour of his patriotism, or the sincerity of his political faith. But according to our firm opinion, the articles of his creed, if carried into practise, would prove destructive of the great principle of human liberty, and compel the many to yield obedience to the few. The principles of government entertained by Marshall were the same as those professed by Hamilton, and not widely different from those of the elder Adams. That both these illustrious men, as well as Marshall, were sincere lovers of their country, and sought to effect, through the means of government, the greatest practicable amount of human happiness and prosperity, we do not entertain, we never have entertained a doubt. Nor do we doubt that among those who uphold the divine right of kings, and wish to see a titled aristocracy and hierarchy established, there are also very many solely animated by a desire to have a government established adequate to self-preservation and the protection of the people. Yet if one holding a political creed of this kind, and who, in the exercise of high official functions, had done all in his power to change the character of the government from popular to monarchical, should be suddenly cut off by death, would it be unjustifiable in those who deprecated his opinions to allude to them and their tendency, while paying a just tribute to his intellectual and moral worth?

Should General Jackson descend into the grave tomorrow, with what propriety could they who denounce him as a tyrant and usurper join their voices to swell the loud note of unmingled eulogium? They might with perfect propriety speak of his honesty of purpose, his bravery and firmness; but they could extend their praise to other topics only by giving the lie to their previous accusations. If they have been honest in representing him as violating the Constitution and trampling on the laws; if they really believe that he has siezed the sword and purse, and has done all in his power to change the Government into an autocracy; the paramount duties of patriotism, rising superior to the mere suggestions of sympathy, would seize the death of such a man as an occasion of adverting to the true character of his principles of action, and of rousing the people from the delusion into which they had fallen.

Of Judge Marshall's spotless purity of life, of his many estimable qualities of heart, and of the powers of his mind, we record our hearty tribute of admiration. But sincerely believing that the principles of democracy are identical with the principles of human liberty, we cannot but experience joy that the chief place in the supreme tribunal of the Union will no longer be filled by a man whose political doctrines led him always to pronounce such decision of Constitutional questions as was calculaten to strengthen government at the expense of the people. We lament the death of a good and exemplary man, but we cannot grieve that the cause of aristocracy has lost one of its chief supports.

THE ABOLITIONISTS.

[*From the Evening Post of August* 8, 1835.]

In looking over the English papers received this morning, we were struck with the following remarks in the London Courier of the 7th ultimo:

"Our readers will undoubtedly recollect that within these few years societies have existed in London and lectures have been given for the purpose of attacking Christianity. A gentleman known by the name of Robert Taylor, who, we must charitably suppose, was out of his senses, took to himself the name, we believe, of the Devil's Chaplain, and in that character was accustomed to address his audience. Some of his followers or friends, or persons who embraced opinions similar to his, undertook to lecture in the provinces on the same subject, and the Clergy of the English Church were, in several places, and on several occasions, both by him and them, challenged to meet and justify or defend the doctrines they taught. Among all reasonable people there was but one opinion as to the indecency of the proceedings of Messrs. Taylor and Co., and there was, we believe, but one opinion as to the propriety of the conduct of the Clergy, who took no notice of the challengers and their assertions. The proper contempt thus exhibited by the Clergy and the good sense of society, have completely put an end to these proceedings. The public now never hear of Mr. Robert Taylor and his friends, and seem not to care what has become of them."

In the above paragraph we have the course pointed out which ought to have been pursued in this country in relation to the fanatical doctrines and proceedings of the immediate abolitionists. It is our firm persuasion, as we have often had occasion to state, that the rapid growth and greatly augmented ardour of the association known by that name are in a very large degree ascribable to the unwise and unjust measures taken to suppress it. If they had been suffered to pour out their zeal unopposed; if their wild doctrines had not been noticed, or, if noticed at all, only with calm and temperate arguments, we feel satisfied that at this day that sect of political fanatics would have embraced much fewer persons that it now numbers, and would have exhibited far less zeal than now characterises its efforts. All history, all experience supports the opinion we express.

We defy any man to point to a single instance in which fanaticism has been turned from its object by persecution, or in which its ardour has not been inflamed and its strength increased when opposed by arguments of brute force. On the contrary, history contains many striking cases of fanatical enterprises languishing and being abandoned, when those engaged in them were suffered to take their own course, without any other hinderance than such as was necessary to prevent their overleaping the safeguards of society.

Fanaticism is a species of insanity and requires analogous treatment. In regard to both, the soothing system is proved by its results to be the most effectual. The mind slightly touched with lunacy, may soon be exasperated into frenzy by opposition, or soon restored to perfect sanity by gentle and assuasive means. So, too, the mind, excited to fanaticism on any particular subject, religious, political, or philanthropic, is but heated to more dangerous fervour by violence, when it might easily be reduced to the temperature of health by the lenitives which reason and moderation should apply.

The first great impulse which the abolition cause received in this city was, we are persuaded, the attempt to suppress it by the means of mobs ; and the greatest promoters of the abolition doctrines have been, in our judgment, not Thompson nor Garrison, but the Courier and Enquirer, the Journal of Commerce and the Commercial Advertiser. We do not speak this in a spirit of crimination ; for our desire is to assuage and conciliate, not to inflame and exasperate. We express the opinion more with a view to its influence on future conduct, than to reprehend that which is past; and we do hope that, in view of the pernicious consequences which have flowed from violent measures hitherto, a course more consistent with the meekness of Christianity, and with the sacred rights of free discussion, will be pursued henceforth.

While we believe most fully that the abolitionists are justly chargeable with fanaticism, we consider it worse than folly to misrepresent their character in other respects. They are not knaves nor fools, but men of wealth, education, respectability and intelligence, misguided on a single subject, but actuated by a sincere desire to promote the welfare of their kind. This, it will hardly be denied, is a true description, of at least a large proportion of those termed abolitionists. Is it not apparent on the face of the matter, that invective, denunciations, burnings in effigy, mob violence, and the like proceedings, do not constitute the proper mode of changing the opinions or conduct of such men? The true way is, either to point out their error by temperate arguments, or better still leave them to discover it themselves. The fire, unsupplied with fuel, soon flickers and goes out, which stirred and fed, will rise to a fearful conflagration, and destroy whatever falls within the reach of its fury.

With regard to the outrage lately committed in Charleston, we do not believe it constitutes any exception to our remarks. The effects of all such proceedings must be to increase the zeal of fanaticism, which always rises in proportion to the violence of the opposition it encounters. Some of the Charleston papers, we perceived, spoke of the attack on the Post Office as *premature*, and thought it ought not to have been made until the result was received of an application which had been forwarded to the General Post Office for relief. Neither the General Post Office, nor the General Government itself, possesses any power to prohihit the transportation by mail of abolition tracts. On the contrary it is the bounden duty of the Government to protect the abolitionists in their constitutional right of free discussion ; and opposed, sincerely and zealously as we are, to their doctrines and practise, we should be still more opposed to any infringement of their political or civil rights. If the Government once begins to discriminate as to what is orthodox and what heterodox in opinion, what is safe and what is unsafe in its tendency, farewell, a long farewell to our freedom.

The true course to be pursued, in order to protect the South as far as practicable, and yet not violate the great principle of equal freedom, is to revise the post-office laws, and establish the rates of postage on a more just gradation—on some system more equal in its operation and more consonant with the doctrines of economic science. The pretext under which a large part of the matters sent by mail are now sent free of postage—either positively or comparatively—is wholly unsound. "To encourage the diffusion of knowledge" is a very good object in itself; but Government has no right to extend this encouragement to one at the expense of another. Newspapers, pamphlets, commercial and religious tracts, and all sorts of printed documents, as well as letters, ought to pay postage, and all ought to pay it according to the graduation of some just and equal rule. If such a system were once established, making the postage in all cases payable in advance, with duplicate postage on those letters and papers which should be returned, not only the flood of abolition pamphlets would be stayed, but the circulation of a vast deal of harmful trash at the public expense would be prevented, creating a vacuum which would naturally be filled with matters of a better stamp.

MR. KENDALL'S LETTER.

[*From the Evening Post, August* 12, 1835.]

THE following letter has been addressed by the Post Master General to the Post Master at Richmond, enclosing a copy of his letter to the Post Master at Charleston, South Carolina.

"Post Office Department,
5th August 1835.

Sir: My views in relation to the subject of your letter of the 3d inst. may be learnt from the enclosed copy of a letter to the Post Master at Charleston, S. C., dated 4th inst.

Very respectfully,
Your obt. servant,
AMOS KENDALL.

Edm'd. Anderson,
Ass't. P. M. Richmond, Va.

Post Office Department,
August 4th, 1835.

P. M. Charleston, S. C.

Sir: In your letter of the 29th ult. just received, you inform me that by the steamboat mail from New-York your office had been filled with pamphlets and tracts upon slavery: that the public mind was highly excited upon the subject, that you doubted the safety of the mail itself out of your possession: that you had determined, as the wisest course, to detain these papers: and you now ask instructions from the Department.

Upon a careful examination of the law, I am satisfied that the Postmaster General has no legal authority to exclude newspapers from the mail, nor prohibit their carriage or delivery on account of their character or tendency, real or supposed. Probably it was not thought safe to confer on the head of an executive department a power over the press, which might be perverted and abused.

"But I am not prepared to direct you to forward or deliver the papers of which you speak. The Post Office Department was created to serve the people of *each* and *all* of the *United States*, and not to be used as the instrument of their *destruction*. None of the papers detained have been forwarded to me, and I cannot judge for myself of their character and tendency; but you inform me that they are, in character, "the most inflammatory and incendiary—and insurrectionary in the highest degree."

By no act, or direction of mine, official or private, could I be induced to aid, knowingly, in giving circulation to papers of this description, directly, or indirectly. We owe an obligation to the laws, but a higher one to the communities in which we live, and if the *former* be perverted to destroy the *latter*, it is patriotism to disregard them. Entertaining these views I cannot sanction, and will not condemn the step you have taken.

"Your justification must be looked for in the character of the papers detained, and the circumstances by which you are surrounded."

In giving place to the above letter, we cannot refrain from accompanying it with an expression of our surprise and regret that Mr. Kendall, in an official communication, should have expressed such sentiments as this extraordinary letter contains. If, according to his ideas of the duties of patriotism, every postmaster, may constitute himself a judge of the laws, and suspend their operation whenever, in his supreme discretion, it shall seem proper, we trust Mr Kendall may be permitted to retire from a post where such opinions have extensive influence, and enjoy his notions of patriotism in a private station. A pretty thing it is to be sure, when the head officer of the

Post Office establishment of the United States, and a member, *ex officio*, of the Administration of the General Government, while he confesses in one breath that he has no legal power to prevent the carriage or delivery of any newspaper, whatever be the nature of its contents, declares in the very next, that by no act of his will he aid, directly or indirectly, in circulating publications of an incendiary and inflammatory character. Who gives him a right to judge of what is incendiary and inflammatory? Was there any reservation of that sort in his oath of office?

Mr. Kendall has not met the question presented by recent occurrences at the South, as boldly and manfully as we should have supposed he would. He has quailed in the discharge of his duty. He has truckled to the domineering pretensions of the slave-holders. In the trepidation occasioned by his embarrassing position, he has lost sight of the noble maxim, *fiat justitia ruat cœlum.* The course which, by neither sanctioning nor condemning the unlawful conduct of the postmaster at Charleston, he has virtually authorized him and the other postmasters at the South to pursue, is neither more nor less than practical nullification. It is worse than that: it is establishing *a censorship of the press*, in its worst possible form, by allowing every two-penny postmaster through the country to be judge of what species of intelligence it is proper to circulate, and what to withhold from the people. A less evil than this drew forth, in former days, the Areopagitica from the master mind of Milton; but we little dreamed that new arguments in favour of the freedom of speech and of the press would ever become necessary in our country.

We are sorry to say that this letter of Mr. Kendall has materially diminished the very high respect we have heretofore entertained for him. It shows a deficiency of courage and independence which we did not expect to see him betray.

THE POSTMASTER GENERAL.

[*From the Evening Post, August* 14, 1835.]

We publish the communication signed *Justice*, in relation to the late extraordinary letter of the Post Master General, because we are friends of free discussion, and not because we by any means agree with the sentiments of the writer. The remarks with which we accompanied Mr. Kendall's letters were written after more reflection on the nature and tendency of the views expressed in that document, that we are fain to believe Mr. Kendall himself bestowed on the subject on which he expressed such strange opinions; for the only extenuation we can find for that individual is that he wrote in haste, under the influence of trepidation or excited feeling. We will not suppose that to curry favour with the south was any part of his motive, for we have too high a respect for his character willingly to admit the idea that he would sacrifice justice for the sake of popularity.

The position assumed by our correspondent that the Postmaster General was obliged to choose between two evils is not tenable. He was not placed between the horns of a dilemma. His duty was single, simple, and positive, and ought to have been performed openly and promptly, without any paltering, shrinking, or evasion. He was not required to *assent* to an interruption either of the whole mail or a part. His refusal to permit a certain portion of the contents of the mail to be culled out and detained or destroyed, might very possibly, and for the sake of the argument we are willing to say very certainly, lead to the forcible interruption of the whole; but for this he would be in no degree accountable, provided all means which the law places at his disposal had been duly employed to prevent such a result. Suppose the postmaster at Charleston, or some other place, should inform the Post Master General that an organized band of robbers, of great numerical strength, had given notice of their intention, unless certain letters containing money were delivered up to them, to waylay the mail and destroy its whole contents: here would be "a strange alternative presented for Mr. Kendall's prompt selection," yet not stranger than the one which has occurred, and obviously not to be decided upon different principles. Would our correspondent justify him, in such a case, for choosing the lesser of two evils, and permitting the money-letters to be given up in order to save the rest of the mail? The difference between us, on the point in dispute, is, that Mr. Kendall was not called upon to choose between evils, but was imperatively called upon to do his duty, and, as far as practicable, to see that those under him did theirs, leaving any violations of public law and order which might ensue to the investigation and punishment of the proper tribunals.

Our correspondent does not see, as we do, in the doctrines of Mr. Kendall's letter, a justification of a most intolerable species of censorship of the press. It is true, the authorizing of every village postmaster to decide what may, and what may not be circulated, by the public mail, through his district of country, does not prevent any body from printing his sentiments, on any subject, just as if there were not ten thousand such self-constituted supervisors of the press. But the publisher of a newspaper who finds himself denied the facilities of the mail is almost as much interdicted from the circulation of his opinions, as if he were denied the use of presses or types.

The mail is the great means of disseminating publications in the newspaper or pamphlet form, and every citizen has an equal right to its facilities. Not a mail is carried between any two given points on the whole map of our country which does not convey matters to the circulation of which, by themselves, we should be sorry to contribute. Yet the individual who should refuse to pay his proportion of the tax, even supposing it a specific one, which constituted the means of defraying the post-office expenses, on the ground of his hostility to the principles avowed in any portion of the publications carried by mail, would be guilty of nullification in its worst possible form.

Should Congress undertake to discriminate, by law, between the different kinds of publications which may be carried by mail, permitting some to be circulated through that medium on the ground of their being sober and orderly, and prohibiting others as violent and inflammatory—should Congress ever assert such powers and exercise such legislation, and the public submit, not merely will our liberties be destroyed, but the very principle of freedom be extinct within us.

Our post-office system, as we have before, on different occasions, admitted, is very bad, and ought to be amended. Indeed, we have expressed the opinion, as doubtless many of our readers recollect—an opinion which event after event but serves to confirm more and more strongly —that it would have been well for this country if the power to establish post-offices and post-routes had never been given to the Government, but left entirely, as a matter of trade, to be regulated by the laws of trade—left to the regulation of the same principles which furnish us with such admirable facilities for the transportation of our persons and packages from place to place, and would have done no less for us in respect to our letters, circulars, and newspapers.

But as this is a theoretical question, it may be out of season to discuss it in the present connexion. Yet, in the reformation of the post-office department, it would be well to conform it as nearly as possible to free-trade principles. The tax of postage, like all other taxes, ought to fall equally on the community ; not as now, the seaboard be made to pay for the interior, and letter-writers for the carriage of newspapers, handbills and pamphlets.

With these hasty remarks, we submit the views of our correspondent to our readers. Though we ourselves feel constrained to take ground against the sentiments of Mr. Kendall's epistle, our correspondent may console himself with the assurance that our example is not likely to be extensively imitated. The opposition papers in this quarter are too anxious to conciliate the good will of the South, and turn the slave question into a weapon against their political adversaries, to find any fault with views which will be so highly relished as those of Mr. Kendall in the slave states. On our side, equally timid and disingenuous sentiments will prevail. The Times dare not speak out for itself on the present, or any other question requiring the least boldness of character ; and the Albany Argus which came to hand this morning is profuse in expressions of admiration of "the prompt, liberal *and just* reply of the Postmaster General," considering his view of the subject as "the only one that could be taken," and avowing the utmost confidence that such will be "the general opinion." Tray, Blanche and Sweetheart, and the whole pack, will yelp responsive to the bark of the leading hound, and a din will instantly be raised in eulogy of the Postmaster General more than sufficient to drown our feeble voice.

TWO-PENNY POSTMASTERS.

[*From the Evening Post, August* 15, 1835.]

We give below the correspondence of one of the "two-penny postmasters" who think with Mr. Kendall, that they owe a higher obligation to the community in which they live than to the laws; or, in other words, that it is of more consequence to play amiable to the south and truckle to its arrogant pretensions, than to obey their oath of office and perform the solemn duties of their station. We may expect to see many patriots now, in quarters which have not been suspected of abounding with patriotism; since, according to the doctrines of the Postmaster General, all that is required to constitute one a Sydney or a Hampden is to nullify the laws.

We were aware that nullification never had any terrors for Mr. Gouverneur, and he has made this obvious enough now by the extraordinary eagerness he has manifested to play the nullifier and foist himself before the community in that character. We cannot, of course, suspect so pure a man of any intention in this matter of creating a southern interest in his favour, and of obtaining southern influence to strengthen the feeble tenure by which he is said to hold his office. He is quite disinterested in the course, no doubt! He pursues it solely because it is pointed out by duty; because it is incumbent on patriotism to disobey the laws. We must pause here, lest Mr. Gouverneur's patriotism should next object to our own journal, and cause him to take the responsibility of refusing to forward it by mail. Should he do so, however, we promise to bring his patriotism to the touchstone of the laws, and give him an opportunity of ascertaining whether a New-York jury approve this new species of nullification, which erects every hot-headed and intemperate postmaster into a Censor of the Press, and authorises him to decide what newspapers may be circulated and what not.

With these remarks we submit the correspondence referred to.

POST OFFICE CORRESPONDENCE.

Copy of a letter addressed to the President and Directors of the American Anti-Slavery Society, by S. L. Gouverneur.

"Gentlemen—I have received a letter from the Postmaster at Charleston, of which the enclosed is a copy. I have transmitted another to the Postmaster General.

"Entertaining full confidence that you will duly appreciate my sincere desire to reconcile a just discharge of my official duties with all the delicate considerations which are in the case presented to me, I have respectfully to propose to you that the transmission of the papers referred to be suspended, until the views of the Postmaster General shall have been received.

"With great respect, &c.

(Signed,) "SAM'L. L. GOUVERNEUR."

"Sam'l. L. Gouverneur, Esq.

"Sir—Your communication addressed to 'the President and Directors of the American Anti-Slavery Society,' has been handed me by Mr. Bates, and shall be laid before the Executive Committee.

"I am, respectfully,

"Your obedient servant,

"ARTHUR TAPPAN,

"President A. A. S. Society."

"New-York, Aug. 7, 1835."

"Anti-Slavery Office,
New-York, 8th Aug. 1835.

"Sam'l. L. Gouverneur, Esq. P. M. New-York.

"Dear Sir—Your favour of yesterday, covering a letter from the Postmaster of Charleston, in regard to the recent violation of the United States mail in that place, and proposing to us to suspend the transmission of our publications until the views of the Post Master General shall be received, has been laid before the Executive Committee of the American Anti-Slavery Society, and I am instructed, very respectfully, to transmit to you the following reply, viz:

"'Resolved, That while we are desirous to relieve public officers from any unnecessary difficulties and responsibilities, we cannot consent to surrender any of the rights or privileges, which we possess in common with our fellow-citizens, in regard to the use of the United States mail.'

"With much respect, your obedient servant,

"E. WRIGHT, Jr.

"Sec. Dom. Cor. Am. A. S. Society."

"To the President and Directors of the American Anti-Slavery Society.

"Gentlemen—I have the honour to acknowledge the receipt of your letter of yesterday, covering a copy of a resolution of certain persons described as 'the Executive Committee of the American Anti-Slavery Society.'

"Early on the morning of the 7th inst., I addressed a communication to you, enclosing a copy of one which I received from the Postmaster at Charleston. Referring you to the peculiarly delicate considerations which were involved in the case he presented, I respectfully proposed to you to suspend the transmission of your papers until the views of the Postmaster General, before whom the whole subject has been laid, could be received. This communication having been delivered to you by Mr. Bates, Assistant Postmaster, I received a verbal assurance that you would cheerfully comply with the proposition I had made. In full assurance that this proposition would not be changed, I gave the necessary instructions to separate the papers referred to, in making up the mail for that portion of the country, and retain them at this office. The resolution to which I have referred, gave me the first intimation of the change of your views; and was received at this office about the time of closing the mail. It was, therefore, too late in fact, to cause a different disposition to be made of these papers. They were accordingly retained here in pursuance of the original understanding with you, nor will they be transmitted by mail until the instructions of the Postmaster General shall have been received.

"Having thus placed you in possession of the facts, I beg leave to refer more distinctly to the resolution of your committee. My views have been much mistaken, if it is intended to imply that I required relief at your hands from 'any difficulty or responsibility,' whatever, as 'a public officer.' Had you declined, in the first instance, the proposition I had offered, my determination would have been promptly announced to you. Placed as I was, in a peculiarly delicate position; appealed to by an officer of the same department at a distance, to lend my aid in preserving the public peace—securing the safe transmission of the important contents of that valuable branch of the mail department—and arresting a course of excitement which could not fail to lead to the most disastrous results, I should not have hesitated to adopt that course which, in my judgment the highest obligations imposed, had it even demanded in some degree a temporary 'surrender of the rights and privileges' you claim to possess. While manifesting so openly your benevolence to the colored people, I thought I had a right to claim some portion of your sympathies for the white population of that section of country—the peculiar situation of which Mr. Huger so fully described. I would respectfully ask, gentlemen, what injury could result from a momentary suspension of your efforts, compared with that which might have occurred, had they been pushed at all hazards?

"I entertain for you, and all your rights, every sentiment of respect which is due, and I deeply regret that a departure from the original understanding, which promised to prevent all excitement and collision, has compelled me to express myself so fully. I have reflected deeply on the subject. The laws which secure to you the rights you claim, also impose the penalties on those who infringe them. I shall assume the responsibility in the case you have made with me, and to the law and my superiors will hold myself accountable.

"With great respect, &c. &c.

"SAM'L. L. GOUVERNEUR."

"New-York, Aug. 9, 1835."

We trust no one will do this journal the gross injustice to construe the censure we have taken leave to express of the extraordinary and disorganising sentiments of the Postmaster General, or of the unlawful conduct of Mr. Gouverneur, as an approval, in the slightest degree, of the course pursued by the Abolition Association. We consider the fanatical obstinacy of that Association, in persevering to circulate their publications in the southern states, contrary to the unanimous sentiment of the white population, and at the obvious risk of stirring up insurrections, which, once commenced, no one can tell where they will end, as reprehensible to a degree for which language has no terms of adequate censure. We have expressed ourselves fully and frequently on this subject; and if any remonstrances which we have the power to frame, or any appeals we could make to the reason or humanity of the abolitionists, could avail to restrain them from prosecuting their designs in the mode which has already led to so much excitement, and which threatens speedily to lead to consequences far more deplorable, our readers may be assured they should not be withheld.

But while we deprecate, as earnestly and sincerely as any person can, in the north or south, the conduct of the abolitionists, we deprecate not less all unlawful and tumultuary means of preventing or counteracting their efforts. We were taught long ago, by the sage precept of Jefferson, that "error may be safely tolerated, where reason is left free to combat it;" and the truth of this maxim has been illustrated by a thousand notorious instances, under our free and tolerant institutions. We believe its orthodoxy would have borne the test of this exciting abolition question, and that if the tenets and conduct of the Anti-Slavery Association had been met only in a temperate and reasoning spirit, all that is really dangerous in them, all that the south has any right to complain of, would long since have been given up. We believe that fanaticism might have been subdued by sound calm argument, while it has only been inflamed to greater desperation and extravagance by the violent assaults it has encountered. We believe it might have been vanquished by Ithuriel's spear, while Antæus-like, it has gained new strength from every blow of the herculean club—the mob weapon which seems to be fast superceding the assuasive exercise of truth and reason.

But whether we are right or wrong in these opinions, we hold fast, nevertheless, to the inviolability of the law, and exert our voice with all possible earnestness against the strange principle and practice of the day, that a mere ministerial servant of the public has power to say when the law shall be executed and when set at nought. If the abolitionists cannot be restrained by reasoning and constitutional law, let them not be restrained by any other weapon. The liberty of speech and of the press are the main pillars in the great fabric of political liberty, and if they are shaken, the whole structure, reared at such cost, and guarded with such sleepless vigilance, will tumble to the dust. Can they be more directly assailed than by the recognition of a principle which puts it at the discretion of every rash and intriguing postmaster — to say what printed matter shall be circulated and what committed to the flames? We trust the laws concerning the Post Office may undergo early and very extensive reformation—a reformation which will throw pecuniary difficulties in the way of the gratuitous circulation of all sorts of political, philanthropical, and sectarian trash. But while they remain as they now are, it is as great an outrage against the equal rights of man, and as audacious an interference with the freedom of the press, to intercept and destroy the pamphlets of the abolitionists, as it would be those of the colonizationists, or any other association, or individual, of whatever sect, party, or name.

We do not like the tone in which our southern brethren speak of matters connected with abolition. There is a great deal too much of the Ercles' vein in it. They are quite too much disposed to threaten; and should the north retaliate in the same braggart style, ill blood might be stirred between us. There is one thing, we, for a single journal, with all due amenity of disposition, but inflexible firmness of temper, shall take leave to assure our fellow-citizens south of Mason aud Dixon's line; namely, that we shall not permit our right to discuss the question of slavery, or any other question under heaven, to be denied. Point us the section or clause in the articles of confederation, or the obligation in any form or any place, which prohibits us from expressing our free opinions on that subject or any subject, and you may prevail upon us to be silent; but by threats of disunion you never can. This *ultima ratio* of dissolving the federal compact has got to be as familiar in the mouths of the southerners as household words. It is held up as a bugbear at every turn. Dissolve the Union, in welcome, if the only tie to hold it together must be wrought out of the sacred right of free discussion—if we must mix the cement with the very heart's blood of freedom. Dissolve the Union! and pray what would the south gain by that? Would that put an end to discussion? Would that prevent men from speaking their thoughts on the subject of slavery? Would that put afar off the evil day which the south is but hastening, with fearful rapidity, by the very method—the ill-judged, fatal method—which it takes to retard it?

We are as much opposed as the Richmond Enquirer, whose menacing language has somewhat moved us from our propriety, to such a discussion of the slave question as can at all interfere with the real prosperity of the south. We are wholly, strongly, inveterately opposed to the discussion of it in the mode adopted by the abolitionists, and deplore that fanatical course of conduct which instead of bettering the condition of the slaves, necessarily subjects them to stricter vigilance and more severity of discipline, which fills the bosoms of the white population with anxiety and alarm, which excites in their minds the most unfriendly feelings towards their brethren of the north, and the fruit of which eventually must be insurrection, murder, and the shedding of blood like water. We need not repeat that we are opposed wholly, warmly, to this course of discussion. Nay we have yielded, and might continue to yield we know not how much longer, to the nervous fears of the south, and totally pretermit the discussion of the slave question in every form and manner, if this were asked of us as a matter of concession, and not demanded, with accompanying threats, as a right. But it is one thing to remain silent through compassion and brotherly concern, and another to be rudely and authoritatively hushed by a vaunting command.

But however displeasing the tone of the south is to us, its vapouring is a matter utterly insignificant compared with the theoretical violation by Mr. Kendall, and the practical violation by Mr. Gouverneur, of the equal rights of all citizens to disseminate their opinions through the mail. This outrage upon the principles of freedom, under the pretence of *patriotism* (fine patriotism, with a vengeance!) is one of a most startling character. The act of the New-York postmaster would give us little concern were it not authorised by the avowed principles of his superior. As it is, where is this course of proceeding to stop? Whose rights are safe? We are all at the mercy of an army of postmasters, and must satisfy the discretion, of their high mightinesses that we mean no treason, before our opinions can have passage free. They stop the abolition journals to-day: who will insure us that they will not stop ours to-morrow? Newspapers are the present object of imperial interdiction: who shall answer that the sanctity of letters will not next be violated, their contents inspected, and their secrets betrayed?

If the strange and startling doctrines we have heard promulgated within the past week are to prevail, we shall wish that Mr. Barry, with all his remissness, pliancy, and inattention, were again at the head of the Post-office, in the place of a man who considers it patriotism to disobey the laws.

THE EVENING POST AND MR. VAN BUREN.

[*From the Evening Post of August* 20, 1835.]

THE Richmond Whig takes some notice of the remarks made by this journal on the letter of the Post-master General, and adds: "Now we are anxious to know if in this matter, the Post, which we understand to be the city organ of Mr. Van Buren, *expresses his sentiments?*" We shall take the pains to answer the Richmond Whig fully and candidly, and trust to the sense of honour and justice of that print to give a conspicuous insertion to our reply.

The Evening Post is not the organ of Mr. Van Buren, or of any other man or set of men whatever, save and except its editors, who are also its proprietors, and who conduct their journal with exclusive reference to their own sense of right and expediency.

They are in no private communication with Mr. Van Buren, directly or indirectly; they know his sentiments only through public channels; and their attachment to him is altogether political, and founded on their sincere estimate of Mr. Van Buren's public services and private virtues—their knowledge of his private virtues being an unavoidable inference from the fact, that the virulence of an opposition which does not hesitate to invade the domestic sanctuary, and even violate the grave, has found nothing in his private character to reprehend.

Mr. Van Buren has no more to do with the contents

of the Evening Post than has the editor of the Richmond Whig ; and he can answer for himself how much that is.

Nay more, an article from Mr. Van Buren's pen, if offered for insertion to-morrow, would be judged of on precisely the same rules that govern in relation to all communications, and would be accepted or rejected with single reference to its sentiments and style, just as would be done in reference to an anonymous contribution.

What Mr. Van Buren's sentiments are in regard to Mr. Kendall's letter we do not know ; but we have confidence from what we do know of Mr. Van Buren's sentiments, that he cannot approve the disorganizing doctrines of that letter.

What Mr. Van Buren's sentiments are on the subject of state rights in regard to negro slavery the Richmond Whig may easily ascertain from public and authentic sources ; and what they are in regard to the expediency of abolishing slavery in the District of Columbia, is equally ascertainable from sources as public and well authenticated.

Finally, there is ample ground for the assertion, and not any for a denial of it, that Mr. Van Buren has no connexion, in any way or shape, with the doctrines or movements of the abolitionists, and that the attempt, on the part of certain prints, to connect him with them is a base party trick, justifiable only according to the tenets of that school of morals which affirms that "*all is fair in politics.*"

MR. VAN BUREN AND SLAVERY.

[*From the Evening Post, August*, 22, 1835.]

The Richmond Whig of the nineteenth instant, commences an article in relation to certain opinions expressed by this paper, by saying: "Mr. Van Buren's organ in the city of New-York most acrimoniously censures Messrs. Kendall, Postmaster General, and Gouverneur, Postmaster of the city of New-York, for their respective letters." In this sentence our readers may see the progress of error. Falsehood seems to possess an inherent, self-propelling power, and its tendency is always to move forward. Thus what one day the Richmond Whig puts forth conjecturally, as supposition, or matter of inference, is next day boldly asserted as matter of positive knowledge. On the 18th it understood this journal to be an organ of Mr. Van Buren, and on the 19th, without any intermediate corroboration of its opinion, surmise had grown into established fact. We are sorry that the Richmond Whig is thus increasing the difficulty of correcting its unfounded statement.

The object of connecting this journal, in respect to its opinions touching the question of slavery, with Mr. Van Buren, is collaterally to injure that individual by imputing to him sentiments unfriendly to southern rights and interests. We must beg of the Richmond Whig, however, in justice to both ourselves and Mr. Van Buren, not to consider us as his mouthpiece, since no imputation can be more unjust, nor to censure him for our opinions, since he never has the least knowledge of them except through the same medium that conveys them to the Richmond Whig, namely, the columns of this newspaper.

The Richmond Whig knows perfectly well that the paragraphs which it has quoted from this paper, it might have taken from the Albany Evening Journal, into which they were immediately copied with expressions of entire concurrence in the sentiments they express, and with an accompanying article as strongly reprehending the course of Amos Kendall as did our own. But if the Richmond Whig had quoted from the Albany Evening Journal, it could not have called it "*Mr. Van Buren's organ*;" since it is notorious that there is not a print in the United States—not excepting even the Richmond Whig—more bitter against Mr. Van Buren than the paper in question. Yet, if a few prints, including some in favour of Mr. Van Buren and others opposed to him, concur in expressing objections to Mr. Kendall's sentiments, and the great majority of prints, without reference to their preferences or prejudices on the question of the Presidency, agree in approval, either explicit or tacit, of those sentiments, how can the Richmond Whig reconcile it to its sense of what honour requires, as well in political warfare as in a contest of any other nature, to single out a particular paper, and by terming it an organ of Mr. Van Buren, disingenuously attempt to fasten upon him opinions with which he has no more connexion than the Richmond Whig itself?

Let Mr. Van Buren stand or fall by his own merits. Do not seek to destroy him by imputing to him opinions with which he has nothing to do. Judge of him by his own acts and sentiments, and if these do not condemn him, attempt not to bolster up a bad cause by resorting to a species of political forgery.

It was modestly intimated in the Letter of Mr. Van Buren, accepting the nomination tendered him by the Baltimore Convention, that he owed his selection more to his being pointed out to the democracy by the persevering attacks of his enemies, than to any positive merit of his own. The merits of Mr. Van Buren may speak unbonneted to as proud a fortune as that to which he is about to be elevated by the free suffrages of the people of the United States; and it did not need that he should become the object of opposition rancour to endear him to the hearts of the democracy, who, in the services he has done the state, in his even and consistent career, his uniform support of popular rights, and his general integrity and worth in all the relations of life, public and private, are furnished with an ample warrant for the esteem in which they hold him. But this we will say: that if there were no positive evidences of Mr. Van Buren's claims to approbation, we yet could find, in the very bitterest prints of the aristocracy, the most abundant negative testimony of his merits. Let the reader look through the journals most violently opposed to that distinguished man—journals which give daily proof of the recklessness with which they overleap the domestic barriers and ransack the secret places of private life. Let him fasten on all he meets with relative to Mr. Van Buren, drag it out into day-light, sift it and examine it, and what does it amount to? Is there a single act alleged against Mr. Van Buren for which he ought to blush?—a single sentiment which he ought to retract?—a single expression which does discredit to his head or his heart? He is called a magician; yet not for the practice of arts inhibited, for all his powers are those only of a superior nature, patriotically exercised for the advantage of his country. He is called an intriguer; yet notwithstanding all the mutations of parties, and all the derelictions of friends which have occurred in the long period that the public gaze has been fixed upon him, the world is boldly challenged to show a single trace of secret plotting. In the absence of fitter themes of censure, his personal habits are chosen as topics of ridicule and reproach; and the proud spirit of aristocracy has descended even so pitifully low as to descant on the style of his equipage and the fashion of his clothes!

The Richmond Whig, however, with a spirit of originality which would be commendable, were it not a spirit of dishonesty also, strikes out a path for itself, and disdaining to comment on the workmanship of Mr. Van Buren's watch-chain or the trimmings of his coach, attacks him on the more important ground of hostility to the rights and domestic institutions of the south. It is unfortunate for the object which the Richmond Whig seeks to accomplish that it has no foundation for its remarks. This does not derogate from the boldness of its effort, but materially interferes with the prospect of success. Mr. Van Buren will hardly be deserted as unfriendly to the south, because the Evening Post has expressed disapprobation of the sentiments of Mr. Kendall's letter.

But we have a word to say on our own score as regards this subject of unfriendliness to the south. There is not a journal even in the trans-Potomack part of the Union which feels a stronger interest in the real welfare of that portion of the confederacy than is entertained by ourselves; there is not one which has a nicer regard for their rights, or would make a greater effort to defend them. We have watched the progress of the question which is now agitating the southern states with the liveliest concern, and have witnessed the rapid increase of abolition fanaticism with the deepest regret, not unmingled with alarm. If aught had been in our power to arrest that frantic sect, we should not have stood an inactive spectator of its progress. If any arguments urged by us could convince them of their fatal error, or if any persuasion would turn them from their course, neither reasoning nor exhortation should be withheld. Nay, further, with all the influence we can possibly exert, we shall support every proper and constitutional effort to throw difficulties in the way of the abolitionists, and protect the south from the subtle poison of their inflammatory and insurrectionary publications. Whatever can be done to promote the security of our brothers of the south, not inconsistently with the paramount obligations of the Constitution, and with those sacred principles of liberty on which the Constitution is founded, we shall do with all our heart and soul and understanding. But the Richmond Whig must excuse us if we pause at that line of demarkation. We cannot trample on the charter of our national freedom to assist the slave-holder in his warfare with fanaticism. We cannot subscribe to those disorganizing sentiments which would elevate ten thousand postmasters above the law, and constitute them censors of the press, however great our respect for the source from whence they proceeded, or however sincere our regret for the particular occasion which elicited them.

Among the matters which our columns contain to-day is the "Calm Appeal," so called, of the Richmond Enquirer to the people of the north on the exciting subject which now engrosses so much of public attention. We need not ask of our readers to give this address a careful perusal, for the topic and the source will alike commend it to their gravest consideration. But great as our esteem is for the writer who thus appeals to the citizens of this section of the confederacy, and ardent as is our desire that the bitter cup, which he seems to think we are raising to the lips of our southern brethren, may pass untasted from them, we cannot permit his address to go forth, without accompanying it with an expression of our disapprobation of much that it contains. Our time will not permit us to go into particular objections; but we may state generally that it claims quite too much in denying the right of the north to discuss the question of slavery, and addresses its arguments too much to our fears. The grand alternative which the Richmond Enquirer seems to have ever in its eye, a dissolution of the Union, might not prove a remedy for all the ills the south is heir to. Far off be the day when the ties which unite our sisterhood of sovereignties shall be sundered; but come that event when it may, there are none on whom the ills of separation will more sorely press than on those states which are ever so forward to "calculate the value of the Union," and to threaten its dissolution.

FANATICAL ANTI-ABOLITIONISTS.

[*From the Evening Post, August* 26, 1835.]

THE call for a public meeting to express the sense of this community on the subject of the efforts of the anti-slavery society is published in our paper this afternoon, with all the signatures attached. We do not like the phraseology of this call, and if the resolutions to be submitted to the proposed meeting should be written in the same spirit, we shall be constrained to withhold our approbation from them. It would be well for those who are chiefly concerned in getting up the meeting to remember that there may be fanaticism as well among the anti-abolitionists as the abolitionists, and that incendiary language is as unjustifiable on the one part as the other. The call of a public meeting, and the proceedings of that meeting when convened, should be calm and temperate, suitable to the gravity of the occasion, and the dignity of the community. Such inflammatory phrases as "imported travelling incendiaries," and "misguided native fanatics" smack too much of the Courier and Enquirer to accord with the seriousness of the subject in regard to which the people are called together to deliberate. It would be a source of endless regret to all right-minded men if this public gathering should degenerate into a mob, and act over the scenes of the former abolition riot. Yet those engaged in drawing up the resolutions, besides the other considerations which strongly recommend moderation in sentiment and expression, would do well to bear in mind that in the present excited state of public feeling, a few inflammatory phrases might easily set men's minds on fire, and give a tumultuous character to an assemblage which can only truly promote the desired end by acting with the most impressive seriousness and decorum.

REWARD FOR ARTHUR TAPPAN.

[*From the Evening Post, August* 26, 1835.]

The southern presses teem with evidences that fanaticism of as wild a character as that which they deprecate exists among themselves. How else could such a paper as the Charleston Patriot advert with tacit approval to the statement, that a purse of twenty thousand dollars has been made up in New-Orleans as a reward for the audacious miscreant who should dare to kidnap Arthur Tappan, and deliver him on the Levee in that city. Revolting to right reason as such a proposition is, we find it repeated with obvious gust and approbation by prints conducted by enlightened and liberal minds—by minds that ordinarily take just views of subjects, achieve their ends by reasoning and persuasion, and exert all their influence to check the popular tendency to tumult. Is the Charleston Patriot so blinded by the peculiar circumstances in which the south is placed as not to perceive that the proposed abduction of Arthur Tappan, even if consummated by his murder, as doubtless is the object, would necessarily have a widely different effect from that of suppressing the Abolition Association, or in anywise diminishing its zeal and ardour? Does it not perceive, on the contrary, that such an outrage would but inflame the minds of that fraternity to more fanatical fervour, and stimulate them to more strenuous exertions, while it would add vast numbers to their ranks though the influence of those feelings which persecution never fails to arouse.

But independent of the effect of the proposed outrage on the abolitionists themselves, what, let us ask, would be the sentiments it would create in the entire community? Has the violence of the south, its arrogant pretensions and menacing tone so overcrowded our spirits, that we would tamely submit to see our citizens snatched from the sanctuary of their homes, and carried off by midnight ruffians, to be burned at a stake, gibbeted on a tree, or butchered in some public place, without the slightest form of trial, and without even the allegation of crime? Are our laws so inert, are our rights so ill-guarded, that we must bear such outrages without repining or complaint? Is our Governor a wooden image, that he would look on such unheard of audacity and make no effort to avenge the insult? These are questions which it will be well for the south to ponder seriously before it offers rewards to ruffians for kidnapping citizens of New-York. If the south wishes to retain its slaves in bondage, let it not insult the whole population of this great free state by threatening to tear any citizen from the protection of our laws and give him up to the tender mercies of a mob actuated by the most frantic fanaticism. Such a proceeding would make abolitionists of our whole two millions of inhabitants.

Mr. KENDALL'S LETTER.

[*From the Evening Post, August* 29, 1835.]

If the letter of Mr. Kendall to the postmaster at Charleston deserved the animadversions which have been passed upon it, that to Mr. Gouverneur, which was published in this paper yesterday, requires stricture in a much greater degree; and it was a source of regret to us that circumstances compelled us to place it before our readers unaccompanied by a full expression of dissent from the extraordinary positions it maintains. We hasten to supply the omission by making it the chief subject of our attention to-day.

The letter of Mr. Kendall, after a passing remark about the "fatuity" of the abolitionists, which must be considered as the expression of a mere personal opinion, and therefore out of place in an official communication, proceeds to acknowledge, in the clearest terms, that, after the fullest consideration of the subject, he is satisfied that the Postmaster General has no authority to exclude any species of newspapers or pamphlets from the mails, and adds that such a power, as it would be fearfully dangerous, has been properly withheld. But in the very face and teeth of this admission, Mr. Kendall goes on to say, that nothing but the want of power deters him from giving a sweeping order to exclude the whole series of abolition publications from the southern mails. How striking a proof he affords of the truth of his own remark, that such a power of censorship or interdiction vested in the head of the post-office department "would be fearfully dangerous, and has been properly withheld!" Ay, most properly! Yet though this fearfully dangerous power has been withheld from the Postmaster General, that functionary is in favour of its exercise by his subordinates, and instead of reprehending Mr. Gouverneur for his lawless conduct, he pats him on the back, and tells him in plain phrase, "if I were situated as you are, I would do as you have done!" We confess that, had not Mr. Kendall's previous letter taken off the edge of our astonishment, this sentiment would have occasioned a keener surprise than we are well able to express in words.

Let us look at the reason of this thing calmly. The Government has carefully withheld from the post-office department a certain power, because it was too fearfully dangerous in its nature to be trusted to the discretion of even the chief officer, under any limitations, however guarded, or responsibilities for its abuse, however heavy. Yet this very power, so jealously and scrupulously withheld from the chief officer, that officer, in the same breath that he acknowledges his lack of it, and commends the wisdom that refused to confer it upon him, applauds his subordinate for usurping, and assures him of the concurrent applause of his country and mankind! Was ever contradiction more manifest? Was ever folly, or "fatuity," if the Postmaster General prefers the word, more palpable?

Postmasters, the letter goes on to say, may, in all cases, lawfully know the contents of newspapers, because the law provides that they shall be so put up as to admit of their being examined. The thirtieth section of the post-office law of 1825 does certainly require "that all newspapers conveyed in the mail shall be under cover, open at one end." And it also ordains that "if any person shall enclose or conceal a letter, or other thing, or any memorandum in writing, in a newspaper, pamphlet, or magazine, or in any package of pamphlets, newspapers, or magazines, or make any writing or memorandum thereon, which he shall have delivered into any post-office, or to any person for that purpose, in order that the same may be carried by post, free of letter postage, he shall forfeit the sum of five dollars for every such offence." Now, here the purpose is distinctly seen why the law requires that the covers of newspapers should be open at one end. It is not that the postmasters may make themselves acquainted with the contents of newspapers, in order to judge whether or not "they are inflammatory, incendiary, and insurrectionary in the highest degree," and to exercise their supreme discretion whether they ought to be forwarded or retained; but it is simply that they may ascertain whether they conceal any such attempt to defraud the Department of postage as is pointed out and made penal by the clause quoted above. If the covers of newspapers are directed to be left open at one end for any other purpose than this, where is that purpose stated? If it is that postmasters may make themselves acquainted with the contents, there surely should exist some word of direction or intimation to that effect. To infer that they may lawfully set themselves down and peruse all the publications which are sent to be circulated through the mail, because those publications are left accessible for an express and very different purpose, is about as wise as to infer that because a pastry-cook leaves his shop-door open for the accommodation of his customers, a street beggar may enter and consume all his pies and tarts without fee or reward.

But fortunately, after the sample we have had of the discretion of postmasters and postmaster generals, this thing is not left to inference. The law is so perfectly explicit that Mr. Kendall's sophistry, ingenious as it is, stands but little chance before it; and he will be driven back, perforce, to his former position, and compelled to derive his authority for this general perusal of newspapers on the part of his subordinates, in their search after incendiary matter, to that obligation which he alleges we owe to the communities in which we live above the laws by which those communities are governed. In the very section that directs that one end of newspaper covers shall be left open, it is ordained that "if any person, employed in any department of the post-office, shall improperly detain, delay, embezzle, or destroy any newspaper, or shall permit any other person to do the like, or shall open any mail or packet of newspapers not directed to the office where he is employed, such offender shall, on conviction thereof, forfeit a sum, not exceeding fifty dollars, for every such offence." We fancy it is not from this clause that the Postmaster General gets his authority for saying that "postmasters may lawfully know, in all cases, the contents of newspapers." Let us state briefly the tenour of some other clauses, that the reader may single out the one from which this alleged right is derived. The law provides that any master of a steamboat carrying the mail who shall fail to deliver to the postmaster, within a specified time, any packet with which he may have been entrusted, shall forfeit thirty dollars for every failure: that if any person shall wilfully obstruct or retard the mail, he shall be fined a hundred dollars: and that if any person employed in the post-office shall detain, open, or destroy any letter or packet of letters, he shall be fined not exceeding three hundred dollars, or imprisoned not exceeding six months. In none of these clauses, we presume, does Mr. Kendall discover his authority for the postmasters reading all the newspapers and pamphlets which pass through their hands. Indeed we are driven to the conclusion that the warrant for doing so exists only in that profound maxim which makes their duty to the community paramount to that which they have solemnly sworn to yield to the laws. Incendiary articles may set whole communities on fire; newspapers and pamphlets may contain incendiary articles;

ergo, it is proved syllogistically, that their duty to the community obliges them to read all the newspapers and pamphlets which come into their hands, the law to the contrary notwithstanding.

And now that this stumbling-block is removed from the path of the argument, and it is established that the postmasters, heaven defend them! ought to read the contents of all packages "open at one end," let us see what is the next position we arrive at. Why, neither more nor less, than that, if they discover the said contents to be inflammatory, "it cannot be doubted that it is their duty to detain them, if not even to hand them over to the civil authorities." This we deny; unless the Postmaster General is going again for his authority to his paramount obligation to the community, and means to thrust the despised law aside as something beneath his notice. If the postmaster's duty is derived from the law: if it is circumscribed by those solemn words, "I do swear that I will faithfully perform all the duties required of me, and abstain from every thing forbidden, by the laws in relation to the establishment of the post-offices and post-roads within the United States;" it seems to us perfectly plain, that his detention of publications, because he deemed them inflammatory, would be flat perjury. Congress has not trusted to the Postmaster General that "fearfully dangerous power" of excluding any species of newspapers from the mails; and it has not trusted it to the postmasters under him: where then the authority which, in the case supposed, or in any supposable case, would make it their duty to detain publications of the kind referred to, or of any kind whatever?

But while the Postmaster General thus proclaims what he considers as beyond a doubt the duty of the postmasters under him in a given case, he is careful to repeat several times that he has no authority to direct them to do so; that "they act on their own responsibility, and if they *improperly detain* or use papers sent to their offices, for transmission or delivery, it is at their own peril, and on their heads falls the punishment." The meaning of the phrase, "*improperly detain*" as used in the Post-office law, is fixed by the stipulations of that law as to what is proper to be done. All unnecessary delay, all voluntary delay, in executing the injunctions of the law is improper delay; but delay arising from unavoidable casualties or unforeseen hinderances of any kind, does not come under that head. Thus, if an unusual number of publications should be poured into the post-office on any occasion, and the means of conveyance should be inadequate to the immediate transmission of them all, the delay which might occur in forwarding a portion would be a necessary and not improper delay. Thus also the delay occasioned by freshets, broken bridges, and a hundred other casualties of the roads, is not improper delay in the meaning of the law. But delay occasioned by postmasters keeping packages back in order to peruse their contents, or having perused them, because they consider them "inflammatory, incendiary, and insurrectionary in the highest degree," is clearly, within the meaning of the law, *improper delay*. It is improper, because it is no part of the postmaster's duty to peruse printed communications through his office, any more than written ones, but on the contrary he his directly forbidden to do so under a penalty; and further, because, if he violates this part of his duty, and peruses them in defiance of the law, the "fearfully dangerous power" is neither entrusted to him nor to his superior, nor indeed is it possessed by the General Government itself, to authorize their detention, on account of their tendency, real or supposed, whether in a religious or moral, a political or social respect.

But while the Postmaster General is so anxious to shift

from his own head all responsibility for this discretionary exercise of unauthorized and "fearfully dangerous" power, he takes care that the load of responsibility shall not rest very heavy on the heads of his subordinates. He talks, indeed, of the "peril" and "punishment" which they will incur if they improperly exercise their unauthorized discretion; but in this most monstrous and flagrant instance, in which a Postmaster has audaciously exercised "fearfully dangerous" powers not only not conferred upon him, but expressly interdicted under heavy penalties, his superior, at whose hands he must be punished if he has incurred punishment, smiles graciously upon him, and tells him, "if I were situated as you are, I would do as you have done," and "you will, I have no doubt, stand justified in that step before your country and all mankind!" More monstrous, more anarchical doctrines, we never heard promulgated. With what face after this, can Mr. Kendall punish a postmaster for any exercise of the fearfully dangerous power of stopping and destroying any portion of the mails? He has but to say, I considered the contents of that portion "inflammatory, incendiary, and insurrectionary in the highest degree," and Mr. Kendall is bound in consistency to reply to him that, in his place, he would have done the same, and that his country and mankind will applaud the proceeding.

The case which the Postmaster General puts, of the discretionary power which it would be proper for a postmaster to exercise in the event of a war, is not analogous. The abolitionists do not deserve to be considered on the same footing with a foreign enemy, nor their publications as the secret despatches of a spy. They are American citizens, in the exercise of the undoubted rights of citizenship, and however erroneous their views, however fanatic their conduct, while they act within the limits of the law what official functionary, be he merely a subordinate postmaster, or the head of the post-office department, shall dare to abridge them of their rights of citizenship, or deny them access to those facilities of intercourse which were instituted for the equal accommodation of all? If the American people will submit to this, let us expunge all written codes, and resolve society into its original elements, where the might of the strong is better than the right of the weak.

The Postmaster General affects to consider the course pursued by Mr. Gouverneur "a measure of great public necessity;" and he enters into a very rhetorical description of the consequences which will result from throwing firebrands into magazines of combustibles. We shall leave Mr. Kendall's figures of rhetoric to take care of themselves, and shall only give our attention to his arguments stripped of their showy integuments. It is by no means clear, then, that the deplorable effects which it is considered would inevitably flow from the circulation of the abolition pamphlets are correctly stated. Mr. Kendall himself does not profess to be personally acquainted with the character of those productions, and the "concurrent testimony" which he alludes to is somewhat too vague and declamatory to be altogether trusted. The abolitionists, many, if not the most of whom, say what we may of their opinions and conduct on the question of slavery, are respectable, intelligent, religious men, and mean well, whatever may be the effect of their efforts—the abolitionists, we say, have peremptorily denied, in official publications, a large part of the matters charged against them. They have denied, for example, that their publications have been addressed to any but respectable citizens, or were intended to circulate among any others. They have denied that they were addressed, directly or indirectly, to the passions of the slave, but wholly to the reason and conscience of the master. The statements of the southern postmasters themselves, as far as they go corroborate this assertion. Here then one important part of the "concurrent testimony" on which Mr. Kendall relies is seen to be defective.

But let us admit that the pamphlets and newspapers of the Anti-Slavery Society are as incendiary as alleged, and that they are intended for the perusal of slaves even more than of masters, still we maintain that a much more effectual, and certainly much more legal means of defeating the object of the abolitionists was in the power of the southern people than disobedience of the law, and violation of their oaths on the part of the public officers of the United States. We are frequently told, with various degrees of vaunting, that on this question of abolition, the south is as one man—that it presents an undivided front—that there is no dissenting voice. By the means then, of quiet and efficient organization, by vigilance committees, and the other measures of internal police which the nature of the evil would naturally suggest to them, they might more certainly prevent the circulation of the dreaded publications, than by any forcible seizure of the post-office, or any violation of his sworn duty by the postmaster in their behalf. If they secure the post-office, either by their own violence, or the treachery of its guardian, they block up but one channel of the stream of free opinion. By the peaceable means which we have suggested they would dam them all. The necessity of vigilance would still press upon them as to other sources of danger, if all fears of the post-office were lulled to rest; so that a little added watchfulness for the few months that must elapse before Congress can revise the post-office laws is not an evil of so greivous a character as to justify Mr. Kendall's denominating the proceeding of Mr. Gouverneur "a measure of great public necessity."

But the most important, the most startling part of Mr.

Kendall's letter we have not yet at all considered. He wishes to throw the question on the popular ground of state rights, and expresses a strong doubt whether the abolitionists have a right to make use of the public mails in distributing their papers through the southern states. The question here arises, who are the abolitionists! The Courier and Enquirer, a print which says more, and therefore ought to know more on the subject than any other in the United States, calls this journal an abolition print. The Albany Argus, has intimated the same thing, and the Lynchburg Virginian, with some foul-mouthed personalties about "the cashiered midshipman," repeats the slander. The American, also, for opposing this new and "fearfully dangerous" species of censorship of the press which the Postmaster General labours so hard to establish, and in which he is so readily seconded by the practical efforts of *Mr. Gouverneur*—the American, also, has been styled an abolition newspaper. Now, we ask, who is to decide what journals are abolition and what not? Is *Samuel L. Gouverneur* to sit in judgment over the American and the Evening Post, and decide whether they shall be permitted to pass to their southern subscribers? whether there is not some law, in some slave state, which would include our sheets within its ban, for daring to exercise the right of free discussion, on a momentous question, under the warrant of that provision in the Constitution, of the United States, repeated in almost every state Constitution which guarantees to every citizen the freedom of speech and of the press?

But let us pass over this difficulty which lies at the threshold, and take a full view of Mr. Kendall's new state rights doctrine as applicable to the post office. When the southern states, he says, became independent, "they acquired a right to prohibit abolition papers within their territories; and the power over the subject of slavery and all its incidents was in no degree diminished by the adoption of the federal constitution." He further states that, under this sovereign power, some states have made the circulation of abolition papers a capital crime, and others a felony; and concludes by asking whether the people have a right to do by the mail carriers and Postmasters,, what if done by themselves or agents would subject them to the most degrading punishment. It is a great mistake to say that the power of the southern states over slavery *and all its incidents* was in no degree diminished by the adoption of the federal constitution. One of the "incidents," the power of importing slaves, was certainly taken away. But every other "incident" of slavery, with which any single provision of the federal constitution conflicts was necessarily diminished. The Constitution, no matter what were the previous laws of the state, became, on its adoption, the supreme fundamental law of the confederacy. So far from the incidents of slavery being in no wise impaired, many of the sagest men in the Virginia Convention, among them Governor Randolph, Mason, and Patrick Henry, were decidedly of opinion that the Constitution gave the General Government the power of abolishing slavery altogether, in various ways, either by the operation of inordinate taxes, or by requiring the slaves to do military service, and emancipating them as the reward. One of the first things, it is true, which the Congress did under the existing Constitution, was to disavow any right on the part of the General Government to interfere with the subject of slavery. But a resolution of Congress has not the force of Constitutional law. Passed at one session it may be rescinded at another, and even expunged from the journals, as we trust will soon be corroborated by a conspicuous instance.

When the several states adopted a Constitution which gave to the federal government the power to establish the post office, and the power also to make all laws necessary and proper to carry that clause into effect, they gave up all right of extending their local penal enactments, as to the circulation of prohibited publications of any kind, so as to include those officers of the General Government who were merely carrying into effect the provisions of a constitutional law, clearly sheltered under the ceded power above referred to. A constitutional doubt of this kind, when it touches the question of slavery, is of a more exciting character, than when it embraces other matters ; but it rests precisely on the same foundation as many other doubts which have been started and settled, and must have the same disposition made of it. The question of the Sunday mail is one of precisely analagous character. Many persons, as fanatical with regard to violations of the Sabbath as the abolitionists are on the subject of slavery, were of opinion that the sovereign power of the states extended over the subject of religion so far as to authorize the stopping of the mails on Sunday. The question was tried, and the result proved otherwise.

Yet if the power "to establish post-offices and post-roads" includes, as a necessary incident, the power to run mails every day and hour, through every state in the confederacy, it must also include the power to preserve those mails inviolable until their contents are safely delivered into the hands to which they are addressed. If the Government possesses the one power it necessarily does the other. If it possesses neither, the post office clause in the Constitution is a mere mockery—the shadow of a shade.

Our article has run out to such an unexpected length that we must now cut it short, though there are still several topics on which we wished to express our views. Mr. Kendall's ingenious, but most heterodox and nullifying letter concludes with the expression of a hope, that Mr. Gouverneur and the other postmasters who have assumed the responsibility of stopping the publications of the Anti-Slavery Society, "will see the necessity of performing their duty in transmitting and delivering *ordinary* newspapers, magazines, and pamphlets, with perfect punctuality." Verily we have fallen on evil times when such a request or injunction from a high officer of the General Government to his subordinates is necessary. Does not that very sentence include within itself a whole volume of commentary?

TROUBLE IN HAVERHILL.

[*From the Evening Post, September* 3, 1835.]

"Last evening, (Sunday,) Mr. May, the abolitionist lecturer, attempted to hold forth in Haverhill, Mass. At the hour of assembling, the meeting-house was filled with numbers of both sexes, and the lecturer commenced his discourse, when a volley of stones and lighted fire-crackers were showerd through the windows into the pulpit and upon the congregation, who immediately dispersed. A piece of ordnance was brought upon the spot, probably to frighten the congregation."

So says Brigg's Boston Bulletin. The rights of free discussion are forsooth marvellously well respected in this land of liberty! Formerly, in frontier settlements, beyond the regular operation of law, and in cases where the offences of criminals were too clear to admit of doubt and too base to deserve the slightest lenity, Judge Lynch, so called, was content with administering a species of *codex robustus*, which the criminal himself did not more dread to encounter, than the thongs and whipping post to which a more authentic judicial tribunal would have condemned him.

But this Judge Lynch, with the proneness to usurpation which characterises all possessors of ill-defined power, has lately extended most fearfully the prescriptive boundaries of his authority. All places are now within the limits of his jurisdiction, and all sorts of crimes, real or imputed, and whether known as such in the statute books or not, are provided for in his unwritten law. The man who—thinking that clause in the Constitution means something which guarantees to every citizen of the United States freedom of speech and of the press—ascends the pulpit, now-a-days, to deliver his sentiments on an interesting subject, may count himself fortunate indeed if he ever descends from it alive; as the probability is he will be hung by the neck to the very horns of the altar by some summary decision under the authority of Lynch law, which, it seems, is entirely paramount to the Constitution and the natural rights of man.

In the case which we copy above, it is matter of marvel that the piece of ordnance, loaded with round shot and grape, was not discharged at the broadside of the meeting-house, the more effectually "to frighten the congregation," which end would have been still more certainly consummated if a few men, women and children had been killed on the spot. It is a thousand pities Judge Lynch, usually inexorable, was so weakly merciful in this instance, since it is now quite possible that the abolitionist he has suffered to escape may attempt again to exercise his freedom of speech, and the same misguided persons may venture to listen to him; which manifestly could not have happened if they had been killed outright.

There is one little doubt which sometimes obtrudes itself into our minds to prevent us from being wholly proselyted to the faith of *Lynchism ;* namely, whether, after all, the best mode of correcting error of opinion is to destroy the freedom of speech. A little stream, which, if left alone, would soon lose itself in marshes and sedgy places, is sometimes, by being dammed up, swelled to a mighty volume, giving propulsive force to engines of enormous power. It may be so with regard to the abolitionists. It is true, if a man utters dangerous doctrines, he is effectually silenced by cutting his throat, and as dead men tell no tales, so neither do they preach immediate abolition. Yet it is a question, which history does not answer altogether to suit the practise of Judge Lynch and his myrmidons, whether the blood so shed sinks into the barren earth, or whether, like that which trickled from Medusa's severed head, it will not engender a brood of serpents which shall entwine themselves around the monster slavery, and crush it in their sinewy folds.

THE ANTI-SLAVERY SOCIETY.

[*From the Evening Post, Sept.* 4, 1835.]

THE annexed address to the public has been sent to us inclosed in a note from an officer of the Anti-Slavery Society, requesting us, in "behalf of the society whose document it is, and in justice to the public who have a right to the information it contains," to publish it in our columns this afternoon. We most cheerfully comply with this request ; and furthermore invite the attention of our readers to this address, as not only one which it is incumbent on them in fairness to peruse, but as one, the sentiments of which, with a single exception, deserve, in our judgment, their approval.

It is quite time, since the South seems determined that

we shall discuss the question of slavery, whether we will or no, that we remember the maxim which lies at the foundation of justice, *Hear the other side.* We have listened very credulously to the one side. We have with greedy ears devoured up all sorts of passionate invectives against the abolitionists, and received as gospel, without evidence, the most inflammatory and incendiary tirades against them. While appropriating to them exclusively the epithets of incendiaries and insurrectionists, we have ourselves been industriously kindling the flames of domestic discord, and stirring up the wild spirit of tumult. It is high time to pause, and ask ourselves what warrant we have for these proceedings? It is time to balance the account current of inflammatory charges, and see which side preponderates, whether that of the incendiaries of the north or of the south.

We have here, in the subjoined official address, signed with the names of men whom we believe too upright to lie, and who certainly have shown that they are not afraid to speak the truth, an exposition of the creed and practise of the Anti-Slavery Society. We have already said that, in our judgment, the matters contained in this document, with a single exception, deserve cordial approval. This expression we wish taken with a qualification. We do not approve of perseverance in sending pamphlets to the south on the subject of slavery in direct opposition to the unanimous sentiments of the slaveholders; but we do approve of the strenuous assertion of the right of free discussion, and moreover we admire the heroism which cannot be driven from its ground by the maniac and unsparing opposition which the abolitionists have encountered.

The particular portion of the subjoined document which we except from our approval is that wherein it is asserted as the *duty* of Congress to abolish slavery in the

District of Columbia. That Congress has the constitutional power so to do, we have not the slightest doubt. But high considerations of expediency, in the largest sense of the word, should be well weighed before an exercise of that power is attempted. A spirit of conciliation and compromise should govern in the matter, as it did in the formation of our sacred *Magna Charta.* Every state in the confederacy should be considered as having an equal interest in the seat of the National Government, and the legislation for it should be of that neutral tint, which results from the mixture of contrary hues of opinion, and is in strong opposition to none. If the free states have a majority in Congress, yet paramount considerations of brotherhood and national amity should prevent them from stirring the question of slavery, by introducing it in any collateral or insidious form. Whenever that question once fully comes into general discussion it is destined to shake our empire to the centre. Let the commotion be then avoided in regard to a spot of ground which is not a pin's point on the map, and in the government of which, more than in almost any other question, the sentiments of the minority ought to be respected.

We are not sure that the Harry Percys of the South, are not by their hot menaces and inconsiderate vaunts precipitating a discussion which must be entered into sooner or later, and may, perhaps, as well be undertaken at once. Be that as it may, their high and boastful language shall never deter this print from expressing its opinion that slavery is an opprobrium and a curse, a monstrous and crying evil, in whatever light it is viewed; and that we shall hail, as the second most auspicious day that ever smiled on our republic, that which shall break the fetters of the bondman, and give his enfranchised spirit leave to roam abroad on the illimitable plain of equal liberty.

We have no right to interfere legislatively with the subject of slavery in our sister states, and never have arrogated any. We have no moral right to stir the question in such a way as to endanger the lives of our fellow human beings, white or black, or expose the citizens of the north, attending to their occasions in the south, to the horrors of Lynch law. Nay, we repeat, what we have often asserted with as sincere earnestness as any loud-mouthed anti-abolitionist, that we deeply deplore all intemperate movements on this momentous subject, in view of the dreadful wrecks which the meeting tides of contrary fanaticism must spread around their borders. But while we truly entertain these sentiments, we know no reason that renders it incumbent on us to conceal how far our views are really opposed to slavery; and while we disclaim any constitutional right to legislate on the subject, we assert, without hesitation, that, if we possessed the right, we should not scruple to exercise it for the speedy and utter annihilation of servitude and chains. The impression made in boyhood by the glorious exclamation of Cato, that

> A day, an hour of virtuous liberty,
> Is worth a whole eternity of bondage,

has been worn deeper, not effaced, by time; and we eagerly and ardently trust that the day will yet arrive when the clank of the bondman's fetters will form no part of the multitudinous sounds which our country continually sends up to heaven, mingling, as it were, into a song of praise for our national prosperity. We yearn with strong desire for the day when Freedom shall no longer wave

> "Her fustian flag in mockery over slaves."

POST-OFFICE PATRONAGE.

[*From the Evening Post, Sept.* 5, 1835.]

Those persons who have been in the habit of looking into this paper, at stated periods, hitherto, to see the post-office list of uncalled for letters, and who may be disappointed at not finding it in our columns any more, are referred to the New-York Times, to which journal that portion of the "government patronage" has been transferred. The object of this change is, we suppose, to punish the Evening Post for maintaining the supremacy of the Constitution and the inviolability of the law, in opposition to the seditious doctrines of the Postmaster General, and the audacious conduct of his deputy, Mr. Gouverneur, the postmaster of this city. Such modes of punishment, however, have been tried on us before without effect. We once expressed dislike, we remember, of the undignified tone of one of Mr. Woodbury's official letters, as Secretary of the Treasury, to Nicholas Biddle; and the Treasury advertisements were thenceforward withheld. The Secretary of the Navy having acted with gross partiality in regard to a matter recently tried by a naval court-martial, we had the temerity to censure his conduct; and of course we could look for no further countenance from that quarter. The Navy Commissioners, being Post-Captains, may naturally be supposed to have taken in high dudgeon our inquiry into the oppression and tyranny practised by their order; and "stop our advertisements!" is the word of command established in such cases. When the Evening Post exposed the duplicity of Samuel Swartwout, the Collector of this Port, it at once lost all further support from the Custom House. And now, having censured the doctrines of Mr. Kendall and the practice of Mr. Gouverneur, the Post-office advertising is withdrawn, of course.

About all this we wish our readers to understand that we do not utter a single complaint; for as we never, directly nor indirectly, solicited any man or institution to take our paper, or give us custom in any shape, so we never shall remonstrate against its being discontinued, at the pleasure of those who bestow it. We merely state the fact for the information of all whom it may concern, and shall take the liberty of adding the assurance, for the accuracy of which the past, indeed, furnishes some vouchers, that the course of this journal cannot be influenced, a hair's breadth, by that species of reasoning which may be termed the *argumentum ad loculum.* The quality of independence would be worth but little if it could stand no sacrifices: ours, at all events is not of so sickly a kind; and any losses we may incur in fearlessly maintaining the right of free discussion and the supremacy of the laws, and in earnestly and undeviatingly pursuing, on all subjects, that path which honesty and honour point out, will always be cheerfully sustained.

The taking away of the post-office "patronage" (execrable word!) has not made Mr. Kendall's letter and Mr. Gouverneur's conduct appear a whit more heterodox and dangerous than they did before; and the restoration of it to-morrow would not render them a jot more sound and harmless in our view. Our opinions on the subject presented by the letters of those two functionaries were formed from a perusal of the letters themselves, not from a consideration of our subscription-book and leger. We never regulate our course by such low and uncertain standards, but endeavour, without extraneous bias, to determine all questions by the immutable principles of truth and reason, and to act accordingly with boldness and zeal, leaving consequences in the hands of the community. We ought to add that our experience, so far, has corroborated the good old maxim, that ***honesty is the best policy.*** There is no danger that the withdrawal of the post-office advertisements will render our minds at all doubtful of the truth of the saying, or of its invariable excellence as a guide of conduct.

ABOLITIONISTS.

[*From the Evening Post, September* 7, 1835.]

THERE is a class of newspaper writers who seem to think that epithets are more powerful than arguments, and who therefore continually bestow on their opponents odious appellations, instead of counteracting the tendency of their views by temperate expositions of their fallacy. To call names certainly requires less effort of mind than to reason logically, and to persons of certain tastes and powers may therefore be the most congenial mode of disputation. But we are not aware that the highest degree of proficiency in this species of dialectics ever threw much light on the world, or sensibly advanced the cause of truth; and it may be doubted if even the fisherwomen of Billingsgate, who we believe stand unrivalled in vituperative eloquence, can be considered as ranking among the most edifying controversialists.

There are those, however, who widely differ from us in this opinion, if we may judge by their practise; who deem a harsh epithet more conclusive than a syllogism, and a personal allusion as comprising in itself subject, predicate, and copula. By this class of reasoners it has been our fortune to have many of our views opposed, and it is amusing to see the air of triumph with which they utter their opprobrious terms, as if each one levelled to the earth a whole file of arguments. Thus the fallacy of our views on banking was unanswerably demonstrated by calling us a lunatic ; the folly of our opposition to monopolies was made manifest by likening us to Jack Cade; and all reasoning in support of the equal righ s of man was summarily overthrown by the tremendous epithet of agrarian. The views which we have felt it our duty to urge on various other subjects were irrevocably scattered by a volley of small shot, among which the phrases "sailor actor editor," and "chanting cherubs of the Post," did the most fatal execution. And now, again, our exertions in support of the sacred right of free discussion, and in defence of the supremacy of the laws, are answered by a single word—by denouncing us as *abolitionists*.

There are persons who might be frightened into silence by the terrors of this formidable epithet; but we have something of the same spirit in us that animates those to whom it more truly applies, and do not choose to be driven back by the mere vulgar exclamations of men who wield no weapon but abuse, and who do not even know the meaning of the words they so liberally employ. The foundation of our political creed is unbounded confidence in the intelligence and integrity of the great mass of mankind ; and this confidence sustains and emboldens us in our course on every public question which arises. We are led by it, not to inquire into individual prejudices or opinions ; not to an anxious examination of the popular pulse on every particular subject ; but to an inquiry, simply, into the abstract merits of the question, and an examination of it by the tests of truth and reason, relying on the popular wisdom and honesty to sustain the line of conduct which such scrutiny suggests. It is so in the present case. There is no terror in the term abolitionist for us ; for we trust to our readers to discriminate between words and things, and to judge of us by our sentiments, not by the appellations which foul-mouthed opponents bestow. The course we are pursuing is one which we entered upon after mature deliberation, and we are not to be turned from it by a species of opposition, the inefficacy of which we have seen displayed in so many former instances. It is Philip Van Artavelde who says—

> All my life long,
> I have beheld with most respect the man
> Who knew himself, and knew the ways before him,
> And from amongst them chose considerately,
> With a clear foresight, not a blindfold courage;
> And having chosen, with a steadfast mind
> Pursued his purposes.

This is the sort of character we emulate.

If to believe slavery a deplorable evil and a curse, in whatever light it is viewed; if to yearn for the day which shall break the fetters of three millions of human beings, and restore to them their birth-right of equal freedom; if to be willing, in season and out of season, to do all in our power to promote so desirable a result, by all means not inconsistent with higher duty: if these sentiments constitute us abolitionists, then are we such, and glory in the name. But while we mourn over the servitude which fetters a large portion of the American people, and freely proclaim that, did the control of the subject belong to us, we would speedily enfranchise them all, yet we defy the most vigilant opponent of this journal to point his finger to a word or syllable that looks like hostility to the political rights of the south, or conceals any latent desire to violate the federal compact, in letter or spirit.

The obligations of the federal compact, however, are greatly misrepresented by those who contend that it places a ban on all discussion of the question of slavery. It places an interdiction on the discussion of no subject whatever ; but on the contrary secures, by an especial guarantee, that no prohibition or limitation of freedom of opinion and speech, in its widest latitude, shall ever be instituted. The federal government cannot directly interfere with the question of slavery, simply because the power of such interference is not included among those conferred upon it; and "all powers not delegated to the United States by the Constitution, nor prohibited by it to the states, are reserved to the states respectively, or to the people." The truth is, the only restraint on the discussion of slavery is that which exists in the good sense and good feeling of the people, in their sentiments of brotherhood, and in the desire which all rational minds must entertain of accomplishing worthy ends by means every way proportioned to the object. Whoever supposes that the question is guarded by any more positive obligation than this, has very imperfectly studied both the Constitution itself, and those documents which illustrate its history, and the sentiments, motives and policy of its founders. The Journal of the Convention which framed the Constitution, and those of the several State Conventions are happily extant. If it is true that the people of the United States are forbidden to speak their sentiments on one of the most momentous subjects which ever engaged their thoughts ; if they are so bound in fetters of the mind that they must not allude to the less galling fetters which bind the limbs of the southern slave ; let the prohibitory passage, we pray, be quickly pointed out ; let us be convinced at once that we are not freemen, as we have heretofore fondly believed ; let us know the worst, that we may seek to accommodate our minds and break down our rebellious spirits to the restricted limits in which alone they are permitted to expatiate.

But how false is the imputed acuteness for which the American people are famed, if they have overlooked this.

principle in their institutions, so deadly hostile to liberty, until now that the assertion of their supposed freedom of discussion has called for the application of it ! Burke, long ago, speaking of America, observed, that "in other countries, the people, more simple and of less mercurial cast, judge of an ill principle in government only by an actual grievance; here they anticipate the evil, and judge of the pressure of the grievance by the badness of the principle. They augur misgovernment at a distance; and snuff the approach of tyranny in every tainted breeze." Little is this compliment deserved at the present day, whatever may have been the case at the period when it was uttered, if we are now for the first time to discover that we have blindly entered into a compact which excludes us from an expression of our sentiments on a subject, not only of vast intrinsic interest to every freeman, but one that hangs like a portentious cloud over the destiny of our country, fraught with direst and hourly accumulating mischief, and threatening to break, sooner or later, in a fearful and desolating tempest. The approach of tyranny, if his is so, was not snuffed afar off, but it closed around us, folding us in its strong embrace, and poisoning the atmosphere with its corruption, before we were aware of our danger.

Strange to say, even they who framed the Constitution, and the sages who deliberated upon it in the several State Conventions, overlooked the startling interdiction of free discussion which it is now said to enjoin. In Virginia, from whence we hear so menacing a voice, no pretence was set up, when the Constitution was adopted, that the federal compact prohibited freedom of speech on any subject whatever. Nay, it was even thought, and openly expressed, by many of her wisest sons, that Congress itself had the power, in various indirect ways, to snap the shackles of the slave and give him freedem. George

Mason complained in the Convention that there was no clause in the Constitution securing to the southern states their slave property, and contended that Congress might lay such a tax on slaves as would amount to manumission. Patrick Henry contended that there was nothing to "prevent Congress from laying a grievous and enormous tax on slaves, so as to compel owners to emancipate them rather than pay the tax." In another speech he argued that Congress would possess the power of abolishing slavery under the clause empowering it to provide for the general defence—that it might pronounce all slaves free, and had ample warrant for so doing. Various other opinions of like import were confidently expressed and eloquently insisted upon.

We refer to these passages in the debates of the Virginia Convention, not as concurring in the views they take of the powers of Congress under the federal compact, but to show that it was not always considered, even in Virginia, which now speaks so authoritatively and hotly on the subject, that the "domestic relations of the south," as it softly phrases the relations between master and slave, were a matter entirely fenced round from all interference beyond the boundaries of the slave states. That there is any rightful power of legislative interference in the general government, direct or indirect, or in the governments of the states, we distinctly deny. But at the same time we as distinctly assert the clear unalienable right of every citizen of the United States to discuss the general subject, and for our own part shall fearlessly and fully exercise that right whenever we are not restrained by paramount considerations of amity or duty. The senseless cry of abolitionist at least shall never deter us, nor the more senseless attempt of so puny a print as the New-York Times to show that we have deserted the democratic party. The often quoted and beautiful saying of the Latin historian, *homo sum—humani nihil a me alienum puto*, we apply to the poor bondman as well as to his master, and shall endeavour to fulfil towards both the obligations of an equal humanity.

SLAVERY NO EVIL.

[*From the Evening Post, September* 9, 1835.]

NOTHING, in these days of startling doctrines and outrageous conduct, has occurred to occasion us more surprise than the sentiments openly expressed by the southern newspapers, that slavery is not an evil, and that to indulge a hope that the poor bondman may be eventually enfranchised is not less heinous than to desire his immediate emancipation. We could hardly have believed, if we had not seen these sentiments expressed in the southern newspapers, that such opinions are entertained by any class of people in this country. But that they are both entertained and loudly promulgated, the extracts from Charleston papers which our columns contain this afternoon afford abundant and sorrowful proof. These extracts are from journals which speak the feelings and opinions of a whole community; journals conducted with ability, by men who weigh their words before they give them breath, and seldom utter sentiments, particularly on momentous questions, which are not fully responded to by a wide circle of readers. We have made our quotations from the Charleston Courier and Charleston Patriot; but we might greatly extend them, did not our sickened feelings forbid, by similar passages from various other newspapers, published in various parts of the south.

Slavery no evil! Has it come to this, that the foulest stigma on our national escutcheon, which no true-hearted freeman could ever contemplate without sorrow in his heart and a blush upon his cheek, has got to be viewed by the people of the south as no stain on the American character? Have their ears become so accustomed to the clank of the poor bondman's fetters that it no longer grates upon them as a discordant sound? Have his groans ceased to speak the language of misery? Has his servile condition lost any of its degradation? Can the husband be torn from his wife, and the child from its parent, and sold like cattle at the shambles, and yet free, intelligent men, whose own rights are founded on the declaration of the unalienable freedom and equality of all mankind, stand up in the face of heaven and their fellow men, and assert without a blush that there is no evil in servitude? We could not have believed that the madness of the south had reached so dreadful a climax.

Not only are we told that slavery is no evil, but that it is criminal towards the south, and a violation of the spirit of the federal compact, to indulge even a hope that the chains of the captive may some day or other, no matter how remote the time, be broken. Ultimate abolitionists are not less enemies of the south, we are told, than those who seek to accomplish immediate enfranchisement. Nay, the threat is held up to us, that unless we speedily pass laws to prohibit all expression of opinion on the dreadful topic of slavery, the southern states will meet in Convention, separate themselves from the north, and establish a separate empire for themselves. The next claim we shall hear from the arrogant south will be a call upon us to pass edicts forbidding men to think on the subject of slavery, on the ground that even meditation on that topic is interdicted by the spirit of the federal compact.

What a mysterious thing this federal compact must be, which enjoins so much by its spirit that is wholly omitted in its language—nay not only omitted, but which is directly contrary to some of its express provisions! And they who framed that compact, how sadly ignorant they must have been of the import of the instrument they were giving to the world! They did not hesitate to speak of slavery, not only as an evil, but as the direst curse inflicted upon our country. They did not refrain from indulging a hope that the stain might one day or other be wiped out, and the poor bondman restored to the condition of equal freedom for which God and nature designed him. But the sentiments which Jefferson, and Madison, and Patrick Henry freely expressed are treasonable now, according to the new reading of the federal compact. To deplore the doom which binds three millions of human beings in chains, and to hope that by some just and gradual measures of philanthropy, their fetters, one by one, may be unlocked from their galled limbs, till at last, through all our borders, no bondman's groan shall mix with the voices of the free, and form a horrid discord in their rejoicings for national freedom—to entertain such sentiments is treated as opprobrious wrong done to the south, and we are called upon to lock each other's mouths with penal statutes, under the threat that the south will else separate from the confederacy, and resolve itself into a separate empire.

This threat, from iteration, has lost much of its terror. We have not a doubt, that to produce a disrupture of the Union, and join the slave states together in a southern league, has been the darling object, constantly and assiduously pursued for a long time past, of certain bad revolting spirits, who, like the arch-angel ruined, think that "to reign is worth ambition, though in hell." For this purpose all the arts and intrigues of Calhoun and his followers and myrmidons have been zealously and indefatigably exerted. For the achievement of this object various leading prints have long toiled without intermission, seeking to exasperate the southern people by daily efforts of inflammatory eloquence. For the accomplishment of this object they have traduced the north, misrepresented its sentiments, falsified its language, and given a sinister interpretation to every act. For the accomplishment of this object they have stirred up the present excitement on the slave question, and constantly do all in their power to aggravate the feeling of hostility to the north which their hellish arts have engendered. We see the means with which they work, and know the end at which they aim. But we trust their fell designs are not destined to be accomplished.

If, however, the political union of these states is only to be preserved by yielding to the claims set up by the south; if the tie of confederation is of such a kind that the breath of free discussion will inevitably dissolve it; if we can hope to maintain our fraternal connexion with our brothers of the south only by dismissing all hope of ultimate freedom to the slave; let the compact be dissolved, rather than submit to such dishonourable, such inhuman terms for its preservation. Dear as the Union is to us, and fervently as we desire that time, while it crumbles the false foundations of other governments, may add stability to that of our happy confederation, yet rather, far rather would we see it resolve into its original elements to-morrow, than that its duration should be effected by any measures so fatal to the principles of freedom as those insisted upon by the south.

These are the sentiments of at least one northern journal; and these sentiments we shall intermit no occasion of urging with all the earnestness of our nature and all the ability we possess. It is due to ourselves, and it is no less due to the south, that the north should speak out plainly on the questions which the demands of the former present for our decision. On this subject boldness and truth are required. Temporizing, like oil upon the waters, may smooth the billows for a moment, but cannot disperse the storm. Reasonable men and lovers of truth will not be offended with those who speak with boldness what reason and truth conspire to dictate. "As for the drummers and trumpeters of faction," to use the language of Lord Bolingbroke, "who are hired to drown the voice of truth in one perpetual din of clamour, and would endeavour to drown, in the same manner, even the dying groans of their country, they deserve no answer but the most contemptuous silence.

REGULATION OF COAL.

[*From the Evening Post, Sept.* 10, 1835.]

A copy of the petition of the Corporation of this city, on the subject of the law regulating the sale of anthracite coal, has been laid before us, and is worthy of a remark. The petition desires that such an alteration of the existing law may be made as shall permit the purchaser to choose for himself whether he will have his coal weighed by an appointed weigher or not. Nothing can be more indisputably reasonable than this. Those who claim that municipal authorities ought to exercise their powers for the regulation of trade, and establish inspectors, guagers, weighers and supervisors, of various kinds, to see that tradespeople do not cheat their customers in quality, strength, weight, or quantity, yet cannot, we should suppose, be so utterly blind to the natural rights of the citizen, as to require that he should not be permitted to cheat himself, if he prefers to do so.

For our own part, as our readers well know, we are opposed to the whole system of legislative interference with trade, which we wish to see left to its own laws, unfettered by any of the clogs and hinderances invented by political fraud and cunning, to extract indirect taxes from the community, and contrive offices with which to reward the selfish exertions of small-beer politicians. We should be glad to see the whole tree, root and branch, destroyed. We should be glad if the whole oppressive and aristocratic scheme of inspection and guaging, whether existing under the General Government, or that of the state, or of the city, were utterly abrogated. We should be glad to see the custom-house swept off into the sea, and the whole army of collectors, surveyors, tide-waiters, and lick-spittles, of various denominations, swept off with it—or at least compelled to resort to some other method of obtaining a livelihood. We should be glad if the inspectors of beef, flour, pork, cotton, tobacco, wood, charcoal and anthracite, and all their brother inspectors, too numerous to mention, were made to take up the line of march, and follow their file leaders into some more democratic species of avocation. The land, freed from this army of incubuses, and from the bad laws which give them being, would then blossom as the rose under the genial influence of free trade ; and then it would be found, we do not doubt, from the alacrity with which the people would bear direct taxation for all the necessary purposes of government, that there was never any reason for the anomaly we have presented in resorting to indirect means for obtaining the public resources, as if the popular virtue and intelligence, on which our institutions are professedly founded, existed but in name, and the necessary expenses of government could only be obtained from the people by some method which prevented them from seeing what they paid.

But putting these ultra views, as some may consider them, entirely out of sight, there cannot be two opinions, one would think, as to the entire propriety of the request now made to the city legislature by the petition to which we have alluded. There are many persons who have greater confidence in the coal dealers than in the public weighers, and we know of no just reason why they should be prohibited by law from indulging their preference.

[*From the Evening Post, September* 19, 1835.]

EXTREMES UNITE.

From the Washington Globe, of yesterday.

"THE Evening Post has, on various occasions, shown a disposition to fly off from the democratic party, by running into extremes. Upon the Tariff it knew no medium. It was free trade, without a reference to the policy of other nations. In regard to Banks no account to be taken of the actual condition of things in the country, but a universal and immediate annihilation was the tendency of all the Post's arguments. The spirit of agrarianism was perceivable in all the political views of the editor, and it seemed as if he was inclined to legislate altogether upon abstractions, and allow the business of the world and the state of society to have nothing to do with it. This Eutopian temper in the Post was perpetually running the Editor's head against a post —some established land-mark set up by the experience and good sense of the people to designate the different interests among us and the principles by which they were to be protected. In its warfare upon the settled principles of Democracy, the Post has ever and anon found itself at loggerheads with the organs which have long been accustomed to reflect the public sentiment. The Richmond Enquirer—the Albany Argus, and other standard republican prints, have been successively the object of its attack. Finally, the Post, as if eager to break with the party to which it has assumed to be devoted, has assailed the Secretary of the Treasury, the Secretary of the Navy, and the Postmaster General. All this might possibly be set down to individual caprice—a sort of innocent ostentation, by way of displaying the independence of the editor. But he has at last (and we are glad of it) taken a stand which must forever separate him from the democratic party. His journal now openly and systematically encourages the Abolitionists. In this, he attacks the compromise which was the foundation of the Union, and commits outrage upon the most devotedly cherished feelings of the whole democracy of the Union. The abolition conspiracy is worse than nullification. The latter only contemplates a dissolution of the Union. The scheme of the Abolitionists involves the destruction of the Confederacy, and brings with it also, as a foretaste, the horrors of a servile and civil war. As this is the tendency of the Post's present course, it must be content, hereafter, to be numbered among those journals with which its extravagance has associated it. The abolition faction is the natural ally of the Nullification and Hartford Convention factions; and while the Post, as a journal, acts with the former, the Democracy will class it with the Telegraphs, the Telescopes, the royal Americans, the Stone and Dwight Advertisers of the day."

We lose no time in placing the foregoing article conspicuously before our readers, and shall willingly part from such as fall off from us in consequence of the excommunication pronounced by the Washington Globe. But they who shall stand by us through the evil report, as they have stood by us through the good report of that paper, and as they stood by us long before that paper had existence, shall have ample occasion to acknowledge that our democracy is of too steadfast a kind to be driven off even by the revilings of those who profess the same political creed with ourselves and act as accredited organs of our party. The principles which govern us in relation to all political questions are such as insure our permanent continuance with the real democracy of the land ; and as the reputation of this journal was in no degree the result of any assistance which it ever derived from the Washington Globe, so we may be permitted to hope that its surcease will not be occasioned by the countenance of that print being withdrawn.

There are certain leading principles in politics which constitute the cynosure by which the course of this journal is guided. The universal political equality of mankind, the intelligence and integrity of the great mass of the people, and the absolute right of a majority to govern, are the fundamental articles of our belief. These actuate us in every movement now, and we trust will continue to actuate us to the last moment of our lives. The political theories which rest on these principles as their basis, though they may sometimes ascend beyond the line of prudence, can never overtop the altitude of truth. but in their most airy elevation will securely lean against that steadfast and eternal support.

We very much regret that the Globe has taken upon itself to denounce this journal, and to give all who believe in its infallibility to understand that they must hereafter consider and treat the Evening Post as belonging to the common herd of the enemies of the democracy. We regret it, both because of the two-fold motive from which the anathema proceeds, and from a consideration of the consequence which it is likely to occasion. But we by no means look upon it as the worst evil which could befall us, and while we remain true to the great interests of democratic freedom, we have little fear either that our own prosperity, or our just influence on public sentiment, will be materially diminished by the proscription or denunciation of a party journal which, in no quality that ought to distinguish the public press, rises much above the level of ordinary party papers, and which derives all its superiority from the mere accident of its semi-official character.

We have alluded to the two-fold motive which has led the Globe to pronounce our exclusion from its list of democratic newspapers. What it says about our tendency to run into extremes is for the purpose of giving a colourable pretext for the course which undivulged motives of secret policy have prompted it to pursue. Our views on the subject of the tariff never before elicited a syllable of disapprobation from that journal. Throughout the great struggle, which involved such extensive interests, excited such angry feelings, and threatened, at one time, to sunder the Union, the Globe, indeed, pursued a cautious silent policy, or, when it ventured to express itself at all, did so in equivocal terms, liable to a double construction, and played to perfection the part of a political Janus, turning one face to the South and the other to the North.

The course of this paper on the subject of banks is wholly and we believe wilfully misrepresented by the Washington Globe, and, at any rate, this is the first time that a word of disapprobation on that subject has been expressed. It is utterly untrue, and every reader of this journal knows it is so, that we have desired a reformation of the bank system "regardless of the actual condition of things," and have insisted upon "universal and immediate annihilation" of the system. The course which we have pursued in regard to banks is the same which the Globe itself, though with much less earnestness, has pursued; it is the same course that has been over and over again recommended by Andrew Jackson, Thomas H. Benton, Churchill C. Cambreleng, and many others of the most prominent and soundest democrats in the land. It is the only course consistent with democratic principles, and we defy the Globe to point out one sentiment in our anti-monopoly warfare in the slightest degree at variance with the doctrines of democracy as taught by Jefferson and illustrated by Jackson.

As to the contemptible slang about Agrarianism and Utopianism, to which the Globe descends for the lack of valid objections against this journal, we deem it wholly unworthy of reply. The assertion that we have warred against "the settled principles of democracy," is an unmitigated falsehood, for which not a tittle or shadow of proof can be adduced. It is false, also, that the Richmond Enquirer has been attacked by us, or that we have assailed the Secretary of the Treasury any further than by mentioning the discontinuance of Treasury advertisements in this paper, with the presumed cause. The Secretary of the Navy we have indeed assailed, for grossly impartial and improper conduct in the case of Captain Read; and the assault, unluckily for him, was fully justified by the facts which occasioned it. We have also assailed the Postmaster General, for the official promulgation of doctrines which strike at the root of government and public order. What we have done in relation to these two functionaries we should do again, were the same cause (which heaven forbid!) again presented; and we know of no ægis which ought to protect their misconduct, any more than that of the humblest member of the democratic party, from the reprehension of the press.

But the real two-fold motive of the Globe is perfectly understood. As far as that motive is connected with a desire to punish us for having opposed the nullifying doctrines of Amos Kendall, we do not deem it worthy of animadversion, and are quite content to let matters take their own course in that respect. As far as it springs from a disposition to appease the south, and thus promote the interests of Mr. Van Buren in that quarter of the confederacy, we certainly do not disapprove the end, however much we may naturally shrink from the honours of martyrdom for that purpose. It has been a source of much regret to us that the discussion which has arisen between the north and south would necessarily tend to alienate in some degree, the minds of southern men from a northern candidate for the office of President; and we have not doubted that, to produce this very result, the discussion was promoted, and the angriest and most imflammatory mode of disputation resorted to, by some of those engaged in it. Yet because dishonest politicians were endeavouring to wrest a great question to their own sinister purposes, we did not feel ourselves at liberty to shrink from an earnest support of what we consider the cause of truth; much less did we feel it incumbent on us to yield to the arrogant demand of the south, that we would not only abstain from all discussion of the question of slavery, but even prohibit its discussion "by the strong arm of the law." Our duty as democrats and as freemen seemed to us to require that we should earnestly oppose this arrogant demand, the more especially as we saw but too plain denotements, in this quarter of the Union, of a disposition to truckle to the South, for the purpose of promoting objects wholly inferior in importance to the great principle of free discussion.

In a sincere desire that Martin Van Buren may be elected President of the United States, we are not surpassed by the Washington Globe or any other journal in this or any other part of the Union. Not for our own behoof, in any way or shape, do we desire this, nor because of any disposition favourable to our private interests or feelings that it would make in either the public offices or emoluments. We desire the success of Mr. Van Buren simply because of his intrinsic fitness for the high office of President, and for the sake of the democratic principles involved in the contest. Whatever we can do to promote his election, not inconsistent with the eternal obligations of truth and justice, shall be freely and strenuously done; and let the Washington Globe, and such of the democracy as follow its bidding, class the Evening Post with what journals they please, and despitefully use us to any extent that their malignity prompts, we shall be found, nevertheless, always in the thickest of the fray, doing battle with all our soul and strength and understanding, under the democratic banner first unfurled by our fathers on the fourth of July 1776, the glorious motto of which is THE EQUAL RIGHTS OF MANKIND!

THE COMMITTEE AND THE EVENING POST.

[*From the Evening Post, Oct.* 10, 1835.]

THE General Committee have at last fired off their big gun which they have been a long time past engaged in loading. We are not utterly exterminated by it, that is certain. We live and breathe and have our being, notwithstanding this *brutum fulmen* has been launched at us. Let us pick up the spent bolt, and exhibit it to our readers. Here it is:

DEMOCRATIC REPUBLICAN GENERAL COMMITTEE.

"At a regular meeting of the Democratic Republican General Committee, held at Tammany Hall, on Friday evening, the 9th day of October, 1835, the following preamble and resolution were adoped;

"*Whereas,* The course of the Evening Post, in continuing to discuss the Abolition question, in our opinion, meets the decided disapprobation of the Democracy of the City and County of New-York, and of an overwhelming majority of the people of the North, and is decidedly contrary to the expressed opinion and views of this Committee; and whereas, the manner as well as the matter of its publications upon that question, are in our opinion dangerous to the peace and safety of the good people of the South, our brethren in the family of this great Republic:—Therefore,

"*Resolved,* That the proceedings of the Democratic Republican General Committee be no longer published in the Evening Post, and that this Resolution be signed by the Chairman and Secretary, and published in the Times, Truth Teller, Jeffersonian, and the German paper, the New-York Gazette.

"DAVID BRYSON, Chairman."

"EDWARD SANFORD, Secretary."

Circumstances prevent us to-day from occupying any considerable space with comments on the foregoing extraordinary proceedings. It is not necessary that we should do so. The preamble and resolution carry on their face, stamped in characters which he who runs may read, and he who reads must despise, full evidence of the most cringing and dishonest spirit which has dictated this proceeding. This paper is proscribed—for what? For having deserted democratic principles? No. For any act of infidelity to the great cause of the people? No. For having slackened in its zeal or industry to promote the diffusion of the doctrines taught and illustrated by Jefferson and Jackson? No. It is proscribed *for being free,* and for persevering in its undoubted right of *free discussion.* It is proscribed for considering the poor negro a man and a brother; for deploring the hard fate which binds nearly three millions of native Americans in galling, endless, hopeless servitude; for deploring this partly on account of the unhappy and degraded wretches themselves, but more on account of those who hold them in bonds; for deploring it on account of the prejudicial influence which slavery exercises on the morals of a people, for the manifold vices which it fosters, and for the paralysing effect which it has on enterprise and industry in every walk of life. This is the reason why we are proscribed.

But is not the question of abolition a party question? No. Is it not one over which the General Committee have legitimate cognizance? No. It is a question too wide to be infolded in the narrow span of party: it is one which they whom the Committee represent never thought of submitting to their action. As well might that committee designate the religious creed of the democratic newspapers, and withdraw their countenance from all such as believed more or less than should be established as the true measure of piety by their standard, as to proscribe a newspaper, because, on a question of universal philanthropy, it takes a side different from that which a majority of the community have espoused.

But though the question of abolition is not a party question, yet the discussion of the subject, it is thought, may exercise an unfavourable influence on the interests of Mr. Van Buren at the South. It hence becomes the policy of short-sighted and knavish partizans, who are ever ready to sacrifice the right to the expedient, not knowing that in the eyes of true philosophy they are identical, to hush up a discussion which may disaffect the slaveholder from a northern candidate for the office of President. Not being able to hush the Evening Post, which decides for itself, wholly independent of dictation or control from any quarter, or on any subject, what to speak, and when to speak, and when to hold its peace, the next best thing to be achieved is to excommunicate it from the pale of the democratic party, and thus show the slaveholders that no advocate for universal emancipation —no journal which has a real veneration for the glorious declaration that *all men* are born with certain unalienable rights, among which are life, liberty, and the pursuit of happiness,—is counted, at the north, as belonging to the democratic party!

The day will come, nor is it far off, when those who compose the majority of the present General Committee will blush for their proceeding of last night. Let Mr. Van Buren be elected through the base, paltry, truckling policy which his friends are exhibiting; and before his administration terminates he will have reason to lament that his northern supporters had not more strictly guided themselves by the only true rule of action, in politics as well as in ordinary affairs of life, *that honesty is the best policy*. Should Mr. Van Buren succeed by keeping down the slavery discussion for a while, it will only break forth with renewed violence after he is elected, and make his whole term of office one scene of rude commotion and perplexity. The question must sooner or later be met, and met boldly. No northern president can ever guide the affairs of this great nation in peace while slavery exists. The discussion at the south has been got up at the present time, in some measure, no doubt, by nullifiers and heated opponents of Mr. Van Buren, for the purpose of defeating his election. But the question, whenever raised, and for whatever object, should always be promptly and boldly met by the presses and the people of the north.

Such, at all events, being our opinion, we shall continue to discuss the momentous topic, notwithstanding the proscription of the General Committee, and with zeal neither inflamed nor abated by that extraordinary proceeding.

FREE FERRIES AND AN AGRARIAN LAW.

[*From the Evening Post, Oct.* 10, 1835.]

THE American, some few days since, in an editorial article, expressed itself in favour of the establishment of free ferries at the public expense. A correspondent of that paper, a day or two afterwards, proposed the establishment, at the public expense, of free carriages to carry people about the city. Both propositions were serious, not ironical. We have not the papers at hand in which they were contained, but believe we do not mistake the purport of the two articles. Now it seems to us that, the epithet *agrarian,* which the American has sometimes applied to this journal, was never so much deserved by any political theory we have advanced, as it is by that paper for the projects referred to. Let us confine ourselves, however, to that which was editorially asserted, namely, the one relative to free ferries, for which we may justly hold the American responsible. This, we certainly think can be demonstrated to be *agrarian,* according to the sense in which that term is employed by politicians of the present day.

The agrarian law of Rome was a law to provide for the equitable division of conquered lands among those who conquered them. It was not altogether unlike our laws for the distribution of prize money; though far more just than they, according to our recollections of its provisions. But the charge of agrarianism, as applied reproachfully at the present day to the radical democracy, imputes to them a desire to throw down the boundaries of private right, and make a new and arbitrary division of property. This charge so far as relates to this journal, and so far, as we sincerely believe, as it relates to any considerable number of individuals, of any name or sect, in our country, has no foundation in truth. Of our own political doctrines we can truly say that they are in every feature the very opposite of agrarianism. They rest, indeed, on the basis of inviolable respect for private right. We would not have even the legislature take private property, except for the public good, directly, not incidentally; and then only in the clearest cases, and by rendering the most equitable compensation. We would never have it delegate that power to any private corporation, on the ground that the public good would be incidentally promoted by the doings of such a body.

But the American, in becoming the advocate of free ferries, leans to agrarianism, in the popular and justly odious sense of the word. It takes the property of A. and gives it to B. It proposes to bestow a valuable gratuity on such persons as have occasion to use the ferry, and pay for this gratuity, for the most part, with money filched from the pockets of those who never step foot in a ferry-boat. Is this not clearly unjust? Is it not to some extent, an agrarian scheme?

The American may answer us that it is but an extension of the same power, the rightfulness of which nobody ever calls in question, which is exercised by all municipal corporations in constructing streets at the public expense, for the gratuitous accommodation of all who choose to use them. Even this power in its nature is agrarian, and is submitted to by universal assent, not because it is right in principle, but because its conveniences overbalance the theoretic objections. But there is a point where the objections equal the conveniences, and to insist on any scheme which lies beyond that point, is to run the risk of being called, with justice, agrarian. Every body has more or less occasion to use the streets; and therefore every body ought to contribute towards the expense of making and preserving them. This expense is taken out of the general fund derived from taxes. The burden of taxes falls, directly or indirectly, on every body, and if not in the precise proportion of relative advantage from the use of the streets, still the difference is too slight to awaken complaint. But the case is widely different with regard to ferries. Thousands of citizens never use them at all; yet according to the agrarian scheme of the American, they would be required to pay as much for supporting them as those who cross the river a dozen times every day. They would find their advantage, the American might argue, in the greater cheapness of market commodities, the increased number of customers to the city traders, and the general improvement of the city. But this advantage would not be diffused equally, and whatever is done by legislation should tend to the equal benefit of all.

But where would the American stop? If free ferries are of advantage, why would not free markets be also? And free warehouses? And free dwelling houses? And free packet ships? And in short free from every thing? The arguments by which alone the American can support its theory of free ferries, are equally pertinent and cogent in defence of a literal *commonwealth.* Who would have thought to see the American turn so ultra an agrarian?

Now, our theory with respect to ferries is liable to no such objections. It is precisely the same as our theory with respect to banks, with respect to railroads, and with respect to every other branch of trade and enterprise. Our theory is the free trade theory. It is simply to leave trade alone to govern itself by its own laws. Ferries are as much a matter of trade, as Broadway stages, or Broadway shopkeeping. Leave the subject open to unrestricted competition. Leave men to run boats where they please, when they please, and how they please, with no other restraint upon them than such municipal regulations as may be requisite for the preservation of public order—some simple rules, such as "turn to the right, as the law directs." When this course is pursued, we shall have ferry boats where they are wanted, and as many as are wanted, and no more. People will not run more boats than yield a fair profit on investment, and where competition is free there will certainly be as many. The ferries, then, between New-York and Long Island, and between New-York and New-Jersey, will be as well conducted, and as well supplied with boats, as are the ferries now between New-York and Albany.

This is our scheme: how does the American like it? The difference between us is that we are for leaving ferries to the regulation of the laws of trade; the American is for controlling them by Agrarian law.*

FANCY CITIES.

[*From the Evening Post, Sept.* 14, 1836.]

A TRAVELLER, once, in Indiana, on setting out early one morning from the place where he had passed the night, consulted his map of the country, and finding that a very considerable town called Venice, or Verona, or Vienna, or by the name of some other European city, beginning with a V, occupied a point on his road but some

* It may be proper to state again here what has been already noticed in the Preface, that Mr. Leggett was attacked by a very severe and protracted illness in October 1835. He did not return to the paper till the fall of the next year.

twelve or fifteen miles off, concluded to journey as far as that place before breakfast. Another equally extensive town, bearing as sounding a name, was laid down at a convenient distance for his afternoon stage; and there he proposed halting for the night. He continued to travel at a good round pace until the sun had attained a great height in heaven, and until he computed that he had accomplished more than twice or thrice the distance which he proposed to himself in the outset. His stomach had long since warned him that it was time to halt, and his horse gave indications which plainly showed that he was of the same opinion. Still he saw no town before him, even of the humblest kind, much less such a magnificent one as his map had prepared him to look for. At length, meeting a solitary wood-chopper emerging from the forest, he accosted him, and inquired how far it was to Vienna. "Vienna!" exclaimed the man, "why you passed it five and twenty miles back: did you not notice a stick of hewn timber and a blazed tree beside the road? That was Vienna." The dismayed traveller then inquired how far it was to the other place, at which he designed passing the night. "Why you are right on that place now," returned the man; "it begins just the other side of yon ravine, and runs down to a clump of girdled trees which you will see about a mile further on the road." "And are there no houses built?" faltered out the traveller, who began to suspect that, as the song says—

"The heath this night must be his bed."

"Oh, no houses whatsomever," returned the woodman; "they hewed and hauled the logs for a blacksmith's shop, but before they raised it the town lots were all disposed of in the eastern states, and every thing has been left just as you now see it ever since."

It is pretty much in the same way that things are left, at the present time, in this portion of the country. If any one should make a map of the lands lying within the compass of some thirty or forty miles from this city, and embrace in it all the improvements, projected as well as actually existing, the spectator, who does not know the true condition of the country, would be astonished at the appearance of dense population which it would present. Cities, towns and villages would be represented as lying scattered around him at every step. The intermediate slips of unoccupied ground would seem hardly large enough even to furnish pasture for the stray cattle of the surrounding towns, much less to supply their inhabitants with all the necessary products of agricultural consumption. We hear no more, now-a-days, of a farm being sold, as a farm, in the vicinity of the city. The land is all divided into lots of a hundred feet by twenty-five ; and it would seem as if, in the visions of speculators, a dense city must soon extend from the Atlantic ocean to the lakes, and from the Hudson river to the borders of Connecticut.

One of the most curious circumstances connected with the universal rage for speculation is the exceeding gullibility of the people. No scheme seems to be too vast to stagger their credulity. The most impracticable plans are received as easy of accomplishment, and the most stupendous projects are entered upon with undoubting confidence, as if they were "trifles light as air." The thought obtrudes itself, apparently, into no man's mind, that there is a stopping place where all this rapid motion must cease—that the machine, urged to too great velocity, will at last fall to pieces. No one seems to anticipate that there must come a time when the towering fabric which speculation is building up, grown too huge for its foundation, will topple on the heads of its projectors, and bury them in its ruins. Every one acts as if there were no fear that the explosion would take place while he is in danger. Each one stretches out his hand to grasp his share of the gambler's spoils, without any idea that, like fairy money, it may turn to worthless rubbish in his hands. A general infatuation has siezed the minds of the community, and each one grows wilder in his lunacy from listening to the ravings of those around him.

In the meanwhile the speculators would indeed seem to have discovered the Midas art. Their touch turns every thing to gold. They are all getting rich. One buys the refusal of a farm for a vast deal more than it is intrinsically worth. He sells it to another for a large advance, before the term of payment has arrived. The second sells it to a third, the third to a fourth; and in this way it probably passes through a dozen hands, before the first instalment of the original price is paid. Each successive purchaser fancies himself rich, and the one into whose possession the property falls last has magnificent plans in prospect, and thinks that he is richest of all. But pay day must come, and come ere long, we fear, to many an unprepared speculator, and rudely wake him from his dream of fancied wealth.

The vast and sudden increase which the paper money circulation of this country has undergone within the last eighteen months is the cause of the feverish thirst of riches which the community now exhibits; and whatever shall check that circulation, and turn it back upon the banks, will arrest the disease, but arrest it with a violence that to many will prove fatal, and give a fearful shock to all. Paper money is, to the people of this country, the insane root that takes the reason prisoner; and they can be restored to sanity only by withholding such stimulating and dangerous aliment. As it now is, their appetite grows by what it feeds on. The demand for money increases with each succeeding day; and every new loan of bank credit but gives rise to new projects of speculation, each wilder and more chimerical than the last.

The effect of this pervading spirit of speculation (or spirit of gambling, as it might with more propriety be called, for it is gambling, and gambling of the most desperate kind) on the morals of the community is dreadful. Its direct and manifest tendency is to blunt men's moral perceptions, and accustom them by degrees to arts and devices of traffic which an honest, unsophisticated mind would shrink from with horror as frauds of the most flagitious dye. It creates a distaste for the ordinary pursuits of industry; it disinclines the mind from gradual accumulation in some regular vocation, and kindles an intense desire, like that expressed in the prayer of Ortogal of Basra, "Let me grow suddenly rich!" To this gambling spirit of the age we may directly trace the most of those prodigious frauds the discovery of which has recently startled the public mind. "Startled the public mind," did we say? The phrase is wrong. The public were not startled. They heard the stories with the most stoical indifference; and if any exclamations were uttered, they conveyed rather a sentiment of commiseration for the criminals, than one of detestation for their stupendous crimes.

But the day of the madness of speculation is drawing to a close. The time must come, nor can it be remote, when some financial or commercial revulsion will throw back the stream of paper circulation to its source, and many a goodly vessel, which had ventured too boldly on the current, will be left by the reflux stranded on its shores. Circumstances may yet defer the evil day for awhile, but it cannot be far off. A failure of the cotton crop, a slight reduction of prices in Europe, or any one of the thousand contingencies to which trade is perpetually liable, will give a shock to the widely expanded currency of the country, which will be felt with ruinous force through every vein and artery of business. Wo unto them in that day who do not now take timely caution. Their cities and towns and villages, which they are now so fertile in planning, as if they thought men might be multiplied as rapidly as paper money, will remain untenanted and desolate memorials of their madness, and the voice of sorrow and mourning, instead of the din of present unreal prosperity, will be heard through the land.

COPY RIGHT LAW NO MONOPOLY.

[*From the Evening Post of Sept.* 27, 1836.]

Some of the newspapers, we perceive, are treating the subject of a copy-right law, as if such laws were grants of monopolies, and rested on precisely the same principles with enactments conferring exclusive trading privileges, as banks, insurance companies, and the like. This is a very erroneous view of the matter. A copy-right law instead of being a monopoly, is the very reverse. A monopoly is a legislative grant, to an individual or association, of exclusive or peculiar privileges or immunities denied to the rest of the community. A copy-right law, on the other hand, confers no new privilege or immunity, but absolutely takes away a portion of an author's right of property in a work of his own creation, and renders no equivalent, except the mere guarding the remainder with some special provisions.

It would be far more proper to call the laws securing to men their rights of property in land monopolies, than those which protect authors and inventors in the productions of their intellectual industry and ingenuity. The rights of property in land are not natural rights. By nature, we are all heirs in common of the earth, as well as of the air and ocean. The origin of individual rights of territory may all be traced, either to the lawless rapacity of might, or the arbitrary enactments of incompetent legislative authorities. The letters patent of an ignorant monarch have granted away a whole continent to the discoverers, though that continent was already in the occupation of numerous tribes of human beings. Such grants may with some propriety be called monopolies.

But an author's right of property in his productions rests on a juster basis. In all ages and all nations of the world, the right of an individual to the creations of his own labour or skill have always been considered sacred. Even the Indians, who hold their hunting grounds in common, and admit of no arbitrary divisions or appropriations of territory among the members of their tribes, respect each other's exclusive claim to the creations of their own efforts, to that species of property which owes its value to individual labour and skill. Thus the red hunter, who ranges free over the face of the earth, who would spurn the idea of being shut in by fences, and mock the claims of personal possession; yet respects the rights of his fellows in their bows and arrows, which they shape from the reeds and saplings; in their wigwams, which they construct of the trees of the forest; and in the wampum and moccasins, which are woven by their own ingenuity. On the same basis rests an author's right of property in the book which he draws from the resources of his mind, and prepares with labour both of the hand and the head. On the same basis, also, rests the right of the inventor to the productions of his ingenuity. These are natural rights, not rights created by law; not rights growing out of kingly grants, or the preponderance of might over justice.

But society, to promote the benefit of the mass, deprives the individual of this inherent natural and perpetual right, after a limited period of time; and the only consideration which it renders in return for the usurpation, is to guard him in the exclusive possession and advantages of his property for the short space he is permitted to retain it. In doing this, however, it does no more for the author, than it is its duty to do for the possessor of every species of property, the grand object for which all government is framed, being to protect men in the peacful enjoyment of life, limb and property. To the author and inventor, then, the law grants no exclusive privilege but curtails them of a natural right—limits them to a few years in the possession of property wholly created by themselves, to which, without such limitation, their claim would be of the same enduring character, as the mechanic's is to the results of his skill, or the farmer's to the products of his industry. Such being the facts, is it not manifestly absurd to call the copy-right law or the patent-law a monopoly?

THE FIRE DEPARTMENT.

[*From the Evening Post, Sept.* 28, 1836.]

Our paper, yesterday afternoon, contained gratifying evidence of such prompt and active public spirit, on the part of a portion of our fellow-citizens, in relation to the condition in which the community are placed by the recent unworthy conduct of a great number of the firemen, as affords strong assurance that, in the event of a conflagration, adequate efforts will be made to extinguish it. Volunteer companies, by the pot neous and energetic action of the highly respectable men composing them, have been already formed to take charge of the engines deserted by their former crews. These new companies including among them citizens whose heads are blanched with years, come forward wit an honourable pledge, that they will unite cordially with the Fire Department, rendering all the assistance in their power to extinguish whatever fires may occur, and discharging the duties which may be assigned to them with alacrity and subordination.

Among those who have distinguished themselves in this manner, and earned the thanks of their fellow-citizens, we notice the proceedings of a meeting in the fourth ward, composed, in part, of old firemen, exempt from further duty by reason of their having performed the term of service required by law. At the head of these is Mr. Daniel Berrian, who officiated as Chairman of the meeting. Mr. Berrian is an old and respectable inhabitant of the fourth ward, a man in affluent circumstances, and considerably advanced in years. Yet, after a life of useful toil, he does not hesitate to come forward in his old age, to resume the arduous duties of a fireman, from which he long since exem ted himself by a full and active discharge of all the required services, and to rebuke, by his example, the concerted rebellion of those who, from dissatisfaction with the Common Council, whether well or ill founded, did not he itate to leave, as they thought and hoped, the city defenceless against its most dangerous scourge. Such conduct as Mr. Berrian and his associates display, richly deserves the approbation of the community, and stands in noble contrast with that of the recusant firemen.

We see it stated in some of the newspapers that a portion of the firemen who have abandoned their places assembled at the fire yesterday, at the corner of Anthony and Centre-streets, and not content with having withdrawn their own aid from the Fire Department, attempted to frustrate the exertions of others, who were not disposed to see the city again desolated by a conflagration. Some of the ringleaders in this most wicked riot were apprehended, and are now in close custody. We trust that no mistaken views of policy or false sympathy may lead to their enlargement till they have been made the subject of exemplary punishment. Let not those laws, which the tribunals are ready enough to enforce against a combination of poor journeymen tailors, who had no worse object in view than to coerce their employers into the payment of increased wages, now lie a dead letter, when a more formidable combination is committing outrages which tend directly to the overthrow of all security both of property and life.

It is most earnestly to be hoped that the opportunity presented by existing circumstances, in relation to the means possessed by the city for the extinguishing of fires, will be turned to its best use in the total revision and reformation of the system which has heretofore been in use. The public attention is now directed with strong interest to the subject, and the public sense demands the adoption of some plan which will not subject the city to be exposed a prey to unresisted conflagration, whenever a capricious body of volunteers shall find or fancy cause of offence in the proceedings of the municipal authorities.

There is no reason, that we are aware of, why the firemen should not be a regularly organized corps of paid men, enlisted by the City Government for a fixed period, and subject to coercive regulations. The protection of the lives and property of the citizens against conflagration is as legitimate an office of government, as their protection against the midnight robber and murderer, or against any of those disorders for which the police is instituted. As well might our marshals and constables, or the watchmen who guard our streets at night, or any other class of men who render a laborious public service be composed of persons doing volunteer duty, as the firemen. And as well might they, for rendering such service, be exempted, like the firemen, from the list of jurors. It might then happen that the Common Council, by some appointment or removal, or some other act, performed with a single view to the public good, should give offence, simultaneously, to a leading or popular watchman, fireman, and police officer. In what condition would the city be left, if, in consequence of a rebellious combination, it should at once be stript of all its defences against fire, robbery, tumult and secret crime?

If the duty of the Fire Department were entrusted to a duly organized corps of men, compensated for their services with a sufficient stipend, and subject to frequent drills and trainings, and all the proper measures of discipline, we should have, in the place of a riotous and licentious body, one that would act with both celerity and decorum, and, in discharging their duties, no further interrupt the quiet of the city than would be inevitable from the nature of the service they perform. The shrieks and shouts and hoarse bellowings, from a hundred clamorous throats, which now accompany every engine, and scare sleep from the lids of the startled inhabitants far around, would then be heard no more; and nothing but the rattling of the wheels, and the necessary words of command from duly appointed officers, would break in upon the stillness of the night.

There is one consideration conected with this subject to which we briefly alluded a few days ago, and which, we think, deserves the attention of the public authorities: the improper character of the immunity extended to the firemen in exempting them from duty as jurors. Whatever diminishe the list of respectable persons liable to render that important service to the community, impairs, in some degree or other, the validity of the great bulwark of our rights—the trial by a jury of twelve peers, taken promiscuously from the whole body of citizens. In a new organization of the Fire Department, it is to be hoped no such privilege will be admitted.

WOOD INSPECTION.

[*From the Evening Post, October* 6, 1836.]

A GENTLEMAN of this city, not long since, having occasion to cut down the trees upon a piece of woodland which he owned at a short distance in the country, concluded to send them to his town-house, in his own farm waggon, and deposit them in his cellar for his winter fuel. He was met on the way by one of that army of municipal officers, called wood-inspectors, who forbade him to proceed until the loads were inspected, the number of cords ascertained, and the amount of the inspection-fees paid. It was in vain that he remonstrated, telling the man that the wood was from his own farm, for his own use, and conveyed to the city in his own vehicle. The inexorable inspector turned a deaf ear to all his arguments, and only reiterated, "my fees! my fees!" And it was only on paying the fees, and having his wood duly measured, that the gentleman was permitted to proceed on his way. This is only one of nnmerous illustrations we might give of the beauties of that system of taxation which forces people to pay enormous duties on the prime necessaries of life for the support of an idle and useless herd of office-holders.

There never was a more gratuitous and tyrannical imposition on the community than those municipal laws which make it obligatory on every citizen to employ a public officer to measure his wood and weigh his coal.

We have no objection that there should be public weighers and measurers for those who choose to employ them, for those who have not confidence enough in the persons with whom they deal to trust to their honesty, or who are too indolent or too busy to attend to their own business. These may make use of inspectors in welcome, and pay them their fees, or what sum they think proper, for their services. But we do contend against that principle of legislation, which, for the accommodation of these distrustful or indolent people, imposes on the whole public the obligation to pay an equal sum for services they would much rather dispense with. We ourselves, for example, stand in no need of any such intermediary agency. We can trust the dealer from whom we purchase our coal and wood, or otherwise we can stand and see that due weight and measurement are given, and do not thank any corporation officer to meddle with our affairs, and demand a fee for his interference.

The aggregate amount of this unjust tax in this city is very great, and the burden falls very heavily on some classes of the community. Why should it not be at once repealed? Can any one give any good reason why our wood and coal inspection laws should not be effaced from the statute book? Is there a single class of persons, save only the office-holders themselves, who fatten on these spoils of a rifled community, that would have the least reason to complain of such an abrogation? Would not the citizens at large, rich and poor, be benefited by the rescinding of those absurd enactments? There can be but one answer to these questions. Would that the Common Council could be induced to act according to the purport of that reply.

CAUSES OF FINANCIAL DISTRESS.

[*From the Evening Post, October* 24, 1836.]

THE financial storm long since predicted by this journal has at last commenced in good earnest, and begins now to be severely felt. For a considerable time past a pressure for money has been experienced in this metropolis, and within a few days it has increased to a degree which has made it the subject of general conversation and complaint. Men now perceive that their projects, sustained on the airy basis of too widely extended credit, are in danger of sudden ruin. A sense of general insecurity is awakened, and alarm and consternation are taking the place of that fool-hardy spirit of speculation, which, but a little while ago, kept hurrying on from one mad scheme to another, as if it possessed the fabled art of turning all it touched into gold. A commercial revulsion has commenced, and we fear will not terminate, till it has swept like a tornado over the land, and marked its progress by the wrecks scattered in its path.

It is always to be expected in this country, when any thing occurs to create extensive dissatisfaction, that newspaper writers, on one side or the other, will strive to turn it to the uses of party; and we accordingly find, in the present instance, that the opposition journals seize the subject of the financial difficulties as a theme for declamation against the government, and ascribe all our pecuniary embarrassments to the mal-administration of public affairs. Some, with singular contempt for the understanding of their readers, deal in mere generalities, and, in all the worn out common places of the political slang vocabulary, denounce the administration as composed of a set of ignorant "tinkers of the currency," or fraudulent speculators, who interfere with the financial arrangements of the country, for the purposes of private gain, perfectly regardless of the wide-spread ruin they may occasion. In the same spirit they call upon the merchants to close their stores and counting-rooms, and go out into the streets as political missionaries, devoting themselves exclusively, for the next twenty days, to the business of electioneering, with a view of putting down a corrupt administration, which is forever trying high-handed experiments with the currency, and obstructing the sources of commercial prosperity. The day has been when the mercantile men of this community suffered themselves to be inflamed by such appeals, and acted in pursuance of such advice. But we trust that day is past, never to return.

Another portion of the opposition papers, with more respect for the intelligence of their readers, endeavour to fortify their charges against the administration by explaining the mode in which they conceive it to be the author of the present difficulties. By some of these, all the embarrassments of the money market are traced to the order of the Treasury Department, requiring payment for public lands to be made in specie. This may do very well as a reason to be urged by those wise journalists who are ever ready to shape their political economy to the exigencies of party; but will hardly satisfy readers of so much intelligence as to demand that the cause shall be adequate to the effect. Any one who will give the slightest attention to the statistics of the land sales, and who will reflect what a vast amount of purchase an inconsiderable sum in specie will pay, in its necessarily constant and rapid circulation from the land office to the neighbouring bank, and from the bank back to the land office, must be perfectly satisfied that the regulation in question cannot have had any perceptible effect in producing the general financial pressure now experienced.

There is a third class of opposition writers who, like

the others, imputing all the difficulties to the administration, yet find out an entirely different and much more adequate cause. These impute it entirely to the Treasury orders, issued to various banks in different parts of the Union against the public funds collected on deposite in the banks of this city. By the natural course of trade, New-York is the great money market and storehouse of bullion for the entire confederacy. At this port, four-fifths of the whole revenue of the country are collected, and would here accumulate, affording a substantial basis of credit and reciprocal accommodation to those who pay it, were it not for that "tinkering with the currency" which subverts the natural order of things. To this extent we sincerely go with those who are declaiming against the government. We agree with them that the condition of affairs, as established by the laws of trade, is deranged by government interference, and that the *treasury orders*, which have the effect to cause a sudden dispersion of the public funds accumulated in this city, and to drain the specie from the vaults of our banks, sending it hither and thither, and for a time, entirely destroying its use, as a foundation of commercial credit, are the immediate cause of the prevailing distress. So far, the opposition writers have our concurrence; but not one step beyond, because, further than this, they are not supported by truth. Let us look calmly at the facts, and see where justice must attach the blame.

The complaint is, that Mr. Woodbury, directed perhaps by the Executive, issues Treasury Orders to banks at various distant points, which they present to the banks in this city, in many cases demanding specie, thus compelling those institutions suddenly to retrench, and spreading consternation and ruin among the merchants. The banks themselves, it is further affirmed, if payment of these orders should continue to be demanded in specie, will soon be exhausted of every metalic dollar, and obliged to suspend the redemption of their notes. We very much fear that there is no exaggeration in all this. But where lies the blame? We are not content to stop at Mr. Woodbury, and shower undeserved obloquy upon him. We cannot charge it to General Jackson; for we have no warrant for believing he would assume such a fearful responsibility. We go further than this: we go to the laws of the last Congress: we go to those enactments which make it obligatory on the Treasury Department to act as it is acting; which leave it no discretion; which compel it to derange the currency, to break up the foundations of commercial credit in this great city, and create all the wide-spread distress which, in the end, must result from the proceeding. One step further will show us the origin of those laws; and there we behold the very men who are now the loudest and angriest declaimers against these consequences: the very party which is endeavouring to convert them into a fatal weapon against their opponents. To the act regulating the deposites of public money, *and more particularly, to the supplementary act, passed on the last legislature day of the session, we impute all the mischief.*

Both these acts were conceived, and matured, and carried into effect by the opposition, aided by such administration members as they could deceive with the illusory promises of advantage which the measures held out to the spirit of sectional rapacity. They considered their carrying them a great party triumph. They had public rejoicings on the occasion, with discharges of artillery, bonfires, and all the etceteras of such electioneering pageants. They now behold the result, or rather *the commencement of the end.* The fruit is of the tree of their planting; if it is bitter, they have themselves to thank. Bad as it is, we fear that worse—much worse is yet to come.

We assert that the Secretary of the Treasury cannot possibly act otherwise than he is now acting. He doubtless sees, and knows, and laments, the consequences of the orders issued from his department; but he has no power to withhold them. The President of the United States has no power to forbid their being issued. It is done in plain pursuance of the positive provisions of the Deposite Law and its supplementary rider—laws devised by the aristocracy, carried by the aristocracy, rejoiced at by the aristocracy. Fain would the President have interposed his Veto, but they were made to assume such a shape as obviated the constitutional objection, and, in the delusion of the moment, too many of the democratic party had joined their opponents to render such a step of any avail. The bills were signed—signed with a strong presentiment, or rather a clear foresight of the evils they would occasion; and the event affords another forcible illustration of the sagacity of that great man whom the people, in happy hour, selected to guide the affairs of state. Other warning voices foretold the ruin that would ensue. The views of Mr. Van Buren were well known at the time, and were immediately after very clearly expressed. In the House of Representatives Mr. Cambreleng raised his admonitory voice, and predicted the very state of things which now exists. But all in vain. The opposition drowned remonstrances with clamour. They won to their side sectional politicians by the hopes which they excited of local advantages. They carried the measure; and now they experience its effects. Not they only, unfortunately; but those who opposed, as well as those who supported the mad, corrupting scheme. The whole people feel the effects, and are doomed to feel them with far greater intensity before many months are past.

The supplementary law to which we have alluded renders it the duty of the Secretary of the Treasury to make "transfers from banks in one State or Territory to banks in another State or Territory, *whenever such transfers may be required,* in order to prevent large and inconvenient accumulations in particular places, or *in order to produce a due equality and just proportion, according to the provisions of said act*"—namely, the Deposite Act. The "due proportion and just equality" *required* by the provisions of that act, is a division, on the first of January next, of the surplus revenue among the states in proportion to their respective representation in the Senate and House of Representatives of the United States; and, in the meanwhile, the Secretary of the Treasury is directed to make transfers from state to state, according to that scale of distribution, and not to suffer to remain in any one deposite bank an amount exceeding three-fourths of its capital. Thus this wise law obliges him to stand in a posture of perpetual vigilance, and keep carting the public money about from bank to bank, the moment the course of business places in any institution a single dollar beyond the limitation of the law. The evil, then, springs from the law and those who made the law, and not from the Secretary of the Treasury.

As for the fact that specie is demanded of the banks in New-York in payment of the Treasury orders, the opposition have again only their own party to thank. It is a notorious fact that a majority of the several directors of nine-tenths of the banks in the United States are members of the opposition. The Treasury orders are issued in the usual form, and it is left entirely discretionary with the banks in whose favour they are issued to make such arrangements with the banks on which the orders are drawn as shall be most for the convenience and interest of all parties concerned. This is a matter with which the Secretary of the Treasury has, of right, nothing to do. He is bound to act according to the invariable usage of the Department; and if the opposition directors of a distant bank choose to demand specie of a New-York bank, for the purpose of embarrassing the institution, crippling its means of accommodating its customers, and thus spread confusion and panic through the community, we know of no way in which Mr. Woodbury can interfere to prevent the result. He but obeys the provisions of a law which clearly prescribes the mode in which he is to act. That he has every disposition so to discharge his imperative duties as to mitigate as much as possible the hardship of their necessary effect on the mercantile community, no man can entertain a reasonable doubt. He has expressed himself, as we see stated in the Journal of Commerce of this morning, ready to arrange the distribution of the surplus revenue in any manner, consistent with the law, which shall best subserve the interests of trade, and promote stability in the money market. That paper says, " no more drafts will be issued at present, and some already issued and transmitted to distant places, will be countermanded. It devolves on the deposite banks here, to point out to the Secretary the manner by which, in their opinion, the objects of the law can be most conveniently accomplished." But the immediate cause of the financial embarrassments is in the law itself, and the Secretary of the Treasury, execute its provisions in what mode he may, cannot prevent commercial distress. In the meanwhile, the condition into which the community are thrown by a few drafts upon our banks for specie, is a forcible illustration, added to the many which had been previously afforded, of the beauties of that banking system of exclusive privileges by which the people have so long suffered themselves to be oppressed.

But the first, great, and all important cause of the pecuniary distress lies much deeper than any which the opposition papers assign. It is neither the Treasury order in relation to the public lands, nor the Treasury orders on deposite banks. These last have, at the very worst, but precipitated an evil, which, had no such orders been issued, or no transfers in any way made, could by no possibility have been long averted. It would have come next winter, and with a pressure greatly augmented by the delay. It would have fallen, like an avalanche, at the very season when revulsion is more fatal, because then the largest amounts of payments are to be made. The distribution law takes effect in January, and had not the necessity of complying with the conditions of the supplementary bill given the present harsh, but salutary check to speculation, the amount of credit, now so prodigiously inflated, would have been still further extended, and the shock of a sudden explosion would have been far more fearful and disastrous.

Without the distribution bill, even, a dreadful commercial revulsion could not long have been avoided. We were rushing on madly at a rate which could not long be continued. The first obstacle must have thrown us from our course, and dashed us to pieces. Look at the present state of the country. When did it ever before present such a spectacle of prodigiously distended credit? When did such a fever of speculation madden the brains of whole communities? When did all sorts of commodities bear such enormous prices? And when, at the same time, was there ever such vast consumption—such prodigality, wastefulness, and unthinking profusion? Is the treasury order the cause of this? Alas, it is one of its remote consequences. What filled your treasury to such overflowing, that some cunning politician was prompted by a consideration of the exuberance to devise the scheme of distribution? Speculation. What excited that spirit of speculation? The sudden and enormous increase of bank capital, and the corresponding inflation of bank currency. In the last eighteen months alone *nearly one hundred millions of bank capital* have been added to the previous amount. Examine the following bank statistics, derived from sources believed to be accurate, and see how prodigiously and rapidly our system of bank credit has been swollen:

Aggregate capital of the Banks in the United States.

In the year 1811 the total amount was		$52,600,000
1815		82,200,000
1816		89,800,000
1820		102.100,000
1830		110,200,000
1835		196,250,000
1836 (August)		291,250,000
Increase in *nine years* preceding	1820	$49,500,000
Do. *ten years*	1830	8,100,000
Do. *six years*	1836	181,050,000

Who can look at this statement, and not feel convinced that the cause of the present financial distress lies deeper than treasury orders, whether in relation to public lands or public deposites? This enormous increase of bank capital in the last six years has been accompanied by a corresponding expansion of bank issues, and by a commensurate extension of private credits. The business of the country has been stimulated into most unwholesome and fatal activity. Circumstances, unlooked for, have occurred to aggravate the epidemic frenzy. The government has obtained the payment of long delayed indemnities from foreign powers; and new formed corporations have contracted large loans abroad. These sums, added to the product of our staples, have been exhausted by the excessive importations. Domestic speculation—speculation in the products of home consumption, in land, in town lots, in houses, in stock enterprises, in every thing, has kept pace, step for step, with the inordinate increase of foreign trade. What is to pay all this vast accumulation of debt? It must come at last out of labour. It must come from the products of industry. We have been borrowing largely of the future, and have at last arrived at the point where we must pause, and wait for the farmer, the mechanic, and patient hewer of wood and drawer of water to relieve us from our difficulties.

Reader, take home to your bosom this truth, and ponder well upon it, it is the bank system of this country, our wretched, unequal, undemocratic system of special privileges, which occasions the difficulty we now begin to feel. It is not pretended that under the free trade system of credit, or under any system, commercial revulsions would not sometimes, and to some extent, take place. They are incident to the nature of man. Prosperity begets confidence; confidence leads to rashness; the example of one is imitated by another; and the delusion spreads until it is suddenly dissipated by some of those rude collisions, which are the unavoidable penalties of a violation of the laws of trade. But such fearful and fatal revulsions as mark the eras of the commercial history of this country, would not, could not, take place under a free trade system of banking.

It is when ignorant legislators pretend to define by law the limits of credit and shaking at one time with unnecessary trepidation refuse to enlarge them to the wants of trade, while at another they extend them far beyond all reasonable scope—it is when such "tamperers with the currency" attempt to control what is in its nature uncontrollable, and should be free as air, that revulsion, panic, and commercial prostration necessarily ensue. While we have restraining laws and specially chartered banks, we shall have periodical distress in the money market, more or less severe, as the period has been hastened or delayed by accidental causes. Party writers may at one time lay every disorder to the removal of the deposites, and at another to a treasury order; but whatever orders the Treasury may issue, the alternate inflations and contractions of the paper currency incident to such a pernicious system as ours will continue to produce their inevitable consequence, unwholesome activity of business, followed by prostration, sudden and disastrous.

We have exhausted our space for the present; but shall have more to say on this subject another day. There are some prophetic passages in the speech of Mr. Cambreleng on the distribution bill last winter, to which we shall take an early occasion to ask the attention of our readers.

In the month of October or November, 1836, Mr. Leggett's connection with the Evening Post ceased, and with his usual activity he immediately undertook the establishment of the *Plaindealer*, which appeared in December of the same year. My remaining selections are made from the last named work.—*Ed.*

THE POLITICAL PLAINDEALER.

PREFATORY REMARKS.

[*From the Plaindealer, December* 3, 1836.]

The first number of the Plaindealer was to be issued so soon after the announcement of an intention to publish such a journal, that it was not thought necessary to precede it with a very elaborate prospectus; the more particularly as the editor's connexion with the Evening Post for eight years previous, during a considerable portion of which time that paper was under his sole direction, had made the public very generally acquainted with his views on all the leading questions of politics and political economy, and with his mode of treating those subjects. Instead of the swelling promises which usually herald a publication of this kind, it was therefore deemed better to let the work speak for itself, and to depend for its success, from the first, as we eventually must, on the intrinsic qualities by which it should be distinguished. The same reasons which obviated the necessity of a particular prospectus, suggest the propriety of indulging in but a brief preliminary address. The Plaindealer is now before the reader, and must speak for itself. There are always circumstances to be encountered at the outset of an undertaking like this which diminish the merits of a first number, and which therefore authorize us to express, with some confidence, a hope that future numbers may be better. We think we can at least safely promise that equal claims shall be maintained.

The title chosen for this publication expresses the character which it is intended it shall maintain. In politics, in literature, and in relation to all subjects which may come under its notice, it is meant that it shall be a PLAINDEALER. But plainness, as it is hoped this journal will illustrate, is not incompatible with strict decorum, and a nice regard for the inviolability of private character. It is not possible, in all cases, to treat questions of public interest in so abstract a manner as to avoid giving offence to individuals; since few men possess the happy art which Sheridan ascribes to his Governor in the Critic, and are able entirely to separate their personal feelings from what relates to their public or official conduct and characters. It is doubtful, too, if it were even practicable so to conduct the investigations, and so to temper the animadversions of the press, as, in every instance, "to find the fault and let the actor go," whether the interests of truth would, by such a course, be best promoted. The journalist who should so manage his disquisitions, would indeed exercise but the "cypher of a function." His censures would be likely to awaken but little attention in the reader, and effect but little reformation in their object. People do not peruse the columns of a newspaper for theoretic essays, and elaborate examinations of abstract questions; but for strictures and discussions, occasional in their nature, and applicable to existing persons and events. There is no reason, however, why the vulgar appetite for abuse and scandal should be gratified, or why, in maintaining the cause of truth, the rules of good breeding should be violated. Plaindealing requires no such sacrifice. Truth, though it is usual to array it in a garb of repulsive bluntness, has no natural aversion to amenity; and the mind distinguished for openness and sincerity may at the same time be characterized by a high degree of urbanity and gentleness. It will be one of the aims of the Plaindealer to prove, by its example, that there is at least nothing utterly contrarious and irreconcilable in these traits.

In politics, the Plaindealer will be thoroughly democratic. It will be democratic not merely to the extent of the political maxim, that the majority have the right to govern ; but to the extent of the moral maxim, that it is the duty of the majority so to govern as to preserve inviolate the equal rights of all. In this large sense, democracy includes all the main principles of political economy : that noble science which is silently and surely revolutionizing the world ; which is changing the policy of nations from one of strife to one of friendly emulation ; and cultivating the arts of peace on the soil hitherto desolated by the ravages of war. Democracy and political economy both assert the true dignity of man. They are both the natural champions of freedom, and the enemies of all restraints on the many for the benefit of the few. They both consider the people the only proper source of government, and their equal protection its only proper end ; and both would confine the interference of legislation to the fewest possible objects, compatible with the preservation of social order. They are twin-sisters, pursuing parallel paths, for the accomplishment of cognate objects. They are sometimes found divided, but always in a languishing condition ; and they can only truly flourish where they exist in companionship, and, hand in hand, achieve their kindred purposes.

The Plaindealer claims to belong to the great democratic party of this country; but it will never deserve to be considered a party paper in the degrading sense in which that phrase is commonly understood. The prevailing error of political journals is to act as if they deemed it more important to preserve the organization of party, than to promote the principles on which it is founded. They substitute the means for the end, and pay that fealty to men which is due only to truth. This fatal error it will be a constant aim of the Plaindealer to avoid. It will espouse the cause of the democratic party only to the extent that the democratic party merits its appellation and is faithful to the tenets of its political creed. It will contend on its side while it acts in conformity with its fundamental doctrines, and will be found warring against it whenever it violates those doctrines in any essential respect. Of the importance and even dignity of party combination, no journal can entertain a higher and more respectful sense. They furnish the only certain means of carrying political principles into effect. When men agree in their theory of Government, they must also agree to act in concert, or no practical advantage can result from their accordance. "For my part," says Burke, "I find it impossible to conceive that any one believes in his own politics, or thinks them to be of any weight, who refuses to adopt the means of having them reduced to practice."

From what has been already remarked, it is matter of obvious inference that the Plaindealer will steadily and earnestly oppose all partial and special legislation, and all grants of exclusive or peculiar privileges. It will, in a particular manner, oppose, with its utmost energy, the extension of the pernicious bank system with which this country is cursed; and will zealously contend, in season and out of season, for the repeal of those tyrannous prohibitory laws, which give to the chartered money-changers their chief power of evil. To the very principle of special incorporation we here, on the threshold of our undertaking, declare interminable hostility. It is a principle utterly at war with the principles of democracy. It is the opposite of that which asserts the equal rights of man, and limits the offices of government to his equal protection. It is, in its nature, an aristocratic principle; and if permitted to exist among us much longer, and to to be acted upon by our legislators, will leave us nothing of equal liberty but the name. Thanks to the illustrious man who was called in a happy hour to preside over our country! the attention of the people has been thoroughly awakened to the insidious nature and fatal influences of chartered privileges. The popular voice, already, in various quarters, denounces them. In vain do those who possess, and those who seek to obtain grants of monopolies, endeavour to stifle the rising murmur. It swells louder and louder; it grows more and more distinct; and is spreading far and wide. The days of the charter-mongers are numbered. The era of equal privileges is at hand.

There is one other subject on which it is proper to touch in these opening remarks, and on which we desire that there should exist the most perfect understanding with our readers. We claim the right, and shall exercise it too, on all proper occasions, of *absolute freedom of discussion.* We hold that there is no subject whatever interdicted from investigation and comment; and that we are under no obligation, political or otherwise, to refrain from a full and candid expression of opinion as to the manifold evils, and deep disgrace, inflicted on our country by the institution of slavery. Nay more, it will be one of the occasional but earnest objects of this paper to show by statistical calculations and temperate arguments, enforced by every variety of illustration that can properly be employed, the impolicy of slavery, as well as its enormous wickedness: to show its pernicious influence on all the dearest interests of the south; on its moral character, its social relations, and its agricultural, commercial and political prosperity. No man can deny the momentous importance of this subject, nor that it is one of deep interest to every American citizen. It is the duty, then, of a public journalist to discuss it; and from the obligations of duty we trust the Plaindealer will never shrink. We establish this paper, expecting to derive from it a livelihood; and if an honest and industrious exercise of such talents as we have can achieve that object, we shall not fail. But we cannot, for the sake of a livelihood, trim our sails to suit the varying breeze of popular prejudice. We should prefer, with old Andrew Marvell, to scrape a blade bone of cold mutton, to faring more sumptuously on viands obtained by a surrender of principle.* If a paper, which makes the right, not the expedient, its cardinal object, will not yield its

* The story to which allusion is here made cannot too often be repeated. We copy it from a life of Marvell, by John Dove. It is as follows: The borough of Hull, in the reign of Charles II. chose ANDREW MARVELL, a young gentleman of little or no fortune, and maintained him in London for the service of the public. His understanding, integrity, and spirit, were dreadful to the then infamous administration. Persuaded that he would be theirs for properly asking, they sent his old school-fellow, the LORD TREASURER DANBY, to renew acquaintance with him in his garret. At parting, the Lord Treasurer, out of *pure affection*, slipped into his hand an order upon the Treasury for 1,000*l*., and then went to his chariot. Marvell looking at the paper, calls after the Treasurer "My Lord, I request another moment." They went up again to the garret, and Jack, the servant boy, was called. "Jack, child, what had I for dinner yesterday?" "Don't you remember, sir? you had the little shoulder of mutton that you ordered me to bring from a woman in the market." "Very right, child. What have I for dinner to day?" "Don't you know, sir, that you bid me lay by the *blade-bone to broil?*" "'Tis so, very right, child, go away. My Lord, do you hear that? Andrew Marvell's dinner is provided; there's your piece of paper. I want it not. I knew the sort of kindness you intended. I live here to serve my constituents; the Ministry may seek men for their purpose; *I am not one.*"

conductor a support, there are honest vocations that will; and better the humblest of them, than to be seated at the head of an influential press, if its influence is not exerted to promote the cause of truth.

THANKSGIVING DAY.

[*From the Plaindealer, December* 3, 1836.]

THURSDAY, the fifteenth of the present month, has been designated by Governor Marcy, in his annual proclamation, as a day of general thanksgiving throughout this state. This is done in conformity with a long established usage, which has been so generally and so scrupulously observed, that we doubt whether it has ever been pretermitted, for a single year, by the Chief Magistrate of any state in the Confederacy. The people, too, on these occasions, have always responded with such cordiality and unanimity to the recommendation of the Governors, that not even the Sabbath, a day which the scriptures command to be kept holy, is more religiously observed, in most places, than the day set apart as one of thanksgiving and prayer by gubernatorial appointment. There is something exceedingly impressive in the spectacle which a whole people presents, in thus voluntarily withdrawing themselves on some particular day, from all secular employment, and uniting in a tribute of praise for the blessings they enjoy. Against a custom so venerable for its age, and so reverently observed, it may seem presumptuous to suggest an objection; yet there is one which we confess seems to us of weight, and we trust we shall not be thought governed by an irreligious spirit, if we take the liberty to urge it.

In framing our political institutions, the great men to whom that important trust was confided, taught, by the example of other countries, the evils which result from mingling civil and ecclesiastical affairs, were particularly careful to keep them entirely distinct. Thus the Constitution of the United States mentions the subject of religion at all, only to declare that "no religious test shall ever be required as a qualification to any office or public trust in the United States." The Constitution of our own state specifies that "the free exercise and enjoyment of religious professions and worship, without discrimination or preference, shall forever be allowed in this state to all mankind;" and so fearful were the framers of that instrument of the dangers to be apprehended from a union of political and religious concerns, that they inserted a clause of positive interdiction against ministers of the gospel, declaring them forever ineligible to any civil or military office or place within the state. In this last step we think the jealousy of religious interference proceeded too far. We see no good reason why preachers of the gospel should be partially disfranchised, any more than preachers against it, or any more than men devoted to any other profession or pursuit. This curious proscriptive article of our Constitution presents the startling anomaly, that while an infidel, who delivers stated Sunday lectures in a tavern, against all religion, may be elected to the highest executive or legislative trust, the most liberal and enlightened divine is excluded. In our view of the subject neither of them should be proscribed. They should both be left to stand on the broad basis of equal political rights, and the intelligence and virtue of the people should be trusted to make a selection from an unbounded field. This is the true democratic theory; but this is a subject apart from that which it is our present purpose to consider.

No one can pay the most cursory attention to the state of religion in the United States, without being satisfied that its true interests have been greatly promoted by divorcing it from all connexion with political affairs. In no other country of the world are the institutions of religion so generally respected, and in no other is so large a proportion of the population included among the communicants of the different christian churches. The number of christian churches or congregations in the United States is estimated, in a carefully prepared article of religious statistics in the American Almanac of the present year, at upwards of sixteen thousand, and the number of communicants at nearly two millions, or one-tenth of the entire population. In this city alone the number of churches is one hundred and fifty, and their aggregate capacity is nearly equal to the accommodation of the whole number of inhabitants. It is impossible to conjecture, from any data within our reach, the amount of the sum annually paid by the American people, of their own free will, for the support of the ministry, and the various expenses of their religious institutions: but it will readily be admitted that it must be enormous. These, then, are the auspicious results of *perfect free trade in religion*—of leaving it to manage its own concerns, in its own way, without government protection, regulation, or interference, of any kind or degree whatever.

The only instance of intermeddling, on the part of the civil authorities, with matters which, being of a religious character, properly belong to the religious guides of the people, is the proclamation which it is the custom for the Governor of each state annually to issue, appointing a day of general thanksgiving, or a day of general fasting and prayer. We regret that even this single exception should exist to that rule of entire separation of the affairs of state from those of the church, the observance of which in all other respects has been followed by the happiest results. It is to the source of the proclamation, not to its purpose, that we chiefly object. The recommending a day of thanksgiving is not properly any part of the duty of a political Chief Magistrate: it belongs, in its nature, to the heads of the church, not to the head of the state.

It may very well happen, and, indeed, it has happened, in more instances than one, that the chief executive officer of a state has been a person, who, if not absolutely an infidel or sceptic in religious matters, has at least, in his private sentiments and conduct, been notoriously disregardful of religion. What mockery for such a person to call upon the people to set apart a day for returning acknowledgments to Almighty God for the bounties and blessings bestowed upon them! But even when the contrary is the case, and it is well known that the Governor is a strictly religious man, he departs very widely from the duties of his office, in proclaiming, in his gubernatorial capacity, and under the seal of the state, that he has appointed a particular day as a day of general thanksgiving. This is no part of his official business, as prescribed in the Constitution. It is not one of the purposes for which he was elected. If it were a new question, and a Governor should take upon himself to issue such a proclamation for the first time, the proceeding could scarcely fail to arouse the most sturdy opposition from the people. Religious and irreligious would unite in condemning it: the latter as a gross departure from the specified duties for the discharge of which alone the Governor was chosen; and the former as an unwarrantable interference of the civil authority with ecclesiastical affairs, and a usurpation of the functions of their own duly appointed ministers and church officers. We recollect very distinctly what an excitement arose in this community a few years ago, when our Common Council, following the example of the Governor, undertook to interfere in a matter which belonged wholly to the clerical functionaries, and passed a resolution recommending to the various ministers of the gospel the subject of their next Sunday discourse. The Governor's proclamation would itself provoke equal opposition, if men's eyes had not been sealed by custom to its inherent impropriety.

If such a proceeding would be wrong, instituted now for the first time, can it be right, because it has existed for a long period? Does age change the nature of principles, and give sanctity to error? Are truth and falsehood of such mutable and shifting qualities, that though, in their originial characters, as opposite as the poles, the lapse of a little time may reduce them to a perfect similitude, and render them entirely convertible? If age has in it such power as to render venerable what is not so in its intrinsic nature, then is paganism more venerable than christianity, since it has existed from a much more remote antiquity. But what is wrong in principle must continue to be wrong to the end of time, however sanctioned by custom. It is in this light we consider the gubernatorial recommendation of a day of thanksgiving; and because it is wrong in principle, and not because of any particular harm which the custom has yet been the means of introducing, we should be pleased to see it abrogated. We think it can hardly be doubted that, if the duty of setting apart a day for a general expression of thankfulness for the blessings enjoyed by the community were submitted wholly to the proper representatives of the different religious sects they would find no difficulty in uniting on the subject, and acting in concert in such a manner as should give greater solemnity and weight to their proceeding, than can ever attach to the proclamation of a political governor, stepping out of the sphere of his constitutional duties, and taking upon himself to direct the religious exercises of the people. We cannot too jealously confine our political functionaries within the limits of their prescribed duties. We cannot be too careful to keep entirely separate the things which belong to government from those which belong to religion. The political and the religious interests of the people will both flourish the more prosperously for being wholly distinct. The condition of religious affairs in this country fully proves the truth of the position; and we are satisfied it would receive still further corroboration, if the practice to which we object were reformed.

PILOTS.

[*From the Plaindealer, December* 3, 1836.]

The loss of the Bristol, some account of which melancholy and fatal shipwreck will be found under the appropriate head, has had the good effect of drawing public attention very strongly to the defects of that bad system of laws in regard to piloting, to which the dreadful casualty is, beyond all question, attributable, and to create a very general and deep conviction of the necessity of immediate reform. The defects of the pilot laws have often before been adverted to in several of the leading public journals, and they have been the theme also, of particular animadversion in the legislature; but all attempts to improve them have hitherto failed. Their evil tendency has now received an illustration, however, which forces the subject on public attention, and occasions so general and earnest a demand for a thorough revision and remodification of the system, that those interested in preserving the present abuses will hardly have influence enough effectually to resist the desired reform. The fondness for monopoly which, in regard to so many matters, has distinguished the legislation of this state, is shown in no instance more signally than in the laws relating to pilots. If the legislators had been all ingenious men, (which we believe has seldom happened to be the case,) and if it had been their express object to frame a set of laws on that subject which should most completely defeat their ostensible object, they could hardly have devised a system more suited to such a purpose than that which they have instituted nominally for the protection of the vast and valuable commerce of this port. The remedy for a system, the natural fruit of which is seen in the dreadful shipwreck which has recently occurred at the very entrance of our harbour, is perfectly simple. The evil results from monopoly, and free-trade supplies the obvious and infallible remedy. A system of unbounded competition; a system which should allow any person to be pilot, who submitted to a competent tribunal, the proper evidences of skill, and gave proper security for a faithful exercise of his functions, would be certain to supply the harbour of New-York with a numerous class of as hardy, intelligent, and enterprising pilots, as are to be met with in any port in the world. Instead of the sleepy and intemperate leeches, who now fatten on our commerce, without rendering it any real assistance, and who vigilantly discharge no part of their calling but that of collecting their unearned fees, we should have a set of men who, in storm and sunshine, would be constantly upon the ocean, venturing far out, and furthest under the most threatening sky. We should have men who would not suffer a noble ship, after having triumphantly encountered the storms of the Atlantic, to be wrecked, and scores of human beings to perish with her, for want of a pilot, in the very mouth of our harbour. We should have men, as the Evening Post forcibly expresses it, "almost amphibious, and caring as little for the storm as the seagull."

BREAD LAW.

[*From the Plaindealer, December* 3, 1836.]

We were hugely disappointed last Monday evening, that the Common Council did not complete their action on the subject of bread. Some weeks ago, Alderman Holly introduced a resolution, which was adopted, in favour of appointing a committee to consider the propriety of re-establishing the old law relative to an assize of bread. If the committee which was appointed under this resolution had acted with half as much celerity as they usually do when eatables or drinkables are the subject of their deliberations, we should probably by this time have had bread of respectable size, instead of the diminutive things—scarcely a mouthful for a hungry Alderman—which the bakers have now the audacity to serve to their customers as shilling and sixpenny loaves.

There are some people so ignorant of the laws of political economy as to pretend that the size of bread ought to be governed by the fluctuations in the price of flour, and to be large when flour is cheap, and small when it is dear. It is strange how such an absurd notion, so utterly opposed to the principles of our entire system of legislation, could ever get into the heads of sensible men. What can the poor man, who buys his shilling loaf of bread of the grocer, be supposed to know concerning the price of flour? He cannot be running about the town to ascertain the variations of the flour market. His time is money, and he cannot afford to spend it in so prodigal a manner. No: it is necessary to protect him from the frauds of dishonest bakers: it is necessary to establish a uniform weight, and to ensure compliance with it by appointing a Bread Weighmaster General, with an ample retinue of Deputies. Is not this the principle which pervades our legislation? Have we not a Weighmaster General of merchandise? Have we not an Inspector of Tobacco? and of Flour? and of Beef? and of Pork? And shall bread, the staff of life, be neglected? "Tell it not in Gath!"

We trust Alderman Holly will take an early opportunity to make his report, and we hope he will recommend a good stout loaf at once, and urge its adoption with all that eloquence and learning for which we understand he is distinguished. The measure may operate rather hard upon the bakers, but will it not be a benefit to the community at large? And why should the profits of a few extortionate bakers stand in the way of a great good to thousands and tens of thousands of people? If the bakers have any patriotism they will themselves not object. But the hardship will be one of only temporary duration. Flour cannot always remain at fourteen dollars a barrel, and wood at three dollars a load. A reaction, by and by, will reduce prices as much below a medium point as they now are above it; and then will come the harvest of the bakers. They will then find the truth of Lord Byron's line, (if they ever read Lord Byron,) that

> Time at last makes all things even.

The wise men who frame our laws have been fully aware of this truth. Hence the usance of money is fixed at seven per cent., not that it is always worth seven per cent. and no more, as there were some long-faced gentry in Wall-street, this very day, who could have testified; but because it is sometimes as much above that rate, as at other times below it, and so the legislature strike an average, for the sake of uniformity, and to protect the community. In the same way they limit the number of pilots to sixty, though there are times when more might find employment. But take one time with another, that number is sufficient, and it is therefore fixed at that, for the sake of uniformity, and to protect the community—an end well accomplished, as a certain recent event has fully proved!

In the same wise spirit which devised the usury law, Alderman Holly now proposes to pass a law, fixing a uniform standard of bread; and we hear it whispered that he next intends to establish a uniform standard for coats and pantaloons, and to impose a heavy fine on every tailor who shall dare to make them larger or smaller than the prescribed dimensions. Very large people and very small people may, it is true, experience some inconvenience from being obliged to wear garments of the medium standard; but there is a great benefit in uniformity, and the community ought to be protected by law against the frauds of tailors, who are somewhat noted for cabbaging. We advise Alderman Holly to persevere, nor pause in his wise undertaking, till he has fixed a standard for every thing by law. Do we not boast of being a people of laws? If it is a thing to boast of, let us then have law enough.

THE STREET OF THE PALACES.

[*From the Plaindealer, December* 10, 1836.]

There is, in the city of Genoa, a very elegant street, commonly called, *The Street of the Palaces.* It is broad and regular, and is flanked, on each side, with rows of spacious and superb palaces, whose marble fronts, of the most costly and imposing architecture, give an air of exceeding grandeur to the place. Here reside the principal aristocracy of Genoa; the families of Balbi, Doria, and many others of those who possess patents of nobility and exclusive privileges. The lower orders of the people, when they pass before these proud edifices, and cast their eyes over the striking evidences which the lordly exteriors exhibit of the vast wealth and power of the titled possessors, may naturally be supposed to think of their own humble dwellings and slender possessions, and to curse in their hearts those institutions of their country which divide society into such extremes of condition, forcing the many to toil and sweat for the pampered and privileged few. Wretched indeed are the serfs and vassals of those misgoverned lands, where a handful of men compose the privileged orders, monopolising political power, diverting to their peculiar advantage the sources of pecuniary emolument, and feasting, in luxurious idleness, on the fruits of the hard earnings of the poor.

But is this condition of things confined to Genoa, or to European countries? Is there no parallel for it in our own? Have we not, in this very city, our "*Street of the Palaces,*" adorned with structures as superb as those of Genoa in exterior magnificence, and containing within them vaster treasures of wealth? Have we not, too, our *privileged orders?* our scrip nobility? aristocrats, clothed with special immunities, who control, indirectly, but certainly, the political power of the state, monopolise the most copious sources of pecuniary profit, and wring the very crust from the hard hand of toil? Have we not, in short, like the wretched serfs of Europe, our lordly masters,

> "Who make us slaves, and tell us 'tis *their charter?*"

If any man doubts how these questions should be answered, let him walk through Wall-street. He will there see a street of palaces, whose stately marble walls rival those of Balbi and Doria. If he inquires to whom those costly fabrics belong, he will be told to the *exclusively privileged of this land of equal laws!* If he asks concerning the polltical power of the owners, he will ascertain that three-fourths of the legislators of the state are of their own order, and deeply interested in preserving and extending the privileges they enjoy. If he investigates the sources of their prodigious wealth, he will discover that it is extorted, under various delusive names, and by a deceptive process, from the pockets of the unprivileged and unprotected poor. These are the masters in this land of freedom. These are our aristocracy, our scrip nobility, our privileged order of charter-mongers and money-changers! Serfs of free America! bow your necks submissively to the yoke, for these exchequer barons have you fully in their power, and resistance now would but make the burden more galling. Do they not boast that they will be represented in the halls of legislation, and that the people cannot help themselves? Do not their servile newspaper mouth-pieces prate of the impolicy of giving an inch to the people, lest they should demand an ell? Do they not threaten, that unless the people restrict their requests within the narrowest compass, they will absolutely grant them nothing?—that they will not relax their fetters at all, lest they should next strive to snap them entirely asunder?

These are not figures of speech. Alas! we feel in no mood to be rhetorical. Tropes and figures are the language of the free, and we are slaves!—slaves to most ignoble masters, to a low-minded, ignorant, and rapacious order of money-changers. We speak, therefore, not in figures, but in the simplest and soberest phrase. We speak plain truths in plain words, and only give utterance to sentiments that involuntarily rose in our mind, as we glided this morning through the *Street of the Palaces*, beneath the frowning walls of its marble structures, fearing that our very thoughts might be construed into a breach of privilege. But thank heaven! the day has not yet come—though perhaps it is at hand—when our paper money patricians deny their serfs and vassals the right to think and speak. We may still give utterance to our opinions, and still walk with a confident step through the *Street of the Palaces of the Charter-mongers.*

ASSOCIATED EFFORT.

[*From the Plaindealer, December* 10, 1836.]

SOME days ago, we observed in one of the newspapers, a paragraph stating that a meeting of mechanics and labourers was about to be held in this city for the purpose of adopting measures of concerted or combined action against the practice, which we have reason to believe exists to a very great extent, of paying them in the uncurrent notes of distant or suspected banks. No such meeting, however, as far as we can learn, has yet been held. We hope it soon will be; for the object is a good one, and there is no other way of resisting the rapacious and extortionate custom of employers paying their journeymen and laborers in depreciated paper, half so effectual as combination.

There are some journalists who affect to entertain great horror of combinations, considering them as utterly adverse to the principles of free trade; and it is frequently recommended to make them penal by law. Our notions of free trade were acquired in a different school, and dispose us to leave men entirely at liberty to effect a proper object either by concerted or individual action. The character of combinations, in our view, depends entirely upon the intrinsic character of the end which is aimed at. In the subject under consideration, the end proposed is good beyond all possibillity of question. There is high warrant for saying that the *labourer is worthy of his hire;* but the employer, who takes advantage of his necessities and defencelessness to pay him in a depreciated substitute for money, does not give him his hire; he does not perform his engagement with him; he filches from the poor man a part of his hard-earned wages, and is guilty of a miserable fraud. Who shall say that this sneaking species of extortion ought not to be prevented? Who will say that separate individual action is adequate to that end? There is no one who will make so rash an assertion.

The only effectual mode of doing away the evil is by attacking it with the great instrument of the rights of the poor—*associated effort.* There is but one bulwark behind which mechanics and labourers may safely rally to oppose a common enemy, who, if they ventured singly into the field against him, would cut them to pieces: that bulwark is the *Principle of Combination.* We would advise them to take refuge behind it only in extreme cases, because in their collisions with their employers, as in those between nations, the manifold evils of a siege are experienced, more or less, by both parties, and are therefore to be incurred only in extreme emergencies. But the evil of being habitually paid in a depreciated substitute for money; of being daily cheated out of a portion of the just fruits of honest toil; of having a slice continually clipped from the hard-earned crust; is one of great moment, and is worthy of such an effort as we propose.

PRIVILEGED ORDERS IN DANGER.

[*From the Plaindealer, December* 10, 1836.]

A DOCUMENT is published in the Washington Globe of last Monday, which we have read with the profoundest attention and the liveliest pleasure, and which we regret that the occupied state of our columns prevents us from taking as full a notice of as the importance of the subject and the ability with which it is treated deserve. This document is a letter from Charles J. Ingersoll, of Philadelphia, in answer to one addressed to him by a number of the members elect of the Pennsylvania legislature, asking him, as he had been chosen a member of the Convention to propose amendments to the Constitution of that state, to express, for publication, the views he entertains in regard to the general powers of the Convention, particularly with reference to the United States Bank, and the question of vested rights. Mr. Ingersoll goes very fully into an exposition of the subjects indicated by these inquiries. At the very outset of his reply, he explicitly declares, as his own deliberate and mature conviction, that *bank-charters may be repealed by act of Assembly, without a Convention, and that such act will not be contrary to the Constitution of the United States.* Mr. Ingersoll shows that such also was the opinion, fifty years ago, of the early democrats of Pennsylvania, not declared merely, but practised, in the repeal of the charter of the Bank of North America, in 1785. This repeal was effected on the broad democratic ground, not that it had violated the conditions of its exclusive privileges, but that such an institution was aristocratic in its nature, dangerous to liberty both in its intrinsic character and as a precedent of evil, and utterly inconsistent with the fundamental principle avowed in the Pennsylvania Bill of

Rights, that government was to be administered for the equal advantage of men, and not for the peculiar emolument of any man, family, or set of men. Mr. Ingersoll also shows that the doctrine of the revocability of charters has been strenuously maintained by some of the greatest British statesmen; among them by Fox and Burke, on the bill for revoking the charter of the East India Company; and he gives a long and pertinent extract from the memorable speech of the latter on that subject. Mr. Ingersoll contends that a bank charter is not a contract within the meaning of the clause of the Constitution of the United States, prohibiting any state from passing a law impairing the obligation of contracts, and he shows that the authorised exponents of the other side of the question, so far as the repeal of the charter of the Pennsylvania United States Bank is in debate, have themselves expressly admitted that their engagement with the state lacks an essential principle to constitute it a contract. The letter of Mr. Ingersoll closes with an admirable passage, descriptive of the present condition of affairs in this country, brought about by exclusively privileged stock-jobbers and money-changers; and contrasts it with the condition in which they would soon be placed, on the accomplishing of that great reformation which shall "restore to the people their equality, to the states their sovereignty, and to the Union its supremacy over coin and currency."

THE COAL QUESTION.

[*From the Plaindealer*, *December* 10, 1836.]

There seems to be no doubt entertained, among those who have investigated the subject, that there is a combination among the dealers in coal, in this city, not to sell under certain stipulated prices. We do not know whether this is so or not; but let us take it for granted that it is, and the question then arises, What are we to do to remedy the evil? The Albany Argus would suggest that "it might be well to inquire whether combinations to raise the price of coal, pork, flour, and other necessaries of life, are not offences against society," which require to be made punishable by law. The Journal of Commerce (a free-trade paper!) would respond affirmatively to the question, and say, "if dealers in the above articles have combined to raise prices, let the law walk into them!"

For our own part, we would neither make a new law to punish the combiners, nor take advantage of Chief Justice Savage's and Judge Edwards's decisions, to inflict upon them the penalty of any existing statute, or of any breach of the common law of England. With all deference to the Journal of Commerce, we must take the liberty to say, that we consider its example better than its precept; and that is by no means a usual occurrence in these days of much profession and little practice. That print informs us that its conductors, "not being disposed to submit to the extortion of the coal combination, took the liberty to order a small cargo from Philadelphia, which cost there, at this late season of the year, $8 50 the long ton of 2240 lbs. broken and screened. The freight will increase the price to about $11 25 the long ton, which is equal to $10 for such tons as are sold by the combinationists. Dumped at the door, the cost will not exceed $11." This, the Journal of Commerce adds, is better than paying thirteen or fourteen dollars, the price charged here, and shows what kind of profits the coal dealers make. Let us add that it is better, also, than making a law, or raking up an old one from the undisturbed dust of antiquity, to punish a combination, (if peradventure any combination exists) which is so very easily circumvented and set at nought.

The Journal of Commerce and the Albany Argus may both rest assured that the laws of trade are a much better defence against improper combinations, than any laws which the legislature at Albany can make, judging by the specimens to be found in the statute books. When a set of dealers combine to raise the price of a commodity above its natural value, they will be sure to provoke competition that will very soon let them down from their fancied elevation. It seems, according to the Journal of Commerce's own statement, that the coal dealers are selling coal by retail in this city at an advance of from eighteen to twenty-seven per cent. upon the net cost of the article delivered here. This is making no allowances for the diminution of weight the coal may undergo during transportation ; nor for the fees of the inspectors of coal, which are to be charged upon it as an item of the cost ; nor for the rent of the coal-yard ; nor for wages of labour in shovelling it to and fro. When all these particulars are added together, and deducted from the price asked, it will be found, we think, to leave but a moderate profit for the coal dealers, notwithstanding the many and loud complaints of their extortion. Truth is truth, and though the price of fuel is enormously high, we ought not to impute all the blame to those of our citizens who deal in the commodity, when our own figures prove that they do not make very extravagant profits after all.

But if the blame does not lie with the coal dealers, where does it lie? We think there is no great difficulty in correctly answering this question. According to our view it lies, then, in the first place, with the legislatures of two or three states, which have given the privileges of a monopoly to certain coal companies, enabling them to fix prices by combination at the fountain head. It lies, in the second place, with those same legislatures, in giving the privileges of a monopoly to certain railroad and canal companies, enabling them to fix the rates of toll and freightage. It lies, in the third place, with Congress, which has placed so heavy a duty on foreign coal as almost to shut it out from competition with the domestic. And it lies, in the fourth place, with our municipal authorities, who increase the burden by appointing measurers of foreign coal, weighers of domestic coal, and inspectors of wood, all of whom are allowed, by law, enormous fees for a duty which they do not half perform, and which, if they performed it ever so thoroughly, would be altogether superfluous.

There is still one other cause which ought not to be omitted from the calculation ; and that is, the diminished quantity of coal mined, in consequence of speculation having withdrawn labour from that employment, during the past summer, to work on railroads, to dig canals, to level hills, and fill up valleys, and, perform the various other services which were necessary to carry out the schemes projected by the gambling spirit of the times. Hence the supply is not more than adequate, at the most, to the demand; and hence those who have a monopoly of the article at fountain head ask the present enormous prices, secure that the citizens must either give them or freeze.

There is one branch of this subject in which we most cordially concur with the Journal of Commerce. That paper suggests the propriety of the institution of benevolent associations, for the purpose of procuring a large supply of coal when it is cheapest, and disposing of it, by retail, at the prime cost and charges, to the poorer classes of citizens, whose means do not enable them to buy much in advance. Such an association might do a vast amount of good, without ever expending a single dollar. Suppose, for example, a hundred citizens, of well known respectability, and sufficient pecuniary responsibility, should enter into an association for the purpose named, and should purchase a given amount of coal at six months credit, each member of the association being jointly and severally responsible for the indebtedness of the whole. The coal might then be put at such a price as, when all was sold, would yield the net cost and charges; and before the obligations of the company should fall due, the money would be in hand to discharge them. This would be a cheap charity on the part of those who engaged in it, and a most valuable one to those classes of citizens for whose benefit it would be intended.

A FINE VOLLEY OF WORDS.

From the Plaindealer of December 17, 1836.

It is related, in one of those instructive fables which we have all read in our school-boy days, that the shepherd, who indulged himself in the innocent pastime of crying wolf, when no wolf was near, for the mere purpose of seeing what effect the startling exclamation would have on the neighbouring herdsmen, found, unfortunately, when the beasts of prey actually descended upon his flock, and were committing unresisted havoc, that the alarm-word, which had been wont to bring instant succour, had wholly lost its salutary efficacy. The moral of this story is susceptible of extensive application. They who invoke aid when none is required, will be doomed at last to have their prayers unheeded, however urgent may be the occasion which then prompts the appeal; and they, too, whose objurgatory temper leads them to indulge in habitual threats, when no cause of offence is intended, will find, in the end, their fiercest denunciations disregarded, without reference to the circumstances by which they may be elicited. Persons who reside near the Falls of Niagara grow familiar with the din, and become, in time, wholly unconscious of the perpetual thunder of the cataract; and it is said that the keepers and medical attendants in a mad-house get so accustomed to the shrieks and yells of the frantic inmates, as to be able to pursue their avocations with as much tranquillity as if the silence was not broken by such horrid sounds.

These truths do not seem to have been present in the mind of Mr. McDuffie, when he prepared his recent message to the legislature of South Carolina. He has shot off, in that document, "a fine volley of words," to use a phrase from Shakspeare; but he seems to have forgotten that the northern people have become so accustomed to such volleys, that they have lost the terror which originally belonged to them. There was a time when a threat of disunion, from a much more insignificant source than the chief magistrate of a great state, in his official communication with the legislature, would have excited a thrill of alarm in the bosom of every true lover of his country, throughout the whole extent of this vast confederacy. There was a time, when every heart sincerely responded to the farewell admonition of Washington, that as union is the main pillar in the edifice of our real independence, we should "cherish a cordial, habitual, and immoveable attachment to it; watching for its preservation with jealous anxiety; discountenancing whatever may suggest even a suspicion that it can, in any event, be abandoned; and indignantly frowning on the first dawning of every attempt to alienate any portion of our country from the rest." There was a time, when the sacrilegious thief, who steals the consecrated chalice from the altar, would not be looked upon, by religious men, with half the horror that a whole people would have regarded the daring wretch who should lisp a recommendation to dissolve the federal compact. But that time is long since past. The bound which restrained, as within a magic circle, the controversies of political disputants, has been overleaped. Southern statesmen (what an abuse of the word!) long ago employed their arithmetic to calculate the value of the Union; and now nothing is more common than the threat of its dissolution. Is it proposed to admit a territory into the Confederacy under such qualifications as shall promote the cause of freedom, and extend and strengthen the basis of human rights? Dissolve the Union! is the cry which at once assails our ears from the south. Is it recommended, by those whose interests are involved in manufactures, to continue, for a while longer, the restrictions on commerce, under which domestic manufactures were first fostered into existence? Dissolve the Union! exclaim the patriots of the south. Is it suggested that it is the duty of Congress to abolish slavery in a district over which the Constitution gives it exclusive jurisdiction? Dissolve the Union! is the frantic shout which is again pealed forth from the south. To dissolve the Union seems to be the ready remedy for every grievance, real or supposed. It is the nostrum which, in the true spirit of reckless and desperate quackery, the politicians of the southern states, and particularly of South Carolina, would administer for every ill. It is the panacea which they appear to consider of universal efficacy. It is the cure which will alike restore the patient to health, whether he suffers from an external hurt or from internal decay; whether his malady be serious or trivial, chronic or acute. Amputation seems to be the only remedial measure known in the political chirurgery of the south.

But Governor McDuffie goes a step further than any

former practitioner. He is for using the knife, not when disease attacks a limb, but the moment it is apprehended. He is for dissolving the Union, not when any measure, militating against "the domestic institutions of the south," is effected; but whenever it is proposed. He would proceed to that extremity, not when the abolition of slavery, in any shape or degree, is accomplished; but the moment the question is discussed. To say that slavery is an evil, is, in his view, a violation of the federal compact; and for Congress to receive a petition on the subject, is, according to his exposition of constitutional law, equivalent to a declaration of war against the states in which slavery exists.

THE CORPORATION QUESTION.

[*From the Plaindealer, December* 24, 1836.]

One of the newspapers which has done us the honour to notice this journal, animadverts, with considerable asperity, upon our declaration of interminable hostility to the principle of special incorporation, and points our attention to certain incorporated institutions, which, according to the universal sense of mankind, are established with the purest motives, and effect the most excellent objects. The ready and obvious answer to the strictures we have provoked is, that it is the means, not the end, which furnishes the subject of our condemnation. An act of special incorporation may frequently afford the persons associated under it facilities of accomplishing much public good; but if those facilities can only be given at the expense of rights of paramount importance, they ought to be denied by all whose political morality rejects the odious maxim that the end justifies the means. It would be a very strained and unwarrantable inference from any remarks we have made, to say that we are an enemy to churches, public libraries, or charitable associations, because we express hostility to special legislation. It would be an unwarranted inference to say that we are even opposed to the principle of incorporation ; since it is only to the principle of *special incorporation* that we have expressed hostility. We are opposed, not to the object, but to the mode by which the object is effected. We are opposed, not to corporation partnerships, but to the right of forming such partnerships being specially granted to the few, and wholly denied to the many. We are opposed, in short, to unequal legislation, whatever form it may assume, or whatever object it may ostensibly seek to accomplish.

It has been beautifully and truly said, by the illustrious man who presides over the affairs of our Confederacy, that "there are no necessary evils in government. Its evils exist only in its abuses. If it would confine itself to *equal protection*, and, as heaven does its rains, shower its favours alike on the high and the low, the rich and the poor, it would be an unqualified blessing." But it departs from its legitimate office, it widely departs from the cardinal principle of government in this country, the equal political rights of all, when it confers privileges on one set of men, no matter for what purpose, which are withheld from the rest. It is in this light we look upon all special acts of incorporation. They convey privileges not previously enjoyed, and limit the use of them to those on whom they are bestowed. That special charters are, in many instances, given for objects of intrinsic excellence and importance, is freely admitted ; nor do we desire to withhold our unqualified acknowledgment that they have been the means of effecting many improvements of great value to the community at large. Let it be clearly understood, then, that we do not war against the good achieved; but seek only to illustrate the inherent evil of the means. A special charter is a powerful weapon; but it is one which should have no place in the armory of the democracy. It is an instrument which may hew down forests, and open fountains of wealth in barren places; but these advantages are purchased at too dear a rate, if we give for them one jot or tittle of our equal freedom. As a general rule, too, corporations act for themselves, not for the community. If they cultivate the wilderness, it is to monopolize its fruits. If they delve the mine, it is to enrich themselves with its treasures. If they dig new channels for the streams of industry, it is that they may gather the golden sands for themselves, as those of Pactolus were gathered to swell the hoards of Crœsus.

Even if the benefits, which we are willing to admit have been effected by companies acting under special corporate privileges and immunities, could not have been achieved without the assistance of such powers, better would it have been, in our opinion, far better, that the community should have foregone the good, than purchase it by the surrender, in any instance or particular, of a principle which lies at the foundation of human liberty. No one can foretell the evil consequences which may flow from one such error of legislation. "Next day the fatal precedent will plead." The way once open, ambition, selfishness, cupidity, rush in, each widening the breach, and rendering access easier to its successor. The monuments of enterprise erected through the aid of special privileges and immunities are numerous and stupendous; but we may yet be sadly admonished

> ———"how wide the limits stand,
> Between a splendid and a happy land."

But, fortunately, we are not driven to the alternative

of either foregoing for the future such magnificent projects as have heretofore been effected by special legislation, or for the sake of accomplishing them, continuing to grant unequal privileges. It is a propitious omen of success in the great struggle in which the real democracy of this country are engaged, that monopolies, (and we include in the term all special corporate rights) are as hostile to the principles of sound economy, as they are to the fundamental maxims of our political creed. The good which they effect might more simply and more certainly be achieved without their aid. They are fetters which restrain the action of the body politic, not motories which increase its speed. They are jesses which hold it to earth, not wings that help it to soar. Our country has prospered, not because of them, but in spite of them. This young and vigorous republic has bounded rapidly forward, in despite of the burdens which partial legislation hangs upon its neck, and the clogs it fastens to its heel. But swifter would have been its progress, sounder its health, more prosperous its general condition, had our law-makers kept constantly in view that their imperative duty requires them to exercise their functions for the good of the whole community, not for a handful of obtrusive and grasping individuals, who, under the pretext of promoting the public welfare, are only eager to advance their private interests, at the expense of the equal rights of their fellow-men.

Every special act of incorporation is, in a certain sense, a grant of a monopoly. Every special act of incorporation is a charter of privileges to a few, not enjoyed by the community at large. There is no single object can be named, for which, consistently with a sincere respect for the equal rights of men, a special charter of incorporation can be bestowed. It should not be given to establish a bank, nor to erect a manufactory;

to open a road, nor to build a bridge. Neither trust companies nor insurance companies should be invested with exclusive rights. Nay, acting in strict accordance with the true principles both of democracy and political economy, no legislature would, by special act, incorporate even a college or a church. Let it not be supposed, however, that we would withhold from such institutions the intrinsic advantages of a charter. We would only substitute general, for partial legislation, and extend to all, the privileges proper to be bestowed upon any. The spirit of true wisdom, in human affairs, as in divine,

> "Acts not by partial, but by general laws."

Nothing can be more utterly absurd than to suppose that the advocacy of these sentiments implies opposition to any of the great undertakings for which special legislative authority and immunities are usually sought. We are opposed only to a violation of the great democratic principle of our government; that principle which stands at the head of the Declaration of Independence; and that which most of the states have repeated, with equal explicitness, in their separate constitutions. A general partnership law, making the peculiar advantages of a corporation available to any set of men who might choose to associate, for any lawful purpose whatever, would wholly obviate the objections which we urge. Such a law would confer no exclusive or special privileges; such a law would be in strict accordance with the great maxim of man's political equality; such a law would embrace the whole community in its bound, leaving capital to flow in its natural channels, and enterprise to regulate its own pursuits. Stock bubbles, as fragile as the unsubstantial globules which children amuse themselves with blowing, might not float so numerous in the air; but all schemes of real utility, which presented a reasonable prospect of profit, would be as readily undertaken as now. That active spirit of enterprise, which, in a few months, has erected a new city on the field lately desolated by the direst conflagration our history records ; that spirit of enterprise, which every year adds whole squadrons to the innumerous fleet of stately vessels that transport our commerce to the remotest harbours of the world ; that spirit of enterprise which seeks its object alike through the freezing atmosphere of the polar regions, and beneath the fervour of the torrid zone, displaying the stars and stripes of our country to every nation of the earth ; that active spirit would not flinch from undertaking whatever works of internal improvement might be needed by the community, without the aid of exclusive rights and privileges.

The merchant, who equips his noble vessel, freights her with the richest products of nature and art, and sends her on her distant voyage across the tempestuous sea, asks no act of incorporation. The trader, who adventures his whole resources in the commodities of his traffic, solicits no exclusive privilege. The humble mechanic, who exhausts the fruit of many a day and night of toil in supplying his workshop with the implements of his craft, desires no charter. These are all willing to encounter unlimited competition. They are content to stand on the broad basis of equal rights. They trust with honourable confidence, to their own talents, exercised with industry, not to special immunities, for success. Why should the speculators, who throng the lobbies of our legislature, be more favoured than they? Why should the banker, the insurer, the bridge builder, the canal digger, be distinguished by peculiar privileges? Why should they be made a chartered order, and raised above the general level of their fellow-men?

It is curious to trace the history of corporations, and

observe how, in the lapse of time, they have come to be instruments that threaten the overthrow of that liberty, which they were, at first, effectual aids in establishing. When the feudal system prevailed over Europe, and the great mass of the people were held in vilest and most abject bondage by the lords, to whom they owed strict obedience, knowing no law but their commands, the power of the nobles, by reason of the number of their retainers and the extent of their possessions, was greater than that of the monarch, who frequently was a mere puppet in their hands. The barons, nominally vassals of the crown, holding their fief on condition of faithful service, were, in reality, and at all times, on any question which combined a few of the more powerful, absolute masters. They made kings and deposed them at pleasure. The history of all the states of Europe is full of their exploits in this way; but the narrative of the red and white rose of England, of the contending houses of York and Lancaster, is all that need be referred to for our present purpose. Corporations were the means at last happily hit upon of establishing a power to counterbalance that so tyrannously and rapaciously exercised by the barons. For certain services rendered, or a certain price paid, men were released from the conditions which bound them to their feudal lords, and all so enfranchised were combined in a corporate body, under a royal charter of privileges and immunities, and were termed "freemen of the corporation." In process of time, these bodies, by gradual and almost imperceptible additions, grew to sufficient size to afford a countercheck to the power of the nobles, and were at last the instruments, not in England only, but throughout Europe, of overthrowing the feudal system, emancipating their fellow-men from degrading bondage, and establishing a government somewhat more in accordance with the rights of humanity.

But in this country, founded, in theory and practice, on an acknowledgment, in the broadest sense, of the universal right of equal freedom, the grant of special corporate privileges is an act against liberty, not in favour of it. It is not enfranchising the few, but enslaving the many. The same process which, when the people were debased, elevated them to their proper level, now, when the people are elevated, and occupy the lofty place of equal political rights, debases them to comparative servitude. The condition of things in free America is widely different from that which existed in Europe during the feudal ages. How absurd then, to continue a system of grants, for which all actual occasion long since ceased, and which are now at utter and palpable variance with the great political maxim that all alike profess! It is our desire, however, in treating this subject, to use no language which may embitter the feelings of those who entertain contrary views. We wish to win our way by the gentle process of reason; not by the boisterous means which angry disputants adopt. It has, in all times, been one of the characteristic errors of political reformers, and we might say, indeed, of religious reformers, too, that they have threatened, rather than persuaded; that they have sought to drive men, rather than allure. Happy is he "whose blood and judgment is so well commingled," that he can blend determined hostility to public errors and abuses, with sufficient tolerance of the differences of private opinion and prejudice, never to relinquish courtesy, that sweetener of social life and efficient friend of truth. In a small way, we seek to be a reformer of certain false principles which have crept into our legislation; but as we can lay no claim to the transcendent powers of the Miltons, Harringtons and Fletchers of political history, so we have no excuse for indulging in their fierceness of invective, or bitterness of reproach.

THE TRUE THEORY OF TAXATION.

[*From the Plaindealer, December* 24, 1836.]

THE Evening Post, in one of its recent excellent articles on the protective system, speaking with particular reference to the impost on coal, expresses the opinion that it is the duty of our rulers to lighten the burdens of the people as much as possible, "especially when they fall on articles of first rate necessity; and it is easy," the Evening Post adds, "to distinguish between those that do, and those that do not."

We are very willing to see the protective system attacked, either in gross or in detail. If we find that we cannot procure the immediate reduction of all duties to the exact revenue standard, as graduated on an equal *ad valorem* scale, we must be content to concentrate our forces upon particular articles or classes of articles, and thus attempt to accomplish the overthrow of the tariff, somewhat after the manner that the redoubtable Bobadil proposed to overthrow an army. We are afraid, however, that this mode of operation, in our case, as in his, will fail of effecting any very important result. But while we are willing to join the Evening Post in bringing about a reduction of the tariff, either by piecemeal or wholesale, we cannot quite agree with the sentiment it expresses, as an abstract proposition, that it is the especial duty of rulers to reduce taxes on necessaries, and to discriminate between those which are so, and those which are not. It seems to us, on the contrary, that the true theory of taxation, whether direct or indirect, whether levied upon commerce, or assessed, without any intermediary agency or subterfuge, upon the property of the people, is that which falls with equal proportional weight upon every variety of commodity. While we should contend, with the utmost earnestness against the imposition of a tax, the effect of which would be to burden the poor man and let the rich go free; we should oppose as positively, if not as zealously, a contrary system, which tended to place the load, in any undue degree, upon the shoulders of the rich. We are for equal rights; for the rights of the affluent and the needy alike; and we would not admit, in any case, or to any extent whatever, the principle of either laying or repealing duties for the special advantage of the one class or the other. We have had too much already of discriminating duties.

If we must raise the revenues of our federal government from imposts on commerce, the true theory to contend for, in our view of the subject, is an equal *ad valorem* duty, embracing every commodity of traffic. The importer of foreign coal will tell you a pathetic story of the hardships and sufferings of the poor at this inclement season of the year. He will borrow perhaps the eloquent language of the Evening Post, to describe the shivering inmates of garrets and cellars, and the poor lone woman who buys her coal by the peck. He will draw you to her wretched abode, and show her surrounded by her tattered offspring, expanding their defenceless limbs over a few expiring embers that mock them with ineffectual heat. When he has raised your sympathy to the proper pitch, he will then call on you to exert your influence to procure the repeal of a duty which places beyond the reach of thousands of shuddering wretches one of the prime necessaries of life, and leaves them to all the horrors of unmitigated winter, as it visits the unfed sides and looped and windowed raggedness of the poor. The dealer in foreign grain will have a similar tale to relate. He will expatiate on the sufferings of the indigent from the high price of bread, and ask you to exempt breadstuffs from taxation. The importers of books and charts, and of mathematical instruments, will talk of the advantages of a wide diffusion of literature and science, and ask for a repeal of duties on those articles in which their trade consists. Colleges will represent that the cause of education requires their libraries and laboratories should come duty free. Railroad corporations will point out the many political and commercial benefits that must accrue to the country from facilitated intercourse between its distant parts, and ask that their engines and other appliances be released from the burden of taxes. All these applications, and many others of a like kind, have something specious to recommend them to a favourable consideration, and some have been listened to and granted. The prayers of corporate bodies have been affirmatively answered, while a deaf ear has been turned to those of the ill-fed and unprivileged poor. In our sense, however, they ought all to be treated alike, and all to be rejected. The only legitimate purpose of a tariff is that expressed by the Constitution, "to pay the debts and provide for the general welfare;" and the debts should be paid and the general welfare provided for, in strict accordance with the great distinguishing principle of our government—the equal rights of the people. This never can be entirely accomplished while imposts on foreign commerce furnish the means of revenue; but it is the obvious duty of legislators to do nothing to increase the unavoidable inequality of the burden.

The true system of raising revenue, the only democratic system, and the one which we trust the people of this Confederacy will some day insist upon adopting, is that of direct taxation. We hope the day will come, (and we think we see the evidences of its approach) when not a Custom House will exist in the land; when tidewaiters and guagers, appraisers and inspectors, will be unknown; and when commerce, that most efficient friend of the best interests of man, and brightener of the links of international amity, will be as free to go and come, as the breeze that fills her sails, or the wave that bears her freighted stores. The system from which we now derive the resources of our government is in utter opposition to the maxim on which our government is founded. We build up our institutions professing the utmost confidence in the intelligence and integrity of the people ; but our very first act betrays distrust both of their sagacity and virtue. We fear they have neither sense enough to see that the expenses of government must be defrayed, nor honesty enough to pay them if directly applied to for that purpose ; and hence we set about, by various modes of indirection, to filch the money from their pockets, that they may neither know how much they contribute, nor the precise purpose to which it is applied. Could a system be devised better calculated to encourage lavish expenditure, and introduce variety of corruption ? To preserve the government simple and pure, the people should know what they pay, and for what object. This would excite men to that degree of vigilance which is necessary to the preservation of their rights ; it would restrain their political agents from neglecting or exceeding their trusts ; and it would prevent government from that otherwise inevitable, however gradual, enlargement of its powers and offices, which, in the end, must prove destructive of the liberties of the people. A system of indirect taxation tends, with steady and constant force, to undermine the basis of popular rights. It is, in its very nature, an aristocratic system, and bears upon its front the evidence of distrust of popular capacity and virtue. A system of direct taxation, on the contrary, is a candid and democratic system. It is built on the presumption that the mass of men have sufficient intelligence to know in what good government consists, and sufficient integrity to pay what is required to maintain their rights. It is, in short, the only true theory of taxation; and the day will be an auspicious one for the great cause of human liberty when it is adopted by the American people.

"YOUR NAPKIN IS TOO LITTLE."

[*From the Plaindealer, December* 24, 1836.]

When the generous Othello was wrought upon by the arts of his false friend to suspect the fidelity of his wife, the agony of his ingenuous mind, unable to dissemble, betrayed itself at once in his countenance; and Desdemona seeing him troubled, and wholly unconscious of the cause, but supposing some mere physical ill afflicted him, offered to bind up his aching temples with her handkerchief. None who have had the good fortune to see the text of Shakspeare illustrated by the acting of Kean or Forrest, can ever forget the deep pathos, and wonderful fulness of meaning, of Othello's brief reply, "Your napkin is too little!"

We take the liberty to use this phrase in reference to the conduct of those political journalists who, on one side as well as the other, seek to tie up the abolition question within the limits of party, and treat it as if it were a subject on which men are divided by the same lines that divide them on the ordinary political topics of the times. Those efforts do not deceive the people, either at the north or south, but only expose the dishonesty of those who make them. The American Sentinel, for example, assures its southern readers that the views expressed in Governor Ritner's message, on the subject of slavery, are those peculiarly entertained by the whig party, as it is styled, and that the democracy of Pennsylvania, after the next annual election, will be represented by a majority in both branches of the legislature, when the abolitionists will no longer have it in their power to do any injury to southern interests. But in making this statement, it departs so widely from what is the notorious fact, that it cannot have the effect to deceive a single mind. The slaveholders know full well, and the American Sentinel also knows full well, while it publishes a contrary intimation, that the opposition to slavery, the desire to see it abolished, and the determination to discuss the subject, are not confined either to one party or the other in Pennsylvania ; but that they are entertained and expressed by multitudes of men, without the slightest reference to party lines, as drawn by other political questions. The Philadelphia Sentinel knows, too, that if the slavery question is to be considered a political question at all, it is so in the highest and most important meaning of the phrase ; and that it has no affinity or connection with other questions that come under that designation. In the soothing words which it addresses to the south on this subject it manifests a desire, it is true, to bind up the throbbing temples of the slaveholders ; *but its napkin is too little.*

There are numerous party journals, in different quarters of the country, which are playing this despicable game of retaliation and mutual crimination on the subject of slavery. In one place, some accidental or irrelevant circumstance is seized hold of and distorted, to convince the south that the abolitionists belong to the democratic party ; and, in another, the direct contrary is established by some equally cogent process of argument or proof. The truth is, and the south sees it, notwithstanding the puling of such prints as the Richmond Enquirer about " the whig legislature of Vermont," and " the whig Governor of Pennsylvania," that this question is not confined within the bounds of party; that it is not a question of whig and democrat, or one that is affected by the ordinary principles and divisions of political antagonism; but that it includes men of every variety of political belief, and extends through every portion of the Confederacy, where the moral leprosy of slavery does not exist. If a desire to abolish slavery, and a deep and earnest abhorrence of it, in all its aspects, are characteristic of one party more than the other, we hesitate not to say that it is of the democratic party; since the institution is in more positive and utter violation of the fundamental article of the creed of democracy, which acknowledges the political equality, and unalienable right of freedom of all mankind.

But let the south not vainly imagine that detestation of slavery is confined to either of the political divisions of the community, or that it can ever hush the question up no matter what party or faction may be in the ascendency. The right of free discussion is a right which we of the north will never relinquish; and that set of public servants who should be so base and so audacious, so lost to all sense of true patriotism, and so ignorant of the temper of the people, as to attempt to fetter opinion by any legislative restraints on its free exercise, would be hurled from their places, by such an instant and overwhelming storm of universal scorn and indignation, as has no precedent in all the political convulsions of our history. There was a time, perhaps, a few years since, when a mild and conciliatory course, on the part of southern writers and speakers, might have delayed, though it could not have stopped, the discussion of the question of negro slavery. But the 'Ercles vein was preferred, and the stale threat of a dissolution of the Union was resorted to. What has been the consequence? Where there was one abolitionist then, there are hundreds now; and instead of a feeble and occasional mention of the subject in a few newspapers, it is now, everywhere, openly, boldly, thoroughly discussed. The day is past, if it ever was, when a party complexion could be given to that great and momentous question, and when politicians, on either side, could be thus deterred from meddling with it, lest it should exercise an untoward influence on mere party objects. The Richmond Whig and the Richmond Enquirer, which seem governed by a spirit of mutual emulation in their efforts to throw the odium of the slavery discussion, each on the opposite party, will yet find that this is an ineffectual way of treating the subject ; they will yet find that *their napkin is too little.*

BEAUTIES OF THE EXCLUSIVE SYSTEM.

[*From the Plaindealer, December* 24, 1836.]

The Independent Republican, published at Goshen, in this state, points out, in the following paragraph, one of the many violations of the equal rights of the people, to which the system of granting special charters of incorporation has led.

"Among the thousand discriminations on our statute books in favour of *associated wealth,* there is none more unjust than that which gives to Railroad Companies the privilege of importing their iron *free of duty,* while every ounce used for agricultural or mechanical purposes is burdened with an impost of 25 per cent. If, however, the amount of duty were the only injury to individual industry resulting from this odious distinction, its evils would be comparatively light. But the exclusive privilege thus granted to incorporated companies, has induced orders to such an extent for railroad iron, that the manufacturers in England have gone almost universally into its fabrication ; thus causing a limited supply for other purposes, and inducing an advance of price equal to at least 50 per cent. It is thus that through a mistaken course of legislation incorporated wealth draws around itself additional immunities, while individual enterprise is cramped by legal disabilities, or burdened by unjust exactions. But the day of exclusive privileges, we trust, is at an end ; and among the first acts of Congress we hope to see an abolishment of that unjust discrimination which now gives to mammoth associations a privilege sedulously withheld from the community at large."

The injustice of this exemption of railroad corporations from a duty which all citizens have to pay, and of its indirect operation to increase the prices of all articles of foreign manufacture in iron, other than irons for railroad tracks, is too obvious to require any illustration. It is too obvious to admit the supposition that Congress, in excepting railroad iron from duty, did not perceive the unequal and unjust effect which the measure would necessarily have. What a view, then, does not this circumstance present of the enormous power which chartered associations already possess, when they can thus openly procure immunities from Congress, at the expense of an imposition of additional taxes and burdens on the people at large—on all not included within the pale of exclusive corporate privileges !

POLITICAL PROSPECTS.

[*From the Plaindealer, December* 31, 1836.]

This number of our paper is issued to its readers on the eve of a new year. Standing at its threshold, let us pause, for a moment, to consider the political character by which it is likely to be distinguished.

"Coming events cast their shadows before;" and an attentive observer may already perceive various pregnant indications of the question relied upon, by the leading spirits of the aristocracy, to keep up the division of parties, and shake the administration of Mr. Van Buren. It may already be seen that the question of a federal bank is to be the great rallying point of the adversaries of democracy. The forces, so signally routed and dispersed by the energy and determination of General Jackson, are gathering again for a new assault, and recombining the elements of their strength. The letters of Mr. Biddle, and the motions and speeches already made, in both houses of Congress, in regard to the imputed causes of the financial pressure experienced by the community, the derangement of the currency, the enormous rates of domestic exchange, and the consequent interruption of many extensive and valuable branches of traffic, are all denotements that point, more or less significantly, to one ultimate object, the re-establishment of a federal banking institution. In what precise form this proposition will come up, and what previous measures will be pursued to convince the people that it presents their only hope of relief from the various evils of a depreciated and discredited currency, are not yet clearly denoted by any of the preliminary steps. It is not probable that the scheme will be openly promulgated during the present session of Congress. It is in embryo, and it will not fairly break the shell, until Martin Van Buren assumes the presidential office.

In the meanwhile, the most sedulous and constant attempts will be made, to excite alarm and distrust; to diffuse the idea that all the evils resulting from overtrading and a frantic spirit of speculation are to be wholly ascribed to the financial mismanagement of the government; and that pecuniary derangement and distress, as it commenced with the prostration of the United States Bank, so it will not terminate till that institution is restored to its original powers and functions. "We must have a national bank!" is the exclamation we already hear in many quarters; and every possible effort, in Congress and out, will be made to strengthen and spread the opinion that a bank, established under federal authority, is the only source to which the community can look for permanent and adequate relief. We have great confidence, however, that the democracy of the country cannot be deceived on this subject. It is hardly possible, in the nature of things, that they can be again exposed to such a wide and desolating financial tempest as that of 1834, when the Bank of the United States, as its last resort, having tried the arts of bribery and cajolery to a prodigious extent, and in vain, poured out its fiercest wrath upon the country, with the view of coercing the people into its measures. They who withstood unshaken the wicked attempts of that period, will hardly be overcome by the efforts which are again about to be exerted against them.

In the engrossing topic presented by the new crusade which the leaders of the various factions of the opposition are devising, all seem to have lost sight of the great man, who was but recently held up to the people as a fit person to fill the chief office of the Confederacy. What has become of General Harrison? Poor man, he has run his course. He has answered, better than could have been expected, the purpose for which he was cruelly dragged from retirement; and having served his little day, as the object "of empty starers and of loud huzzas," he is permitted to slink back into congenial obscurity, where there are "none so poor as do him reverence." We could not but pity the weak old man, when we saw him carried round the country, "as our rarer monsters are," by a set of designing individuals, who, profusely zealous in dishonest homage, cared not a rush for him they pretended to honour, further than the profit they hoped to make by the exhibition.

> ———————— The statesman of the day,
> A pompous and slow moving man, he came.
> Some shouted, and some hung upon his car,
> To gaze in 's eyes, and bless him. Maidens waved
> Their kerchiefs, and old women wept for joy;
> While others, not so satisfied, unhorsed
> The gilded equipage, and turning loose
> His steeds, usurped a place they well deserved,
> Why? what thus charmed them? Had he saved the state?
> No. Did he purpose its salvation? No.
> ——————————But the wane has come,
> And his own cattle must suffice him now.

The bank is the question now, and the popular ear will be dinned no longer with the exploits of the hero of Tippecanoe. *Requiescat in pace!*

It is a happy thing for the cause of true democracy, that the man whom the people have chosen to preside over the Confederation is voluntarily pledged, with the utmost positiveness and solemnity, to oppose, by all the means in his power, the re-establishment of a federal bank, in any shape, or with any limitations that can possibly be devised. We do not think it is possible for language to furnish the materials of a more absolute and comprehensive engagement, than that which Martin Van Buren, of his own motion, solemnly entered into with the people of the United States, as the great condition on which he was willing to accept the office of Chief Magistrate. In his celebrated letter to Sherrod Williams, speaking on the subject of a United States Bank, he says, "*My objection is that the Constitution does not give Congress the power to erect corporations within the states. It is an objection which nothing short of an amendment of the Constitution can remove. It is a historical fact, that the Convention refused to confer that power on Congress, and I am opposed to its assumption by it on any pretence whatever. I am not only willing, but desirous, that the people of the United States should be fully informed of the precise ground I occupy on this subject.*"

In the face of this ample and explicit pledge, there are persons who believe, or affect to believe, that Martin Van Buren will encourage, not openly, but secretly, the views of those who seek to establish another federal bank ; and that he will finally sign a bill to that effect, under the pretext of yielding to the public voice. What measure of his whole life, we would ask, stamps him such a knave and renegade, as to afford countenance to the belief? What act of treachery has he committed of so black a die as furnishes ground for the opinion? What single event is recorded in his history that gives to the slanderous conjecture the least shadow of probability? There is none. Martin Van Buren, "were damned beneath all depth of hell," to use the strong language of Shakspeare, if he had furnished the slightest reason for this wild and most erroneous surmise. He would not only expose himself, by such a course to the scorn and hisses of mankind while he lives, but his memory would stink in the nose of succeeding ages, and his name would be mentionod hereafter only as that of a very paragon of political treachery and falsehood. But the idea is absurd on its face, and is too monstrous even for credulity itself to believe.

The opposition have no hopes of gaining Martin Van Buren over to their purposes. Their object is not to proselyte him, but to destroy him. Their aim is to overthrow the democratic ascendancy and erect a federal bank on its ruins. To this end, they will cast every possible embarrassment in the way of his administration.

They will create all the financial confusion in their power, and exaggerate all that occurs, no matter from what cause, ascribing every difficulty to the want of a great fiscal institution, like that which the veto of General Jackson destroyed. By these constant efforts they hope to effect a gradual change in public opinion, and at last prepare the popular mind to receive a bank created by a two-thirds vote in Congress. We see the beginning of these measures already; but we see it without alarm. They who, like us, entertain a sincere belief in the fundamental maxim of democracy, which, in recognising the right of a majority to govern, acknowledges the capacity and virtue of the people, may contemplate, without apprehension, these renewed exertions of the leaders of a baffled combination of factions. It is the old struggle of the antagonist principles of our government. It is a recommencement of that contest between the aristocracy and the democracy, which has been often waged before, and in which the cause of popular liberty has always triumphed. There is less ground of fear now, than in any previous conflict, that victory will desert those on whom it so long has smiled; since the people more thoroughly understand, than at any former period, the insidious and dangerous nature of all gigantic moneyed institutions, and the enormous power of evil they exercise, when brought into the field to control the political elements of the country.

That the bank question will furnish the line of party division, and the object of party strife, through the coming year, we have not a doubt. The contest will probably be carried on with much excitement and animation, and, in the commercial districts especially, will be marked with that deplorable bitterness and rancour of mutual crimination and retort, which are naturally created by discussions that affect the pecuniary interests of men. But, without claiming the gift of prophecy, we think we can see through the clouds which lower on the political prospect, and discern that the year will terminate auspiciously for the great principles of human freedom, and in the discomfiture of those who desire to restrain the unbiassed expression of the popular voice.

AMERICAN NOBILITY.

[*From the Plaindealer, December* 31, 1836.]

A WRITER, of uncommon eloquence and ingenuity, has appealed, in the columns of the Evening Post, under the signature of *Anti-Privilege,* and has undertaken to prove the unconstitutionality of the restraining law, on the ground that it is a violation of that clause of the federal constitution which declares that *no state shall grant any title of nobility.* It is obvious, from the whole tenor of the article, that this is not undertaken as a mere exercise of ingenuity; but that, "just in his views or not, the writer is in earnest." We have read his remarks with attention, and profess ourselves to be of the opinion he so cogently maintains, that the restraining law is, in effect, if not in letter, a grant of titles of nobility to those whom its provisions protect in their special privileges and immunities. We cannot better appropriate a portion of our space, than by inserting an extract from this able essay.

"It is not merely titles of nobility, as they are defined in England, or France, or Germany, or Spain, that are prohibited by the Constitution, but titles of nobility in the broad and comprehensive import of the term. Now what is it that constitutes *nobility?* Not noble descent. In this all nations and all writers are agreed. Not the possession of large domains. Not hereditable honours.

Not the exercise of high political authority. Not worth, nor wealth, nor talent, nor strength, nor beauty. It is neither of these things. By the unanimous testimony of those who have gathered the true meaning of the word, from the various senses in which it has been used, it signifies a quality, which by virtue of some document put forth by due authority, places the subject of it in the enjoyment of civil rights denied to the mass of the community. A *noble* is defined by English writers to mean 'a person who has a privilege which raises him above a commoner or peasant.' On the continent the word *noble* is less restricted than in England. The French Academy thus define the word : '*Qui par droit de naissance ou par lettres du prince, fait partie, d' une classe distinguée dans l' état.*' 'One who by right of birth, or by patent from the prince, makes part of a distinguished class in the state.' In every part of Europe, it is *civil privilege* which constitutes the nobleman ; and since the progress of intelligence has stripped many of this order of the immunities they once enjoyed, the title of nobility, in numerous instances, is understood to be one of custom and of courtesy only, possessing no validity, because conferring no distinction. Now what is the quality which a charter confers upon the citizens who can obtain it by their merits, their importunities, or their bribes? *Civil privilege*—gainful, enviable civil privilege. Privilege denied to their unchartered brethren. Privilege more valuable by far than the immunities of a German Baron, a French Duke, a Spanish Grandee, or an Italian Prince. Laying political authority aside, there is not in all Europe, (the assertion is deliberately made,) a nobleman among them all, that possesses peculiar privileges as much worth having, as the special civil powers of the Bank Directions of America. Even the banking system of Europe is infinitely more democratic than our own.

Among the moneyed men of the old world, whatever license one has, all have; whatever restriction falls on one, is made to fall on all. But how is it with us?

"Few of our charter-holders have reflected much upon the nature of the privileges they enjoy, and fewer still have felt compunction at the thought that what they are thus enjoying has been denied to the rest of the community. But known to them or not, it is nevertheless true. The want of consciousness of their advantage relieves them from the charge of deliberate exclusiveness. Still the fact is not the less a fact, that the Chartered Bankers of America enjoy favours without a parallel in nobility-ridden Europe. To be an American bank director is to be raised high above the heads of the unchartered million. To be an American bank director is to exercise a prerogative, vast at all times, but at this moment almost princely. It is to wield a power that, if it pleases, may subdue the proud to the most humiliating sacrifices, buy over by timely largesses the venal and the weak, and terrify into submission the gentle and the good. It is to hold the purse-strings of a boundless commerce, with an exclusive right to sell, drop by drop, the natural nutriment of trade. To be an American bank director is to be an American nobleman without the publicity and the disadvantage of the visible decoration. Let me hear the answers to this allegation. It will perhaps be said that a charter is not a title of nobility, because it does not come by right of birth, or by patent from the prince. Was this the meaning of the Constitution when it solemnly decreed that no *state* shall grant a title of nobility? Most surely not. It contemplated noble privileges, emanating from the *legislative* power. It may be urged that a bank charter is not a *title* of nobility, because it only grants exclusive *powers* and not distinctive *appellation*. A state, we shall be gravely told, may grant *nobility* but not *titles of nobility.* It may, for due considerations, lay in the lap of some great family the monopoly of grain, the *regie* of cotton or tobacco, the special privilege of dealing in exchange, or the imperial franchise of printing the acknowledgments of its debts. But it may not deck it with a sounding adjective. It may not designate it "Illustrious," or "Serene." It may grant to the meanest citizen all the prerogatives that make a prince; it may give away for ever the very essence of its sovereignty, but a sonorous epithet it shall not give. It may *make* a man a monarch, but it shall not *label* him a lord. Need I answer an assumption so unspeakably absurd?"

The author of the above new view of a very important subject has promised to continue his speculations, and we hope, for the sake of the public good which such investigations are calculated to effect, that he will redeem his pledge. We have been in the habit for a long time, of speaking very freely on the subject of the exclusive privileges of our chartered aristocracy, and have frequently, for the purpose of bringing the system into disrepute, termed those who are enjoying its advantages, the scrip nobility, and the noble order of the money-changers. The peculiar privileges which they exercise (and exercise very tyrannously at times,) we really considered, in point of fact, fully equal to those of any order of European nobility, and, in their tendency to undermine our democratic institutions, highly insidious and dangerous. But we have not before been led to reflect that the act which constitutes the exclusiveness of these rights and immunities is a grant of titles of nobility, in positive contravention of an express provision of the Constitution of the United States. We tender to *Anti-Privilege* our cordial thanks for the flood of new and useful light he has shed upon this subject.

We have heretofore looked on the restraining law as

an unequal, unnecessary, and unjust restraint on the natural freedom of capital and industry. We shall hereafter look upon it with augmented abhorrence as a positive violation of the Constitution of the United States, in a respect which was meant to guard the American people from the approaches of aristocracy. We have heretofore looked upon banking incorporations, which that law encircles and protects, as possessed of privileges incompatible with the principle of equal rights, a principle which constitutes the very foundation of human freedom. We shall hereafter look upon them with increased aversion, as the possessors of actual titles of nobility, distinguished by more objectionable features than the patents of the European aristocracy; and we shall labour with renewed zeal to enfranchise the community from their degrading subjection to the noble order of the money-changers.

THE INEQUALITY OF HUMAN CONDITION.

From the Plaindealer, December 31, 1836.

THE venerable Sir Thomas More, in a work wherein he has availed himself of the convenient latitude of fiction to utter many important political maxims and opinions, which might not have been tolerated, in his days, had they been put forth in the sober guise of literal truth, has expressed numerous sentiments in regard to the errors and abuses of government, which apply with as much force and accuracy to our times and country, as to his. "Is not that government both unjust and ungrateful," he asks, "that is prodigal of its favours to those who are goldsmiths and bankers, and such others as are idle, and live either by flattery, or by contriving the arts of vain pleasure; and, on the other hand, takes no care of those of a meaner sort, such as ploughmen, colliers, and smiths, without whom it could not subsist? After the public has reaped all the advantage of their service, and they come to be oppressed with age, sickness, and want, all their labours, and the good they have done, is forgotten; and all the recompense given them is that they are left to die in great misery. The richer sort are often endeavouring to bring the hire of labourers lower, not only by their fraudulent practices, but by the laws which they procure to be made to that effect; so that, though it is a thing most unjust in itself to give such small rewards to those who deserve so well of the public, yet they have given those hardships the name and colour of justice, by procuring laws to be made for regulating them."

Who, that knows anything of our legislation, can read this passage, without perceiving that it applies as strongly to the condition of things among ourselves, as if it had been written purposely to describe them, and not those which existed in England three centuries ago? Our government, like that against which the complaint was urged, is prodigal of favours to bankers and others, who choose to live in idleness by their wits rather than earn an honest livelihood by the useful employment of their faculties; and like that, it makes no laws conferring privileges and immunities on the "common people," who look to their industry for their support. The farmers, the labourers, the mechanics, and the shopkeepers, have no charters bestowed upon them; but the only notice they receive from the law is to forbid them, under heavy penalties, from interfering with the exclusive rights granted to the privileged few.

A very casual and imperfect survey of society, in regard to the vast disparity of condition it presents, must satisfy any reflecting mind that there is some great and pervading error in our system. If the inequalities of artificial condition bore any relation to those of nature ; if they were determined by the comparative degrees of men's wisdom and strength, or of their providence and frugality, there would be no cause to complain. But the direct contrary is, to a very great extent, the truth. Folly receives the homage which should belong only to wisdom ; prodigality riots in the abundance which prudence has not been able to accumulate, with all his pains ; and idleness enjoys the fruits which were planted and cultivated by industry. It is not necessary to state these facts in figurative language, in order to render them worthy of serious and attentive consideration. Look through society, and tell us who and what are our most affluent men? Did they derive their vast estates from inheritance? There are scarcely a dozen wealthy families in this metropolis whose property descended to them by bequest. Did they accumulate it by patient industry? There are few to whom an affirmative answer will apply. Was it the reward of superior wisdom? Alas, that is a quality which has not been asserted as a characteristic of our rich. Whence, then, have so many derived the princely fortunes, of which they display the evidences in their spacious and elegant dwellings, in their costly banquets, their glittering equipages, and all the luxurious appliances of wealth? The answer is plain. They owe them to special privileges; to that system of legislation which grants peculiar facilities to the opulent, and forbids the use of them to the poor ; to that pernicious code of laws which considers the rights of property as an object of greater moment than the rights of man.

Cast yet another glance on society, in the aspect it presents when surveying those of opposite condition. What is the reason that such vast numbers of men groan and sweat under a weary life, spending their existence in incessant toil, and yet accumulating nothing around them, to give them hope of respite, and a prospect of comfort in old age? Has nature been less prodigal to them, than to those who enjoy such superior fortune? Are their minds guided by less intelligence, or their bodies nerved with less vigour? Are their morals less pure, or their industry less assiduous? In all these respects they are at least the equals of those who are so far above them in prosperity. The disparity of condition, in a vast multitude of instances, may be traced directly to the errors of our legislation; to that wretched system, at war with the fundamental maxim of our government, which, instead of regarding the equality of human rights, and leaving all to the full enjoyment of natural liberty in every respect not inconsistent with public order, bestows privileges on one, and denies them to another, and compels the many to pay tribute and render homage to the few. Take a hundred ploughmen promiscuously from their fields, and a hundred merchants from their desks, and what man, regarding the true dignity of his nature, could hesitate to give the award of superior excellence, in every main intellectual, physical, and moral respect, to the band of hardy rustics, over that of the lank and sallow accountants, worn out with the sordid anxieties of traffic and the calculations of gain? Yet the merchant shall grow rich from participation in the unequal privileges which a false system of legislation has created, while the ploughman, unprotected by the laws, and dependent wholly on himself, shall barely earn a frugal livelihood by continued toil.

In as far as inequality of human condition is the result of natural causes it affords no just topic of complaint; but in as far as it is brought about by the intermeddling of legislation, among a people who proclaim, as the foundation maxim of all their political institutions, the equality of the rights of man, it furnishes a merited reprehension.

That this is the case with us, to a very great extent, no man of candour and intelligence can look over our statute books and deny. We have not entitled ourselves to be excepted from the condemnation which Sir Thomas More pronounces on other governments. "They are a conspiracy of the rich, who, on pretence of managing the public, only pursue their private ends, and devise all the ways and arts they can find out, first, that they may, without danger, preserve all that they have so acquired, and then that they may engage the poor to toil and labour for them, at as low rates as possible, and oppress them as much as they please."

[*From the Plaindealer, December* 31, 1836.]

A MORNING print in this city, contained a long article, on Wednesday, in which it was maintained, that the right of a free discussion of the question of negro slavery ought to be put down by popular clamour and violence. The writer admits that there is "no remedy at law," and "no constitutional safeguard," against a free discussion of the subject; and therefore recommends to the people, in open and express terms, to silence the opponents of slavery by tumult. The following is the passage:

"Let them crush and overpower their ravings, by noises still louder, and hiss them from the community. We allow the remedy is extreme, but so is the disease. We know that we shall be denounced as the advocate of mobs, just as the popular leaders of the revolution, in this city and elsewhere, were stigmatized as demagogues, because they appealed to the people, when those who made and administered the laws, had not the power, or lacked the patriotism to protect them against their enemies. Be it so: we shall not the less continue to call upon the people, and invoke the popular feeling to rise in self-defence and in defence of their peace and their Union."

"Just as the popular leaders of the revolution were stigmatized as demagogues!" The seditious print desires to place itself in a noble category: but we are glad it admits that the measure proposed *is revolutionary*, and we trust there is strength enough in the laws, and energy enough in their ministers, to teach the leader in theatrical brawls, that he is now laying violent hands on something too sacred to admit of further forbearance. The leaders of the revolution were "popular," because they sought to overthrow a government which denied men "the blessings of liberty;" the leaders of a revolution who seek to overthrow "the blessings of liberty," and establish the worst of tyranny instead, that dreadful despotism which denies the freedom of speech, will, we think, hardly find themselves on the popular side.

"We know we shall be denounced as the advocate of mobs!" Prophetic journal! It sees the sentence that awaits it, as clearly as the felon foresaw his doom when the executioner's cart was carrying him to Tyburn. What a pity to denounce, as the inciter of mobs, the print that only calls upon the people to break tumultuously into the halls where men of worth and intelligence are quietly engaged in grave and lawful deliberations, and drown their proceedings with senseless and frantic clamour! But it advises no violence. Oh no! Tar and feather them a little, tweak their noses, spit upon them, and bestow a few gentle kicks perhaps; but not a jot of violence. Strange, that such moderate counsels should expose one to be denounced "as the advocate of mobs!"

FRANKING PRIVILEGE.

[*From the Plaindealer, December* 31, 1836.]

WE have received a letter from Washington, from a private individual, on his own private business, enclosed in an envelope, franked by a Member of Congress. These frauds upon the government, we have reason to believe, are very common; but as we do not choose to be an accomplice, even after the fact, in a piece of swindling, we shall expose every such instance of cheatery in which it is attempted to make us a participant.

LEADING PUBLIC OPINION.

[*From the Plaindealer, January* 21, 1837.]

THERE are several public journals in this country which, owing to circumstances of position, deserve and receive a good deal of attention from the newspaper press generally, to which very little respect would be due on account of any intrinsic qualities they possess.

What is leading public opinion? Public opinion we take to be composed of the opinions of individuals. When the sentiments of a majority of the thinking men of a community concur, on any given subject, their opinions are the public opinion. Any person who, whether by the mere influence of his character, or by argument, seeks to change, to any extent, the prevailing opinion, or the views of any individual of the prevailing number, may be said, in a certain sense, to assume the character of a leader of public opinion. Every man's example is, in a greater or less degree, a leading influence; and it is not merely the undoubted right, but it is the imperative duty of a good citizen, to do all within the compass of his opportunities, to lead the public opinion aright ; to lead it in the direction which he conceives will most effectually promote general prosperity and social order and happiness.

If this is the duty of a private individual, it becomes, in a much stronger point of view, that of the conductor of a newspaper press. His vocation is emphatically that of a public leader. Its obligations are very imperfectly and impotently discharged, if he confines himself to the mere drudgery of chronicling events. It requires him to maintain principles, investigate measures, expose the evil motives and effects of erroneous public conduct, tear off the veil in which sophistry conceals its object, and assist the cause of truth with every argument that reason can furnish, and every embellishment that fancy affords. To discharge fully the duties of a public journalist would be to elevate the vocation to the loftiest summit of human dignity and usefulness. A public journalist, animated with a due sense of the obligations of his responsible trust, and gifted with the faculties, intellectual and physical, for their adequate performance, would well deserve to be a public leader in a more extended signification of the phrase than that in which we desire it should be understood. He should have a mind filled with a great variety of human learning, and a ready command of all its stores. He should have a head cool, clear, and sagacious; a heart warm and benevolent; a nice sense of justice ; an inflexible regard for truth ; honesty that no temptation could corrupt; intrepidity that no danger could intimidate; and independence superior to every consideration of mere interest, enmity, or friendship. He should possess the power of diligent application, and be capable of enduring great fatigue. He should have a temperament so happily mingled, that while he easily kindled at public error or injustice, his indignation should never transgress the bounds of judgment, but, in its strongest expression, show that smoothness and amenity which the language of choler always lacks. He should, in short, be such a man as a contemporary writer described that sturdy democrat, old Andrew Fletcher, of Saltoun—"a gentleman steady in his principles; of nice honour; abundance of learning; brave as the sword he wears, and bold as a lion; a sure friend, and irreconcilable enemy; who would lose his life readily to serve his country, and would not do a base thing to save it." This is the *beau ideal* of the character of a conductor of a political newspaper.

When Imlac, in *Rasselas*, was in the full torrent of his enthusiastic description of the various qualifications necessary to constitute a poet, he was suddenly interrupted by the Prince with the exclamation, "Enough! thou hast convinced me that no human being can be a poet. Proceed with thy narration." In the same way, the reader may be disposed to interrupt us here, and tell us that we are drawing an outline of an editor which no human being can fill. It is nevertheless the model which all who undertake the vocation should propose to themselves, and according to the degree in which their emulation succeeds is the approbation they deserve. When Cowper described the character of Paul as the object of clerical imitation, it was with no hope that the most devout and diligent of the priesthood could ever fully emulate the excellence of the apostle's character; and it was certainly with no intention of imputing to even the humblest of that class a spirit of arrogance in undertaking the functions of the holy office. In the same way, it seems to us, the charge of arrogance is misapplied, when aimed at those who, like ourselves, have neither the natural nor acquired talents necessary to the most perfect discharge of editorial functions. Circumstances thrust one man into one vocation, and another into another;

and all that can justly be required of him, is that he should exercise with diligence and fidelity such talents and skill as he has, to promote the interests of truth and of his fellow-man. Every physician cannot be a Boerhaave or a Rush; every lawyer a Coke or a Hamilton; nor every newspaper editor an Ames or a Bryant. But it is in the power of every one to be an honest man, and to exert his powers, with constant assiduity and integrity, for the promotion of sound principles of public government, or, in other words, to lead the public opinion aright. The conductor of the humblest newspaper occupies the centre of a circle of larger influence, than more commanding intellects, if shut out from access to the press; and the duty to obey punctually, *but censure freely,* which Jeremy Bentham sets down as a maxim for the government of every good citizen, should be considered especially incumbent upon him.

THE MASSACHUSETTS MADMAN.

Though this be madness, yet there's method in it.—HAMLET.

[*From the Plaindealer, January* 21, 1837.]

THE phrase which we make use of as a title for this article is furnished by the *Albany Argus.*

"It will be seen, by the congressional report, that Mr. Adams, and the abolition members of Congress, have started the old game of agitation in the House of Representatives. No doubt the design is to waste as much as possible of the public time, at this short session, upon a question not less fruitless than mischievous. How discreditable is it to the country, that the *Massachusetts madman* is permitted, not only to outrage all order and decorum in the house, but to scatter incendiary evil and excitement throughout the country!"

What an exquisite sense of "order and decorum" the *Albany Argus* displays! What dignity, what respect for the character which should distinguish the state paper, and what deference for a man who has filled the highest office in our republic, this modestly worded paragraph evinces! There is something in the circumstance of Mr. Adams being *permitted* to make a motion in the House of Representatives, which, we must confess, deserves strong rebuke; and our only wonder is that the *Albany Argus* could so admirably command its temper, as to confine itself to so gentle a reprimand. "The Massachusetts Madman" merits harsher treatment. He should have been denounced, in the bitterest terms, as a bald-headed and paralytic dotard, for the unparalleled audacity he has been guilty of, in presenting a petition of his constituents to the House of Representatives, and asking that it might be appropriately referred. Such atrocious conduct could proceed only from the weakest head and the worst heart; and we are surprised that the *Albany Argus* lets him off so easily. We cannot refrain, however, from inviting the attention of our readers to its paragraph, as a model of newspaper suavity and decorum.

That Mr. Adams is a madman there is medical authority for asserting. A physician being called on as a witness, not long since, in this city, in the case of a trial before one of our courts, in which an attempt was made to prove one of the parties insane, defined madness to consist in conduct or opinions differing from those of the mass of mankind. Mr. Adams differs very widely, alas! from the mass of mankind, both in conduct and opinions, if we are to take the House of Representatives as a fair criterion of public sentiment. He strangely believes that slavery is an evil; that Congress has constitutional jurisdiction, in all respects, over the District of Columbia; that the right of petition is guaranteed to all citizens by the federal compact; and that the right of speech justifies him in expressing his sentiments, even on the tabooed question of abolishing involuntary servitude. To these crazy opinions, he adds the crazy conduct of persisting in expressing them ; and thus comes doubly within the category of madman. To express unpopular opinions, now-a-days, is not only deemed madness, but madness of that aggravated kind which calls for the harshest treatment of bedlam. The soothing system is out of place here. That is proper to be applied only in the milder forms of lunacy. But the man who is so utterly frantic as to express unpopular opinions, should be dealt with somewhat after the fashion that keepers of insane hospitals deal with their raving and delirious patients. Instead of ordinary habiliments, his limbs should be swathed in a species of straight waistcoat—an unguentous integument, composed of molasses and boiling tar ; he should be placed on a diet of rotten eggs ; and for exercise, ridden a few miles, at a sharp trot, on a wooden rail. This is the mode of treatment which the madness of uttering unpopular opinions is considered as calling for, and we faithfully copy the prescription from the latest edition of the Political Pharmacopœia, a chapter of which was transcribed from the *Westchester Spy* in the last number of our paper.

It has been discovered, we believe, of late years, in Great Britain, that a free use of the *halter* is not the best possible mode of preventing petty crimes ; and there are some who will probably question whether *tar and feathers* are a sovereign specific for the disease of abolitionism. Insanity, of the kind which the Massachusetts Madman displays, is certainly wonderfully on the increase. It has got to be an epidemic in the land ; and what is most surprising, cases of the most aggravated description, and in the greatest numbers, occur in those neighbourhoods where the remedial measures have been most energetically applied. We have our doubts even, if some patriotic practitioner, should administer a dose of tar and molasses to Mr. Adams, whether the result would not be, not to effect a cure, but to spread the disease. The operation seems to be somewhat like that of the means adopted by the British Government to plant the Episcopal Church in Ireland, which, according to the London Examiner, have done more to advance the cause of Popery, than could have been effected by a hundred Colleges *de Propaganda.* A hundred thousand undisturbed lecturers on abolition, at all events, could not have done half so much to spread their doctrines, as has been effected by the violence of those who sought to suppress them. They have but pricked the sides of their intent. They have but spurred them to more rapid progress. Their opposition has but inflamed the spirit which it could not vanquish. Like the matadores and picadores of the Spanish national game, their darts and javelins torture, but do not kill, and only exacerbate the spirit of those baited men, who needed no additional impulse to sting them into activity.

The abolitionist, while fastened with galling ligatures to the stake, with his limbs shrinking and shrivelling under a flood of seething tar, if, in that moment of nature's extremest agony, his mind can rise superior to physical torture, has this glorious source of consolation before him: that the pangs he suffers will not be lost, but will awaken, in a thousand bosoms, such sympathy for his sufferings, and such indignation against his persecutors, as will do more than volumes of argument to draw attention to the evils of slavery, and promote the great and holy cause of universal emancipation. Mr. Adams, too, may patiently bear the abuse poured upon him, when he reflects that the feelings it is calculated to arouse in the minds of all honourable men will have a salutary influence in preparing them for a due consideration of those important truths, of which he has shown himself such a fearless champion. The *Albany Argus* has done a service to the cause of freedom, by terming that venerable statesman the *Massachusetts Madman.*

RIGHTS OF AUTHORS.

[*From the Plaindealer, January* 21, 1837.]

We welcome, thrice welcome, the estimable *Veto* to the columns of the Plaindealer, albeit he makes his first appearance as the opponent of views we have but recently and earnestly expressed. But truth is the spark struck out by the collision of opposite opinions ; and as it is truth alone which we desire to elicit, our correspondent is not less welcome than if he appeared on the same side of the argument with ourselves. His communication has commanded our attentive perusal ; and it deserves that of our readers. It proceeds from a mind animated with the most liberal motives, capable of comprehending the largest subjects, habituated to logical investigations, and possessing that power of lucid and perspicuous exposition, which usually distinguishes those who think with accuracy and order. We have read his essay, however, without being convinced of the soundness of its views ; and shall embrace this occasion of adverting to the subject, to state a few reasons for our difference of opinion.

The whole question of the propriety of an international copyright law, or a copyright law at all, resolves itself, we think, into the enquiry whether such a regulation would promote the greatest good of the greatest number. This is the principle which we conceive constitutes the basis of the most important rights of property. They are artificial rights, not rights of nature. They are created by laws, not merely confirmed by them. This is obviously the case with regard to that species of property which the political institutions of all civilized countries regard with peculiar deference, and secure with particular care, and to which the distinctive appellation of *real estate* is given. The right of property in land, like the right to breathe the vital air of heaven, is, by nature, common to all mankind; and the only just foundation of individual and peculiar rights is furnished by the laws of the land. Locke, who goes as far as any writer in tracing the right of property to inherent causes existing anterior to political institutions, does not maintain that any thing gives to an individual a distinct and exclusive right to land, except in as far as by occupying it and mixing his labour with it, it becomes his own in such a sense that you cannot take it away without also taking the fruits of his labour, which, he contends, are his own by nature. Paley, on the contrary, in his book on Relative Duties, considers the law of the land the only real foundation of territorial property.

But let us, in conformity with the opinions of Locke and other accredited writers, concede that men have a natural right of property in the productions of their own industry and skill; that the mechanic, for example, has an exclusive right to the article he manufactures; the fisherman to the fish he catches; and the fowler to the birds he shoots. To the same extent the author has an exclusive natural right of property in the book he composes; that is, he has a natural right to the manuscript, so long as he chooses to retain it to himself. The process by which the mechanic fabricates a particular article is his property, so long as he keeps it secret. The peculiar arts of the fisherman and fowler are their property, in the same way, until they communicate them. And the thoughts of the author are his property, equally, until he publishes them to the world. In all these cases, alike, so far as natural rights are concerned, they then become common property. Every body is at liberty to imitate the article manufactured by the mechanic; to practice the artifices of the fisher and fowler; and to copy the book of the author. Any further exclusive or peculiar property in them has no other foundation than the law.

The right of exclusive property, of the exclusive use and benefit of the fruits of one's own labour, is the great and secure foundation of social order and happiness. Without it, man would never rise above a semi-barbarous condition; and in those communities where it is most securely guarded, we invariably find the highest degree of moral and intellectual refinement, the greatest general prosperity, and the most advanced condition of all the arts which sustain and embellish life. But we would have it understood, in passing, that this important and fundamental right is violated as fatally by unequal laws, by laws which give peculiar facilities for the acquisition of wealth to the few, and deny them to the many, as by those more obviously arbitrary edicts, which directly and openly deprive the labourer of his reward. The true security of the right of property consists in equal legislation.

If we are correct in the position assumed, that the exclusive natural right of an author to his production, like that of a mechanic to the fashion or device of his table or chair, extends no further than to his immediate copy, the question for society then to determine is, whether it is proper to create and guard this right by legal enactments; and the decision of it, in our view of the subject, should rest solely on the consideration of the effect it would have on the interests of the great mass of mankind, or, to repeat Bentham's phrase, it should be decided according to the principle of "the greatest good of the greatest number." It is entirely within the competency of the law to make a literary production property, either absolutely and in perpetuity, or in a qualified sense, and, for a limited period of time. If government should choose to do neither, but leave the published book as free to be copied, as a new device in cutlery, a new style in dress, the author would be without reasonable ground of complaint, since he entered into the vocation without the prospect of any other advantage, than what necessarily and inalienably belongs to the opportunity of the first use of the fruits of his labours.

But if the law undertakes to establish a certain kind of property in the productions of authorship, "in the fruits of intellectual exertion," to use the language of our correspondent, it must fix the limit somewhere; and those intellectual labourers excluded from the vineyard, (and there would necessarily be many such) would then have some reason to complain of partial legislation. The farmer who, by a long and careful study of the processes of nature, discovers an improved method of tillage and culture, by which he can make his field yield a harvest of twofold abundance, ought surely not to be excluded from the category of those who benefit mankind by the fruits of intellectual exertion; yet the neighbouring farmer, who ploughs the adjoining field, copies his mode of tillage, and no one ever thinks of instituting a law to give the first a right of property, and secure to him the exclusive advantages of his discovery. The artist who spends days and nights of patient intellectual toil in devising tasteful and symmetrical patterns for the lace worker and silk weaver, sees the fruits of his intellectual labour copied as soon as they are exhibited; and does not dream of asking the security and advantage of any peculiar legal rights. The natural advantage of the inventor, that he is first in the market, presents a sufficient stimulus to exertion, and secures, in most cases, an adequate reward.

If the principle of copyright were wholly done away, the business of authorship, we are inclined to think, would readily accommodate itself to the change of circumstances, and would be more extensively pursued, and with more advantage to all concerned than is the case at present. It is very much the fashion of the day to deride and decry cheap publications. We are not of the number who can join in the censure. The great good which the invention of printing originally effected, was to diffuse literature, and make books accessible to myriads, who were precluded from them before, by reason of the enormous prices at which manuscript copies were sold, What the first rude efforts of the printing-press were, in comparison with the slow and painful manipulations of the cloistered scribe, the art of cheap printing of the present day is to that art as it was practised by our fathers. It is spreading literature over the entire land. It is penetrating with it into every nook and corner of society. It is offering its golden fruits, ay, richer than gold, to the poor and ignorant, as well as to the rich and educated. It is awakening millions of human beings to a sense of their birthright; to acknowledge that they are God's creatures, and not beasts that perish. We are the friend of cheap literature, for it is the friend of humanity, and is exercising an important influence in the illustration of the most interesting problem of morals, the infinite perfectibility of man. If there were no copyright laws, all literature would take a cheap form, and all men would become readers. It would take a cheap form to preclude competition; and it would be widely diffused because of its cheapness. Instead of an edition of two, or three, or five thousand copies, which never constitute, as a general rule, the maximum of a popular author's success, twenty, thirty, and perhaps a hundred thousand would be readily disposed of. Let us withdraw our attention, for an instant, from a contemplation of the interests of authors, to consider those of mankind at large. Who can fail to see how vastly the general benefit would be promoted? What a noble spectacle an entire nation of readers would present! With what intelligence and order would not its affairs be conducted! And if knowledge is power, what a vast influence it would exercise in the counsels of nations, and in directing the destinies of mankind!

But there is no need that we should throw the interest of authors out of sight in this consideration. On the contrary, we believe the benefit to themselves would be in an equal ratio with that to the community at large. If they were left without the protection of a copyright, their business would assume new forms. They would connect themselves, in schemes of extensive publication, with those whose facilities would put competition at defiance. The advantage of a first copy is in itself incalculable. With publishers of large capital, whose measures are wisely taken, it is worth more than ordinary copyrights. The Harpers, if we are correctly informed, pay British writers, for a duplicate copy in advance of publication in London, as much as some of the copyrights of some of the most favoured authors at home will command. Nobody attempts to reprint the Penny Magazine and Penny Cyclopœdia upon Jackson; simply because, having by arrangement with the British publishers, the benefit of a first copy, he puts it in so cheap a form, and prepares so vast an edition, that competition is intimidated, as it has everything to lose and but little to gain. The advantages of a first sale, when the preparatory steps are duly and discreetly taken, are prodigious. They constitute the author's natural and inalienable right; and we repeat our strong conviction that if he were left alone, the interest of both author and public would be most effectually promoted.

If we are right in the view we have taken of this subject; if it can be shown that the present system is wrong in itself, as tried by the greatest good principle; the argument in favour of the extension of the copyright law, so as to embrace the authors of other countries, falls to the ground. It is the same argument which we constantly hear used in favour of extending the grants of special charters. But if an evil exists in our system, it is the duty of good citizens to endeavour to abolish it, not to make it an excuse for instituting other evils. Our correspondent says truly and eloquently, that there is no ground on which our Congress can be bound to act according to a decision of the House of Lords, nor on which they are not at liberty, setting authority and precedent aside, to revert to the first principles of justice and expediency. Our institutions are founded on a maxim widely different from the fundamental principle of other governments; and it is proper that our legislation should be marked by an equally distinctive character. It is for this young and vigorous republic to set an example to the nations of the old world; and after those glorious principles of equal liberty which constitute the basis of our political fabric, we hardly know a measure which would tend in a larger degree to promote the best interests of mankind, than the enfranchisement of the press from the exclusive privileges of authorship.

OUT, DAMNED SPOT!

[*From the Plaindealer, January* 28, 1837.]

This blot, that they object against your house,
Shall be wiped out in the next Parliament.

SHAKSPEARE.

We expressed, in a very brief paragraph in our last number, our sincere satisfaction that the blot which had been too long suffered to stain the journal of the United States Senate, had at length been expunged, through the persevering and praiseworthy efforts of Mr. Benton. We thank him, from the bottom of our heart, for the constancy he has exhibited in this good cause, and we rejoice most sincerely in the success by which he is at last rewarded.

The resolution upon which the brand of infamy and the sentence of expurgation is now passed, was adopted at a period of unprecedented party excitement. Of those who voted in favour of it, there is probably hardly an individual, who, were the matter to do over, would again record his vote in the affirmative. The judgment of men was blinded at the time by passion. Madness ruled the hour. The questions at issue were of the vastest moment; and they were, besides, precisely of that kind which most effectually appeal to the passions and prejudices of our nature, and most completely drown the still small voice of reason. Never, since the formation of our Confederacy, had any contest arisen, in which the two great antagonist principles that each yielded a grudging assent to the federal compromise, were again brought so thoroughly into active opposition, as in that struggle. The question that called them into strife, too, was a money question—it was one that directly and deeply affected the pecuniary interests of the community. On both sides, and among all classes of people, the war was carried on with the most ruthless fury. In the epidemic frenzy of the period, argument was thrown wholly aside as a useless weapon, and abuse and declamation were greedily snatched up in its stead. The press did all it could to exacerbate the delirium, and the halls of Congress echoed and re-echoed with criminatory and vituperative language, much fitter for the stews than for the council chambers of a great republic. It was during that period of political madness that the resolution was passed, pronouncing the President guilty of having violated the Constitution; and we repeat our firm conviction that, were the act yet to do, under the altered and happier temper of the present time, hardly one who voted for the measure would be willing now to occupy the same ground.

That the resolution condemning the President was unconstitutional, that it was not merely without the warrant of constitutional law, but in direct and palpable violation of the express provisions of the federal charter, seems to us a matter too clear for argument. We should almost as soon think of proving the axioms of geometry, the self-evident propositions of Euclid. It was a violation, moreover, not merely daring and flagitious in its immediate character and object, but, as a precedent, fraught with the direst mischief. If we even admit that to expunge this resolution is also a violation of the Constitution, we think there are few who will deny that, at worst, it is an offence of a far more venial and innocuous kind. One might infer, however, from the solemn and lugubrious protest which Mr. Webster has thought proper to deliver on the occasion, that this expunging process was an act fatal to the liberty of the country. We have seldom met with anything more supremely ridiculous than the stilted, mock-tragedy style of this speech, considered in reference to the occasion which elicited it. It commences in the following manner:

"Mr. President: Upon the truth and justice of the original resolution of the Senate, and upon the authority of the Senate to pass that resolution, I had an opportunity to express my opinions at a subsequent period, when the President's protest was before us. Those opinions remain altogether unchanged.

"And now, had the Constitution secured the privilege of entering a protest on the journal, I should not say one word on this occasion; although, if what is now proposed shall be accomplished, I know not what would have been the value of such a provision, however formally or carefully it might have been inserted in the body of that instrument.

"But, as there is no such constitutional privilege, I can only effect my purpose by thus addressing the Senate; and I rise, therefore, to make that protest in this manner, in the face of the Senate, and in the face of the country, which I cannot present in any other form.

"I speak in my own behalf, and in behalf of my colleague; we both speak as senators from the state of Massachusetts, and, as such, we solemnly protest against this whole proceeding.

"We deny that senators from other states have any power or authority to expunge any vote or votes which we have given here, and which we have recorded, agreeably to the express provision of the Constitution.

"We have a high personal interest, and the state whose representatives we are, has also a high interest in the entire preservation of every act and parcel of the record of our conduct, as members of the Senate.

"This record the Constitution solemnly declares shall be *kept;* but the resolution before the Senate declares that this record shall be *expunged.*

"Whether subterfuge and evasion, and, as it appears to us, the degrading mockery of drawing black lines upon the journal, shall or shall not leave our names and our votes legible, when this violation of the record shall have been completed, still the terms 'to expunge' and the terms 'to keep,' when applied to a record, import ideas exactly contradictory; as much so as the terms 'to preserve' and the terms 'to destroy.'

"A record which is *expunged.* is not a record which is *kept,* any more than a record which is *destroyed* can be a record which is *preserved.* The part expunged is no longer a part of the record; it has no longer a legal existence. It cannot be certified as a part of the proceedings of the Senate for any purpose of proof or evidence."

The play on the words *kept* and *expunged* is worthy of the occasion. As there were no solid reasons to offer against the course which Mr. Benton's resolution proposed, this jingle of antithetical expressions was resorted to as a melancholy substitute for argument, and with most amusing and lackadaisical gravity does Mr. Webster tinkle and clink these two harmless words together, producing all possible dissonance from the clashing of their unsonorous syllables. To expunge is not to keep, and to keep is not to expunge; that which is expunged is not kept, and that which is kept is not expunged: this is the burden of his diatribe. Like Dicky Suett, "he trolls on the stock of those two words, richer than the cuckoo."

We agree with Mr. Webster, that the part of the journal expunged, no matter what the mode in which the act of expunging is performed, or, in a mere literal sense, how complete or incomplete the process, is no longer any part of the record; that it has no longer a legal existence. If not a single letter be effaced or obliterated by the lines which circummure in disgraceful imprisonment the audacious resolution, thus penned up in perpetual infamy, it nevertheless ceases, in a legal sense, to be any portion of the record, as much as if the page which contains it were torn out and consumed in the fire. But in admitting this, Mr. Webster admits somewhat too much for his argument. He admits the constitutionality of the proceeding, and thus his sounding protest, uttered with such "awful state," falls to the ground, the only prop on which it stood being torn away by the same hand that took so much pains to build it up. If the majority of the Senate, in passing the expunging resolution, have transcended their constitutional warrant, the journal is not expunged, but merely blotted; it is no more expunged in a legal sense, than if the Clerk of the Senate had accidentally spattered a little ink upon the page. It can still be certified, for any purpose of proof or evidence, as a part of the proceeding of the Senate; and should it be objected to as having been expunged, the answer obviously would be, that certain unauthorised persons, availing themselves of their right of access to the Senate chamber, had audaciously embraced the opportunity to disfigure the journal of its proceedings. If Mr. Benton and those who acted with him were without constitutional warrant, what they have done is of no great effect in impairing the legal validity of the resolution expunged, than if the same thing had been effected by some mischievous boy in the lumber garret of the capital. The resolution is either constitutionally expunged, or it is not expunged at all.

But we maintain that it is expunged, and we rejoice at it. We maintain that it is expunged, because we think it is susceptible of the clearest proof that the act was fully within the constitutional power of the Senate. We rejoice at it, because the original resolution was a manifest and shameful usurpation of power, expressly prohibited to the Senate by the most imperative terms of the federal charter; and as such ought to be distinguished from all other proceedings, and made conspicuously odious, by such marks of deliberate reprobation as those which now encircle it and are inscribed upon its front. Mr. Webster can find but one meaning to the word *keep*, and that as synonymous with *preserve*. To keep a diary, however, is not to preserve a diary; to keep a set of books is not to preserve them; and to keep a journal is not to preserve it. The meaning of the word, as used in connexion with a written record of any kind, is clearly established by all usage, not as synonymous with *preserve*, but as synonymous with *write*, or *record*. Thus, you say of your clerk, he *keeps* your accounts; though his duty may merely be to *write* or *record* your accounts in a book, of which you retain the custody yourself. Your book-keeper is the recorder of your accounts, not the preserver of your books, which, as a totally separate and distinct office, he may or may not perform. If it had been the intention of the constitution to enjoin the preservation of the journal, and to forbid all subsequent alteration of any portion of the record, the phraseology of the clause would doubtless have been less ambiguous. As it now stands, it presents, according to Mr. Webster's reading, the anomaly of using one word in a double sense. "Each house shall *keep* a journal of its proceedings;" that is, "each shall *write* a journal of its proceedings," and "each house shall *preserve* a journal of its proceedings." This would truly be an instance of singular economy in language, if the framers of the constitution were so solicitous, as Mr. Webster seems to think, to have the clause understood in its twofold import.

We quote another passage from Mr. Webster's "Protest."

"We have seen, with deep and sincere pain, the legislatures of respectable states instructing the senators of those states to vote for and support this violation of the journal of the Senate; and this pain is infinitely increased by our full belief, and entire conviction, that most, if not all, these proceedings of states had their origin in promptings from Washington; that they have been urgently requested and insisted on as being necessary to the accomplishment of the intended purpose; and that it is nothing else but the influence and power of the executive branch of the Government which has brought the legislatures of so many of the free states of this Union to quit the sphere of their ordinary duties for the purpose of co-operating to accomplish a measure, in our judgment, so unconstitutional, so derogatory to the character of the Senate, and marked with so broad an impression of compliance with power.

It would have been edifying if Mr. Webster had condescended to explain, in this connexion, the influences which were employed to procure the passing of the resolution which has now happily been expunged for ever from the record. If we were to admit that the "legislatures of respectable states" have been operated upon in the manner alleged by him, we should still maintain that it was far less shameful to be moved by the influence and power of the President of the United States, than to stand at the beck and nod of the nimble-tongued money-changer, whose largesses and bribes caused so many senators to crouch at his feet, and submissively avow their readiness to perform his behests.

Mr. Webster's speech, as it draws near its conclusion, waxes more and more solemn.

"We make up our minds to behold the spectacle which is to ensue. We collect ourselves to look on, in silence, while a scene is exhibited which, if we did not regard it as ruthless violation of a sacred instrument, would appear to us to be little elevated above the character of a contemptible farce."

He prepares to die with dignity ; to muffle up his face in his senatorial mantle, and fall at the feet of the murdered constitution, which all the while runs blood. But his courage fails him in the trying moment. The conspirators advance—the secretary raises the fatal pen—the imprisoned resolution is shut up in its eternal walls of black—the Constitution is violated—and where is Daniel Webster? He had made up his mind to behold the spectacle ; his heart was as brave as a lion ; but his legs were cowardly, and had ran away with him.

Upon the whole, we are free to say that Mr. Webster made out, in the unpleasant circumstances in which he was placed, quite as well as could have been expected. It was an awkward business he had to perform at best, and the character of a stickler for the Constitution was one in which he was making his first appearance. If he had begun his practice in the part in 1834, he would have avoided altogether the occasion of this last and mortifying display.

As for Mr. Benton, he has redeemed his pledge nobly. He promised, almost in the words we have placed as a motto at the head of this article, that he would pursue that wicked resolution, which condemned the President, without a trial and without a hearing, until it should be effaced from the journal of the Senate. The oath which he took over the violated Constitution was characterized by all the fervour of that of Junius Brutus over the violated body of Lucretia, and faithfully has he kept his vow. He has redeemed the character of the Senate ; he has effaced the disgraceful record ; he has wiped out the "damned spot."

WORDS ARE THINGS.

[*From the Plaindealer, January* 28, 1837.]

"It is understood that General Santa Anna had an interview, with the President of the United States, at the Palace, on Thursday, and was kindly and courteously received by him. They met again, it is said, a second time, yesterday. The subject of this conference may be inferred probably from the tenor of the official papers, of which copies were sent to the Senate on Thursday last."

We copy the above paragraph from the *National Intelligencer*, of last Saturday, for the purpose of animadverting on its phraseology. "Words are things," and by acquiring a habit of using familiarly terms which belong appropriately to a state of things the opposite of those which exist under our institutions, the mind may be gradually led to regard the things themselves with less dislike. The above paragraph is meant as a serious and plain announcement of a fact in which it was thought the public would take an interest. The word *palace*, therefore, as applied to the President's house, is entirely out of place. A palace is a royal residence, the abode of a prince. We have no palaces in this country, as we have no princes. The nomenclature of monarchies and aristocracies is wholly inapplicable to the institutions of a federal democracy. The word *palace* has but two significations; the one literal, a royal residence; and the other figurative, a house pre-eminently splendid. In neither signification is it truly applicable to the President's house, which is simply the abode of a fellow-citizen, having no princely rights or immunities, but merely filling a delegated trust, of limited powers, and for a limited duration of time; and which is besides very far inferior in splendour to the residences of many private citizens. This abuse of words would hardly have elicited attention, and certainly would not have provoked a comment, had we met with it in a newspaper which habitually indulges in the cant dialect of party. We do not know that we should have noticed it had it appeared in one of the vulgar paragraphs of the Globe; but in a journal usually so accurate and circumspect as to manner, as well as matter, in all statements of facts, as the *National Intelligencer*, we own it occasioned us some surprise. If the President's house is to be seriously spoken of as the Palace, the President himself will next be designated by some appellation of royalty. The term *palace,* in this application grates harshly enough on the ear, when it is used in the derisive or ironical language of party exasperation; but in a calm and decorous statement, such as that of the National Intelligencer was doubtless meant to be, of a mere circumstance of personal news, in which it was thought the public would feel an interest, without the slightest reference to party divisions, it seems to us singularly out of place and improper.

FREE-TRADE POST OFFICE.

[*From the Plaindealer, February* 4, 1837.]

A BILL, it will be seen, is now before Congress, reported by the Post Office Committee, the object of which is to carry into effect the recommendation in the Postmaster General's last annual report, on the subject of epistolary communication between the inhabitants of this country and Great Britain. That report, it will be recollected, contained the following passage:

"The attention of the undersigned has been urgently called by the deputy postmaster general of the British North American Provinces to the insecurity of correspondence carried on through the packet ships between Canada and the United States on the one side, and the British isles on the other. Valuable letters and packets sent from Canada through the port of New-York, and from various parts of the United States, never reach their destination. The only effectual remedy which suggests itself, is, a regular mail across the ocean, and a direct connexion between the post offices of the two countries. By a reciprocal arrangement, mails might be interchanged between the post offices in New-York and Liverpool, or any other foreign port, to be conveyed by the packets, or other vessels under contract. The number of letters now crossing the ocean is so great, that a moderate postage on them would pay the cost of their transportation. There is scarcely a doubt that such an arrangement may be effected, if Congress shall think it expedient to grant the necessary power."

This power, we presume, will be granted by Congress, and it is not improbable that the bill will have been passed into a law before these remarks are presented to our readers. It is therefore with no expectation of arresting or changing, in the slightest degree, the course of action on the subject, that we choose it as the theme for our speculations in the present article; but merely because it may answer a useful purpose to invite the reader's mind to a consideration of what constitute the proper functions of political government, and how far the principle of unrestricted competition may be safely left to form its own laws and supply the wants of society.

Everybody must admit that the Post Office, as a branch of the Government, is an institution obviously and inevitably liable to the most prodigious abuses. Under the present system, there are some twelve or fifteen thousand postmasters, holding their appointments directly from one man, and removable at his mere will. Nearly all this numerous army of postmasters, at least a full myriad of them, have subordinates under their control; and if we include in the estimate the contractors, drivers, carriers, and the various other persons more or less dependent for support on the enormous system, it will probably yield an aggregate of not much less than half a million of persons under the immediate direction, to some extent, of a single individual, seated at the head of the federal government. Can any one be so blind as not to perceive, at a glance, that this is a monstrous power, at all times susceptible of being exerted, with the most dangerous effect, for the advancement of objects hostile to the true interests of the people? We do not ask the question with reference to the present, or the past, or any future administration, or with particular reference to any event which has occurred or is likely to occur; but simply in reference to the subject in the abstract, and to the aspect it presents under all the changes and fluctuations of party affairs.

It is not only the vast means of undue influence which the present system gives to a single federal officer, in enabling him, to some extent, directly to control the suffrages of a numerous body of organized dependents; but the facilities it furnishes for the rapid and simultaneous diffusion of political intelligence which it may be desired to circulate, for the obstruction of that of a contrary tenor, and for the exercise of all the arts of political espionage, also render the Post Office, as a branch of government, a dangerous institution. If this is a danger not necessary to be incurred; if the duties which it performs are a matter of trade which might safely be left to the laws of trade; and if the transmission of our letters and newspapers, from place to place, might be submitted, with salutary results, to the operation of the same principles which now secure the carrying of our merchandize and our persons, there are many who will readily admit that the free trade system, as tending to simplify the offices of government and restraining its powers, would be better than one of political regulation. We are ourselves strongly inclined to the belief, that if the clause in the federal charter which gives to Congress the control of the Post Office had never been inserted, a better system would have grown up under the mere laws of trade. The present system, let it be conducted as it may, can never, in the nature of things, be wholly free from political abuses, and is always in danger of being converted into a mere political machine. The abuses which are its inevitable incidents, will necessarily increase from year to year, as the population swells in numbers, and spreads over a wider surface. It must always, managed by political intermediaries and rapacious subordinates, be attended with a vast amount of unnecessary expense; and this expense must be drawn from the people by a method of taxation in utter violation of their equal rights.

Should the history of this Confederacy stretch out for ages, it will probably never exhibit to the world the spectacle of a chief magistrate combining more exalted qualities than distinguish him who now occupies that lofty station. Sincerer patriotism and more unbending integrity no man can ever possess. Sagacity, firmness, restless activity, and unceasing vigilance, are also among his characteristics. Yet even under his administration, what numerous and not unfounded complaints have vexed the the ears of the people of the errors and mismanagement of the Post Offices! Much of the clamour, beyond all question, arose out of party motives, and had no reasonable foundation; but much, on the other hand, was prompted by real delinquency, and was little exaggerated beyond the warrant of truth. If these abuses have existed during the administration of Andrew Jackson, it is not probable that they will not recur under future Presidents. They are inseparable from the system. It is a government machine, cumbrous, expensive, and unwieldly, and liable to be perverted to the worst of uses.

On what principle is the line drawn which separates the matters which are left to the laws of trade, from those which are deemed to require political regulation? The Post Office is established for the purpose of facilitating intercourse by letter between different places. But personal intercourse, though less frequently necessary, is not less positively so, than communication by correspondence. The intertransmission of merchandize is as necessary as either. Why should the government confine its mediation to the mere carrying of our letters? Why not also transport our persons and our goods? These objects, it will be answered, are readily accomplished by the laws of trade, and may therefore properly be left to individual enterprise. But what constitutes this the precise point where the laws of trade become impotent, and where individual enterprise needs to be substituted by political control?

If the clause of the Constitution under which the Post Office establishment exists were struck from the instrument to-morrow, is any one weak enough to suppose that the activity of commerce would not soon supply a system of its own? Modes of conveyance would be instituted at once; they would speedily be improved by the rival efforts of competition; and would keep pace, step by step, with the public demand. It may be said that places far inland and thinly inhabited would suffer by the arrangement. The solitary squatter in the wilderness might not, it is true, hear the forest echoes daily awakened by the postman's horn, and his annual letter might reach him charged with a greater expense than he is now required to pay. But there is no place on the map which would not be supplied with mail facilities by paying a just equivalent; and if they are now supplied for less, it is because the burden of post office taxation is imposed with disproportional weight on the populous sections of the land. But there is no reason why the east should pay the expense of threading with the mail the thick wildernesses of the west, or of wading with it through the swamps and morasses of the south. This is a violation of the plainest principles of equal rights.

The subject of a free trade Post Office presents many considerations which it would be tedious to the reader to pursue to the end in all their ramifications. It is enough for the present that we lay before him a theme of meditation, which will exercise his ingenuity, and afford a not unprofitable incentive to thought. We open the mine, and leave him to trace its various veins of ore. Some of these lay obvious to view. The curse of office-hunting, for example, an inseparable incident of popular government, every year exercises, and in a ratio of prodigious increase, a pernicious influence on the political morals of the country. Under a free trade system of post office business this epidemic evil would necessarily be abated in a vast degree. But would you withdraw, it may be asked, the stimulus which our post office system, by extending mail routes through the wilderness, furnishes to emigration; which provokes a spirit of enterprise to explore the wilds of the west, and to plant colonies in the interminable woods and on the boundless prairies; which causes towns and villages to spring up where the wolf howled and the panther screamed but the week before; and covers with the activity of social life and industry the desert which, but for the impulse furnished by the government, would continue desolate and solitary for ages?

We have no hesitation to answer in the most direct

and unequivocal affirmative. All government bounties, of every shape and name, are as much opposed to our notions of the proper freedom of trade, as government restraints and penalties. We would withdraw all government *stimulants*, for they are bad things at best. But let no man suppose the progress of improvement would be thus retarded. Its direction might be changed, but its advance would be unobstructed. The country would continue to grow, from year to year, not less rapidly and more healthfully than now. Instead of the forcing system, which exhausts the soil, and brings forth only sickly and immature productions, we should merely adopt one of nature and of reason. We should merely leave water to flow in its proper channels, instead of endeavouring to compel its current, without reference to the laws of gravitation. The boundaries of population would still continue to enlarge, like ripples on a sheet of water, circle beyond circle; but they would not be forced into unnatural irregularities, and to shoot out this way and that, according to the schemes of politicians and speculators, who, through interested agents in the halls of Congress, should choose to open roads and penetrate with the mails into places which, if left to the natural course of things, would sleep for centuries in the unbroken solitude of nature.

The project now before Congress, to which we adverted in the outset of this article, is liable to no objection, in our view, except that it adds new complication, and gives greater extent and firmness to the post office system under its political organization, thus rendering more distant and feeble our present slight prospect of economic reform.

THE NEWSPAPER PRESS.

[*From the Plaindealer, February* 4, 1837.]

By thee, religion, liberty, and laws,
Exert their influence, and advance their cause;
By thee, worse plagues than Pharaoh's land befell,
Diffused, make earth the vestibule of hell;
Thou fountain, at which drink the good and wise,
Thou ever bubbling spring of endless lies!

COWPER.

NOT long since, we enriched our columns with a liberal extract from a pamphlet by Dr. Channing, on the subject of abolition.

The sentiments expressed in this extract are those of a calm and philosophical mind, elevated high above the mists of passion and prejudice, and looking down on the strife and turmoil with a benignant spirit, desirous only that the struggle may result in promoting the permanent interests of truth and virtue. The importance of the newspaper press to effect this object are not overrated; and the difficulties which embarrass its action, and render it less efficient for good, than it is capable of being rendered, are stated with accuracy, clearness, and force.

The power of the newspaper press in this country, and more particularly of the diurnal press, is prodigious; and every man, touched at all with the divine enthusiasm of philanthropy, must join in the wish expressed by Dr. Channing, that it might be placed, to a greater extent than it is, in the hands of men of superior ability and stern independence, who would take truth and public utility as their sole guides of conduct. That this is not the case, is the fault, not so much of those immediately connected with the press, who, generally, are absolutely dependent on the fruits of their labours for support, and

17*

whose necessities therefore compel them to consult the very prejudices of the public, as it is of those affluent men of intelligence, integrity, and independence, sprinkled through every community, who, by association, have it perfectly in their power, without any sacrifice of means, to establish newspapers on such a basis as would enable them to stand, unshaken, assaults of prejudice, now fatal to them in the unassisted hands of single and comparatively indigent individuals.

They manage this important branch of public business much better in England than we do here. The principal newspapers there are joint-stock property, many of them having hundreds, and some of them, we believe, even thousands of owners, whose interests are attended to by a committee of directors of their own selection. The editors and editorial subordinates are employed at liberal salaries, and are rendered wholly independent of the proprietors, within a wide limit of general principles. Men of superior intellectual and moral characters are selected to fill those stations ; and the consequence of the system is, that the London newspapers, notwithstanding all the restrictions on the press which there exist, are conducted with a much higher degree of intelligence and independence, than characterize the journals in any of the principal cities on this side of the ocean. If the limits to which we are obliged to confine ourselves permitted, we might illustrate our remark by instances on all the main questions which have occupied the public mind of Great Britain for ten years past. On this very question of slavery, which has drawn forth Dr. Channing's remarks, the English press generally exhibited a degree of fearlessness and true independence, that have but few parallels among the journals of our own country. The influence they exercised on public sentiment, and on legislative action, was immense ; and it was an influence for good, not for evil, as is proved by the auspicious result.

Among us, the newspapers are the property of single individuals; and as it is found that administering to the depraved tastes and appetites of the community, consulting the passions and caprice of the hour, and guiding their course by the variable breath of the multitude, is a more profitable, as well as an easier task, than steering undeviatingly by fixed principles, referring all subjects to the touchstone of truth, and addressing themselves with inflexible constancy to the judgments of men, it is not to be wondered at, however much it is to be deplored, that they adopt the readiest and most lucrative mode of discharging their functions, and forego the glorious opportunity their vocation affords, of effectually advancing the great interests of mankind.

The censure falls with greater weight on the community, than on newspaper conductors. They "who live to please, must please to live." Their business, their very being, is held by a tenure too frail, to allow of their stemming the rough current of popular opinion. There is a deficient moral sense in the public which lies at the bottom of the evil. He who strives to be a reformer, and to discharge his high trust with strict and single reference to the responsibilities of his vocation, will be sadly admonished by his dwindled receipts that he has not chosen the path of profit, however much he may be consoled by knowing it is that of honour. We might point to the daily newspaper press of this city, morning and evening, for exemplifications of our remark. The journal, of both classes, which has notoriously the largest and most profitable support, is not that which is conducted with the highest intelligence or the purest morality. It is as true now, and in reference to this particular subject, as it was in the days of Juvenal, and in the more general application of the poet, that,

———Probitas laudatur et alget:
Criminibus debent hortos, prætoria, mensas,
Argentum vetus, et stantum, extra pocula caprum.

———Worth is praised and starves:
While vice, with gardens, villas, costly boards,
Rare plate, and cups embossed, the world rewards.

How is the evil to be remedied? How is the newspaper press to be rendered what it can and should be? Are there not a hundred readers of this journal, in whose minds the question awakens a ready response? How many men of moderate affluence would it require to form a joint-stock association, with a capital of fifty or a hundred thousand dollars? For any ordinary purpose of trade, which held out a reasonable prospect of reward, a larger sum would be subscribed in a moment. But such a newspaper as such a sum, judiciously expended, might establish, would be sure to yield a fair return in money, and oh! what a large return in public good!

DIVINE ORIGIN OF SLAVERY;

OR MR. CALHOUN'S VERSION OF THE DECREES OF PROVIDENCE.

[*From the Plaindealer, February* 4, 1837.]

Is there—as you sometimes tell us—
  Is there One who dwells on high?
Has he bid you buy and sell us,
  Speaking from his throne, the sky?
Hark! he anwers; wild tornadoes,
  Strewing yonder coast with wrecks,
Wasting towns, plantations, meadows,
  Are the voice with which he speaks.

Our readers will see, in our summary of the proceedings of Congress, that when the petition of certain inhabitants of the District of Columbia was before the Senate last week, asking for an act of incorporation for the District Colonization Society, Mr. Calhoun assumed the ground that slavery has been brought about, in this country, by the special interposition of heaven, and that to endeavour to emancipate the negroes is rebellion against the will of God. "A mysterious Providence," he said, "had brought the two races of men together into this country from different parts of the earth; the European to be the master, and the African the slave. These relations could not be overthrown; and every society founded on the principle of separating them acted on the basis of error."

According to this version of the origin of negro slavery in America, the free states have committed a grievous sin in breaking the fetters of the poor negro, and they might better make all haste, if they would avoid the retributive wrath of heaven for their wickedness, to replace him in bondage. The men who carried on the slave trade, too, instead of having been the inhuman wretches the world has generally accounted them, were ministers of divine Providence, commissioned to bring together, in the new world, the European and African race, to fill their pre-ordained capacities, the one as masters, the other as slaves. When those fierce kidnappers stole the poor untutored black man, as, unconscious of danger, he reclined, in the cool of the evening, beneath his native palm tree, inhaling the night breeze from the ocean, and listening to the refreshing music of the waves breaking on the shore, they committed no act of treachery or cruelty, but executed a holy office, by the especial appointment of God, whose canon, "thou shalt not steal," and whose precept, "love thy neighbour as thyself," were suspended to permit the deed. When they crowded the poor negroes into the suffocating holds of their ships, loaded their galled limbs with fetters, fastened them down to the deck, and hushed their cries of agony and despair with sharp instruments of torture forced between their distended jaws, they were still agents of mercy, in a rough disguise, and still faithfully performing their allotted part in the mysterious designs of Providence. The relationship into which the wretched Africans were brought by these means with the European race in America, was not for a day, nor a year, nor a century, as we are assured by Mr. Calhoun, but for all time; and they who undertake, by any means, to overthrow it—to sunder these heaven-wove ties—are guilty of attempting to violate the clear intentions of Omnipotence.

Strange as this doctrine may sound to some of our readers, it is not original with Mr. Calhoun. It was proclaimed with equal energy in Great Britain, many years ago, when certain incendiaries and lunatics set about the wicked project of abolishing the African slave trade. They were warned, almost in the language which Mr. Calhoun now uses, of the iniquity of their attempt. They were assured that its flagitiousness was only equalled by its impracticability; that, like the warfare of the fallen angels against the hosts of heaven, it would result in displaying at once the enormity and the utter impotence of the effort; and that, in the end, they would be hurled

> With hideous ruin and combustion, down
> To bottomless perdition.

We have a volume this moment lying before us, (Boswell's Life of Johnson) in which, on this very subject, the following passage meets our eye:

"I beg leave to enter my most solemn protest against his (Dr. Johnson's) general doctrine with respect to the slave trade. For I will resolutely say, that his unfavourable notion of it was owing to prejudice, and imperfect or false information. The wild and dangerous attempt which has for some time been persisted in to obtain an act of our legislature, to abolish so *very important and necessary a branch of commercial interest*, must have been crushed at once, had not the insignificance of the *zealots*, who vainly took the lead in it, made the vast body of planters, merchants, and others, whose immense properties are involved in that trade, reasonably enough suppose that there could be no danger. The encouragement which the attempt has received excites my wonder and *indignation*; and though some men of superior abilities have supported it, whether from a love of temporary popularity when prosperous, or a love of general mischief when desperate, my opinion is unshaken. To abolish a *status*, which in all ages God has sanctioned, and man has continued, would not only be *robbery* to an innumerable class of our fellow-subjects, but it would be extreme cruelty to African savages, a portion of whom it saves from massacre, or intolerable bondage in their own country, and introduces into a much happier state of life; especially now when their passage to the West Indies, and their treatment there, is humanely regulated. To abolish that trade would be to

'——shut the gates of mercy on mankind.'

"Whatever may have passed elsewhere concerning it, the House of Lords is wise and independent:

'Intaminatis fulget honoribus;
Nec sumit aut ponit secures
Arbitrio popularis auriæ.'

For the benefit of the unclassical reader, we will thus translate this scrap of Latin, which, by the way, in the original, (one of the odes of Horace,) is said of *virtue*, a much fitter application of the sentiment, than to the House of Lords, in its aspect as the protector and champion of the slave trade.

> ' In stainless honours bright it shines,
> The axe nor seizes nor declines,
> At the vain rabble's breath.'

But the House of Lords, notwithstanding this classical compliment, did yield at last, if not to the variable popular breeze, to the steady and strong tempest of indignation which the horrors of the slave trade provoked throughout the kingdom of Great Britain. It was no shifting and transitory wind of doctrine ; but it had all the force and constancy of truth. It blows yet, freshly and steadily, from the same quarter, and will not subside into a calm, until it has swept every vestige of slavery from the civilized world. This is no *popularis aura*, no transient humour, no temporary excitement, no evanescent flame, rising suddenly into great volume, as suddenly to sink and smoulder in the thin ashes of unsubstantial fuel. It is a wind and a fire of a different description. It comes from the land of the tornado and hurricane.

> ——*Mugiat Africis*
> *Malus procellis.*

It cracks the mast of the labouring bark with an *African* storm. The gale is laden with the groans of slavery and the shrieks of despair. Are these the sounds in which Mr. Calhoun distinguishes the mysterious decrees of Providence that he construes as injunctions to hold his wretched fellow-beings " guilty of a skin not coloured like his own," in perpetual and irremediable bondage ?

Do these furnish the warrant to buy and sell his brother man, like cattle, in the shambles? He will yet learn that the voice of this moral whirlwind, like that of the natural one described by Cowper, is susceptible of a different interpretation. He will learn that it was no part of Providence to create one race of men as bondmen for another; and that ere long, unless the chains which bind the slave are cast off, goaded at last to madness, in a despairing effort, he will rend them asunder. Who shall answer for his moderation in the first drunkenness of sudden freedom? Well for the master will it be if in that hour he become not the victim.

TREASON AGAINST THE STATE.

From the Plaindealer of Feb. 4, 1837.

THE reader who noticed that Mr. Shepard had introduced a bill into the Assembly of this state, on the subject of slavery, which that body refused to entertain at all, or even order to be printed, may very naturally have concluded that it contained some revolting and monstrous proposition. It is not at all likely, however, that his mind can have fully conceived the unparalleled atrocity of Mr. Shepard's design. It was no less than to abolish slavery in the state of New-York! Here is the diabolical document in his own words:—

"No person shall hereafter be held to service or labour, as a slave, or as the child of a slave, within this state; every person now held to such service or labour, within this state, is hereby discharged therefrom, and is henceforth free. Every person born, or who shall hereafter be born within this state, is, and shall be free; and every person held to service or labour as a slave, or as the child of a slave, who shall be imported, introduced, or brought into this state under any pretence whatever, shall be free. So much of the revised statutes of this state, as is inconsistent with the intent and meaning of the preceding section, is hereby repealed."

This is the naked proposition of Mr. Shepard in all its wickedness. He has been guilty of an effort to make this state really and thoroughly free ; to diffuse the spirit of freedom through its very atmosphere, and impart to its soil a quality of corrosion that should eat into the fetters of the slave, and cause them to drop from his enfranchised limbs. He would do for this state what the spirit of liberty has done for England.

> " Slaves cannot breathe in England ; if their lungs
> Receive our air, that moment they are free ;
> They touch our country and their shackles fall."

This is the unhappy condition to which Mr. Shepard desired to reduce this state, in utter disregard of the " domestic institutions " of the southern slaveholder, when, with his negroes at his heels, he chooses to honour us with his presence ; and in utter disregard of the mysterious providence of God, in foreordaining, as we are assured by Mr. Calhoun, the European and African races to meet upon this continent, and become indissolubly united in the tender and endearing relations of master and slave. It was probably in reference to this latter view of the subject that the Assembly so promptly refused to have anything to do with Mr. Shepard's bill. " What God joins together let not man put asunder." In the true spirit of liberty, not less than of religion, they extend this injunction beyond the matrimonial connexion, to that which exists between the slaveholder and the poor negro, and frown indignantly on every attempt to sunder or weaken the heaven-appointed union. What " true friend of the constitution," or jealous defender of the "blessings of liberty," can regard the attempt of Mr. Shepard as better than high treason against the state?

THE RIGHTS OF AUTHORS.

[*From the Plaindealer, February* 11, 1837.]

ABLE pens are wielded against us on the subject of literary property. But as we have no end to answer which is not equally that of truth, we insert the arguments of our antagonists with as much readiness as our own, certain that the ultimate result of discussion, in this, as in regard to every topic within the embrace of human reason, must be the establishment of sound principles. We should shrink dismayed from the correspondent whose communication deservedly fills a large space in our present number, if we were not doing battle on what we yet esteem, notwithstanding his powerful and perspicuous reasoning, the right side of the question. If the reader knew the estimable source of that article, the knowledge would add unneeded influence to the intrinsic weight of its opinions, and extort a smile, perhaps, at our temerity in disputing the field with such an opponent.

The *American Monthly Magazine*, too, in its last number, assails our opinions on the copyright question, in an article written with characteristic eloquence and generous zeal.

It is true that too many of those whose genius has rendered them immortal, have employed their noblest efforts to embellish the solid structure which tyranny erects on the prostrate liberties of man. The two divinest bards, that ever addressed their strains of undying harmony to the enraptured ears of mortals, were the flatterers and upholders of aristocratic pride, and the scoffers of the rights of the people. Homer and Shakspeare "licked absurd pomp," and taught men to regard as a superior order of beings those whose only claims to pre-eminence were founded in rapine and outrage. But when we look back through the bright list of names which English literature presents, we do not find this censure to be of general application. He from whom the remark is derived, as to the potent influence of those who frame a nation's ballads in forming the national character—sturdy old Andrew Fletcher of Saltoun—did not address himself to a caste; he addressed himself to the people, and stood forward ever the eager and intrepid champion of their rights. Milton did not address himself to a caste, but to mankind; and Marvell and Harrington were animated in their writings by the single and exalted motive of improving the political condition of their race.

But we need not contest the sentiment to which we have offered this brief reply, since it does not touch our argument. It is for the very purpose that "the Republic of Letters" may be upheld by *the people*, and that it may be composed *of* the people, that we desire to see the principle of literary property abrogated. We do not wish to deny to British authors a right; but we desire that a legal privilege, which we contend has no foundation in natural right, and is prejudicial to "the greatest good of the greatest number," should be wholly annulled, in relation to all authors, of every name and country. Our position is, that authors have no natural right of property in their published works, and that laws to create and guard such a right are adverse to the true interests of society. We concede at once, and in the fullest manner, that if the propriety of establishing a right of property in literary productions can be shown, the principle ought to be of universal application; that it ought not to be limited to any sect, or creed, or land, but acknowledged, like the plainest rights of property, wherever civilization has extended its influence. An author either has a natural and just right of property in his production, or he has not. If he has, it is one not to be bounded by space, or limited in duration, but, like that of the Indian to the bow and arrow he has shaped from the sapling and reeds of the unappropriated wilderness, his own exclusively and forever.

With regard to the influence which British literature exercises in forming the popular mind and character in this country, we see no cause to fear unfavourable results, if American literature, to which we naturally look to counteract the evil tendencies of the former, is not excluded, by reason of the incumbrance of copyright, from an equally extensive circulation. Leave error free to flow where it listeth, so that truth is not shut out from the same channels. Give both an equal opportunity, and who can doubt to whom will belong the victory? "Who knows not," says John Milton, "that truth is strong, next to the Almighty? She needs no policies, nor stratagems, nor licensings, to make her victorious. Those are the shifts and the defences that error uses against her power." It was under the influence of British literature exclusively, and in many instances of education obtained in British colleges, that our national independence was asserted and achieved; and it would be strange, indeed, if we should be rendered now unmindful of its value, by the tawdry and sickening aristocracy which bedizens the pages of British novels and romances. "The men who write the ballads" are not those whom a copyright stimulates into the exercise of their powers; and if they were, the Americans, thank heaven! are not the people whom ballads move with irresistible influence. We go to our political affairs, as mathematicians go to their abstruse labours; with their intellectual energies screwed to too high a pitch, to be shaken from their purpose by the sounding of brass or the tinkling of cymbals.

We turn now to a consideration of the article of our correspondent, who has ingeniously erected his structure of logical arguments on a foundation furnished by ourselves. Our position that an author has an exclusive natural right of property in his manuscript, was meant to be understood only in the same sense that a mechanic has an exclusive natural right of property in the results of his labour. The mental process by which he contrived those results are not, and cannot properly be rendered, exclusive property; since the right of a free exercise of our thinking faculties is given by nature to all mankind, and the mere fact that a given mode of doing a thing has been thought of by one, does not prevent the same ideas presenting themselves to the mind of another and should not prevent him from a perfect liberty of acting upon them. The right which we concede to the author is the right to the results of his manual labour. The right which is claimed for him is the right to the ideas which enter into his mind, and to which he gives a permanent and communicable form by writing them down upon paper.

But when we pass from corporeal to incorporeal property, we immediately enter into a region beset with innumerable difficulties. The question first naturally arises, where does this exclusive right of property in ideas commence? The limits of corporeal property are exact, definite, and always ascertainable. Those of incorporeal property are vague and indefinite, and subject to continual dispute. The rights of corporeal property may be asserted, without the possibility of infringing any other individual's rights. Those of incorporeal property may obviously give rise to conflicting claims, all equally well founded. If you catch a fish in the sea, or shoot a bird in the forest, it is yours, the reward of your patience, toil, or skill; and no other human being can set up an adverse claim. But if you assert an exclusive right to a particular idea, you cannot be sure that the very same idea did not at the same moment enter some other mind. This is obviously and frequently true with respect to single thoughts, and it will readily be conceived that it may happen with respect to a series. Language is the common property of all mankind, and the power of thought is their common attribute. Shall you then say to a person who has expressed certain ideas in certain words, you shall have an exclusive right of property in those ideas so expressed, and no other human being shall ever use the same sentiments, without incurring a penalty for his tresspass?

If the author has a natural right of property in the ideas of his mind, once committed to paper, it is a right which ought to be universally acknowledged, and he should be allowed to enjoy exclusively the profit of the use of his property in every civilized nation of the world. But where does this right commence? How many ideas must be joined together before they constitute a property? If a man construct an edifice, every brick or board of the entire fabric is his. He may sell it, or lend it, or convert it to what use he will; but no one can take it against his consent without committing a robbery. Is the author's edifice of ideas equally his, in its component materials, as well as in their aggregate combination? Every sentence, perhaps, contains an idea, so natural that it is likely to occur to many minds, and expressed in such obvious language, that the same terms substantially would probably suggest themselves to all. His work is made up of such sentences. In what then consists his right of property? Is each particular sentence a property? Or do they not become property until joined together?

But the subjects of books are various. Some are flights of imagination; some are records of facts. In one, history relates her sober details; in another, science demonstrates his abtruse propositions. In all these, intellectual labour is exerted; but is the fruit of that intellectual labour property in all cases alike? Are the meditations of the poet property in the same sense with the calculations of the mathematician; and has each an exclusive right to the results of his labour? Before you answer this in the affirmative, you should reflect that the processes of mathematical calculation are the same throughout the world, and that the end aimed at by them is also identical. A book of mathematics is a book of calculations, conducted according to certain invariable and universally acknowledged principles; and though to compose it requires perhaps intense intellectual exertion, yet it calls for no original ideas or discoveries. Two mathematicians, one in France, for instance, and the other here, may easily be supposed toiling through the same processes at the same moment, and accomplish results exactly the same. Which has the exclusive right of property in his production? Which shall be permitted to publish his book, and proclaim to the other, and to all the world, I alone am invested with the rights of authorship?

Many of the most interesting and valuable works are mere records of discoveries in experimental science. But two philosophers may at the same time be engaged, in different parts of the world, in the same series of experiments, and may both hit on the same result. The discovery, as mere property, is only valuable perhaps through the medium of publication; yet shall the right of publishing be restricted to one, and if the other presume to tell the same philosophical facts, shall he be considered a species of felon? The law of patents rests confessedly on the same principle as the law of copyright. They both pretend to have natural and obvious justice for their foundation. The inventor of a new application of the principles of mechanics claims a right of exclusive property in the fruit of his intellectual labour, not less than the writer of a poem or a play. Yet some of the most valuable iuventions which have ever been given to mankind have been produced simultaneously, by different minds, in different parts of the world. It is uncertain to this day to whom men are indebted for the application of the magnetic needle to navigation; and the honour of the discovery of the art of printing is yet a matter of dispute. While Franklin was pursuing his electrical experiments in Philadelphia, the philosophers of Paris were engaged in similar investigations, and with similar success. Rittenhouse, when he planned his complicated and ingenious *Orrery,* knew not that such an instrument had already been completed, which was destined to perpetuate the name of its inventor. Newton and Leibnitz each claimed the exclusive honour of their method of fluxions; and many more instances might be adduced, if we had leisure to pursue the subject, of such jarring and incompatible claims to exclusive property in the fruits of intellectual labour. The cases we have stated will sufficiently show that there cannot be, in the nature of things, a positive and absolute right of exclusive property in processes of thought, which different minds may be engaged in at the same moment of time. Two authors, without concert or intercommunion, may describe the same incidents, in language so nearly identical that the two books, for all purposes of sale, shall be the same. Yet one writer may make a free gift of his production to the public, may throw it open in common; and then what becomes of the other's right of property?

The remarks which we have thus far offered go merely

to assail the position of the natural right of property in ideas, as existing anterior to law, or independent of it. It is essential to the establishmeat of such a natural right, that it should be shown to be distinct property, which absolutely and wholly belongs to some one individual, and can belong to no other than he. The labour of your hands belongs to you; for no other individual in the world performed that labour, or achieved its particular results. But the labour of your mind can produce only ideas, which may be common to many minds, and which are not susceptible of being distinguished by marks of peculiar property. Another person falling, under similar circumstances, into the same mood of cogitation, may produce ideas—not merely similar—not another set of perfect resemblance to the first—not a copy—but identically the same. There is an inherent difficulty in fixing limits to incorporeality. The regions of thought, like those of the air, are the common property of all earth's creatures.

We do not offer the crude observations which we have here made as a full answer to our correspondent's argument; for we mean to reserve the question for a more deliberate and careful discussion in another number. But we merely put them forth as some of the reasons which lead us to deny that the author and inventor have any property in the fruits of their intellectual labour, beyond that degree in which it is incorporated with their physical labour.

A VIOLENT STORM AT WASHINGTON.

[*From the Plaindealer, February* 11, 1837.]

Blow wind and crack your cheek! rage! blow!
You cataracts and hurricanoes, spout
Till you have drench'd our steeples, drown'd the cocks!
You sulphurous and thought-executing fires,
Vaunt couriers to oak-cleaving thunderbolts,
Singe my white head!
Here I stand
A poor, infirm, weak, and despised old man:
But yet I call you, servile ministers!

SHAKSPEARE.

BOTH houses of Congress, on Monday last, exhibited a stormy scene. In both, the question of the abolition of slavery was the cause of commotion, and it came up in both on the presentation of memorials: thus showing how utterly absurd is the attempt of the southern members, and of those recreant men of the north who colleague with them, to stave off discussion, and stifle the freedom of speech. In the Senate, Mr. Calhoun put himself prominently forward again, as the champion of slavery. This statesman has many properties which force the mind continually to draw an analogy between him and the chief of the fallen angels, as described by Milton. "Bad ambition" is his prevailing characteristic, and his desire to rule engrosses every sentiment and motive of action. In regard to slavery, he unscrupulously stands forward as the asserter of the most monstrous and startling paradoxes. He is not content to speak of slavery as an incurable ill, entailed upon the southern states by a former race of men, which they are now obliged to endure, as there is no mode of remedy that is not worse than the disease; but he avows, in the most positive and authoritative manner, that slavery is not an evil; that it is a heaven-appointed institution: that it is a condition attended with the happiest and most benign results to both masters and slaves, to both the European and African race; and that he who would put an end to it is not only an enemy to the south, but to the great cause of human happiness. Such was the tenor of Mr. Calhoun's remarks last Monday; and Mr. Rives, by admitting slavery to be an evil, drew down upon himself from the dictatorial Senator a rebuke so sharp as to sound almost like a malediction. Mr. Calhoun was not content with eulogizing the happy and Arcadian condition of the slaves of the south, but he must needs launch derisive and scornful epithets at those whom he was pleased to consider as *the white slaves of the north*, namely, the honest and free labourers, who earn their livelihood by voluntary and requited toil, working when they please, and for whom they please, and when they please resting from their labours. Mr. Calhoun must know very little of human nature, if he is not aware that remarks of this kind aggravate, rather than check, the zeal of those engaged in the cause of abolition. He must know still less of human nature, if he supposes that the insolence and indignity with which the prayers of thousands of respectable petitioners are treated, are calculated to abate their zeal in the cause in which they have engaged. Violence and contumely are not the weapons by which enthusiasm is turned aside from its object. They who madly stamp upon a fire, but anger its sparks to fly into their own faces. "Obstructing violence" (such is the language of the Areopagitica) "meets, for the most part, with an event utterly opposite to the end which it drives at. Instead of suppressing sects and schisms, it raises them and invests them with reputation." Mr. Calhoun's course in regard to abolition is strongly calculated to have this effect.

The tempest raged much more furiously in the House of Representatives than in the Senate, and Mr. Adams, the MASSACHUSETTS MADMAN, as the *Albany Argus* terms him, was the chief object of its fury. This gentleman had the audacity to ask the Speaker if a petition which he held in his hands, purporting to come from certain *slaves*, was to be considered as embraced in the resolution adopted on the 10th of last month, to the effect that all petitions and memorials, relating to the subject of slavery, directly or indirectly, should be laid on the table without discussion. We are free to admit that we do not entirely approve the course taken by Mr. Adams on this subject. Slaves have no absolute constitutional right of petition; and to offer a petition from such persons, therefore, or bring it in any way to the attention of the house, was calculated to excite angry feelings, without the warrant of that clear and indisputable right on which Mr. Adams has stood secure in all his previous proceedings. He had a most undoubted right to ask the question of the admissibility of the petition, however; and the violence which the simple inquiry gave rise to is a strong illustration of the unhappy temper of the south, in relation to a question which must and will be discussed, and which every attempt to put off by violence but causes to be pressed upon them with more earnestness and zeal. It is strange that they should be infatuated to such a degree of blindness on this subject as not to perceive that the very measure they were on the eve of perpetrating—the expulsion of Mr. Adams from the House of Representatives for the exercise of freedom of speech, not only within the bounds of the Constitution, but even within the rules of parliamentary practice—would have done more to advance the abolition of slavery, than all his legislative efforts, if listened to without interruption, and answered with temper and decorum, could possibly effect in a much longer period than probably yet remains to him to exercise his heroic zeal and firmness in the great cause of human emancipation.

Nothing can be more preposterous than the ground taken by Mr. Bynum, "that an attempt to present a memorial from a slave or a free negro is a contempt of the House." That a slave has no express constitutional right to petition is readily conceded; but it is certainly within the constitutional competency of a member to ask if it be the pleasure of the house to listen to a petition from a slave. As for the free negro, the act which emancipates him makes him a citizen, and invests him with an inalienable right of petition—a right equal to that of Mr. Bynum, or of any other citizen whatever. The Constitution makes no distinctions as to creed or colour, but secures to "the people," be they white or black, "the right peaceably to assemble, and petition the Government for a redress of grievances." If the resolution, therefore, had been passed, in any of the forms in which it was proposed, and Mr. Adams had been called to the bar to receive the censure of the House, Congress would have been guilty of such a gross and palpable violation of the Constitution, and such an outrage on one of the trusted and honoured representatives of the free citizens of a great state, as would have raised a storm of indignation, to which the hubbub among the slaveholders in the House of Representatives would be but as the commotion of a turbulent pool compared with the angry heavings of the ocean in a tempest.

MEEK AND GENTLE WITH THESE BUTCHERS.

[*From the Plaindealer, February* 18, 1837.]

It will be seen, by our paragraph under the proper head, that Mr. Brady introduced a proposition into the Board of Aldermen last Wednesday evening, the object of which is graciously to permit all butchers to sell meat in their own shops, provided they take out a license, at an expense of fifty dollars, and enter into some sort of security that they will open only a single shop. This proposition is not to be considered as containing the views of its mover as to the degree of freedom which the citizen should be permitted to enjoy in the business of dealing in meat; for that individual has distinguished himself, for a good while past, as the earnest opponent of the unjust and arbitrary restraints and limitations which are imposed on that branch of traffic, giving a monopoly to a few, and forcing the citizen to pay a price much greater than would be asked, if competition were left free to regulate the supply to the demand. But the resolution of Mr. Brady was probably framed with reference to his prospect of success in any measure tending towards an enlargement of the bounds of the butchers' monopoly; and in that view of it he is entitled to thanks for the measure. But what a sorry picture does not this proceeding exhibit to us of the ignorance and tyranny of our municipal legislators! It is solicited, as a measure of freedom, that a free citizen, as free and intelligent as any member of the Common Council, may be permitted to follow a respectable and useful calling, provided he brings proof that he faithfully served the full term of apprenticeship to that branch of business, gives bonds that he will pursue it only within a specified limit, and pays into the public treasury a large sum of money for the gracious permission which the fathers of the city vouchsafe to him! Can any thing be a greater outrage of common sense than these stipulations? Can any thing be in more palpable and direct violation of the most obvious natural rights? Can any thing, even under the despotic government of Czars, Autocrats, and Grand Seignors, be more arbitrary, unequal, oppressive, and unjust? The prohibitions and restrictions within which butchers are circumscribed, may, with equal warrant of propriety, be drawn round other callings. There is as much reason why the Common Council should take upon themselves to regulate your private affairs, reader, or our own. They may, with equal grace, ordain that no carpenter, or tailor, or hatter, or shoemaker, shall open a shop, except he served a regular apprenticeship to the business, gives bonds that he will open but one, and pays a large bonus into the general coffers for "the blessings of liberty," in that case extended to him. Doctors, lawyers, merchants, and ministers of the gospel, are not less liable than butchers to this municipal supervision and control; and there is quite as much reason, in relation to every one of those vocations, why it should be limited and regulated by the Common Council, as there is in the case of butchers. We hope that among those who have undertaken this business on free trade principles, there are some citizens spirited enough to resist the present ordinances, and defy the inquisitorial power which attempts to tyrannize over them. We should like to see the question tried whether we are, in fact, mere serfs and vassals, holding our dearest privileges but by the sufferance of our municipal servants, or whether we are in truth freemen, possessed of certain inalienable rights, among which is that of pursuing, unmolested, and in our own way, any calling which does not interfere with the rights of others, subject only to the impositions of an equal tax.

THE WAY TO CHEAPEN FLOUR.

[*From the Plaindealer, February* 18, 1837.]

Our paper contains, under the appropriate head, an account of the daring and causeless outrage which disgraced our city last Monday evening. There never was a riot, in any place, on any previous occasion, for which there existed less pretence. There is no circumstance to extenuate it, in any of the aspects in which it can be viewed. The only alleged excuse is the high price of flour, and a suspicion which it seems was entertained, that the price was in part occasioned by a combination among the dealers. But this suspicion has not only no foundation in fact, but if it were well founded, if it were an established truth too notorious for contradiction, it would afford no sort of justification or shadow of excuse to any portion of the community to commit acts of violence, and much less to that portion which was chiefly concerned in this disgraceful tumult.

The chief actors in the riot of Monday evening were, beyond question, members of some of the numerous associations of artisans and labourers affiliated under the general name of the *Trades Union.* What, let us ask, is the very first and cardinal object of the Trades Union? To enable *labour,* by the means of combination, and of extensive mutual countenance and co-operation, to command its own price. And is not *labour* as much a necessary of life as *flour*? Is it not, in fact, more indispensable? Is it not the chief, the prime, the very first necessary of man, in his social organization? What would this city do for a week, nay, for a single day, if *labour*, in all its varieties of form and application, should wholly and obstinately refuse to perform its offices? It does not require any great fertility of imagination to picture the social anarchy, the chaotic confusion, into which the whole frame of things would be thrown. Yet it is to enable it, on occasion, to do this, or, as the only alternative, to compel *capital* to pay whatever price it chooses to exact, that the combination of different mechanic and operative crafts and callings has been formed. And these very people, thus combining to create, in effect, a monopoly of the chief necessary of life, are so enraged by the mere suspicion that the dealers in flour—a commodity for which there are many substitutes, and not indispensable if there were none—have followed their example that they assault the doors and windows of their storehouses with stones, crowbars, and levers, break down all barriers, scatter their property to the winds, and even tear, into irrevocable fragments, their most valuable books and accounts!

Was there ever a more causeless and disgraceful outrage? It is disgraceful to the city, that a sufficient portion of its inhabitants to commit such causeless destruction should be animated by such a fiendish spirit. It is more disgraceful, that its municipal authorities, those to whom the preservation of the public peace is entrusted, should sleep so soundly on their posts, when the loud roar of riot is on the gale, and the work of ruthless violence is going on, deliberately and without interruption, in broad day, and in one of the most frequented and populous parts of the metropolis. If ever the municipal history of the American cities shall be written, that portion which relates to New-York should be inscribed on a page of black. Nothing can provoke our dull and comatose police to the show of a little timely vigilance. At one time, stirred up by a seditious print of the most profligate character, an incendiary spirit breaks out in the community, first brutally attacking the poor negro in the street, then rushing to assault the dwellings of those distinguished as the negro's friends ; and finally breaking tumultuously into the churches dedicated to the worship of God ; and it is not till the last moment, till the very altars are desecrated, that the police awake from their slumbers, and, rubbing their drowsy eyes, inquire what all the tumult is about ? At another time, the same inflammatory journal calls upon the people, amidst the excitement of a most angry political contest, "to arm and strike a blow for liberty," and to "kill the damned Irish !"—and again the police doze in unstartled security, until the pavements are actually stained with human blood ! On a third occasion this same ruffian leader of tumult and sedition gives open and audacious warning to the magistrates that he means to lead a mob to the theatre, and drive an unoffending actor from the stage. "To be forewarned is to be forearmed," according to the old saying ; but it does not apply to the municipal authorities of this city. They take no steps to prevent the premeditated outrage. They have no force stationed to meet the ruffian at the threshold, and hurl him back from his bad design. He is permitted to go on without interruption ; and it is only when the work of malice is accomplished, that the police awake, and ask what is the matter ? In regard to this latest outrage, a foreknowledge of the intentions of those who instigated the disorder seems to have been equally without effect, unless it was the effect to throw them into a more perfect apathy. It will be seen by the statement which we have copied, that a previous intimation of the meditated outrage fell into the hands of the municipal authorities, by an accident which almost looks like providential interposition. But if the dead should rise from the grave to warn them, it is doubtful whether the supernatural visitation would rouse our magistrates into timely activity.

With regard to the question of combination we wish to be distinctly understood. If the dealers of flour had combined to monopolize the article, and to fix a high price upon it, we would hold them answerable for their conduct neither to the civil law nor to mob law, but to the inevitable penalties of a violation of the laws of trade. In the same way, when labourers combine to fix the price of labour, we would hold them responsible only to those natural and immutable principles of trade which will infallibly teach them their error, if they do not graduate the price according to the relations of demand and supply. We are for leaving trade free ; and the right to combine is an indispensable attribute of its freedom.

That the price of flour is not the result of combination, but of causes which lie much deeper, we fully believe. One of those causes is a deficient crop ; but the chief cause of the enhancement in price, not of that article alone, but of every variety of commodity, is the vast inflation which the paper currency has undergone in the last two years. It is not that exchangeable commodities have risen in value, but money, or that substitute for money which the specially privileged banks issue, has depreciated. The fluctuations in the currency must necessarily occasion equal fluctuations in money prices; and these fluctuations must necessarily be exceedingly oppressive to many, since all commodities do not instantly rise and fall in exact relative proportion, but require, some a longer, and some a shorter time, to be adjusted to new standards. The clergyman and the accountant on stated salaries, the tradesman who sells his articles according to a price fixed by ancient custom, and very many others, cannot immediately increase their demands as the price of other things increase ; and such are affected most injuriously by the continual augmentation of paper money, resulting from the incorporation, every year, of whole herds of specially privileged bankers.

The true way to make flour cheap, and beef cheap, and all the necessaries of life cheap, is, not to attack the dealers in those articles, and strew their commodities in the streets, but to exercise, through the ballot boxes, the legitimate influence which every citizen possesses to put an end, at once and forever, to a system of moneyed monopolies, which impoverish the poor to enrich the rich; which, building up a class of lordly aristocrats on the one hand, and degrading the mass into wretched serfs on the other; and which has already exercised a vast and most pernicious influence in demoralizing both the educated and the ignorant classes of society—both those who fatten on the spoils of the paper-predatory system, and those from whose very blood the spoils are wrung.

RIGHT OF PROPERTY IN THE FRUITS OF INTELLECTUAL LABOUR.

[*From the Plaindealer*, *February* 25, 1837.]

We have provoked such odds against us, in the contest on the subject of the rights of property in intellectual productions, that we do not know but that it would be "the better part of valour" to quit the field incontinently. To emulate the conduct of the bold knight whose determined heroism is recorded in *Chevy Chase*, and who, when his legs were off, "still fought upon his stumps," might seem, in such a dispute as we are engaged in, rather censurable obstinacy, than praiseworthy courage. Or if it provoked a smile, it would probably be one, not of approbation, but of that kind which we bestow on the logical prowess of Goldsmith's *Schoolmaster*, who could argue after he was vanquished, as ***Bombastes Furioso*** continues to fight after he is killed.

There is one motive, however, which might not be without some weight with us to persist in the controversy, even after being convinced we had espoused the wrong side. If our doing so would continue to draw such writers into the field as we have heretofore had to contend with, we should not be without excuse; as their forcible reasoning and perspicuous style would far more than counterpoise the influence of our erroneous opinions, exert what ingenuity we might to establish them.

But we choose to deal ingenuously with our readers. We took up arms to battle for the truth, and shall lay them down the moment we find we have inadvertently engaged on the side of her adversaries. That we are shaken in the opinions we have heretofore expressed, we freely admit. The idiosyncracies of style, to use the term aptly employed in the eloquent communication annexed, are marked with such distinctness, that a bare phrase of three or four words, from a writer of admitted genius, is often so characteristic and peculiar, as to indicate its source at once, even to those who have no recollection of its origin, but who judge of it as a connoisseur does of a painting.

How far this peculiar mode of expression can be considered property on the principles of natural justice, the question in dispute. We are not entirely convinced that we have taken wrong ground on this subject; yet we by no means feel so confident of the correctness of our opinions as we did when we put them forth. One thing seems to us, and has all along seemed, very clear: if the author has a natural right of property in the products of his intellectual labour, it ought to be acknowledged as extensively as the capitalist's right of property in his money, or the merchant's in his goods. It is a common law right, not a right by statute, maugre all decisions to the contrary. If, on the other hand, his right is derived from a law founded on views of expediency, instead of the principles of natural justice, we revert to our first position, that the greatest good of the greatest number would be more effectually promoted by the total abrogation of copyright property.

Let the claim of natural right be established, and we should be among the last to invade it; but concede that the question rests on any other basis, and we think we should have no great difficulty in showing that the general welfare would be advanced by abolishing the principle of exclusive property in written compositions, as it is never asserted in those which are merely spoken.

THE BLESSINGS OF SLAVERY.

[*From the Plaindealer, February* 25, 1837.]

An extraordinary colloquy took place in the United States Senate, some short time since, between Mr. Rives and Mr. Calhoun, on the subject of slavery, in which the latter senator maintained, with much vehemence, that slavery is not an evil, but "a good, a great good," and reproached Mr. Rives, in sharp terms, for admitting the contrary. As his remarks were reported by the stenographers, at the time, they contained some very insulting allusions to the free labourers of the northern states, whom Mr. Calhoun spoke of in the most contemptuous terms as serfs and vassals, far beneath the negro bondmen of the south in moral degradation. An elaborate report was some days afterwards published in the Washington papers, which probably had undergone the revision of the several speakers; and from that the offensive expressions relative to the free citizens of the north were wholly omitted.

What is left of Mr. Calhoun's remarks contains only the sentiments which, it is presumed, he stands ready, after leisure for careful meditation, to maintain before the world; and we shall therefore use only that report for comment.

The holding that slavery is not an evil, "but a good, a great good," is not "in the slightest degree inconsistent with the highest principles of freedom!" Not at all; no more than holding that despotism is better than a representative government is inconsistent with the principles of democracy; that tumult and sedition are better than social order is inconsistent with those principles which constitute the foundation of society; or that atheism and blasphemy are inconsistent with the principles of pure religion. Mr. Calhoun's proposition is a truism in the same degree that it would be to say, that a part is greater than the whole, or that two and two are nothing.

But we must not continue in this strain. We are not of the opinion with the dramatist described by Sheridan, who had discovered that the follies and foibles of society are subjects unworthy of the comic muse, which he contended should be taught to stoop only at the greater vices and blacker crimes of humanity. Such monstrous sentiments as are avowed by Mr. Calhoun do not seem to us to afford a suitable theme for irony. They require to be treated in a tone of strong indignation. They call for the severest animadversion. They demand the most serious and earnest strictures from every journalist who is really animated by the principles of freedom, and desires to render the newspaper press such a palladium of liberty as it is susceptible of being made.

We have Mr. Calhoun's own warrant for attacking his positions, with all the fervour which a high sense of duty can give; for we do hold from the bottom of our soul, that slavery is an evil, a deep, detestable, damnable evil; an evil in all its aspects; an evil to the blacks, and a greater evil to the whites; an evil, moral, social, and political; an evil which shows itself in the languishing condition of agriculture at the south, in its paralyzed commerce, and in the prostration of the mechanic arts; an evil that stares you in the face from uncultivated fields, and howls in your ears through the tangled recesses of the southern swamps and morasses. Slavery is such an evil that it withers what it touches. Where it is once securely established, the land becomes desolate, as the tree inevitably perishes which the sea-hawk chooses for its nest; while freedom, on the contrary, flourishes like the tannen,* "on the loftiest and least sheltered rocks," and clothes with its refreshing verdure what, without it, would frown in naked and incurable sterility.

If any one desires an illustration of the opposite influences of slavery and freedom, let him look at the two sister states of Kentucky and Ohio. Alike in soil and climate, and divided only by a river, whose translucent waters reveal, through nearly the whole breadth, the sandy bottom over which they sparkle, how different are they in all the respects over which man has control! On the one hand, the air is vocal with the mingled tumult of a vast and prosperous population. Every hill side smiles with an abundant harvest; every valley shelters a thriving village; the click of a busy mill drowns the prattle of every rivulet, and all the multitudinous sounds of business denote happy activity in every branch of social occupation.

This is the state which, but a few years ago, slept in the unbroken solitude of nature. The forest spread an

*The Alpine fir tree. See Childe Harold, canto IV. 20th stanza.

interminable canopy of shade over the dark soil, on which the fat and useless vegetation rotted at ease, and through the dusky vistas of the wood only savage beasts and more savage men prowled in quest of prey. The whole land now blossoms like a garden. The tall and interlacing trees have unlocked their hold, and bowed before the woodman's axe. The soil is disencumbered of the mossy trunks which had reposed upon it for ages. The rivers flash in the sunlight, and the fields smile with waving harvests. This is Ohio, and this is what *freedom* has done for it.

Now let us turn to Kentucky, and note the opposite influences of *slavery*. A narrow and unfrequented path through the close and sultry canebrake conducts us to a wretched hovel. It stands in the midst of an unweeded field, whose dilapidated enclosure scarcely protects it from the lowing and hungry kine. Children half-clad and squalid, and destitute of the buoyancy natural to their age, lounge in the sunshine, while their parent saunters apart to watch his languid slaves drive the ill-appointed team a-field. This is not a fancy picture. It is a true copy of one of the features which make up the aspect of the state—and of every state where the moral leprosy of slavery covers the people with its noisome scales. A deadening lethargy benumbs the limbs of the body politic. A stupor settles on the arts of life. Agriculture reluctantly drags the plough and harrow to the field, only when scourged by necessity. The axe drops from the woodman's nerveless hand the moment his fire is scantily supplied with fuel; and the fen, undrained, sends up its noxious exhalations, to rack with cramps and agues the frame already too much enervated by a moral epidemic, to creep beyond the sphere of the material miasm.

Heaven knows we have no disposition to exaggerate the deleterious influences of slavery. We would rather pause far within the truth, than transgress it ever so little. There are evils which it invariably generates a thousand times more pernicious than those we have faintly touched. There are evils which affect the moral character, and poison the social relations, of those who breathe the atmosphere of slavery, more to be deplored than its paralyzing influence on their physical condition.

Whence comes the hot and imperious temper of southern statesmen, but from their unlimited domination over their fellow-men? Whence comes it that "the church-going bell," so seldom fills the air with its pleasant music, inviting the population to religious worship? Whence comes it that Sabbath schools diffuse to so small a number of their children the inestimable benefits of education? Whence comes it that the knife and the pistol are so readily resorted to for the adjustment of private quarrel?

The answer to these and many kindred questions, will sufficiently show that slavery is indeed an evil of the most hideous and destructive kind; and it therefore becomes the duty of every wise and virtuous man to exert himself to put it down.

The proof which Mr. Calhoun adduces of the blessings of slavery, so far as the slaves themselves are concerned, that they double in numbers in the same ratio with the whites, is, alas! susceptible of a very contrary interpretation. Do we not know that propagation is encouraged among them without reference to the limitations of morality? That promiscuous intercourse, without respect even to the barriers of consanguinity, is not merely permitted, but approved? That the slaveholders say, in effect, "to 't luxury, pell-mell, for we lack soldiers?" The institution of marriage among the slaves is treated as an idle ceremony, and the restraints on sexual intercourse as of no more obligation than upon the birds of the air, or the beasts of the field. This is a theme on which we are not desirous to expatiate; but it is a truth which ought to be told; and more particularly ought it to be hurled back into the teeth of the southern champion of the blessings of slavery, when he adduces the fecundity of the slaves as a proof of the happiness of their condition.

THE POWER OF CONGRESS OVER SLAVERY IN THE DISTRICT OF COLUMBIA.

[*From the Plaindealer, February* 25, 1837.]

In our last number, we briefly alluded to a question submitted to us by a correspondent, under the signature of "*Citizen.*" That question was, whether, in our opinion, Congress possesses the power to abolish slavery in the District of Columbia, and if so, what article or clause of the Constitution confers that power. We have since received another communication from the same source, renewing the question in a modified form: namely, whether Congress possesses the power to abolish slavery in the District of Columbia, *without paying to the owners of the slaves an equivalent in money.*

In our opinion, the power of immediate and unconditional abolition is as clear as any other power conferred on the federal government. We consider it given by the sixteenth section of the eighth clause of the Constitution, which bestows on Congress the power "to exercise exclusive legislation, *in all cases whatsoever,*" over that District. Nor do we look upon the final clause of the fifth article of the amendments, which provides that private property shall not be taken for public use, without a just compensation, as at all abridging or defining the original substantive power, so far as this question is concerned. Congress, in the case supposed, would not take property for the public use.

If we divide the phrase, *take property for public use,* into three several parts, each part will sustain an argument to bear out our position. Congress does not "*take*" anything; it is not "*property*" which is taken; and it is not taken "*for the public use.*"

In the first place, Congress *takes* nothing, in the Constitutional sense. It merely amends or repeals a law or institution, under which persons, held to service under a peculiar tenure, are said to possess a peculiar value as property, in a limited signification of the term. The property is the labour of the slave, and it is not held absolutely, but under certain conditions, imperative on the masters. Congress, in abolishing slavery, merely changes those conditions, but *takes* nothing. It has an unquestionable constitutional power, in the same way, to abolish, instantly and wholly, the system of protective duties. You may contend that the hasty exercise of this power would be a breach of public faith; and all sudden and violent changes of legislation, under which capital has been largely invested, or industry drawn into particular channels, undoubtedly are so, to a greater or less extent, according to the circumstances. But this does not touch the question of power. You could not contend, with any show of reason, that such a repeal would be a violation of constitutional law. The Supreme Court would not set it aside on that ground. Yet, in such a case, Congress would *take* private property in the same sense that it would by abolishing the system of involuntary servitude in the District of Columbia. It would not, in either hypothesis, *take* perperty in the constitutional meaning of the word. It is within the indisputable competency of Congress to abolish the Post Office system, by which act a myriad of citizens would be suddenly deprived of their means of livelihood. Yet it would *take* nothing in the sense of the provision that enjoins the rendering a just compensation. It might change the seat of government, by which the property of the citizens of Washington and its neighbourhood would undergo a vast depreciation, and, in some cases, absolute annihilation. Yet still it would *take* nothing demanding compensation.

Again, the next branch of the phrase, "*property*," supplies the foundation for an equally cogent argument. The Constitution does not recognize slaves as *property*, in an absolute sense. It does not recognize them as property, in any sense, in the District of Columbia. It recognizes certain rights of masters, *in the several states*, in regard to "persons held to service or labour" under the laws of such states; but it nowhere gives any countenance to the idea that slaves are considered *property* in the meaning of the term as it is used in the fifth article of the amendments. The legislative power of Congress over the District of Columbia, "in all cases whatsoever," will be readily admitted to be as great as that of any state legislature over such state. Yet the conditions on which slaves are held to labour, in the slave states, is always, both in theory and practice, admitted to be a matter of legislative regulation. The legislative authority of every state makes regulations concerning the slaves, all of which have some tendency, more or less, to increase or diminish their value as mere property. But the principle that the state is bound to make compensation for any diminished value which may result from such rules has never been asserted. Thus, for example, the number of hours that a slave shall be required to labour is matter of regulation, in the discretion of the legislature. And if it decrees that he shall be compelled to labour but six hours where he was before obliged to labour ten, it obviously diminishes his value as property. Yet the right to set up a claim, on this ground, for compensation, "for private property taken for public use," has never been asserted. If the legislature may diminish the hours of slave labour to six, it may diminish them to three, or two, or one, or nothing. And Congress certainly possesses as great latitude of legislative power over the ten miles square which have been rendered up to its exclusive control, "in all cases whatsoever."

The third division of the phrase, "*for public use*," furnishes as broad a basis for argument. If the slaves were taken from their masters in the District of Columbia, to work in the dock-yard, or the arsenal, or on board the government vessels, or in any other way from which the public would derive the advantage of their labour, there might be room to demand compensation "for private property taken for public use." But if we admit that they are *taken*, and that they are *property*, we shall still deny that they are taken *for public use*. They are not *taken*, but enfranchised; and not *for the public use*, but for their own; or rather, not *for use* at all, but in compliance with an exalted sense of the inalienable rights of humanity.

But again: with regard to the condition of "*just compensation*." Here, if driven to the last outpost, we have still the means of making a successful stand. Congress cannot, in the nature of things, abolish slavery in the District of Columbia, without rendering compensation; and that it would be *a full equivalent* the slaveholders are themselves ready enough to maintain, when the argument answers their purpose. While slaves are held to service, masters are bound to support them. They are bound to support them in health and sickness alike, in infancy and age, in the vigour of their strength, and in the feebleness of decrepitude. This, as we often hear boastfully averred, is more than adequate compensation for their services. Southern orators are fond of expatiating on the arcadian condition of their blacks, whose lives are past under a patriarchal system, whose wants are supplied without any solicitude on their part, to whom the vicissitudes of the seasons and the storms of state bring no anxiety, and whose hearts, free from corroding cares, may be yielded wholly up to happiness. The laws impose all the duties of protection and maintenance on the masters, who, in that form, allege that they pay, for the services they receive, more than could be earned by any other mode of requiting them. If this is true—and it is an argument which is in every slaveholder's mouth, urged with all the fervour of conviction—then Congress, by abolishing the relation which now exists, would, in releasing masters from their obligations, yield more than "a just compensation for private property taken for public use."

Thus, in whatever light we view this question, as limited by the last inquiry of our correspondent, we come to an affirmative conclusion with respect to the power of Congress over the subject of slavery in the District of Columbia. We are of opinion, notwithstanding, as we before stated, that a careful consideration of *expediency,* in the most exalted meaning of the word, would restrain that body from the immediate exercise of its powers, in the respect in question. As this, however, is a branch of the subject not embraced in the interrogatory of our querist, we shall not pursue it at the present time.

THE RETIREMENT OF ANDREW JACKSON.

[*From the Plaindealer, March* 4, 1837.]

This day the administration of Andrew Jackson expires. This day completes a period that will shine in American history with more inherent and undying lustre, than any other which the chronicler has yet recorded, or which perhaps will ever form a portion of our country's annals.

How full of great events, greatly met, and conducted to great issues, have been the eight little years which have now elapsed since Andrew Jackson was summoned to the helm of state ! Equal to every exigency ; animated by a single and strong desire to promote the true interests of his country and of mankind ; possessed of firmness which no danger could shake, and sagacity which no artifice could delude, how admirably he has discharged his momentous trust ! The inflexible honesty, the intrepid heroism, and the ardent love of country, which distinguish his character, have been eminently displayed in all the various and difficult events of his lofty career. That career is now drawing to a close, and he retires to spend the brief remainder of his existence in the seclusion of private life. He is accompanied by the benisons of a grateful people, and the plaudits of an admiring world.

For a little while longer, the clouds of prejudice, which forever brood over the field of party conflict, may obscure from the vision of some, still battling beneath them, the transcendent lustre of this heroic man's character ; but the day is at hand when his fame, composed in an extraordinary degree of all the best elements of greatness, will be acknowledged by every tongue, and wake emotions of gratitude in every heart. The champion of equal liberty, how constant, how earnest, how successful, have been his efforts in that high object of political achievement! By him have been established landmarks of popular rights which will stand as guides for the legislation of ages. By him, the tide of aristocratic innovation, which was silently washing away the basis of our political fabric, has been turned back to its source, and stayed by an impassable barrier. Schemes of legislation, which, under delusive names were slowly and surely changing the character of our government, have by him been overthrown. Improvident and corrupting expenditures have been arrested. An institution, which had struck its poisonous shoots into every state of the Confederacy, and was fast consolidating our system of sovereignties into an unmingled mass of empire, to become the prey of unbridled ambition, has been lopped from the republic, and cast prone upon the earth.

In retiring from public life, Andrew Jackson leaves his government at a pinnacle of democratic greatness which renders it the gaze and wonder of the world. He found it involved in debt; he leaves it with a redundant treasury. He found it engaged in complicated negotiations with foreign powers; he leaves it with all conflicting claims adjusted, all entangled questions disintricated, and all long protracted obligations fulfilled. Steadily adhering to that simple and sublime rule of national conduct, which he proclaimed at the outset, to ask nothing that is not clearly right, and submit to nothing that is wrong, the direct and manly character of American diplomacy, stamped with his own impress, has won the undisguised respect of all the cabinets of Europe.

Already do those who survey our country from a point of distance that gives to their judgment something of the calmness and impartiality which will distinguish that of posterity, assign to Andrew Jackson a high place among those who stand highest on the records of fame. To that list which comprises the names of those few most illustrious of men, whom all mankind admire for their abilities and revere for their virtues, who attract regard by the splendour of their achievements and rivet it by the exalted purity of their motives and conduct; to that list, when the voice of both party detraction and praise, and the last echo of political or personal enmity or friendship shall long have passed away will the future historian add the name of Andrew Jackson. While intrepid bravery, earnest patriotism, keen sagacity, nice honour, inexorable honesty, and invincible firmness, are qualities to attract regard, so long will posterity treasure that name, and repeat it to their children, to waken emulation in their youthful minds.

The time is past when eulogy could be stigmatized as the fulsome clamour of dissembling selfishness; and it has just begun, when the voice of sincere praise, no longer hushed by the dread of ungenerous imputation, will speak out, louder and louder, till it swells into one universal and enduring acclaim, constituting "the applause of ages."

DIGNITY OF THE PRESS.

[*From the Plaindealer, March* 4, 1836.]

"Your paper should take a more dignified stand; and not condescend to notice the assaults of the degraded penny press. The price of your journal is such that it is taken only by readers of the more intelligent classes; readers who despise the vulgarity of the penny newspapers, and who have cause to feel themselves affronted when you give so large a space, or any space, indeed, to a refutation of their absurdities. It seems to me, that a proper respect for your own dignity, as well as a proper respect for those into whose hands your lucubrations chiefly fall, ought to restrain you from giving additional circulation to the trash of the minor prints, which are suited only to the taste and capacities of the lower classes of people."—*Extract from a letter to the Editor of the Plaindealer.*

The admonitions of our correspondent seem to us to proceed from a very narrow and incorrect view of the subject on which he touches. The real dignity of a public journal is to consult the dignity of truth; and its proper object to exercise whatever influence it may possess to advance the cause of public morals. The penny newspapers, with a single exception, will bear a very favourable comparison with those of higher prices; and surely the mere circumstance of cheapness ought not to exclude them from the pale of honourable controversy. The small sum at which they are afforded does not diminish their dignity, but increases it; because it enlarges the sphere of their circulation, and, in the same proportion, augments their opportunity of usefulness. There are but few vocations, indeed, of superior elevation and importance, to that of the conductor of a penny print, if animated with a due sense of the responsibility of his office, and possessed of sufficient intelligence, integrity, and firmness, for the adequate discharge of its functions. It is not true that his labours are confined to "the lower classes," and it is no argument against them if they were. Persons in all the gradations of society read those newspapers. You will find them on the merchant's desk and the lawyer's table, on the tradesman's counter and the mechanic's shopboard. They penetrate into the library of the divine, and the closet of the retired student. Go where you may, you will discover that they have preceded you. You meet them in the mansions of the rich, and the hovels of the indigent. You encounter them in stages and on board of steamboats; they salute you at the landing-places, and you find them in every tavern sprinkled along the road. One of the penny papers, we observe, claims a daily circulation of *thirty thousand copies*. If we allow that there are from three to four readers to every copy, which is a moderate estimate, we find, then, that the conductor of that print daily addresses himself to the minds, and, if he conducts his vocation with tolerable ability and integrity, exercises a large influence in forming the opinions and guiding the conduct, of a hundred thousand fellow-beings! Is this a vocation without dignity?

But it does not need that we should revert to the statements of the penny papers with regard to the prodigious extent of their circulation, when the proofs of it obtrude themselves upon our attention at every step. And we are not of those who repine at this, but rejoice at it. We are not of those, either, who sneer at the penny press; but are disposed to meet it on equal terms, and, by answering its arguments with the same courtesy, and by detecting and exposing what may seem to us its fallacies, with the same moderation and care, that we should exercise towards any of the larger papers, or towards any other antagonist, do what belongs to us to raise and refine the character of a means of public intelligence, the importance of whichcan hardly be overrated. We consider the establishment of the penny newspaper press as forming a new era in the history of civilization; and we anticipate from it vast benefits to mankind.

If it were true that the readers of the penny newspapers are chiefly confined to what our correspondent chooses to term the "lower classes," it would be a argument, not against them, but in their favour. Those who come within the embrace of that exotic phrase are an immense majority of the American people. It includes all the honest and labouring poor. It includes those whose suffrages decide the principles of our government; on whose conduct rests the reputation of our country; and whose mere breath is the tenure by which we hold all our dearest political, religious, and social rights. How ineffably important it is, then, that the intelligence of these "lower classes" should be cultivated; that their moral sense should be quickened; and that they should have the means within their reach of learning the current history of the times, of observing the measures of *their* public servants, and of becoming prepared to exercise with wisdom the most momentous privilege of freemen. This great desideratum the penny press supplies, not as well and thoroughly, perhaps, as the philanthropist could wish, but to such a degree as to be necessarily productive of immense benefit to society. It communicates knowledge to those who had no means of acquiring it. It calls into exercise minds that before rusted unused. It elevates vast numbers of men from the abjectness of mere animal condition, to the nobler station of intelligent beings. If usefulness constitutes the true measure of dignity, the penny press deserves pre-eminence, as well on account of the character of its readers, as the extent of its circulation. He who addresses himself to intelligent and cultivated minds, has a critic in each reader, and the influence of his opinions must necessarily be circumscribed. But he who addresses himself to the mass of the people, has readers whose opinions are yet to be formed; whose minds are ductile and open to new impressions, and whose intellectual characters he, in some measure, moulds. He becomes the *thinker*, in fact, for a vast number of his fellow-beings.

His mind tranfuses itself through many bodies. His station renders him, not an individual, but a host; not one, but legion. Is this not a vocation of inherent dignity?—to address, daily, myriads of men, not in words that fall on cold and inattentive ears, and are scarce heard, to be immediately forgotton; but in language clothed with all that undefinable influence which typography possesses over oral communication, and claiming attention, not in the hurry of business, or admidst the distractions of a crowded assemblage, but when the thoughts have leisure to concentrate themselves upon it, and follow the writer in all the windings of his argument.

If the censures were well founded which are lavished on "the vile penny press," as some of the larger papers are prone to term their cheaper rivals, they should but provoke minds governed by right principles to a more earnest endeavour to reform the character of an instrument, which must be powerful, either for evil or for good. That they are so vile we do not admit. We have found, ourselves, honourable and courteous antagonists among them; and if those who apply to them the harshest epithets, would treat them instead, with respectful consideration, copying from their columns as readily as from those of other journals, when intrinsic circumstances presented no particular motive of preference, and contesting their errors of opinion on terms of equal controversy, they would do far more towards raising the character and increasing the usefulness of that important branch of popular literature, than general and sweeping condemnation can possibly do to degrade it. For ourselves, professing that our main object is to promote the cause of truth in politics and morals, we should consider ourselves acting with palpable inconsistency, if we were governed, in any degree, by so narrow a principle of exclusion as that which our correspondent recommends. That newspaper best consults its real dignity which never loses sight of the dignity of truth, nor avoids any opportunity of extending its influence.

LEGISLATIVE INDEMNITY FOR LOSSES FROM MOBS.

[*From the Plaindealer, March* 4, 1837.]

The late disgraceful riot in this city has been followed by its natural consequence: impaired confidence in the security of private right in this community. Persons at a distance, having commercial relations with us, are fearful of trusting their property within the reach of men, who have shown themselves so regardless of the first principles of social order, and so little apprehensive of municipal opposition. The owners of flour and grain, in particular, and of other articles of such universal daily consumption as to be classed among the necessaries of life, hesitate to send them to a city where they may be seized, on their arrival, by an infuriated mob, and scattered to the winds of heaven. The result of this must inevitably be an exacerbation of the misery which the poor now experience. Prices, exorbitant as they are, must rise to a still higher pitch, as the supply, receiving no augmentations from abroad, becomes less and less adequate to the demand. And those miserable creatures, who, in their delusion, thought to overthrow the immutable laws of trade, and effect, by a sudden outbreak of tumultuary violence, what no force of compulsion, however organised and obstinate, could possibly accomplish, will be among the very first to reap the fruit of their folly: for, as they are among the very poorest members of the community, any additional advance in the price of flour must put it wholly beyond their means. Thus even handed justice commends to their own lips the chalice they had drugged for others.

One of the evidences of the consternation which the recent tumult has occasioned in the minds of persons having commercial dealings with this city, particularly in articles of necessary food, is shown in the terms of a memorial which the manufacturers of flour in Rochester have addressed to the Legislature, praying for the enactment of a law to protect their property in New-York from the destroying fury of mobs.

It is signed by eighteen flour manufacturing firms of Rochester. The trepidation and anxiety which it betrays on the part of all concerned in the flour trade of that city, may serve to show what must be the general feeling throughout the country, and what must be its necessary consequence in withholding from us a further supply of flour, thus inevitably increasing the burden of which we now complain. But while we copy this memorial, for the lesson it furnishes to those who seek to reform legislative abuses, or to relieve themselves from oppressive burdens, by tumultuary violence, we must not suffer it to be inferred that we approve the object of its prayer.

The power which the legislature is asked to exercise seems to us to lie beyond the proper province of government. The legitimate functions of a democratic government are simply to *protect* the citizens in life and property, not to provide *indemnification* for the loss of either. The government is the mere representative or agent of the community, appointed to guard the rights of each individual, by protecting him from the aggressions of others. This duty includes the defending of him from aggression, in the first place, and the punishing of those who commit it, in the second. But it does not extend to the punishment of an entire community for the offences committed by an inconsiderable portion, which is the position assumed by the Rochester petitioners. It is one of the first and most obvious duties of society, in the outset of its political organization, to make provision for the defence of the rights of its members, in whatever form of violence they may be assailed. The legislative agents of each community, in the discharge of this duty, make such provisions, as the general circumstances of the times, and the particular circumstances which lie within their own jurisdiction, may seem to require. Thus, while in thinly inhabited townships a few guardians of the peace, clothed with the simplest powers, are sufficient, in cities an extensive and complicated system of defence is found to be necessary. Guardians of the night, and guardians of the day, an organized force to protect property from conflagration, and an armed force to protect both life and property from riot and insurrection, are necessary in every populous town, requiring to be extended and modified, according to the increase of numbers, or the deterioration of morals. The principle of self-preservation gives rise to these precautionary and defensive measures, in the first place, and the same principle, ever active, demands that they shall be enlarged and improved, from time to time, as new exigencies arise. If anything occurs to show that the municipal authorities of any community are deficient in requisite vigilance, energy, or power, their deficiency is a proper subject of complaint; and all who are aggrieved, whose rights are in any way invaded or jeoparded through such remissness, have unquestionable ground of petition or remonstrance to a higher legislative tribunal. But no tribunal in this country, under the maxims which we acknowledge as the foundation of our political edifice, has the power to inflict the penalties incurred by a few ruffians, concerned in a violation of private right, on those who not only had no share in the offence, but who perhaps exerted themselves to the utmost to prevent it. This would be in dereliction of the plainest principles of natural justice.

Let us suppose a case. A person, residing at the Battery, by some unguarded speech or action, gives offence to a particular class of persons living in his immediate neighbourhood. The cause of umbrage is reported from one to another, with the natural exaggerations of anger. Bad passions are aroused, and some inflammatory demagogue seizes the occasion—perhaps for the gratification of private malice, or perhaps for the opportunity of plunder—to excite the irritated multitude to acts of violence. They rush to the house of the unconscious offender. Their numbers are rapidly augmented by additions from the crowd of such persons as are ever ready to take part in tumult. Their shouts and cries, echoed from one to another, are as fuel to fire, and increase the fury of their exasperation. They attack the property of him who is the object of their ire, demolish his store-house or dwelling, break its contents into fragments, and scatter them in the streets, or consume them in flames. In the meanwhile the public authorities, informed of the tumult, hasten to the scene. They are joined by numerous bodies of good citizens, desirous to aid them in the suppression of disorder; and, in a little while, but not before the work of destruction is completed, the riot is suppressed, and the chief actors in it apprehended, and committed to safe custody for trial and punishment. But this whole event, from first to last, has occurred, before the tidings can reach other extremes of the metropolis. The citizen at Bloomingdale or Harlem is quietly pursuing his vocation, unconscious of the disorders which disturb the community at another point of the city. Yet the legislation asked for by the petitioners of Rochester would make him responsible for the crimes of others, with which he not only had no participation, but which, could he have known they were meditated, he would have exerted himself with the utmost zeal and diligence to prevent. He would have done so, not only from a sentiment of philanthropy, but from a motive of self-preservation ; as one whose individual rights were exposed to similar hazard ; as a portion of the body politic, which must always suffer, when it shows itself incompetent to protect its individual members from outrage.

The principle involved in this Rochester memorial might, with equal propriety, be extended to embrace indemnity for losses sustained in consequence of individual outrages. It is no less the duty of a community to protect the property of citizens from the attacks of single ruffians, than from those of ruffians in numbers. If the flour manufacturers of Rochester had visited this city to receive payment from their agent whose store-house was attacked, and if the wretch, who directed the attention of an excited multitude to that store-house, had, instead, chosen to waylay those manufacturers singly, and, assailing them with a bludgeon, forced them to surrender the proceeds of their merchandise, it seems to us that they would have equal ground for a petition to the legislature, asking for a law to compel the city of New-York to indemnify them for the amount of which they had been robbed. The principle of *indemnity* is not included in the principle of *protection. Protection* is an obvious duty of humanity, as well as an obvious measure of self-preservation ; but the claim for *indemnification* as obviously rests on the unjust and arbitrary principle that the good should be punished for the crimes of the bad, and the weak for the outrages of the strong. Is there any reason, in natural justice, that the lone widow, frugally living, in some obscure corner of this city, on the slender means picked up by perpetual industry, should be burdened with a tax to compensate the flour merchant of Rochester for his losses from an outrage of which she could have had no knowledge, and over which she could exercise no control? Is there any reason why any person in this city, not implicated in the transaction, should be punished in the way proposed, that does not apply as strongly to every inhabitant of the state? If this community, in its corporate capacity did not exercise due vigilance and energy to prevent the riot in question, and protect the property destroyed, it may be that there is good ground for an action for damages ; but there is surely none for a law to punish the entire community in all cases, whether the outrage was within or beyond municipal control.

The principles which should guide legislation are always reducible to the simplest elements of natural justice. The code for the government of a community of three hundred thousand persons should stand on the same basis of clear undeniable right, with that which would be instituted for a community of only three. If A, B, and C, enter into a social compact, A is clearly bound to assist B, against any violation of his rights attempted by C. But if before A can render assistance, or in spite of it, C succeeds in rifling the property of B, and escapes with it, or destroys it, any claim which might then be set up by B, for indemnity from A, would be so clearly without foundation in justice, as to shock the natural moral sense of all the rest of the alphabet, supposing them living by themselves, in an entirely distinct community.

The *Journal of Commerce*, we perceive, expresses approbation of the object of the memorial we have copied. It pronounces the plan "a good one," and thinks "it should be made general, applying to all property, and to all the cities and towns in the state." We cannot think the *Journal of Commerce* has given its usual attention to this subject; though this is not the first time it has shown a willingness to strengthen government at the expense of men's equal and inalienable rights.

COMMENCEMENT OF THE ADMINISTRATION OF MARTIN VAN BUREN.

[*From the Plaindealer, March* 11, 1837.]

The inauguration of Martin Van Buren, as President of the United States took place at the Capitol, in Washington, on Saturday last, at noon. The day was serene and temperate, and the simple and august ceremonial was performed in the presence of assembled thousands. Mr. Van Buren delivered an Inaugural Address on the occasion, which, probably, most of our readers have already perused, but which, as a portion of the history of the times we insert in our paper. It is longer than the Inaugural Address of his immediate predec essor, but does not contain a tithe part of its pith. It professes to be an avowal of the principles by which the new President intends to be guided in his administration of the government; but with the single exception of the principle of opposition to the abolition of slavery in the District of Columbia, which it expresses with most uncalled for and unbecoming haste and positiveness, he might, with as much propriety, have sung *Yankee Doodle* or *Hail Columbia*, and called it "an avowal of his principles." With the exception of that indecorous announcement of a predetermination to exercise his veto against any measure of abolition which Congress may possibly think proper to adopt during the next four years, the address contains no expression of political principles whatever. It gives a correct and pleasing account of the formation of the federal compact, and expatiates with considerable fervour and eloquence on the value and importance of preserving the Union. It concludes with a statement, in general terms, that Mr. Van Buren intends to adhere strictly to the letter and spirit of of the Constitution; but as this is a duty imposed upon him, in the most explicit manner, by the terms of his oath of office, it cannot be considered of any weight as a separate avowal of the principles by which he will be guided. The address, therefore, as an avowal of guiding principles—save only the principle of extreme opposition, under all possible circumstances, to the abolition of slavery—is little better than a nonentity. Mr. Van Buren commences his administration as a man of *a single principle.*

One of the administration journals of this city, the *Evening Post,* excuses the vagueness of Mr. Van Buren's address, on the ground that an inaugural speech does not present an occasion for the proposal and discussion of particular measures which, it thinks, are more properly reserved for an annual message to Congress. We should acquiesce in the justice of this remark, if Mr. Van Buren had not himself put this address before his countrymen as "an avowal of his principles;" but having done so, we are compelled to try it by the standard he has furnished. The *Evening Post* further says, that for aught it can see, Mr. Van Buren "has laid down the general rules by which he intends to be guided with as much particularity and distinctness as any of his predecessors." We are afraid the *Evening Post,* at the time of making this remark, had neither the inaugural speech of Jefferson nor that of Jackson within the sphere of its vision.

But it is not so much for what it has omitted to say, as for what it says, that we feel dissatisfaction with this inaugural address. We dislike exceedingly both the tone and spirit of its remarks on the subject of slavery. On that one topic, there is, indeed, no want but a superabundance of "particularity and distinctness." Mr. Van Buren is the first President of the United States who, in assuming that office, has held up his veto power, *in terrorem*, to the world, and announced a fixed predetermination to exercise it on a particular subject, no matter what changes might take place in public opinion, or what events may occur to modify the question on which his imperial will is thus dictatorially announced.

Nothing but the clearest warrant of constitutional obligation could excuse this precipitate expression of a determination to exercise a power lodged in the executive, not for the purpose of holding it up to intimidate a co-ordinate branch of the government, and restrain it from the freest exercise of its functions; but for the better purpose of being discreetly used, in the last event, after a subject had undergone all the investigation and discussion that might be deemed necessary as preparatory to legislative action, uninfluenced by any premonition or threat from the executive department of government. For Mr. Van Buren, standing on the threshold of his administration, to announce to the world that he will veto any bill which Congress may pass on a particular subject, is as gross a breach of public decorum, and as violent a stretch of his proper duties, as it would be for the Supreme Court to pass a solemn resolution, declaring that if Congress enacted such or such a law, they would pronounce it unconstitutional, and set it aside accordingly, the moment any question under it should come before them for adjudication. The illustrious man who has just retired from the office of Chief Magistrate has not hesitated to exercise his constitutional negative, whenever called to do so by a sense of duty; but, dictator as he has been freely termed by his opponents, he never so far transcended the obvious bounds of political propriety, as to announce to the people, *in advance*, that he meant to use that power in a supposititious case.

Nothing, we repeat, but the clearest warrant of constitutional obligation could possibly excuse the step which Mr. Van Buren has thought proper to adopt. Is any such warrant alleged? Does the address state any clear constitutional interdiction of a legislative power in Congress over slavery in the District of Columbia? Does Mr. Van Buren venture to affirm that such a law as he declares his intention of vetoing would be a violation of any article or clause in the federal compact? No! he believes that such a course will be "in accordance with the spirit which actuated the venerated fathers of the republic," but does not pretend that such a spirit has made itself palpable and unequivocal in any of the written provisions of the instrument which he has sworn to maintain. If this early announcement of his intentions with regard to one subject which, if raised, he is determined to exorcise with the spell of the veto, is justifiable, why not carry out the new scheme of government, and favour the world with a full list of topics, on which Congress must not act without the fear of the President's negative before their eyes? It might save much fruitless legislation to have the predetermination of the executive formally made known on all questions of legislation; but without such an avowal of them, conjecture may go widely astray, since there is no other very certain mode of ascertaining what is not, in Mr. Van Buren's belief, according to "the spirit which actuated the venerated fathers of the republic."

When a President announces that the letter of the Constitution shall be his guide of public conduct; when he takes as his rule of action a strict construction of the express provisions of that instrument, we may form some tolerable notion of what will be his course. But when he undertakes to steer by the uncertain light of the spirit, we are tossed about on a sea of vague conjecture, and left to the mercy of winds and waves. Hamilton was guided by the *spirit* in proposing the first federal bank; but Jefferson adhered to the *letter* in his argument against that evil scheme. The high tariff system claims for its paternity the *spirit* of the Constitution; but the advocates of a plan of equal taxation, adjusted to the actual wants of the government, find their warrant in the *letter*. The internal improvement system, the compromise system, the distribution system, and every other unequal and aristocratic system which has been adopted in our country, all claim to spring from the *spirit* of the Constitution; but Andrew Jackson found in the *letter* of that instrument his rule of conduct, and it was fondly hoped that his successor meant to emulate his example. Appearances now authorize a fear of the contrary. The first step is certainly a deviation from the path.

Mr. Van Buren's indecent haste to avow his predeterminations on the subject of slavery has not even the merit of boldness. It is made in a cringing spirit of propitiation to the south, and in the certainty that a majority at the north accord with his views. His sentiments on the subject of slavery, so far as it can become a question for federal legislation, were well understood before. They had been distinctly expressed, and he had been supported with a clear knowledge of his opinions on that topic, and a clear apprehension of what would in all probability be his course, should executive action become necessary. There was not the slightest proper occasion, therefore, for anything, beyond a calm repetition of his previously expressed sentiments. The *Veto Pledge* is the peace-offering of an ignoble spirit to appease the exasperated slave-holders at the south. What a mockery it would now be, if, in the course of the next four years, such a change should take place in the public mind (and such a change is clearly within the scope of possibility) as that a large majority of the people should demand the abolition of slavery at the seat of the federal government, and Congress, in compliance with the demand, should pass a bill to that effect—what a mockery, we say, it would be, to present the measure to the President for his approval. He would answer, "I am pledged to use my veto." But the opinions of men have changed since that pledge was given. "No matter: it was unconditional, and must be fulfilled." But the facts elicited in the discussion of the subject prove incontestibly that the measure is demanded by a regard for the prosperity of the country. "No matter: I am pledged." But the free states have solemnly resolved that they will no longer be bound in union with the slave states, if the condition of the league requires the perpetuation of slavery in the ten miles square placed under the executive control of the federal government, and therfore this measure is necessary for the preservation of the union. "No matter: I am pledged. I am pursuing a course in accordance with the spirit which actuated the venerated fathers of the republic, and I cannot be moved from my fixed and predetermined purpose. I told the people in the outset of my administration what I meant to do. They had ample warning, and ought not to have changed their minds, for, being solemnly pledged to veto any bill for the abolition of slavery in the District of Columbia, I cannot now recede."

There is a single phrase in the anti-abolition portion of Mr. Van Buren's address upon which we shall make one additional comment, and then dismiss the subject. Alluding to the pro-slavery mobs and riots which have taken place in various parts of the country, he says, "a reckless disregard of the consequences of their conduct has exposed individuals to popular indignation." This is an admirable version of the matter. The issuing of a temperate and decorous newspaper, in which a question of great public moment was gravely discussed, showed, beyond all question, a most "reckless disregard of consequences," deserving the harshest rebuke ; and the conduct of the mob that broke up the press, demolished the house which contained it, and shockingly maltreated the person of the editor, was merely a natural and justifiable expression of "popular indignation." They who thought the Constitution vouchsafed to them the freedom of speech and of the press, were criminal to act under that singular delusion ; while they who dragged these atrocious men from the sanctuaries of God, from their firesides and from the pulpit, pelted them with stones, tore their garments from their limbs, steeped them in seething tar, and heaped all manner of injuries on their defenceless heads—these men were "true friends of the Constitution," and animated by "the spirit which actuated the venerated fathers of the republic." Mr. Van Buren does not say so in express terms ; but he alludes to their atrocities in language so soft and sugary, as to sound almost like positive approval.

On the whole, we consider this Inaugural Address as constituting a page of Mr. Van Buren's history which will reflect no credit upon him in after times.

THE THEATRE.

[*From the Plaindealer, March* 11, 1837.]

A CORRESPONDENT, for whose motives and intelligence we have great respect, has addressed a letter to us on the subject of theatres, from which we make the annexed extracts.

"I wish the expression of your opinion in regard to our

present theatrical establishments. In alluding to them, however, I trust I shall not be misunderstood. Although, as a professed christian minister, my opinions of the stage may be supposed to be weighed, like the purchases of old, by the unalterable shekels of the sanctuary, yet I solemnly assure you that I am not moved by the impulses of jealousy or revenge. Some years of my early life were spent in connexion with the stage, but though I saw things behind the scenes which led me, in my better moments, to think more and more of the truth that practice and precept do not always go hand in hand together, yet I can conscientiously say, if the theatre, as now conducted, is capable of doing good, heaven grant it may ! I wish your answer to these few questions.

"1. Has not the theatre been originated, and generally sustained, by the bad passions of mankind ?

"2. Have not nine out of ten of the stars in the firmament of the stage been persons of questionable moral character ?

"3. Have not the pleasures afforded by the play-house been more than counterbalanced by the evils of late hours and intense nervous excitement ?

"4. Have not many of the popular tumults, in all ages, been engendered in the heat and unthinking enthusiasm of a theatrical audience ?

"5. Have not the idleness and expense attending the theatre been ever a source of unpleasant reflection to its more thoughtful devotees ?

"6. Might not the redeeming spirits of the stage, such as FORREST, and others, accomplish more for the benefit and rational amusement of mankind in methods of action less exceptionable than the theatre ?

"7. Is it not better, therefore, for real patriots to encourage the theatre, as it is, to a smaller extent, and useful lectures and publications more ?

"I am aware that these questions may seem to you crude and common-place; but I write under the pressure of extensive pastoral engagements. My only object is truth. I respect genius every where, not the less because it 'walks in beauty' on the boards of the theatre, providing it is serving the great end of society—'the greatest good of the greatest number.'"

To reply to the interrogatories of our querist with that fulness of discussion to which we feel invited by the nature of the subject, and the wide scope embraced in his questions, would require greater space than is left at our disposal by the other matters which crowd the columns of our present number. We shall therefore make our immediate answer as brief as possible, and reserve a more ample consideration of the subject for a season when legislative proceedings, and the various topics they furnish for comment, shall no longer press their paramount claims upon our attention.

The nature and tendency of theatrical exhibitions are subjects on which we had maturely reflected, before we resolved to devote one of the departments of this paper exclusively to the drama. That there are some very great and deplorable evils connected with the theatre, is a fact of the utmost notoriety; but these we consider, not inherent, but extrinsic; while the good that belongs to it is essential, and, in our view, even as now conducted, far more than counterbalances the bad. But if we admit that the preponderance lies the other way, it would still seem to us the province of true wisdom, rather to seek to defecate the theatre of the impurities which have collected there, and remove the unwholesome excrescences which licentious custom has engrafted upon it, than to apply the axe to the root, and overthrow utterly what, in its original and inherent nature, contains abundantly the elements of goodly fruit.

The mere fact of the existence of adventitious abuses never furnishes a cogent argument for the abandonment of objects worthy in themselves, unless it can be shown that the supervenient evil has become so closely and thoroughly incorporated with them, as to be inseparable, without greater cost of effort than is justified by the nature of the end to be achieved. That this is not so with regard to the theatres is a position too plain to need that it should be very elaborately enforced. No writer and no combination of writers, no matter how highly gifted with talent, and how strongly animated with enthusiasm in the undertaking, could hope to overthrow them utterly. They might possibly succeed in casting so much temporary odium upon them, as to deter the better portion of society from partaking the amusements they afford; but in so doing they would but remove a check that now counteracts the downward tendency which the theatre partakes with all human institutions, and thus increase the evil of histrionic exhibitions to that portion of the community on whose minds and conduct the acted examples of the stage exercise the strongest influence, and for whose sake it is most desirable that the theatre should be a school of morals, as well as a place of mere innocent dissipation.

To reform the theatre; to oblige managers to exclude from the audience those who come unblushingly in the open character of prostitution, and to expel from the scene those lascivious and indecent spectacles, for which the great moral lessons of Shakspeare are often thrust aside: these are objects perfectly within the reach of public opinion; and to the accomplishment of these, therefore, it becomes a duty of the press to exert its energies. Such, at least, are the general views which we entertained and expressed in the outset of the *Plaindealer;* and we have met with nothing since to show us they are incorrect. If we have been remiss in the execution of that branch of our duty, the deficiency must be imputed to broken health, which for the most part disinclines us to mix with crowds and breathe the close atmosphere they create. Rightly conducted, there is no department of this journal which we could hope might prove to be the instrument of more good, than that in which we offer these remarks; for we think so well of the moral sense of this community, as to believe that it might be efficiently aroused against the more prominent evils connected with the theatres, even by so feeble an advocate as ourselves. The subject might easily be presented to the attention of fathers and mothers, and of husbands and brothers, in such a way, as to awaken in them a spirit which would not be satisfied, short of the total expulsion of lascivious dancers from the stage, and painted strumpets, in the undisguised character of harlotry, from the boxes. Our confidence in the moral sense of the community, as it relates to theatres, is strengthened by the ill success which has attended a late experiment upon its depravity. That audacity of licentiousness which the managers of the National Theatre displayed, in throwing open the best part of their house to the filthiest followers and cullies of debauchery, thus seeking to allure, with the meretricious attractions of the stews, those who could not be won by their wretched stage performances, has met with such a significant rebuke from the outraged public, in the shape of empty benches, that they have been obliged to resign the theatre into the hands of a person, who being himself a man of respectability and honour, better knows what is due to public morals and decorum, and will promptly reform the abuses which, beyond question, led to the ill success of the National Theatre under its previous conductors.

We now turn to the specific questions of our correspondent, and shall give to each a brief reply.

1. The origin of theatres we conceive to have been, in all times and countries, the mere love of amusement; a perfectly innocent passion, in itself, and susceptible of being turned to the promotion of incalculable good. Dr. Johnson has said that he who enlarges the boundaries of innocent amusement, deserves to be ranked among the benefactors of mankind. The theatre, in its intrinsic nature, is not merely a source of innocent entertainment, but of refined instruction. The opening lines of Pope's celebrated prologue describe, with as much justice as eloquence, the real purposes and tendency of scenic exhibitions.

2. What proportion of players have been persons of loose morals is more than we can answer; though from a very limited personal knowledge of those of our own time and city, we are clearly of opinion that the interrogatory of our querist is founded on an exceedingly incorrect estimate. There are circumstances incident to the profession of an actor, which naturally lead to dissipation in some respects; and one of these circumstances, which the more tolerant and enlightened spirit of the present age is daily diminishing, is that prejudice which has made them, in some measure, a proscribed class. But the private moral character of individual performers no more affects the question of the propriety of encouraging theatrical representations, than the dissoluteness of tailors does the question of the propriety of wearing coats. Dr. Johnson's occasional excess in wine does not diminish the pleasure or instruction we derive from the perusal of the Rambler; the wild and dissipated character of Benvenuto Cellini does not impair the satisfaction with which we survey the productions of his genius; nor the lax morality of Sir Thomas Lawrence abate the delight

with which we contemplate his speaking portraits. If we go to the theatre to see Hamlet, it is no concern of ours that the actor, when he has shuffled off the integuments of the philosophic Dane, recruits himself from his exhaustion in a neighbouring cellar, over a pint of porter or a glass of punch.

3. If we answer this question in the affirmative, it makes nothing for the argument of our querist. But the question does not admit of either a general affirmative or general negative reply. It is one for every individual to answer for himself; as every one must answer for himself whether the pleasure of his cup of coffee or cigar is not purchased at too great a cost of nervous excitement. Excitement, in great cities, is a necessary of life, and that which is produced through the instrumentality of such agents as make up the sum of theatrical exhibitions is less harmful than the excitement which would probably supply the place if theatres were abolished.

4. The popular tumults which have been stirred up by scenic representations, have been the insurrections of oppressed men, rising up against their oppressors. The stage has been the friend of liberty ; and hence the institution, under governments of unequal laws, where the policy of the rulers was to keep the people down, of licensers, to see that no dangerous lessons of freedom should be taught in the acted examples of the stage. The argument implied in the question might be cogent, in the mouth of a conservative, and an oppressive government ; but it has no application to things as they exist in this country.

5. *Desipere in loco.* No one can be always busy ; and all amusements cost something. He who cannot afford the amusement of the theatre, yet indulges in it, errs ; but the error is his own, not the theatre's.

6. Possibly they might ; but circumstances, not choice,

decide most men's professions, and he who "acts well his part" is generally considered as fulfilling the just claims of society. The combination of talents which fit a man to be a great actor, would probably not render him as great in any other pursuit. The saying *poeta nascitur*, as far as it is true at all, is true in a much wider application than merely to poets. The question of our correspondent runs *against the grain of nature*. If Sterne had eschewed humourous writing, and made the grave eloquence of Jeremy Taylor's sermons his model, he might have accomplished more good, but more probably he might have failed in the attempt, and accomplished no good at all. If Shakspeare had turned field preacher instead of play writer, he might have been considerd as devoting himself to the more exalted calling, but we doubt whether he would as usefully have employed his godlike faculties. Our correspondent might perhaps more usefully have employed the time which it cost him to address his communication to us; but if, instead of obeying the laudable impulse, he had paused to meditate how he might most profitably spend the period, and to compare the relative merits of different modes of occupation, the season for action might have passed away without anything being done. He generally proves to be the most useful member of society, who goes to work earnestly at that which is before him. Circumstances placed the stage before Mr. Forrest as his field of action. He went to work upon it earnestly, and he has achieved such progress as to stand now, at the age of thirty, far in advance before all competitors. That he is doing good, much good, and in various ways, we do not doubt; while we think it questionable whether, in any other pursuit, he could achieve equal eminence, and exert an equal influence in promoting the ends of society. But why ask the player to doff the buskin and don the cowl or stole? Why require the painter to throw by the pencil, and seize the pen; or the poet to turn from the muses, and devote himself to the austerer worship of Minerva? *Non omnia possumus omnes,* to use the line from Virgil which honest Partridge in Tom Jones, was fond of quoting. Many men are qualified for excellence in some one thing, but few in more. Let each, then, follow the bent of his genius, or yield to the force of circumstances, and strive to do well what it falls to his lot to do.

7. We come now to the last question, which we suspect of having a particular reference to ourselves. We have already answered it, in part, in the general remarks with which we commenced our reply. The mind is so constituted that it requires variety of occupation and variety of amusement. The broadest grimace of the theatre sometimes diverts a weary spirit, that could not be won by attractions of a more elevated kind. Lectures are good things, and so are books good things—very good; but one does not desire always to hear lectures nor always to read books. Partridges are good things, capital things, in their proper place and season; but our correspondent doubtless remembers the pathetic exclamation of the sated monk, who was obliged to dine on them every day in the year—*toujours perdrix!* exclaimed the melancholy ecclesiastic, *toujours perdrix!* The theatre, too, is a good thing in its place and season; and being an amusement that attracts vast numbers of people, it becomes a proper subject for the comments of the press, for a double reason. In the first place, judicious comments, approving what is really good, and condemning what is bad, must have a continual tendency to raise the character of stage performances, and refine the morals of the theatre. Such notices, in the second place, increase the attraction of a newspaper to a large class of readers, and thus extend the field of its usefulness in re-

gard to other subjects of comment and discussion. The subscribers to a newspaper are made up of persons of a great variety of tastes and pursuits. Some are chiefly attracted by its political articles; others by its literary notices; and a third class, perhaps, by its theatrical strictures. But whatever the prevailing motive, most readers, particularly of a weekly journal like our own, do not lay it aside, till they have perused, more or less thoroughly, all its leading topics. They are thus led to the consideration of subjects which, presented separately, would not have won their attention, and thus the great ends of a newspaper are promoted by that very diversity, which is a blemish in the eyes of some, who would have it confine itself to matters of the gravest character and the directest utility. For our own part, it is a source of regret to us that circumstances have prevented our making the theatrical department of our paper more worthy of the perusal of those of our readers who take a lively interest in what relates to the drama. Against the abuses of the theatre we stand ever ready to speak in earnest reprehension; but his censure is most effectual who, discriminating between good and evil, indulges, not in sweeping condemnations, but while he sharply animadverts upon what calls for rebuke, is equally prompt to applaud what merits praise.

GENERAL BANKING LAW.

[*From the Plaindealer, March* 11, 1837.]

The bill which has been introduced into the legislature, under this name, proposes a very great enlargement of the present narrow bounds, in which craft and folly have combined to shut up the business of banking; but it is by no means strictly entitled to the appellation it claims. It is a mitigation of legislative restrictions, but not a repeal of them. We have not space for particular comment, but must express, in general terms, the satisfaction which the introduction of this measure affords of the rapid progress that free trade principles are making in the minds of the people at large. Two or three years ago, such a proposition as that now brought forward by Mr. Robinson would have caused its mover to be hooted at and derided in the most contemptuous and derogatory terms. A charge of lunacy and Jacobinism has been frequently preferred against some of those who made the earliest stand in defence of free trade and equal rights, for recommending measures much less adverse to the present monopoly system, than that now introduced into the legislature by Mr. Robinson. But those who were then ever foremost to shout *Jack Cade* and *Agrarian!* now show, by a decent silence, or faint approval, their consciousness that a vast change has taken place in the minds of the people, and that the universal sentiment is setting strongly against the curse of monopoly legislation and exclusive chartered privileges. We copy an abstract of Mr. Robinson's bill, which we consider only as a precursor of a more perfect reform. "Revolutions never go backwards;" and a revolution, fraught with the vastest consequences to the happiness of mankind, is now taking place, the end of which will be the demolition of all restraints and impediments in the way of complete political and commercial freedom and equality.

RECEPTION OF MR. WEBSTER.

[*From the Plaindealer, March* 18, 1837.]

THE dullness of these piping times of peace was somewhat enlivened on Wednesday last, by the arrival of Mr. Webster in this city, and the public ceremonies of his reception. Arrangements had been made on a pretty large scale, some time previous, by a number of the political friends and partisans of that statesman, to give him a grand reception, and the note of preparation had been constantly sounding, for a week or more in their leading newspapers. The day was bright and temperate, and it is natural to presume that the concourse assembled on the occasion was very large. Those who had to borrow money at three per cent. a month, and those who had money to lend at that rate, probably preferred Wall-street to the Battery; but no doubt the latter place was crowded with many of those happy creatures, who, having neither money to lend, for want of means, nor money to borrow, for want of credit, can yet generally command abundance of leisure to run about after shows and spectacles.

As we did not ourselves witness the reception of Mr. Webster, and as we wish to come as near the truth as possible in our account of it, we copy the statements of two leading newspapers, of opposite sides in politics, but about of equal character for varacity and general respectability.

* * * * * *

We have placed these accounts side by side, that the reader, whose curiosity moves him in the matter, may the more easily compare their conflicting statements, and draw his own conclusions from them. The political newspapers of this city, with two or three honourable exceptions, are valuable rather as enabling one to conjecture the truth, than to ascertain it; as a bad watch sometimes enables one to guess the hour, by making a large allowance for the irregularity of its movements.

The same disparity which the two foregoing accounts display in regard to a simple matter of fact, of which the version of each journal professes to be that of an eye-witness, pervades, more or less, all the party statements of the newspaper press. It is a mortifying fact, but it is an undeniable one. So few newspapers are conducted with a spirit of strict varacity, that the reader, unless he be one of the most credulous and gullible of mortals, seldom yields full faith to their assertions in regard to any matter which has the slightest party relation or bearing. He waits to compare contrary statements, and to gather oral testimony, before he surrenders his belief. One of the two papers from which we have copied the statements of Mr. Webster's reception tells a wilful falsehood, probably both. But whatever was the exact truth, it was not matter of opinion, or matter of feeling, to such a degree as to allow us to believe that both the narratives could have been written in a spirit of sincerity and truth. One writer tried to swell the reception into something very magnificent, the other to sink it into something very mean. For their reward, neither of them will be believed, but every reader will make a large allowance for the magnifying grandiloquence of the one, and the lessening and diminuent sneers and sarcasms of the other.

We have no doubt that Mr. Webster was very warmly received by several thousand people; for he is a leading man of a party, under better organization at the present time than it has been for many years before, and all the usual means of party preparation were adopted to give effect and eclat to the ceremonial. Independent of this Mr. Webster is a great man, and is very sincerely and warmly admired by multitudes of people. We are not, ourselves, among those who admire his political principles, and there have been some things in his political conduct which we cannot approve, even judging it by the scale of his own principles. But we admire his talents, and can very readily conceive how those who accord with him in his fundamental political doctrines, may easily be warmed into enthusiasm, on an occasion like that which his public reception has presented.

We are well pleased with the recent movement on several accounts. In the first place it never displeases us to see the whigs make the most of their great men; for entertaining an abiding and unfaltering confidence in that great fundamental article of democratic faith which recognizes the intelligence and integrity of the people, we have no fear that these mere cavalcades and triumphs can turn the public mind from a contemplation of cardinal principles, or dazzle it so as to render it unable to distinguish between truth and error. This ovation to Mr. Webster has been got up avowedly on the ground of his great services and sacrifices in the cause of the Constitution; but the mass of the people, entertaining a different theory of constitutional obligation from that of Mr. Webster and his followers, turn their eyes to the white headed veteran now slowly journeying across the solitudes of the Alleganies to his secluded home in the far west, and to him—to him against whom Mr. Webster's political life, for the last eight years, has been one perpetual and violent struggle—their hearts pay the involuntary homage of gratitude, as the great champion of the Constitution and of freedom.

But we are pleased with these public honours to Mr. Webster, inasmuch as they afford some evidence that the opposition party of this quarter of the country are determined to rally around him as their foremost man,

They are, no doubt, ashamed of having been led to abandon a statesman of real talents, to make shift with so poor and feeble an "available" as General Harrison, with nothing in the wide world to recommend him but a military title, and we believe a blameless and inoffensive private life. They come back to Mr. Webster with the usual force of retroaction, when the forward movement has been against the bent of nature. This pleases us, and we hope they will keep it up. We shall be delighted to have Mr. Webster put before the country in real earnest as the whig candidate for President. We are tired of contending against "availables," men of no fixed political character, but ready to mould themselves to any new opinion and suit their doctrines to the varying hour. It is contemptible of the whig party to seek refuge under the petticoat of General Harrison. Let them stand out before the world in their true colours, and select a candidate of a known creed, that people may divide themselves according to opinion on antagonist questions, and not be influenced by mere personal preferences or dislikes. If Mr. Webster were the candidate for the chief office of the government, the people would have before them an eminent and learned follower of the school of Hamilton, a man whom they could not but respect for his talents and acquirements, and admire for his bold and manly eloquence. We should contend against him with all the zeal of a sincere conviction that his political creed is adverse to the principles of liberty—we should contend against him early and late, in season and out of season—but our efforts would always be tempered with that respect which such qualities as Mr. Webster possesses must naturally command. It would be a strife of antagonist political principles, and would serve much better to test the relative strength of their adherents, than a contest involving complicated motives of policy and expediency, but carefully removed from the true ground of warfare, as defined by the ultimate aims of the two great parties of this country, the democracy and the aristocracy, the friends of a strong government and the friends of a strong people.

Mr. Webster, on Wednesday evening, addressed a numerous audience in a long speech at Niblo's Saloon, and on Thursday received the salutations of such as chose to pay him a visit of honour or curiosity at the City Hall.

THE DESPOTISM OF THE MAJORITY.

[*From the Plaindealer, March* 25, 1837.]

Words undergo variations in their meaning to accommodate them to the varying usages of men. Despotism, though originally confined, according to its derivation, to the government of a single ruler, and considered a term of honour, rather than reproach, is now employed to signify unlimited tyranny, whether exercised by one or legion, whether by a single autocrat, wielding all the power of the state, or by the majority of a community, combined under strict party organization, and ruling the minority with dictatorial and imperious sway. The two most prominent instances which the world now presents of these different classes of despotism, is that of a single tyrant in Russia, and that of a multitudinous tyrant in America ; and it is a question which some seem to think not easily answered which is the worse, that of an autocracy, of that of a majority.

The intolerance, the bitter, persecuting intolerance, often displayed by a majority in this country, on questions of stirring political interest, towards the rights and feelings of the minority, has come to be a subject of comment by enlightened minds in Europe, that are eagerly watching the results of our great democratic experiment, and drawing arguments in favour of aristocratic government from every imperfection we exhibit. Thus, in the eloquent speech recently delivered by Sir Robert Peel, at Glasgow, there are some allusions to the intolerance of dominant parties in this country, which no candid person can peruse without admitting they contain enough of truth to give great point and sharpness to their sarcasms.

We cannot be suspected of any sympathy with Sir Robert Peel in the purpose with which he made this reference to America. Our love for the democratic principle is too sincere and unbounded, to allow us to have a feeling in common with those who desire to conserve aristocratic institutions. The democratic principle is the only principle which promises equal liberty, and equal prosperity to mankind. We yearn with intense longing for the arrival of that auspicious day in the history of the human race, when it shall everywhere take the place of the aristocratic principle, and knit all the families of mankind together in the bonds of equal brotherhood. Then shall the worn out nations sit down at last in abiding peace, and the old earth, which has so long drunk the blood of encountering millions, grow young again in a millenial holiday.

No American, having sense and soul to feel and appreciate the ineffable blessings of equal liberty, would answer Sir Robert Peel's interrogatory as he supposes. The effeminate popinjays, whom the land, overcloyed with their insipid sweetness, yearly sends abroad to foreign travel, and who prefer the glitter of courtly pomp to the widely diffused and substantial blessings of freedom, might utter such a dissuasion against the adoption of democratic principles. But no honest and manly American, worthy of that name, with intelligence enough to know, and heart enough to feel, that the best and loftiest aim of government is, not to promote excessive and luxurious refinement among a few, but the general good of all—"the greatest good of the greatest number"—would ever lisp a syllable to dissuade England from adopting the glorious democratic principle of equal political rights.

But while we thus differ from Sir Robert Peel in the tenor and purpose of the remarks we have quoted, we are forced to admit that there is but too much truth in the charge of despotism against the majority in our political divisions. The right of the majority to rule, is a maxim which lies at the bottom of democratic government; but a maxim of still higher obligation makes it their duty so to rule, as to preserve inviolate the equal rights of all. This rule of paramount authority is not always obeyed. We have seen numerous and frightful instances of its violation, in those outbreaks of "popular indignation," which men have drawn upon themselves by the fatal temerity of expressing their views on a subject of deep interest to every American, on which their sentiments differed from those of the majority. The wild excesses of riot are not chargeable alone to the madness and brutality of those who take part in them, but to the approval of others, who set on the human bull-dogs to bait the abolitionists, by calling the latter all sorts of opprobrious names; and encouraging the former by bestowing laudatory appellations on their ferocity. They are "true friends of the Constitution," they are men "who appreciate the blessings of liberty," they are "champions of union," they are patriots and heroes; while those against whom their drunken rage is directed are pointed out as fanatics, of the most diabolical temper ; as incendiaries, ready to burn to the ground the temple of freedom ; as murderers, ready to incite the negro against his master, and incarnadine the whole south with the blood of promiscuous and discriminate slaughter.

But to descend from the terrible instances of despotism, which the conduct of the majority on the slave question displays, we see the consequences of the same tyranny in a thousand matters of less startling moment. Does not our newspaper press show marks of the iron rule of despotism, as exercised by a majority ? Whence comes its subserviency ? Whence comes it that each journal goes with its party in all things, and to all lengths approving what the party approves, whether men or measures, and condemning what it condemns ? Why is it that no journalist dares, in the exercise of true independence, to act with his party in what he deems conformable with its political tenets, and censure its course when it varies from them ? Why is it that if, forgetting for a moment that he is not a freeman, he honestly blames some erroneous step, or fails to approve it, his reproach, or his very silence, is made the occasion of persecution, and he finds himself suddenly stripped of support ? Whence comes this we ask, but from the despotism of a majority, from that bitter intolerance of the mass, which now supplies an argument to the monarchists and aristocrats of the old world, against the adoption of the principles of popular government ?

The book press of our country is not less overcrowed by the despotism of the majority than the newspapers. The very work from which Sir Robert Peel makes his quotation affords us a ready illustration. Thousands are burning to read the production of De Tocqueville, and a hundred publishers are anxious to gratify the desire. But they dare not. The writer has not hesitated to express his opinions of slavery; and such is the despotism of a majority, that it will not suffer men to read nor speak upon that subject; and it would hinder them, if it could, even from the exercise of thought.

There are some bold spirits yet in the land, who are determined to battle against this spirit of despotism, and to assert and defend their rights of equal freedom, let the struggle cost what it may. They will speak with a voice that the roar of tumult cannot drown, and maintain their ground with a firmness that opposition cannot move; and if forced at last to surrender, it will be their lives, not their liberty, they will yield, considering it better to die freemen, than live slaves to the most cruel of all despots—a despotic majority

---

OMNIPOTENCE OF THE LEGISLATURE.

[*From the Plaindealer, April* 1, 1837.]

In one of George Colman's metrical oddities, that writer advances the bold opinion that,

> ———What's impossible can't be,
> And never, never comes to pass.

This seems, however, to be a great mistake. The wisdom of modern legislation is continually performing impossibilities. The laws of physics and metaphysics, of mind and matter, are every day abrogated by the laws of man and the march of improvement is so rapid, that it would scarcely be surprising if the whole system of things should shortly be taken wholly under the control of our lawgivers.

Judge Soule, of our state legislature, has lately made a great step towards that consummation. He has introduced a bill to fix the value of money, under every variety of financial circumstances, at precisely seven per cent. a year, and he has framed its provisions with such profound sagacity, that money lenders and money borrowers will never attempt to evade them. This will be glad news to those who are at present paying three per cent. a month.

The notable project of Judge Soule provides that bonds, bills, notes, assurances, all other contracts or securities whatsoever, and all deposites of goods or other things whatsoever, whereupon or whereby there shall be received or taken, or secured or agreed to be reserved or taken, any greater sum, or greater value, for the loan or forbearance of any money, goods or other things in action, than the legal rate of seven per cent. per annum, shall be void; and any bond, bill, note, assurance, pledge, conveyance, contract, and all evidences of debt whatsoever, which may have been sold, transferred, assigned or indorsed upon, for or upon which any greater interest, discount or consideration may have been reserved, obtained or taken than is provided in the first section of the said title shall be absolutely null and void; and no part of any such contract, security or evidence of debt, shall be collectable in any court of law or equity. It also declares every violation of the provisions of the act to be a misdemeanor, subjecting the person offending to fine or imprisonment, or both.

There was a certain philosopher who spent his life in bottling moonbeams. Judge Soule seems to belong to the same school.

The Astronomer in Rasselas, by a long and attentive study of the heavenly bodies, at length discovered the secret of their governments, and qualified himself to direct their courses, and regulate the seasons. "I have possessed for five years," said he to Imlac, "the regulation of the weather and the distribution of the seasons:

the sun has listened to my dictates, and passed from tropic to tropic by my direction ; the clouds, at my call, have poured their waters, and the Nile has overflowed at my command ; I have restrained the rage of the dog-star and mitigated the fervours of the crab. I have administered this great office with exact justice, and made the different nations of the earth an impartial dividend of rain and sunshine. What must have been the misery of half the globe, if I had limited the clouds to particular regions, or confined the sun to either side of the equator ! "

Judge Soule has now taken upon himself an office not less important in the financial system, than that of the learned astronomer in the planetary. He is for dividing the rain and sunshine of the money-market with an impartial hand, and giving equal portions to borrower and lender. In doing this he perhaps may be thought to carry the principle of equality to an undue extent, since it places all borrowers on a level, whatever the difference in the nature of the security they offer, or in the precariousness of the objects to which the loan is to be applied. But Judge Soule is too much of a philosopher to regard such slight circumstances of difference. He looks down on the money-market from such a height as reduces both bulls and bears to uniformity of stature.

The Astronomer, in Rasselas, confessed that there was one thing, in the system of nature, over which he had not been able to obtain complete control. "The winds alone," said he, "of all the elemental powers, have hitherto refused my authority, and multitudes have perished by equinoctial tempests, which I found myself unable to prohibit or restrain." We are afraid that the astronomer's worthy prototype in our legislature will also find there is likewise one thing which is beyond his authority. Judge Soule will yet discover, we imagine, that the interest on money is as variable as the winds, and that as the latter sometimes whisper in zephyrs and sometimes rave in tempests, so the former, in spite of all his efforts will sink down and almost die away, and at others swell and rage to the tune of three per cent. a month.

It is a matter of astonishment to us that any man, having sense enough to recommend him to his constituents for a seat in the legislature, can be so blind as not to see that usury laws are essentially and necessarily unjust and arbitrary. The value of money depends on a thousand very varying contingencies, as much so as the value of any other commodity. A failure of our chief articles of export, either as to quantity or price, immediately increases the demand for money, and at the same time decreases the security of the borrower. An abundant crop and large prices have, as certainly, the opposite result. This is a difference which affects whole communities. The differences which distinguish individual borrowers are not less obvious. One has ample security to offer ; another has none. One needs money to aid him in a pursuit which promises certain profit ; another needs it to prosecute an enterprise of exceeding hazard, which, if successful, promises a large return, but if unsuccessful, leaves no hope of re-payment. One borrower, has health, activity and prudence; another is infirm, indolent and rash. Judge Soule is for making up a Procrustean bed for all alike, without reference to the variety of form and stature. We recommend him to the muse of *Croaker*, as a fit subject for poetic honours, and in the meanwhile apply to him a stanza addressed by that writer to a great leveller in another line:

Come, star-eyed maid, Equality !
  In thine adorer's praise I revel,
Who brings, so fierce his love to thee,
  All forms and faces to a level.

THE MUNICIPAL ELECTION.

[*From the Plaindealer, April* 8, 1837.]

On Tuesday, Wednesday, and Thursday next, the election for municipal officers is to be held. On those days the people of this city are to decide by their suffrages who is to be Mayor for the next year. "There be *three* Richmonds in the field." In the first place, there is John I. Morgan, nominated by the democratic party at Tammany Hall: next we have Moses Jaques, nominated by the equal rights party in the Park; and thirdly and to conclude, there is Aaron Clark, the *ci-devant* lottery dealer, nominated by "platoons, squadrons, battalions, and regiments" of whigs in Masonic Hall, together with the resigned firemen in their strength, with Gulick at their head.

We must confess there are some very serious objections urged against the first named candidate. It is charged, and has not been denied, that he wears flannel next to his skin. There is grave authority for this accusation. It has been asserted by nearly all the whig papers, and the *American* of Thursday evening repeats the charge, in a modified form. It does not, indeed, positively aver that Mr. Morgan wears flannel *next to his skin!*—this degree of atrocity is not alleged. But that he wears flannel is roundly affirmed. What democrat can vote for Mr. Morgan, unless this imputation on his character is clearly proved to be a slander?

But it is not merely the sin of wearing flannel that is preferred against him. The *American* further charges that he is "addicted to umbrellas!" Prodigious wickedness! "Addicted to umbrellas!"—what a blot on his escutcheon. Is there any citizen so lost to patriotism, so lost to manhood and to virtue, as to vote for a man who is "addicted to umbrellas?" We pause for a reply.

Moses Jaques is not much better than Mr. Morgan. He is strongly suspected of wearing flannel likewise, though some affirm that it is only buckskin. But we believe it must be admitted that he is a good deal "addicted to umbrellas." He is addicted to one or two other things not less heinous in the eyes of the aristocracy. He is addicted to the opinon that all men possess equal political rights; and hence he is denominated an agrarian. He is addicted to the opinion that no citizen can be lawfully arrested, even by so potential a body as the New-York legislature, except on a warrant, for probable cause, supported by oath or affirmation; and hence he is considered a leveller. These things, together with flannel shirts and silk umbrellas, put his election out of the question.

The third candidate is Aaron Clark. It is not affirmed, on any hand, that Mr. Clark wears flannel shirts, or is "addicted to umbrellas." He may, or may not, be guilty of these offences against society, but no charge to that effect is brought against him. On the other hand, the virtues of Mr. Clark are great and various. He is "fortune's favourite." He once kept a lucky lottery-office, and sold vast numbers of tickets to poor people for ready money, some of which drew prizes. The business of keeping a lottery-office was one of great dignity and honour. It placed an opportunity within the reach of men of very small means to become suddenly affluent. The keeping a lottery-office was a calling "to which" (we quote the American) "reverend divines appealed to aid churches, to which men of letters and high moral standing appealed to endow colleges and promote education." This was the calling of Aaron Clark, and hence he is called upon to be a candidate for Mayor, and hence the people are called upon to give him their support.

Can they resist the invitation?

In view of the fact that Mr. Morgan wears flannel, and is addicted to umbrellas, the American triumphantly asks, "what control could such a person exercise over the fierceness of the democracy in an uproar?" Though put in an interrogative form, this is an argument that settles the question. No man who wears flannel and is "addicted to umbrellas" could quell a riot, no matter how many flannel-shirted constables and watchmen he had at his heels. The thing is impossible.

As for Mr. Jaques, he is himself one of the fierce democracy, and a chief rioter, since he presides over meetings of the "populace" and "common people" in the Park. What business have the "common people" to hold meetings?

Aaron Clark, then, is the man for the money? Buy your ticket at Clark's. He pursued a calling tolerated by the laws, and reverend divines and heads of colleges were glad to get a share of the money he paid for his license, as they no doubt would be glad to get a share of the city funds, if they were derived, in part, from licensed stews and gambling houses.

If we elect Aaron Clark for Mayor, who knows but he may get up some "splendid scheme," and insure "a grand prize" to every man who assisted in making him manager of the municipal lottery. Huzza for Clark, Fortune's Favourite!

MISS TREE.

[*From the Plaindealer, April* 8, 1837.]

WE have seen *Beatrice*—we will not call it Shakspeare's *Beatrice*, or Miss Tree's *Beatrice*, but *Beatrice* herself. We have seen the identical Sicilian lady, the high-born, beautiful, witty, gay-hearted and volatile, yet loving and constant woman of Messina ; whom Shakspeare imagined, but whom Miss Tree *is*. Other actresses have given us particular traits of her character with liveliness and effect ; but Miss Tree infuses life and soul into them all, and combines them into one with inimitable harmony and grace.

What wonderful individuality there is in the characters of Shakspeare ! No two of them are alike. They may belong to the same class, but the shades of difference are not less obvious, than the features of resemblance they possess in common. It is not merely that they are placed in different circumstances, but they are essentially different. Other dramatists have sometimes copied from themselves, but Shakspeare always copied from nature, and his works are distinguished by the same endless diversity. " Custom could not stale his infinite variety."

If this remark is true of his characters generally. it is more strikingly so of his females. From *Miranda* to *Lady Macbeth*, from *Ophelia* to *Constance*, there is a whole world of interval, filled up with women of every gradation and combination of moral and intellectual qualities. Who, for example, is like *Beatrice ?*

The character of *Beatrice* we do not think has usually been correctly appreciated on the stage. She is spirited, witty, and talkative, and the mere words of her raillery, if we consider separate phrases by themselves, have sometimes a sharpness not altogether consistent with the general idea of amiableness in woman. But if we examine her character more thoroughly, we shall find that her keenest strokes of satire, her sharpest repartees and liveliest jests, are but the artillery with which a proud woman guards the secret of unrequited love. It seems to us the clue to *Beatrice's* character is, that she is conscious of a secret attachment to *Benedick*, and believing her passion unreturned by the determined bachelor, she makes him the object of constant raillery, that she may thus more effectually hide her true feelings from observation. She talks of *Benedick*, and to *Benedick*, because *Benedick* fills her heart, and "out of the abundance of the heart the mouth speaketh," but she talks mirthfully and scornfully, that none, and least of all himself, may suspect the sentiment which is hid beneath her sparkling repartees. The first words *Beatrice* utters are an inquiry concerning *Benedick;* yet with the ready tact of woman, she asks after him by a name that implies a taunt, that the real anxiety which prompted the question, might not be seen. The same feeling, directly after, urges her to inquire who is his companion, and the motive of concealment induces her lightly to add, "He hath every month a new sworn brother."

The reader of the play is prepared, in the very first scene, to set down *Benedick* and *Beatrice* as intended for each other. *Leonato* informs us that they are perpetually waging a kind of merry war, and that "they never meet, but there is a skirmish of wit between them." We soon perceive this very skirmishing is the result of mutual attachment, but with a difference: for *Benedick* is unconscious of the nature of his feelings for *Beatrice*, and really supposes himself proof against all the shafts of blind Cupid, while *Beatrice* is aware of her love, but resolves in the true spirit of maidenly propriety, to hide it deep in her heart, until it shall be called forth in requital for the proffered love of *Benedick*. She is not of the disposition, however, to "let concealment, like a worm i' th' bud, feed on her damask cheek." She is too proud, too gay, too volatile by nature, to be easily dejected. She is of the sanguine, not the melancholic temperament, and looks on men and things in their sunniest aspects.

Leonato tells us "there is little of the melacholy element in her;" and she herself says, she was "born to speak all mirth, and no matter." *Beatrice* is not a creature of imagination, but of strong intellect, and strong feeling. Her volatility relates only to her spirits, not to her affections; she is distinguished by gaiety and airiness of temper, not fickleness of heart. That she is constant in friendship, her fidelity to her cousin *Hero* proves, for when the breath of slander blackens her character, and all, even her own father, believes the tale of guilt, *Beatrice* alone stands up, the asserter of *Hero's* innocence, and indignantly exclaims, "O, on my soul, my cousin is belied!"

But the firmness of her attachment does not show itself only in words. Her lover had just been led to a discovery of the true character of his feelings towards her, and had declared his attachment; and she demands from him, as the first proof of his love, that he should challenge his friend *Claudio*, who had renounced *Hero* at the altar, and traduced her, "with public accusation, uncovered slander, unmitigated rancour." It is no proof of a want of love for *Benedick*, that she is thus willing to risk his life to avenge the wrong done to her cousin; but it only proves that her sense of female honour, and of what is due to it, outweighs love.

She is of that temper that she might well have used the lines of the old English Earl:—

> "I could not love thee, love, so much,
> Loved I not honour more."

She sets *Benedick* to do only what she herself would gladly have done, could she have exchanged sexes with him. "Oh, God! that I were a man!" she exclaims, in the intenseness of her indignation, "I would eat his heart in the market-place!" The thought that *Benedick* could be foiled in the enterprise, and that he might fall beneath the sword of *Claudio*, never once entered her mind. The spirit of the age, and the spirit of the woman, alike repelled the idea. Right and might were deemed to go hand in hand together in such contests. She could think only of the slanderer being punished, and her cousin avenged. Her imagination presented her lover returning triumphant, the champion of injured female innocence; it refused to paint him lying prostrate and bleeding beneath the sword of the calumniator.

That *Beatrice* loves *Benedick*, and levels her raillery at him only to turn attention from her secret, is borne out by the effect of the pleasant stratagem played off upon her, when she is decoyed—

> "——into the pleached bower,
> Where honey-suckles, ripened by the sun,
> Forbid the sun to enter."

that she may overhear the discourse of *Ursula* and her cousin, concerning the pretended love of *Benedick*. Her exclamation, as she emerges from her hiding-place, is,

> "Contempt farewell, and *maiden pride*, adieu!"

These are the disguises she has worn hitherto, but she now casts them off, on finding that she is beloved by *Benedick*. She at once fully acknowledges his worth—

> "Others say thou dost deserve—and I
> *Believe it better than reportingly.*"

Her heart had long before felt the truth of such commendations, and now that she is assured those feelings are returned, she permits her tongue to join in the praise of *Benedick.*

The ideas we have here imperfectly expressed of the character of *Beatrice* seem to be the foundation of Miss Tree's performance. She gives us a living portraiture of a fine, spirited, intellectual, and highly cultivated woman of the world, of a happy temper, and gay and voluble as a singing bird. But while she bears in mind that the quickness and brilliancy of *Beatrice's* wit and repartee constitute a chief element in her character; she does not forget, and does not suffer her audience to forget, that there are other elements necessary to compose the perfect whole, and present, faithfully embodied, the *Beatrice* which Shakspeare drew.

Feminine delicacy is one of the attributes of woman's character, which Miss Tree is not willing to dispense with; and while other actresses give the utmost sharpness and acerbity to every sarcasm and jest that *Beatrice* utters, we find Miss Tree occasionally delivering a repartee with a downcast air and softened tone, that show her innate sense of the propriety of Shakspeare's admonition, "not to overstep the modesty of nature."

Much of *Beatrice's* share in the brilliant dialogue between herself and *Benedick*, depends, for its character, on the style of the speaker—it is modest, if modestly spoken, and the reverse, if uttered only with a view to give it the greatest possible degree of point. But they who adopt the latter method, represent *Beatrice* as a vixen and termagant, whose ready wit and vivacity may excite admiration, but who has no counterbalancing quality to attract esteem. We are amused by her sallies, because they are not directed towards ourselves, for we feel that they must wound as well as dazzle; and we are disposed to commiserate *Benedick*, not to congratulate him, when he is caught in the trap set for him by the *Prince*, and becomes entangled in the toils of matrimony. We dismiss him to his nuptials as one who is about to realize the truth of his own jeers against marriage, and with a certainty that if the drama were continued through another act, we should see him arrayed in the livery he had foretold for the husband of *Beatrice*, "a predestinate scratched face."

But very different are the emotions created by the *Beatrice* of Miss Tree. The softness of woman's tenderest tone, and the witchery of woman's kindest and most feminine smile, qualify the meaning of her words. The arrows of her voluble wit are shot off with a playful air that shows they are aimed only in sport; and her most scornful jests are delivered in a voice silvery and gentle, and accompanied by such a mirthful glance of the eye, that we see there is no league between her heart and her tongue. It is all "mirth, and no matter." We enjoy the encounter of her nimble wit with that of *Benedick*, because his character as a professed contemner of the power of love renders him a fair mark for such shafts as she aims at him; and we are pleased to see him foiled by so fair an antagonist, in a contest which he had himself provoked.

We accompany them to the altar with a sense of gratification that two such congenial spirits are to be united in wedlock; and when the curtain falls upon the drama, our imagination completes the story, by allotting such happiness to the married pair, as young persons of mutual intelligence and good humour, with mutual attachment founded on the basis of esteem, may reasonably count upon enjoying.

The *Benedick* of Mr. Mason would have elicited higher commendation, if that of Charles Kemble had not disqualified us from appreciating moderate excellence in the part. The latter was the perfection of acting; and other *Benedicks* tried by the standard thus furnished, must always be pronounced wanting. This comparative criticism is not fair, when it is avoidable; but Mr. Kemble has not left us a free agent on the subject, and we shall never again see *Benedick* personated, or read a line of the part, without thinking of him.

The *Claudio* of Mr. Fredericks, and the *Don Pedro* of Mr. Richings, were both creditable performances. There was not as much of "the May of youth and bloom of lustyhood" in the appearance of the former, as a strict regard to the text would have required; and a more melancholy bearing in the scene where he is sought by *Benedick*, that he may challenge him for the wrong done to *Hero*, would have been more in consonance with truth and nature.

The *Hero* of Mrs. Gurner was a delicate and graceful personation.

An air of premeditation and design on the part of *Dogberry*, in the delivery of his blunders, impaired their comic effect. They did not fall from his tongue as if he entertained no doubt of the perfect accuracy and eloquence of his language.

The characters, generally, were well sustained; and the music of *Balthazar* and his companions in the second act, deserves this praise, at least—that it answered exactly the description given of it in the text, when *Benedick* says, "An he had been a dog that should have howled thus, they would have hanged him." The audience seemed very much of the same opinion.

THE QUESTION OF SLAVERY NARROWED TO A POINT.

From the Plaindealer of April 15, 1837.

———————Farewell remorse!
Evil be thou my good! By thee, at least,
——I more than half, perhaps, will reign.

MILTON.

THE temperate and well-considered sentiments of Mr. Rives on the subject of slavery, as expressed in the Senate last winter, when certain petitions against slavery in the District of Columbia were under consideration, do not meet with much approval in the southern states. But the violent language of Mr. Calhoun is applauded to the echo. Mr. Rives, it will be remembered, admitted, in the most explicit manner, that "slavery is an evil, moral, social, and political;" while Mr. Calhoun, on the other hand, maintained that "it is a good—a great good."

We have a paragraph lying before us, from the *New-Orleans True American,* in which the sentiments of Mr. Calhoun are responded to with great ardour, and the admission that slavery is an evil is resisted as giving up the whole question in dispute. The writer says:

"If the principle be once acknowledged, that slavery is an evil, the success of the fanatics is certain. We are with Mr. Calhoun on this point. He insists that slavery is a *positive good* in our present social relations—that no power in the Union can touch the construction of southern society, without actual violation of all guaranteed and unalienated rights. This is the threshold of our liberties. If once passed, the tower must fall."

Reader, contemplate the picture presented to you in this figurative language: the tower of liberty erected on the prostrate bodies of three millions of slaves. Worthy foundation of such an edifice! And appropriately is the journal which displays such anxiety for its stability termed the *True American.*

"Evil, be thou my good," is the exclamation of Mr. Calhoun, and myriads of true Americans join in worship of the divinity thus set up. But truth has always been a great iconoclast, and we think this idol of the slaveholders would fare little better in her hands than the images of pagan idolatry.

If the question of the abolition of slavery is to be narrowed down to the single point whether slavery is an evil or not, it will not take long to dispose of it. Yet it would perhaps not be an easy thing to prove that slavery is an evil, for the same reason that itwould not be easy to prove that one and one are two; because the proposition is so elementary and self-evident, that it would itself be taken for a logical axiom as readily as any position by which we might seek to establish it. The great fundamental maxim of democratic faith is the natural equality of rights of all mankind. This is one of those truths which, in our Declaration of Independence, the Bill of Rights of this Confederacy, we claim to be self-evident. Those who maintain that slavery is not an evil must repudiate this maxim. They must be content to denounce the attempts to abolish slavery on the same ground that Gibbon* denounced the petitions to the British Parliament against the slave trade, because there was "a leaven of democratical principles in them, wild ideas of the rights and natural equality of man," and they must join that full-faced aristocrat in execrating "the fatal consequences of democratical principles, which lead by a path of flowers to the abyss of hell." If they admit man's natural

* See his letter to Lord Sheffield, Miscellaneous Works, vol. 1, p. 349.

equality, they at once admit slavery to be an evil. "In a future day," says Dymond, in his admirable work on morals, "it will probably become a subject of wonder how it could have happened that, on such a subject as slavery, men could have inquired and examined and debated, year after year; and that many years could have passed before the minds of a nation were so fully convinced of its enormity, and of their consequent duty to abolish it, as to suppress it to the utmost of their power. This will probably be a subject of wonder, because the question is so simple, that he who simply applies the requisitions of the moral law finds no time for reasoning or for doubt. The question as soon as it is proposed is decided."

But if we shut our eyes upon the moral law, and decide whether slavery is a good or an evil with sole reference to the test of utility; if we consider it merely a question of political economy, and one in which the interests of humanity and the rights of nature, as they affect the slave, are not to be taken into account, but the mere advantage of the masters alone regarded, we shall still come to the same conclusion. The relative condition of any two states of this Confederacy, taking one where slavery exists, and one where it does not, illustrates the truth of this remark. But it would not be difficult to prove, by a process of statistical arguments, that slave labour is far more costly than free, wretchedly as the wants and comforts of the slaves are provided for in most of the southern states. So that, limiting the inquiry to the mere question of pecuniary profit, it could be demonstrated that slavery is an evil. But this is a view of the subject infinitely less important than its malign influence in social and political respects, still regarding the prosperity of the whites as alone deserving consideration. When the social and political effects on three millions of black men are superadded as proper subjects of inquiry, the evil becomes greatly increased.

But to enter seriously into an argument to prove that slavery is an evil would be a great waste of time. They who assert the contrary do so under the influence of such feelings as are evinced by the ruined archangel, in the words from Milton which we have quoted at the head of these remarks. They do so in a tone of malignant defiance, and their own hearts, as they make the declaration, throb with a degrading consciousness of its falsehood.

The position that no power in the Union can touch the construction of southern society without violating guaranteed rights, will no more bear the test of examination, than the assertion that slavery is not an evil. There is no power, we concede, in the federal government to abolish slavery in any state, and none in any state to abolish it except within its own limits. But in as far as a free and full discussion of slavery, in all its characteristics and tendencies, may be considered as touching the construction of southern society, the right belongs to every citizen; and it is by this mode of touching it that it is hoped eventually to do away entirely with the deplorable evil. It cannot always exist against the constant attrition of public opinion.

The right to discuss slavery exists in various forms. It is claimed, in the first place, that Congress has absolute authority over that subject, so far as it relates to the District of Columbia. Every state, also, has authority over it within its own limits. And the people of the United States have absolute authority over it, so far as it presents a question to be considered in reference to any proposed amendment of the federal constitution. Suppose, for example, it should be desired by any portion of the people, to change the basis of southern representation in Congress, on the ground that slaves, being allowed to have no political rights, but being considered mere property, ought not to be enumerated in the political census, any more than the cattle and sheep of northern graziers and wool-growers. The Constitution is amenable in this, as in every other respect, with the single exception of the equal representation of every state in the federal Senate; and it is consequently a legitimate subject of discussion. Yet the discussion of this subject involves, naturally and necessarily, a consideration of slavery in all its relations and influences. Suppose, again, any portion of the citizens of a state where negroes are not held to bondage, but are not admitted to equal suffrage, as in this state, should desire those distinctive limitations to be removed. This is a legitimate question to be discussed, and the discussion of this brings up the whole subject of slavery. Or suppose, thirdly, that any persons in a free state should desire to re-instate negro slavery. The south would scarcely quarrel with them for seeking to carry their wishes into effect; yet they could only hope to do so through the means of a discussion which would legitimately embrace every topic connected with slavery, nearly or remotely.

It is by discussion alone that those who are opposed to slavery seek to effect a reconstruction of southern society; and the means, we think, if there is any virtue in truth, will yet be found adequate to the end. If slavery is really no evil, the more it is discussed, the greater will be the number of its advocates; but if it is "an evil, moral, social and political," as Mr. Rives has had the manliness to admit, in the very teeth of Mr. Calhoun's bravado, it will gradually give way before the force of sound opinion.

THE POWER OF THE FEDERAL GOVERNMENT OVER THE DISTRICT OF COLUMBIA.

[*From the* ***Plaindealer***, *April* 15, 1837.]

We copied, a fortnight ago, the resolution adopted in the lower branch of the Massachusetts Legislature, on the subject of the right of petition and the right of abolishing slavery in the District of Columbia. Since that time the Senate of Massachusetts has adopted the following resolutions, the first by a unanimous vote, and the second with but one dissenting voice.

"*Resolved*, That Congress having exclusive legislation in the District of Columbia, possesses the right to abolish slavery and the slave trade therein; and that the early exercise of such right is demanded by the enlightened sentiment of the civilized world, by the principles of the revolution, and by humanity.

"*Resolved*, That slavery, being an admitted moral and political evil, whose continuance, wherever it exists, is vindicated mainly on the ground of necessity, it should be circumscribed within the limits of the states where it has been already established; and that no new state should hereafter be admitted into the Union whose constitution of government shall sanction or permit the existence of domestic slavery."

The resolutions were not concurred in by the other branch of the legislature, upon which the Senate receded from them, and adopted the resolutions of the popular branch, as heretofore given in this paper.

The proceedings of the Legislature of Massachusetts have elicited much and various comment. Some journals, with that contemptible desire of twisting every circumstance to the uses of party, which distinguishes the newspaper press of this country, treat these resolutions as a whig measure, while others are equally anxious to charge them upon the democrats. The *Washington Globe*, the *Richmond Enquirer*, the *Albany Argus*, and the American of this city, are the leading prints that seek to give a party complexion to the proceeding. The *National Intelligencer* takes higher ground, and speaks of the resolutions according to its opinion of their intrinsic character and tendency, without rushing in the face of notorious facts to impute them to either of the parties into which men are divided on other questions of politics.

"The right of the people peaceably to assemble, and to petition the government for a redress of grievances," is declared in the first article of the amendments to the Constitution, and Congress is expressly forbidden to make any law abridging that right. The question which arises on the terms of the article is whether the right extends no further than to the mere offering of a petition, or whether it includes an obligation upon the government to receive it, and to make such disposition of it as may seem proper under the circumstances. It seems to us, clearly, that a *law* of Congress, refusing to receive petitions on any particular class of subjects, would be a violation of the plain intent and meaning of the Article. *A resolution* of either house of Congress, to the same effect, does the work of a *law*, and seems to us equally a violation of the constitutional provision. But as the *Intelligencer* waves this point as a matter of argument, and confines itself to a simple expression of opinion, we shall also content ourselves, for the present, with stating in these general terms our contrary view of the duty of Congress in regard to petitions.

The alleged power of Congress to abolish slavery and the traffic in slaves in the District of Columbia, presents a topic which the *Intelligencer* deems worthy of more particular notice. It pronounces it a "despotic power," and enters its "solemn protest" against the doctrine. Despotic power is a phrase somewhat revolting to democratic ears, because people are accustomed to associate the idea of despotism with that of the unlimited and arbitrary rule of a single tyrant; but despotic power is neither more nor less than absolute power, whether exercised by one or many, by an autocrat at the impulse of his mere will and pleasure, or by the representatives of a people, according to the written provisions of a constitutional charter as their own creation. Despotic power is neither more nor less, to use the constitutional phrase, than the power "to exercise exclusive legislation, in all cases whatsoever," over the district given up to such legislation. The power of Congress over the District of Columbia is in very truth *despotic power;* that is, it is absolute power; that is, it is the power of exclusive legislation in all cases whatsoever.

The states of Virginia and Maryland, when they ceded the territory to the federal government which now constitutes the District of Columbia, surrendered it to this power of exclusive legislation. The federal government could receive it upon no other condition than that specified in the Constitution, that it should possess the right to exercise over it absolute rule in every possible respect not expressly interdicted by the Constitution. They who then resided or owned property in that limit, if they were dissatisfied with the surrender could remove or dispose of their possessions. The being put to that inconvenience and possible loss constituted a fair subject of petition for indemnity to the sovereign power of their own state. If they chose to remain and suffer themselves and their possessions to be transferred from state to federal authority, they did so with a full knowledge that their rights of personal property then came under the "exclusive legislation of Congress in all cases whatsoever," with no limits whatever upon its power, but those expressed in the provisions of the Constitution. The foundation of the right of property in every country is the law of the land. The foundation of the right of property in Virginia and Maryland is the law of Virginia and Maryland. When Virginia and Maryland surrender a portion of their territory to another government, relinquishing to that other government exclusive right of legislation in all cases whatsoever, the foundation of the right of property in the territory so relinquished then rests in the legislative power to which the surrender is made. The owners of property hold their possessions subject to the control of a despotism. This is the case with the inhabitants of the District of Columbia, and so much for the legal right of Congress to abolish slavery there. The moral right, or what the *Intelligencer* terms the expediency of the measure, constitutes another question which we do not feel called upon to discuss at the present time.

A FEW WORDS TO THE ABOLITIONISTS.

[*From the Plaindealer, April* 22, 1837.]

THE temper in which some of the newspapers, devoted to the abolition of slavery, treat that momentous subject is exceedingly reprehensible—hardly less so, indeed, than that opposite spirit of fanaticism and persecution against which we have so repeatedly and earnestly exerted our voice. The emancipation of three millions of human beings from degrading servitude is a great and noble object, and the means should partake of the same character. Exciting and opprobrious language, insulting jeers, angry denunciations, and uncalled for imputations of unworthy motives, should be scrupulously avoided. They who are governed by the right spirit in endeavouring to accomplish the enfranchisement of the blacks, aim to achieve a great good to the master, as well as to the slave. They aim to do away an evil, moral, social and political, and one that exercises a pernicious influence on all classes of men where it exists. A motive of so much benevolence and philanthropy is best and most effectually shown, in its true character, by kind and assuasive means. But such are not the means resorted to by several of the leading abolition papers. Their language is acrimonious; their condemnation of the slaveholders is sweeping and malignant; their jibes and taunts are full of sharpness and asperity; and the grossest imputations are uttered in bold assertions, without being supported by a syllable of proof. All this is bad, very bad, and tends to retard the good work, which they profess themselves desirous to promote.

It is difficult, we readily concede, for we have experienced it to be so on more than one occasion, to temper with becoming moderation the expressions which indignation naturally prompts on perusing the accounts of those outrages which the negroes and their defenders constantly suffer. We do not know that it is even desirable that, on such occasions, a writer should strive to give vent to his emotions of abhorrence and reprobation in a rill of soft and musical words. Let him pour out his sentiments in a torrent of manly eloquence; let him express himself freely and warmly; let his pen obey the dictates of his heart; let him "cry aloud and spare not." But while we do not condemn, but rather commend, such fervour as honourable, when provoked by the immediate spectacle of wrong and outrage, we would not always come to the consideration of the question of slavery in such an excited temper. It is a question for calm discussion. It is a question of facts and arguments. It is a question which involves vast interests. It is fraught with momentous consequences. It concerns the peace, happiness, and prosperity of millions of fellow-beings. It is inseparably connected with political considerations of the gravest and holiest kind. It is, in short, a question, more than any other which can arise in our Confederacy, that imperatively calls for caution, temperance, and kindness, in the discussion of it. We should not approach it with malevolence in our hearts, either towards the master or slave. We should not approach it as partisans or sectarians. We should come to it only as friends of freedom and humanity, as champions of equal rights, solely desirous of accomplishing that noble end of democratic effort—the greatest good of the greatest number of our fellow men.

This is not the spirit which some of the abolition prints display. The following article, for example, from a recent number of the *Boston Liberator* will not stand the test of the rule we have laid down. It is acrimonious, vindictive, intolerant, and unjust, and unworthy, in every respect, of the cause in which that newspaper is engaged.

The article referred to, after alluding to certain religious anniversaries which are about to be held in this city, Philadelphia and Boston, continues in the following wise:

" It is expected that many slaveholding ministers and christians from the south will be in the above named cities in May. They are coming on to pray and make speeches at our anniversaries.

" But let our coloured citizens beware of these southern ministers and christians. They *may* have another object in attending our anniversaries, besides praying and making speeches. This object very nearly concerns our coloured citizens. These slaveholders think all coloured people ought to be slaves. They look upon you as property, and when they see you and your wives and children walking through the streets, instead of thinking how to do good and save your souls, they think how much you would bring in the market, if they could get you to Baltimore, Washington, Richmond, or New-Orleans.

"So after having made a long prayer and a good speech at an anniversary, perhaps you will find them at night lurking about your houses, to catch you and carry you off to the south. As you come out of your doors, it may be they will spring upon you, knock you down, gag you, chain and fetter you, give you a good cowhiding to keep you still; and then take you to some ship in the harbour and send you to the south.

"Especially, if there has been a contribution at the anniversary, and they have given any thing, then it especially stands you in hand to beware. You may expect that they will indemnify themselves by stealing your wives and children. They know our city authorities will not protect you. They know the ministers and christians of New-York and Boston will think just as well of them if they do kidnap a goodly number of our citizens.

"I warn you to keep in doors. Lock, bolt and bar your doors. Close your shutters. Be careful how you appear at the anniversaries. How do you know but while the slaveholder is making a speech, he may mark you out for his prey? I tell you, slaveholding ministers are accustomed to steal men, women and children every day. It is the first great object of their lives. The next is praying and preaching.

"Up, watch, look out for slaveholding ministers and christians, or your wives and children may be torn from your embrace, and dragged away to weep, to pine and die in the land of tears and blood."

Can anything be in a worse temper than this? It is such articles, and such conduct as naturally and almost necessarily flows from the circulation of such articles, that cause the opponents of slavery to be denounced as fanatics and incendiaries. There is certainly both a fanatical and incendiary spirit and tendency in the remarks we have copied. The abolitionists may rely upon it that they do not advance their object by ebullitions so intolerant and denunciatory. Their natural effect is to exasperate opponents and abate the zeal of friends.

CONNECTION OF STATE WITH BANKING.

[*From the Plaindealer*, *May* 6, 1837.]

A PARAGRAPH from a recent number of this paper, under the head of *Political Meddling with Finance,* is copied by the *Richmond Whig*, and commented upon as a concession that the "experiment" of the last administration, with regard to the currency, has failed. That journal holds the following language:

"The following article from the *Plaindealer*, the ablest and most honest Van Buren paper with which we are acquainted, makes the important concession that the great '*Experiment*' of the *hero* has failed. This conveys no information to our minds, for we have never for one moment been so far deluded as to believe that the result of the tinkering of the currency would be otherwise than it is. Apart from the concession of the failure of the '*Experiment*,' the reason assigned for that failure is worthy of notice. 'Instead of dissolving all connexion between the government and the banks, that connexion has been rendered more complicate,' says the writer, by the new system. Of course it has. That the government might have indisputable control of the banks, and employ them as partisan engines, was the consideration which prompted the '*Experiment*.' All who were honest, and had any acquaintance with finance and commerce, foresaw and foretold that the prostitution of the currency of the country to party would bring ruin."

We thank the *Richmond Whig* for the complimentary terms in which it speaks of us; though, without any affectation of modesty, we must disclaim the justice of its praise, while an administration newspaper, published in this very city, comes daily under our notice, conducted not only with strict integrity, but in the most enlightened and philosophical spirit of political discussion, and showing, in almost every leading article, rare scholarship, great copiousness of logical resources, felicitous command of language, earnest patriotism, large views of public economy, and firm devotion to the cause of truth, joined with such kindness of temper as strips controversy of its bitterness, and leaves the decision of questions to the unclouded judgment of its readers. It would be a happy thing for the people, if there were more newspapers, on both sides of the dividing line of parties, directed by a spirit of so much purity and intelligence. We need not add that we allude to the *Evening Post.*

There is another point in the commendation of the *Richmond Whig* which requires to be set right. This is not a Van Buren paper. The great purpose of our journal is to advance the cause of political truth. We do not adopt, as our maxim, the stale and deceptive cant of *principia non homines,* which is usually the motto of those whose purposes are utterly selfish and base. We contend for men, as well as principles; but for the former as the means, and the latter as the object. For this reason, we are friendly to Mr. Van Buren, considering him as the instrument chosen by the democracy of the country to carry into effect democratic principles in the administration of the federal government. So far as he is true to that great trust, he shall assuredly have our zealous support; but we shall support him in no deviation, however slight, from the straight and obvious path of democratic duty, and should he, in any instance, stray widely from it, he will assuredly encounter our decided opposition. Of this we have already given an earnest, in our condemnation of the strange and startling avowal with which he commenced his executive career—his precedaneous exercise of the veto power. It is an unwarrantable use of political metonymy, then, to call the *Plaindealer* a Van Buren journal. It is a democratic journal, and is ambitious of no higher name.

With regard to the imputed concession made by this paper, we only ask that our language should not be strained to larger uses than its obvious purport justifies. We do not consider that the "*experiment*" has failed, if by that party catchword is meant the measures of the last administration in regard to the United States Bank. We approved then, and approve now, the veto of the bill to recharter that institution. We approved then, and approve now, the removal of the federal revenues from its custody. And we should consider the reinstitution of a bank, in the popular sense of that word, by the federal authority, as one of the very worst evils which could befall our country. What we disapprove now, and what we have always disapproved, is that the government should connect itself, in any way, or to any extent, with the business of banking. When it removed its money from the federal bank, it should not have deposited it with the banks which exist under state authority. It should have stood wholly aloof from such institutions. The only legitimate use which it has for its funds is, in our view, to pay its necessary expenses; and the only legitimate keeper of them in the meanwhile is itself. The treasures of the United States are raised by taxation, in specified modes, for the purpose of paying the debts and providing for the common defence and general welfare of the country. The Constitution recognizes nothing as money but gold and silver coin; and the government should therefore receive its revenues in nothing else. It recognizes, in strictness, nothing as an object to which those revenues are to be applied but the necessary expenses incurred in conducting the general political affairs of the Confederacy. The safe keeping of the money, then, is the only object to be effected, between the collection and the disbursement of it. For this purpose the government is itself fully competent. It has but to establish a place of deposit, under proper guardians, in the commercial focus of the country, and pay the various branches of public service with checks or drafts on that depositary. It has, properly, nothing to do with the exchanges of the country. They are an affair of trade, which should be left to the laws of trade. It has, properly, nothing to do with the currency, which is also an affair of trade, and perfectly within the competency of its own natural laws to govern. Let the government confine itself to its plain and obvious political duties. Let it have nothing to do with a "credit system." Let it connect itself neither with corporations nor individuals. Let it keep its own money, taking care that it is *money*, and not *promises;* and let it leave it to unfettered sagacity and enterprise to devise and carry into effect whatever system of exchange and credit may be found most advantageous to the commercial interests of society.

The first objection which will probably suggest itself to these views is, that they contemplate the keeping of a vast fund of the precious metals hoarded up from use, which might be profitably employed as the basis of commercial credit. But is it not necessary that the fund should be vast? and, on the contrary, it is admitted by politicians both of the democratic and aristocratic sects, the former on general political principle, and the latter from aversion to the dominant party, or distrust of its integrity, that the revenue should be adjusted to the scale of expenditure. The keeping of the surplus safely locked up in the shape of money, would afford an additional motive to both parties to increase their efforts to reduce the revenue to the minimum amount. Again, as to this money being susceptible of being usefully employed as a basis of credit. Credit to whom? The government does not need it; for it has no business to transact on credit. The people collectively do not need it; for it is as much a part of the substantial wealth of the country under the lock and key of the federal treasury, as it would be under that of any bank or individual. And no bank or individual needs it; for the credit of every bank and of every person is sufficiently extended when it covers the basis of their own real wealth. If extended beyond this, on the basis of a loan or deposit from the government, it is obvious such bank or individual would be deriving an advantage by jeoparding the money of the government; that is, of the people; that is, the rights of the many would be endangered for the benefit of the few.

Another objection to our theory may be urged, that if the government gathered its revenue for safe keeping at any one point, its checks on that fund, in some quarters where payments would be necessary, would be below par, and the receiver of them would thus be defrauded of a portion of his dues. This would not be so, in fact, in any part of our country, if the commercial focus of the Confederacy were selected as the place for the federal depositary. Should it happen, however, in relation to any branch of the public service, say, for example, some military outpost, the government would but be under the necessity of transporting the requisite amount of funds to such outposts ; and the cost of doing so would be as much the legitimate expense to be defrayed out of the general fund, as any other expense incurred in the conducting of our political affairs. The same remark will hold good of the cost of conveying the revenues from the various points where collected, to the place of general deposit.

These are, in brief, our views as to the duty of the federal government, in regard to the collection and disbursement of its revenues. The great object which we desire to see accomplished, and to the accomplishment of which, we think, the course of things is obviously tending, is the utter and complete divorcement of politics from the business of banking. We desire to see banking divorced not only from federal legislation, but from state legislation. Nothing but evil, either in this country or others, has arisen from their union. The regulation of the currency, and the regulation of credit, are both affairs of trade. Men want no laws on the subject, except for the punishment of frauds. They want no laws except such as are necessary for the protection of their equal rights. If the government deposites its money with a corporation, a voluntary association, or an individual, it does so either on the condition of some return being rendered, or none. If none, an advantage, which is the property of the whole people, is given to one or a few, in manifest violation of of the people's equal rights. If it receives a return, that return is either an equivalent or not. But no corporation, association, or individual would render an exact equivalent, since only the profit of the trust would present a motive for assuming it. If the return is not an equivalent, it is still manifest that one or a few are benefited at the expense of the many.

We are no enemy to banking. It is a highly useful branch of trade. It is capable of accomplishing many important results, the advantages of which, without legislative control or impediment, would naturally diffuse themselves over the whole surface of society. Banking is an important wheel in the great machine of commerce; and commerce, not confining the word to merchants, who are mere intermediaries and factors, but using it to express the stupendous aggregate of that vast reciprocal intercourse which embraces alike the products of agriculture and art, science and literature—commerce is the efficient instrument of civilization and promoter of all that improves and elevates mankind. We cannot therefore be an enemy of any essential part in so beneficent a whole. Our hostility is not directed against banking, but against that legislative intermeddling, by which it is withdrawn from the harmonious operation of its own laws, and subjected to laws imposed by ignorance, selfishness, ambition and rapacity.

The "experiment" of the last administration, so far as it was an experiment intended to separate the government from connexion with banks, and to bring about the repudiation of every thing but real money in its dealings with the citizens, has our warmest approbation. The specie circular, for the same reason, is an "experiment" which we wholly approved, and Mr. Van Buren has strengthened our good opinion of him by his firmness in adhering to that measure, against the clamour of which it has been made a prolific theme. Glad should we be, if a law, of a tenor corresponding with that order, were enacted in relation to the payments at the customs. We should be rejoiced if the federal government should set so noble an example to the monopoly-loving legislatures of the states, and teach them that the money of the Constitution is the only money which should be known to the laws. They who ascribe the present embarrassments of trade to the "experiments" of Andrew Jackson are not wholly in the wrong. Much of the present evil, we do not question, might have been avoided, had the United States Bank been quietly re-chartered, without opposition, and without curtailment of its powers. It would then have had no motive for its alternate contractions and expansions, beyond the mere desire of pecuniary gain, unless, indeed, it had chosen to play the part of "king-maker," and dictate to the people whom they should elect to fill their chief political trusts. But not being quietly re-chartered, it undertook to coerce the administration to do what it was not disposed to do of its own free will, and hence was tried, in the first place, the efficacy of a sudden pressure, and afterwards of a sudden expansion. It was this course which gave the original impulse to the spirit of wild speculation, and led to the creation of such a large number of banking institutions by the several states. The result, probably, was not wholly unforeseen by the late President, when he refused his signature to the act renewing the charter of the United States Bank. The path of duty, however, lay plain before him; and to turn aside from it would have been as inexcusable, as would be the conduct of that judge who should pardon an atrocious criminal from the fear that, if executed, his confederates might embrace the occasion to excite a tumult, and throw the community into temporary disorder. The course of justice ought not to be stayed by such a consideration in the one case more than in the other.

If the community desire a banking institution, capable of regulating the currency and the exchanges, and possessed of all the power for good which distinguished the United States Bank, without that enormous power of evil by which it was more distinguished, let them, through the ballot-boxes, insist on the abolition of all restraints on the freedom of trade. Enterprise and competition, if they were free to act, would soon build up a better bank than it is in the power of Congress to create, putting out of sight the constitutional objection ; and they would regulate its issues, ensure its solvency, and confine it within the proper field of bank operations, far more effectually than could the most cunningly devised checks and conditions which legislative wisdom ever framed. This is the great "experiment" which has yet to be tried ; and it requires no spirit of prophecy to foresee that one of the great dividing questions of politics for some years to come will resolve itself into a demand, on the one hand, for a federal bank, and, on the other, for the total separation of bank and state. We have provided with great care against the union of politics and religion ; but in our judgment a hierarchical mixture in our government is not more to be deprecated than an alliance between legislation and banking. *Church and State*, has an evil sound ; but *Bank and State* grates more harshly on our ears.

THE CRISIS.

"Laissez nous faire."

[*From the Plaindealer, May* 13, 1837.]

THE community is now experiencing a beautiful illustration of the excellence of the monopoly system. All the banks in this city suspended payment on Wednesday last, and it is to be presumed the example will be followed far and wide. Here, then, is an end of the safety fund bubble, the best system of banks and currency ever devised by human ingenuity, if we may believe the *Albany Argus*, and its followers of the monopoly school, and one of the worst that ever fraud imposed upon credulity, if we will but examine it by the lights of wisdom and experience.

We say here is an end of the safety fund bubble; but this position is conditional on the people's asserting their equal rights, and demanding the absolute divorcement of legislation from the business of banking, and from all supervisory connection with trade and credit, further than the mere enforcement of the obligations of contracts, and the punishment of frauds. If the present condition of things does not impel them to do this, they are sunk in a depth of fatuity beyond all hope of redemption. It is as palpable to the mind, as the universal light of day to the senses, that the present anarchical and chaotic condition of financial affairs is the result, the direct and inevitable result, of the unholy alliance between politics and banking. The union of bank and state in this country is crushing the people under the weight of a despotism as grievous as was ever imposed upon mankind by the union of church and state. Better, far better, to be under the dominion of a hierarchy, than under the galling and ignoble rule of legislation money-changers.

What a world of wisdom there is in the brief phrase we have placed as a motto to this article! Society, recovering from the delirium excited by the stimulus of special legislation, begins to see that true wisdom consists, not in regulating trade by a system of artificial checks and balances, perpetually liable to be thrown into disorder, which the very complication of the contrivance then renders almost irremediable, but simply *in letting trade alone*. There are abundant indications around us that we shall not long stand unaided in the views we have frequently expressed of the utter folly and inevitable evil of all legislative intermeddling with the natural laws of trade. Banking is a good thing enough in its intrinsic nature; but government should have no connection with it, and should recognize nothing as money but silver and gold.

We are not an enemy to a paper representative of money, any more than we are to confidence between man and man in any other shape it may naturally assume, for mutual convenience, in the transaction of necessary dealings. We are not an enemy to banking, any more than we are to any other branch of traffic instrumental in carrying on the great commercial intercourse of society. We are an enemy only to a mixture of politics with banking; to the vain attempts to regulate the channels in which trade shall run; to that legislative intermeddling which withdraws credit from the harmonious operation of its own laws, disturbs its equal flow, and leaves the community to be at one time deluged with a cataclysm of paper money, and at another exposed to all the horrors of financial drought.

It would be a happy thing for this country, if the doubtful power under which banks are created had been positively withheld. It would be a happy thing if all right of interference with trade, either by immunities or prohibitions, by restraining laws or special charters, had been solemnly interdicted. More misery, more immorality, more degradation of the many for the undue elevation of the few, than can even be conjectured, have resulted from the vain attempts to regulate the currency. Let commerce, and let the currency, which is but an appendage and accident of commerce, regulate themselves; and let the government confine its attention strictly to the purposes which constitute the sole legitimate ends of political organization, the mere protection of person and property. We should then soon present to the world the spectacle of a people more free, more equally prosperous, and more happy, than has ever yet furnished a subject to the historian. The history of the past is but a Newgate Calender on an extensive scale; the history of the future would be a work of a sublimer character.

In the midst of the financial desolation which has been brought upon us by the inevitable operation of monopoly legislation—by the wretched charlatanry which seeks to prop up an artificial system of credit with special statutes, and hedge it round with penalties and prohibitions—the community has an ample opportunity to contemplate the consequences of that folly which would substitute the laws of man for those of nature, and wholly change the irreversible order of causes and effects. Can any man who has eyes to see, or ears to hear, or understanding to conceive, survey the deplorable wrecks of commerce and credit strewn on every side, the broken columns and arches of the great fabric of trade, or listen to the groans of an agonized community lying prostrate beneath the ruins, without the conviction rushing into his mind, that the melancholy result must be ascribed to those, who, clothed in brief legislative authority, interpose their fantastic expedients in place of that natural system which constitutes the eternal fitness of things. Each fragment of our shattered commerce bears, stamped in characters which he who runs may read, the forceful inscription—"THIS IS THE FRUIT OF MONOPOLY LEGISLATION."

We were forewarned, timely forewarned, and by one whose counsel we had reason to respect, of the embarrassments in which special legislation would involve us. The messages of Andrew Jackson are replete with lessons of admonitory wisdom. But the passion of avarice had seized upon our hearts, and the desire of sudden riches outweighed the suggestions of reason. We behold now the consequences of our infatuation. We are now admonished by that sternest of teachers, experience. But the lesson, though rude, will lead only to good, if we have the sense to pause, and read it aright.

The banks are broken, and, without legislative intervention, will soon forfeit their charters. We have been sorrowfully taught the miserable impotence of legislation; it is the fountain from which the waters of bitterness have flowed; let us not then again unseal it, that it may effuse another desolating flood. What can legislation do? Insult the community, by confirming the special privileges of money changers, after their own acts have declared their utter worthlessness? Enable a band of paper-money depredators to prey more voraciously than before on the vitals of the people? Authorize them to pour out a fresh torrent of their promises, now really of no more value than the paper on which they are writ? Will the community tolerate such an enormous fraud?

Let the Banks perish! Let the monopolists be swept from the board! Let the whole brood of privileged money-changers give place to the hardy offsprings of commercial freedom, who ask for no protection but equal laws, and no exemption from the shocks of boundless competition. We commisserate the innocent who suffer by the downfall of the banks; but we cannot consent that a mitigation of their troubles shall be purchased by the perpetuation of a system fraught with so much evil to the entire community. Now is the time for the complete emancipation of trade from legislative thraldom. If this propitious moment is suffered to pass by unimproved, the fetter, now riven almost asunder, will be rivetted anew, and hold us in slavery forever. The choice is presented to us of freedom or perpetual bondage. Let us demand, then, as with one voice, the reintegration of our natural rights; let us protest against the renovation of that cumbrous fabric of legislative fraud and folly, which has fallen of its own weight, and, if raised again, will again topple before the first commercial revulsion, to bury other myriads in its ruins.

If we knew any form of speech which would arrest the attention of our reader, or any mode of argument which would satisfy his reason, that we have not again and again used, we would employ it now, with all the earnestness of a sincere conviction of the importance of the subject, to persuade him that the only true ground of hope for the enduring prosperity of our commerce, in all its vast and complicated relations, consists in giving freedom to trade. Free banking is the system pursued in Scotland, and that country escapes revulsions, while England and America are exposed to continual paroxysms and collapsions, to expansions that unsettle all the foundations of property, and contractions that reduce whole communities to wretchedness and want. England, with all the monarchical and aristocratic potentiality of its government, has never yet been able to regulate the currency, with its stupendous machinery of finance. But Scotland, without any separate government, and without any legislative machinery of finance, has enjoyed a staple and uniform currency, because it has wisely been left to the natural laws of trade.

If the wants of the community require a great banking institution, capable of regulating the currency and exchanges, set trade free, and it will supply such an institution of its own accord. We need not go as humble petitioners either to our state or federal government, and beseech it to bestow special privileges on a few, that they may regulate the affairs of the many : we have only to adopt the franker and manlier course of demanding back those natural rights, of which we have been defrauded by dishonest and ignorant legislators. We need seek no immunity, but only claim our own. We need ask for the imposition of no new statute on the overburthened people, but only for the abrogation of laws which now weigh them to the earth. We desire nothing but the common privilege of pursuing our own business, in our own way, without a legislative taskmaster to say how much we shall do, what equivalent we shall have for our toil.

The same enterprise which freights the ocean with our products, which breaks our rivers into a thousand eddies with the revolving wheels of steamboats, which permeates the land with canals, and binds state to state in the iron embrace of railroads, would be abundantly able to perform the humble functions of banker, without the aid of legislative favour, or protection. Enterprise would build up, and competition would regulate, a better system of banks than legislation ever can devise. We have tried, to our cost, the competency of the latter, and we are now tasting the bitter consequences of our credulity.

Let us now test the experiment of freedom. It cannot place us in a worse condition than that to which we have been hurled by the terrible avulsion of the monopoly system.

THE SAFETY FUND BUBBLE.

[*From the Plaindealer, May* 20, 1837.]

——— Help me, Cassius, or I sink !
SHAKSPEARE.

THE prayer of the insolvent Banks has been granted by our monopoly legislature, and they are permitted, in the teeth of their own confession of inability to perform their contracts, to continue to issue their worthless and lying promises, which the community are virtually obliged to receive as real money. Was there ever a piece of grosser legislative fraud than this? Here have been merchants failing by scores for months past. Many of them show, to the entire satisfaction of their creditors, that their property far overbalances their debts. The difficulty of obtaining ready money has obliged them to suspend their payments; but it is rendered manifest, by a full exposition of their affairs, that not a dollar will ultimately be lost by those having claims upon them. The immediate cause which compelled these persons to suspend their business was the impossibility of obtaining money on any kind of securities. But that impossibility was itself the effect of another cause: and if we trace the connexion of cause and effect to the beginning, we shall find that the whole evil grew out of the monstrous expansion of bank credit, which provoked a most inordinate thirst of speculation, and stimulated men to undertake the wildest enterprises. These enterprises were of a nature to require a continually increasing expansion of bank credit. But there was a limit which the banks did not dare to overpass. When that limit was reached, the demand for money to sustain the mad projects which had been undertaken led to the freely giving of the most exorbitant rates of interest to private money dealers. These rates of interest soon consumed the actual means of speculators, and they were forced to sacrifice their property to meet the further demands upon them. Capitalists, seeing that the financial revulsion had commenced, withdrew from the field in alarm. The banks, fearful of a demand for specie, began to retrench as rapidly as they had expanded; and the merchant, in the meanwhile, who had pursued the even tenor of his way, neither enlarging nor diminishing his business, but keeping within those bounds which all former experience told him were compatible with safety, now began to experience the bitter consequences of folly in which he had had no share. In vain he offered triple and quadruple securities for the sums necessary for the transaction of his business. The extravagance and rapacity of the banks had produced, as their natural fruit, a general prostration of commercial confidence. Individuals were afraid to lend; for in the midst of the fictitious values which speculation had given to every thing, they could not decide whether the proffered security was real or illusory, whether substantial or a mere phantom of property, which would melt to nothing in their grasp. The banks could not lend, for they were involved in the meshes of their own wide-spread net; and to extricate themselves, as the result has shown, was a task beyond their strength. They had been potent instruments in producing the general derangement, but were utterly powerless to remedy it. The consequence was, that many a sound and solvent merchant was arrested by inevitable necessity, in the midst of a prosperous career, and obliged to trust his affairs entirely to the mercy of his creditors, and to the sport of accident.

While these deplorable bankruptcies were taking place, we heard of no proposition of relief from our legislature; but the instant that the banks, those prolific fountains from which the streams of mischief flowed, became insolvent, all other business of the state was laid aside, and the sole question deemed worthy of consideration was what means should be devised for propping up the worthless monopoly institutions. As the result of legislative wisdom, employed on this commendable object, we have the following law.

* * * * * *

To discuss the particular provisions of the law which we have submitted to our readers would be a waste of their time and our own. It is enough that is the law. The measure, which the exigency of the times could not but suggest to every mind at all imbued with the true principles of economic freedom, has not been accomplished; but in its stead, a measure has been adopted, by an overwhelming majority, to continue the privileges of an affiliated league of monopolies, after the condition on which those privileges were originally granted has been violated, and the object they were designed to effect has utterly failed. The chartered banks should have been left to their fate. If they are solvent, no loss could occur to any connected with them, nearly or remotely, by such a course; and if they are insolvent, on what principle of justice are they permitted to continue their depredations on the community? The repeal of all the restraints on the trade in money would open the field of banking to universal enterprise and competition; and enterprise and competition, in that branch of business, as in every other, would lead to the happiest results.

It was once feared that religion could not flourish, if separated from the supervision of government; but the success of the voluntary principle in this country has refuted the theories of hierarchists. The success of the voluntary principle in banking would be not less exemplary. The day is coming, we are convinced, when men will universally deprecate all connexion between *Bank and State,* with as much abhorrent earnestness as they now deprecate a connexion between *Church and State.* We have no established religion; why need we have an established bank? One of two things is absolutely certain: either we must utterly dissolve the affairs of politics from those of trade; or we must go back to the system of federal supervision. We must either have no chartered bank, or we must have a national bank. We must either leave trade wholly free, or place it under effectual control. Bad as is the scheme of a federal bank, worse evils are to be dreaded from the fraud and folly of state monopolies. The only true system—the system which has been proved to be good in every thing to which its principles have been applied—the system in entire accordance with the fundamental maxims of liberty—is to confine politics to the affairs of government, and leave trade to its own laws. When our federal Government and our State governments separate themselves entirely from banking and credit, recognizing nothing as money but money, keeping their own revenues in their own custody, and leaving men to form their own system of currency and credit, without intervention, further than to enforce the obligation of contracts, or exact the penalty of violating them—then, and not till then, shall we be a happy and a prosperous people.

NEWSPAPER NOMINATIONS.

[*From the Plaindealer, May* 20, 1837.]

In our last number, when commenting on the "no partisan" professions of the whig travelling committee, we stated that the proceedings of that veracious body had a direct reference to an intended nomination, at no distant day, of Mr. Webster, as a candidate for the office of President. Circumstances have forced this nomination to be made, in an informal manner, at an earlier day than was anticipated. The *Evening Star*, of Thursday last, having intimated, in pretty positive terms, that Mr. Clay is entitled to the support of the aristocracy, as their next candidate for the chief executive office of the Confederacy, the *Commercial Advertiser* and the *American* of the following evening eagerly reprehended the movement of their contemporary, and protested that Daniel Webster was their man. We are sorry to observe any signs of division in the ranks of our adversaries. We should be much better pleased to see them all unite, with one mind and heart, on a single individual; and we should be still better pleased if that individual were Mr. Webster. This would bring the strife on the true ground of antagonist political principles. It would call upon the people to array themselves under the standard either of democracy or aristocracy. It would show conclusively whether the intelligence of this country acknowledges the maxim that "PROPERTY IS THE TEST OF MERIT," or whether it still holds to the opposite maxim, "THE EQUALITY OF HUMAN RIGHTS."

The aristocratic party ought to select Mr. Webster for their candidate. They acted scurvily towards him in the last contest. To thrust him aside from the field, that they might array themselves under the petticoat banner of so poor an "available," such a mere effigy of a leader, as General Harrison, was, to say the least, mortifying treatment. They owe Mr. Webster reparation. They owe it to themselves, too, to pursue a more dignified course. Their political projects, heretofore, have been palpable confessions of inferiority. They have sought to disguise the true issue. They have seized hold of temporary and local questions. They have selected candidates, not with reference to their capacity or principles, but solely with reference to their supposed power of healing divisions, and uniting separate interests. It is time they should come out in their true characters, and avow the real objects for which they contend. Let them declare, then, their rooted distrust of the intelligence and integrity of the mass of the people; their belief that property is the test of merit, and should be the basis of suffrage; their opinion that the duty of government is to take care of the rich, leaving it to the rich to take care of the poor; and their desire, for the furtherance of these objects, to establish a federal bank, with sufficient capital to buy up men and presses, like cattle in the market. At the end of such a confession of faith, nothing could be in better keeping than the nomination of Daniel Webster for the office of President.

Mr. Webster is certainly a great man. We should oppose him, wholly, heartily, and with all the zeal of a firm conviction that his principles are hostile to liberty. But we do not hesitate to call him a great man ; a man of strong and capacious mind, much information, vigorous powers of reasoning, and an uncommon flow of stern and majestic eloquence. He is greater as a lawyer than as a statesman ; but in both characters he stands in the foremost rank. We admire the energy of his faculties. When passages of his speeches come before us, separate from a consideration of the questions which elicited them, we always peruse them with delight. The pleasure they afford us is but the involuntary homage which the mind pays to a superior intellect ; but it changes, by a natural transition, to an opposite feeling, when we are led to reflect upon the nature of the objects for which he is exerting his abilities. Not to assist in enfranchising his fellow-man ; not to hasten that glorious day-spring of equal liberty, which is beginning to dawn upon the world ; not to spread wider and wider the principles of democratic freedom, and break down the artificial and aristocratic distinctions, which diversify the surface of society with such hideous inequalities, does Mr. Webster raise his voice in the Senate-house. The dogmas of his political creed, like the dogmas of an intolerant religion, would confine the blessings of government, as the latter would those of heaven, to an exclusive few, leaving all the other myriads of men to toil and sweat in a state of immitigable degradation. This is the true end and aim of the aristocratic creed. This is the true and inevitable tendency of their measures who contend for a national bank. This is their open profession when they proclaim that property is the proof of merit, and, by the unavoidable converse, that poverty is the proof of unworthiness. For those who acknowledge such sentiments and motives, Mr. Webster is the proper candidate. He has talents and acquirements that must command respect; his personal character is unimpeached; and he has toiled long and strenuously in their service. We are glad that they are about to do all in their power to render a grateful return. The democracy will now have something to contend against, as well as something to contend for. There will be glory in overthrowing such an antagonist, as well as great gain in preserving the supremacy of their principles. With such an opponent as Harrison, we enter languidly into the contest, as a task of mere duty; with such a one as Webster, we shall rush into it eagerly, as a matter of pride as well as patriotism.

THE MORALS OF POLITICS.

[*From the Plaindealer*, *June* 3, 1837.]

Public moralists have long noticed with regret, that the political contests of this country are conducted with intemperance wholly unsuited to conflicts of reason, and decided, in a great measure, by the efforts of the worst class of people. We apply this phrase, not to those whom the aristocracy designate as the "lower orders;" but to those only, whether well or ill dressed, and whether rich or poor, who enter into the struggle without regard for the inherent dignity of politics, and without reference to the permanent interests of their country and of mankind; but animated by selfish objects, by personal preferences or prejudices, the desire of office, or the hope of accomplishing private ends through the influence of party. Elections are commonly looked upon as mere game, on which depends the division of party spoils, the distribution of chartered privileges, and the allotment of pecuniary rewards. The antagonist principles of government, which should constitute the sole ground of controversy, are lost sight of in the eagerness of sordid motives; and the struggle, which should be one of pure reason, with no aim but the achievement of political truth, and the promotion of the greatest good of the greatest number, sinks into a mere brawl, in which passion, avarice, and profligacy, are the prominent actors.

If the questions of government could be submitted to the people in the naked dignity of abstract propositions, men would reason upon them calmly, and frame their opinions according to the preponderance of truth. There is nothing in the intrinsic nature of politics that appeals to the passions of the multitude. It is an important branch of morals, and its principles, like those of private ethics, address themselves to the sober judgment of men. A strange spectacle would be presented, should we see mathematicians kindle into wrath in the discussion of a problem, and call on their hearers, in the angry terms of demagogues, to decide on the relative merits of opposite modes of demonstration.

The same temperance and moderation which characterize the investigation of truth in the exact sciences, belong not less to the inherent nature of politics, when confined within the proper field.

The object of all politicians, in the strict sense of the expression, is happiness—the happiness of a state—the greatest possible sum of happiness of which the social condition admits to those individuals who live together under the same political organization.

It may be asserted, as an undeniable proposition, that

it is the duty of every intelligent man to be a politician. This is particularly true of a country, the institutions of which admit every man to the exercise of equal suffrage. All the duties of life are embraced under the three heads of religion, politics, and morals. The aim of religion is to regulate the conduct of man with reference to happiness in a future state of being; of politics, to regulate his conduct with reference to the happiness of communities; and of morals, to regulate his conduct with reference to individual happiness.

Happiness, then, is the end and aim of these three great and comprehensive branches of duty; and no man perfectly discharges the obligations imposed by either, who neglects those which the others enjoin. The right ordering of a state affects, for weal or wo, the interests of multitudes of human beings; and every individual of those multitudes has a direct interest, therefore, in its being ordered aright.

"I am a man," says Terence, in a phrase as beautiful for the harmony of its language, as the benevolence and universal truth of its sentiment, "and nothing can be indifferent to me which affects humanity."

The sole legitimate object of politics, then, is the happiness of communities. They who call themselves politicians, having other objects, are not politicians, but demagogues. But is it in the nature of things, that the sincere and single desire to promote such a system of government as would most effectually secure the greatest amount of general happiness, can draw into action such violent passions, prompt such fierce declamation, authorize such angry criminations, and occasion such strong appeals to the worst motives of the venal and base, as we constantly see and hear in every conflict of the antagonist parties of our country? Or does not this effect arise from causes improperly mixed with politics, and with which they have no intrinsic affinity? Does it not arise from the fact, that government, instead of seeking to promote the greatest happiness of the community, by confining itself rigidly within its true field of action, has extended itself to embrace a thousand objects which should be left to the regulation of social morals, and unrestrained competition, one man with another, without political assistance or check? Are our elections, in truth, a means of deciding mere questions of government, or does not the decision of numerous questions affecting private interests, schemes of selfishness, rapacity, and cunning, depend upon them, even more than cardinal principles of politics?

It is to this fact, we are persuaded, that the immorality and licentiousness of party contests are to be ascribed. If government were restricted to the few and simple objects contemplated in the democratic creed, the mere protection of person, life, and property; if its functions were limited to the mere guardianship of the equal rights of men, and its action, in all cases, were influenced, not by the paltry suggestions of present expediency, but the eternal principles of justice; we should find reason to congratulate ourselves on the change, in the improved tone of public morals, as well as in the increased prosperity of trade.

The religious man, then, as well as the political and social moralist, should exert his influence to bring about the auspicious reformation. Nothing can be more self-evident than the demoralizing influence of special legislation. It degrades politics into a mere scramble for rewards obtained by a violation of the equal rights of the people; it perverts the holy sentiment of patriotism; induces a feverish avidity for sudden wealth; fosters a spirit of wild and dishonest speculation; withdraws industry from its accustomed channels of useful occupation; confounds the established distinctions between virtue and vice, honour and shame, respectability and degradation; pampers luxury; and leads to intemperance, dissipation, and profligacy, in a thousand forms.

The remedy is easy. It is to confine government within the narrowest limits of necessary duties. It is to disconnect bank and state. It is, to give freedom to trade, and leave enterprise, competition, and a just public sense of right to accomplish by their natural energies, what the artificial system of legislative checks and balances has so signally failed in accomplishing. The federal government has nothing to do, but to hold itself entirely aloof from banking, having no more connexion with it, than if banks did not exist. It should receive its revenues in nothing not recognized as money by the Constitution, and pay nothing else to those employed in its service. The state governments should repeal their laws imposing restraints on the free exercise of capital and credit. They should avoid, for the future, all legislation not in the fullest accordance with the letter and spirit of that glorious maxim of democratic doctrine, which acknowledges the equality of man's political rights. These are the easy steps by which we might arrive at the consummation devoutly to be wished.

The steps are easy; but passion, ignorance, and selfishness, are gathered round them, and oppose our ascent. Agrarian, leveller, and visionary, are the epithets, more powerful than arguments, with which they resist us. Shall we yield, discouraged, and submit to be always governed by the worst passions of the worst portions of mankind; or by one bold effort, shall we regenerate our institutions, and make government, indeed, not the dispenser of privileges to a few for their efforts in subverting the rights of the many, but the beneficent promoter of the equal happiness of all? The monopolists are prostrated by the explosion of their overcharged system; they are wrecked by the regurgitation of their own flood of mischief; they are buried beneath the ruins of the baseless fabric they had presumptuously reared to such a towering height.

Now is the time for the friends of freedom to bestir themselves. Let us accept the invitation of this glorious opportunity to establish, on an enduring foundation, the true principles of political and economic freedom.

We may be encountered with clamorous revilings; but they only betray the evil temper which ever distinguishes wilful error and baffled selfishness. We may be denounced with opprobrious epithets; but they only show the want of cogent arguments. The worst of these is only the stale charge of *ultraism,* which is not worthy of our regard. To be ultra is not necessarily to be wrong. Extreme opinions are justly censurable only when they are erroneous; but who can be reprehended for going too far towards the right?

"If the two extremes," says Milton, in answer to the same poor objection, "be vice and virtue, falsehood and truth, the greater extremity of virtue and superlative truth we run into, the more virtuous and the more wise we become; and he that, flying from degenerate corruption, fears to shoot himself too far into the meeting embraces of a divinely warranted reformation, might better not have run at all."

"ABOLITION INSOLENCE."

[*From the Plaindealer, July* 29, 1837.]

UNDER this head, the *Washington Globe* copies, from a Boston newspaper, the following paragraph:

"The insolence of some of the reckless agitators who

attempt to excite the people by their mad practices, is insufferable. On the fourth, the American flag—the flag of the Union—the national banner—was suspended from a cord extended from Concert Hall to the *Illuminator* office nearly opposite. In scandalous derision of this glorious emblem, every star and stripe of which is as dear to every true American citizen as 'the apple of his eye,' a placard emanating, as we learn, from the *Illuminator* office, was suspended by the side of the flag, bearing in large letters, on one side, 'Slavery's Cloak,' and on the other 'Sacred to oppression.' It remained only till it was noticed, when it was soon torn down. It is creditable to the assembled citizens who saw the scandalous scroll, that their insulted feelings were not urged to violent exasperation against the perpetrators of the outrage, and that the deed was treated with the contempt it deserved."

The insolence of the abolitionists, in the case here adduced, owed its *insufferableness* to its truth. While the people are told that the spirit of the federal compact forbids every attempt to promote the emancipation of three millions of fellow-beings, held in abject and cruel bondage, and that even the free discussion of the question of slavery is a sin against the Union, a "reckless disregard of consequences" deserving the fiercest punishment which "popular indignation" can suggest, we are forced to consider the emblem of our federal union *a cloak for slavery* and *a banner devoted to the cause of the most hateful oppression.* The oppression which our fathers suffered from Great Britain was nothing in comparison with that which the negroes experience at the hands of the slaveholders. It may be "abolition insolence" to say these things; but as they are truths which justice and humanity authorize us to speak, we shall not be too dainty to repeat them whenever a fitting occasion is presented. Every American who, in any way, authorizes or countenances slavery, is derelict to his duty as a christian, a patriot, and a man. Every one does countenance and authorize it, who suffers any opportunity of expressing his deep abhorrence of its manifold abominations to pass by unimproved. If the freemen of the north and west ould but speak out on this subject in such terms as their consciences prompt, we should soon have to rejoice in the complete enfranchisement of our negro brethren of the south.

If an extensive and well-arranged insurrection of the blacks should occur in any of the slave states, we should probably see the freemen of this quarter of the country rallying around that "glorious emblem" which is so magniloquently spoken of in the foregoing extract, and marching beneath its folds to take sides with the slaveholders, and reduce the poor negroes, struggling for liberty, to heavier bondage than they endured before. It may be "abolition insolence" to call this "glorious emblem" the standard of oppression, but, at all events, it is unanswerable truth. For our part, we call it so in a spirit, not of insolence, not of pride speaking in terms of petulent contempt, but of deep humility and abasement. We confess, with the keenest mortification and chagrin, that the banner of our country is the emblem, not of justice and freedom, but of oppression; that it is the symbol of a compact which recognizes, in palpable and outrageous contradiction of the great principle of liberty, the right of one man to hold another as property; and that we are liable at any moment to be required, under all our obligations of citizenship, to array ourselves beneath it, and wage a war, of extermination if necessary, against the slave, for no crime but asserting his right of equal humanity—the self-evident truth that all men are created equal, and have an unalienable right of life, liberty, and the pursuit of happiness. Would we comply with such a requisition? No! rather would we see our right arm lopped from our body, and the mutilated trunk itself gored with mortal wounds, than raise a finger in opposition to men struggling in the holy cause of freedom. The obligations of citizenship are strong, but those of justice, humanity and religion stronger. We earnestly trust that the great contest of opinion which is now going on in this country may terminate in the enfranchisement of the slaves, without recourse to the strife of blood; but should the oppressed bondmen, impatient of the tardy progress of truth urged only in discussion, attempt to burst their chains by a more violent and shorter process, they should never encounter our arm, nor hear our voice, in the ranks of their opponents. We should stand a sad spectator of the conflict; and whatever commiseration we might feel for the discomfiture of the oppressors, we should pray that the battle might end in giving freedom to the oppressed.

THE NATURAL SYSTEM.

[*From the Plaindealer, August* 19, 1837.]

The opposition party and the monopoly democrats are alike the friends of an exclusive banking system, but differ widely, as to the authority on which such a system should rest. The one side advocates the monarchical principle of a great central bank established by federal authority, and the other is equally strenuous in favour of the aristocratic principle of state institutions. They both agree in the most extravagant eulogiums of "the credit system," and consider it the source of all the blessings and advantages which we enjoy. They alike disclaim, with seeming enthusiasm, on the resources of wealth which our country contains, on the activity of its industry, the boldness of its enterprise, and the fertility of its invention, ever on the stretch for new and speedier modes of gain; and they alike demand, with an air of triumph, what has caused these resources of wealth to be explored, what has given energy to industry, confidence, and enterprise, and quickness to the inventive facilities of our countrymen, but the happy influence of "the credit system?" It is this, they tell us which had dug our canals, constructed our railroads, filled the forest, and caused the wilderness to smile with waving harvests. Every good which has happened to our country they ascribe to the credit system, and every evil which now afflicts it they allege may be effectually remedied by its aid. But they differ widely as to the mode of remedy; a cordon of state monopolies being the object aimed at on the one side, and a great central money power the darling project of the other.

For our own part, we are free to acknowledge that if we were confined to a choice of these evils we should not hesitate to decide in favour of the central bank. We are not alone in this sentiment. There are myriads and tens of myriads of true-hearted democrats in the land who, if the unhappy alternative were alone presented to them of a federal bank or a perpetuation of the system of exclusively privileged state monopolies, would decide promptly and earnestly in favour of the former. Better a single despot, however galling his rule, than more galling tyranny of a contemptible oligarchy. While a federal bank is not more dangerous to the principles of political liberty, its influence would be less extensively pernicious to public morals. They who live in the purlieus of a monarch's court may draw out but a sickly existence; but the moral health of a whole country suffers, when it is under the domination of a league of petty tyrants who fix their residences in every town, and taint the universal atmosphere with the contagion of luxurious example. Bad as is the monarchical principle of a federal bank, the aristocratic principle, which would distribute the same tremendous power among a thousand institutions scattered throughout the confederacy, is worse. Mankind suffered heavier oppression under the rule of the feudal barons, than they had ever before suffered when the political power was centered in the throne. But they arrived not at the rich blessings of freedom, until monarchical and feudal tyranny were both overthrown, and the doctrine of divine right and exclusive privilege gave way before that of universal equality.

He who compares the financial history of Europe with its political, will be surprised to find how perfect is the analogy between them. Her ingenious and philosophical mind would be well employed in running the parallel. It would be found that political revulsions, as well as commercial, are the inevitable result, sooner or later, of conferring exclusively on the few privileges that belong, by nature, in common to all; and that all violations of the holy principle of equal rights, while in politics, they produce tumults, insurrections, and civil war, in economy, exercise a corresponding influence, and are followed by panic, revulsion, and a complete overthrow of all the established commercial relations of society.

The fundamental maxim of democracy and of political economy is the same. They both acknowledge the equal rights of all mankind, and they both contemplate the institution of "a wise and frugal government, which shall restrain men from injuring one another, shall leave them otherwise free to regulate their own pursuits of industry and improvement, and shall not take from the mouth of labour the bread it has earned." The preservation of man's equal rights is the be-all and the end-all of the natural system of government. The great maxim which acknowledges human equality is, in the political world, what gravitation is in the physical—a regulating principle, which, left to itself, harmoniously arranges the various parts of the stupendous whole, equalizes their movements, and reduces all things to the most perfect organization. Monarchy, aristocracy, and all other forms of government, are founded on principles which deny the equal rights of mankind, and they all attempt to substitute an artificial system for that of nature. The effect is sometimes to produce a seeming increase of prosperity for a time; but nature avenges her violated laws sooner or later, and overthrows the unsubstantial fabric of presumption and pride.

The great end which is alone worthy of the efforts of the champions of democratic and economic truth, is to institute the natural system in all matters both of politics and political economy. Let them aim to simplify government, and confine it to the fewest purposes compatible with social order, the mere protection of men from mutual aggression. We need but few laws to accomplish this object. We need particularly few in regard to trade. What is the whole essence and mystery of trade, but an exchange of equivalents to promote the convenience of the parties to the barter? Leave the terms, then, to be settled by men's own notions of mutual convenience and advantage. There is no need of political interference.

Extreme simplicity is usually considered as the condition of barbarism, before man has raised himself by science and art from the degradation of mere animal nature. But the saying that extremes meet is as true in politics as in any of its applications. Simplicity may be the goal, as well as the starting-point, of social effort. Is it not a fact verified by the observation of every man of cultivated mind, that in religion, in literature, in art, and in the conventional manners of a community, simplicity and refinement go hand in hand? As society advances it throws off its cumbrous forms and ceremonies; it follows more and more the simple order of nature, which does nothing in vain, but carries on its stupendous operations by the directest processes, linking cause and effect, without superfluous complication, and adapting its means with the utmost exactness to the end. Compare the nations of the earth, and see if simplicity and refinement are not always found together, in whatever respect the comparison is instituted. In architecture, why are the gorgeous edifices of Constantinople, glittering with "barbaric pomp and gold," deemed inferior to the plainer structures of the cities in western Europe? In literature, why are poems crowded with oriental splendour of imagery, and heaped with elaborate ornaments of diction, thrown aside by the reader of taste for those which breathe the unstudied sweetness of nature? In manners, why do those seem the most refined which seem most truly to flow from the promptings of native amenity and elegance of soul? It is because that is most excellent which comes nearest to the simplicity of nature. Nature does nothing in vain.

Simplicity in government is not less a proper object of those who wish to raise and refine the political condition of mankind. Look at those governments which are the the most complex, and you will find that they who live under them are the most wretched. As governments approach simplicity, the people rise in dignity and happiness; and all experience as well as all sound reasoning on the certain data of induction, bears us out in the conclusion, that when they conform most nearly to the simplicity of nature, then will mankind have reached the utmost bound of political prosperity. Then will the cumbrous artificial and arbitrary contrivance of "the credit system," be abandoned, for the harmonious and beneficial operation of natural, spontaneous credit, the free exercise of confidence between man and man.

My selections from Mr. Leggett's published works here close. I had hoped to be able to add to this Collection some extracts from his correspondence. But want of space prevents it. I cannot resist, however, the temptation of closing these volumes with the following beautiful expression of his free and proud spirit. Another occasion may hereafter offer of laying before the public further specimens of his epistolary style. The annexed letter refers to the Congressional election of 1838, when Mr. L. was candidate in the nominating committee.

Copy of a Letter from WM. LEGGETT, *to* ————.

AYLEMERE, NEW ROCHELLE, October 24th, 1838.

MY DEAR SIR—Your kind letter of last Sunday came duly to my hands, as I trust this will to yours. The sanguine terms in which you express yourself, and in which you are not alone, do not inspire me with equal confidence of the result you anticipate. I have but faint expectations that the nomination of ———— can be set aside, and another name substituted in place of his. The same influences which carried him through the committee will force him down the throats of the people. The retainers and myrmidons of the office-holders are a numerous, active, and disciplined band, and their leaders have possession of the secret passes of our camp. The great meeting can be packed, as well as the nominating committee. And when you add to the number of those whom venal motives will directly actuate, the smaller, but not contemptible numbers, who will ignorantly, but honestly, approve the ticket as it stands, from fear of creating division in our party, should they do otherwise; and another number, smaller than either, perhaps, (so at least my self-love whispers me,) who are opposed to me, because they deem me rash, impetuous, and inexperienced, or that I would weaken a ticket to its undoing, otherwise strong enough to be carried—when you add these several elements of opposition to me together, you will find, I think, that they make a sum total much greater than the aggregate of those who regard me in that favourable light in which I am happy to be esteemed by you.

But though we cannot very confidently hope to effect our object entirely, I consider it fully in our power to teach the democracy a good lesson. We may teach them to distrust nominating committees, and all that worse than worthless machinery of party which places the selection of men, and, consequently, the decision of great measures, so far from the direct control of the popular will. They who are loudest and most incessant in the advocacy of regular nomination and established usages, know well what powerful weapons such nominations, and such usages, place in the hands of craft and chicanery.

What I am most afraid of is, that some of my friends, in their too earnest zeal, will place me in a false position before the public on the slavery subject. I am an abolitionist. I hate slavery in all its forms, degrees, and influences; and I deem myself bound by the highest moral and political obligations, not to let that sentiment of hate lie dormant and smouldering in my own breast, but to give it free vent, and let it blaze forth that it may kindle equal ardour through the whole sphere of my influence. I would not have this fact disguised or mystified, for any office the people have it in their power to give. Rather, a thousand times rather, would I again meet the denunciations of Tammany Hall, and be stigmatized with all the foul epithets with which the anti-abolition vocabulary abounds, than recant, or deny one tittle of my creed. Abolition is, in my sense, a necessary and a glorious part of democracy; and I hold the right and the duty to discuss the subject of slavery, and to expose its hideous evils in all its bearings, moral, social, and political, as of infinitely higher moment than to carry fifty sub-treasury bills. That I should discharge this duty temperately, and should not let it come in collision with other duties; that I should not let hatred of slavery transcend the express obligations of the Constitution, or violate its clear spirit, I hope and trust you think sufficiently well of me to believe. But what I fear is, (not from you, however,) that some of my advocates and champions will seek to recommend me to popular support, by representing that I am not an abolitionist, which is false. All that I have written gives the lie to it. All I shall write will give the lie to it.

And let me here add, (apart from any consideration already adverted to,) that, as a matter of mere policy, I would not, if I could, have my name disjoined from abolitionism. To be an abolitionist, is to be an incendiary now, as, three years ago, to be an anti-monopolist, was to be a leveller, and a Jack Cade. See what those three short years have done in effecting the anti-monopoly reform; and depend upon it, that the next three years—or, if not three, say three times three, if you please, will work a greater revolution on the slavery question. The stream of public opinion now sets against us; but it is about to turn, and the regurgitation will be tremendous. Proud in that day may well be the man who can float in triumph on the first refluent wave, swept onward by the deluge which he, himself, in advance of his fellows, had largely shared in occasioning. Such be my fate! and, living or dead, it will, in some measure, be mine. I have written my name in ineffaceable letters on the abolition record; and whether the reward ultimately come in the shape of honours to the living man, or a tribute to the memory of a departed one, I would not forfeit my right to it, for as mauy offices as ——— has in his gift, if each of them was greater than his own. What has led me into all this idle, and perhaps you may think, vain-glorious prate, is an apprehension created in my mind by the article in the New Era, prefacing an abridged copy of my letter to ———. That article—written, unquestionably, in the kindest spirit, speaks of my letter as showing that I am *not* an abolitionist. It shows no such thing; and if I had thought it liable to such a construction, it should never have left my hands. ——— abridged and altered my communication, on his own responsibility, and as soon as I heard from him, that he intended to do so, I wrote to him, admonishing him not to place me in a false position. But I stand by what ——— has done. He has changed my language slightly, and made some omissions: but the letter, as published, represents me truly, as far as it goes.

The New Era, however, goes much further, and jumps to a conclusion wide, Heaven knows, of the truth. As yet, I do not perceive that there is any absolute need of my interfering in the matter, but let me solicit of your friendship, to have a personal eye, as far as you can, to the doings of these gentry. Their next step may possibly be, to place me before the commuty, as a pro-slavery champion. Keep them, for God's sake, from committing any such foolery, for the sake of getting me into Congress. Let ——— and ——— and others of like kidney, twist themselves into what shapes they please, to gratify the present taste of the people, but as for me, I am not formed of such pliant materials, and choose to retain, undisturbed, the image of my God.

Excuse me for scribbling all this farrago to you; but I am really anxious not to be placed before the public in a false and discoloured light. I do not wish to cheat the people of their votes. I would not get their support, any more than their money, under false pretences. I am, what I am! and if that does not suit them, I am content to stay at home, praying God, in the meantime, to mend their taste, which prefers a "mought and a mought," not democrat, to one who is, at least, honest and zealous in their cause.

Yours' truly,

WM. LEGGETT.